Roth Unbound

Also by Claudia Roth Pierpont

Passionate Minds: Women Rewriting the World

Roth
Unbound

A WRITER AND HIS BOOKS

Claudia Roth Pierpont

Jonathan Cape

London

Published by Jonathan Cape 2014

2 4 6 8 10 9 7 5 3 1

First published in the United States in 2013 by
Farrar, Straus and Giroux, New York

First published in Great Britain in 2013 by
Jonathan Cape
Random House, 20 Vauxhall Bridge Road,
London SW1V 2SA

www.vintage-books.co.uk

Addresses for companies within The Random House Group Limited can be found at:
www.randomhouse.co.uk/offices.htm

The Random House Group Limited Reg. No. 954009

A CIP catalogue record for this book is available from the British Library

ISBN 9780224099035 (Hardback edition)
ISBN 9780224099042 (Trade paperback edition)

The Random House Group Limited supports the Forest Stewardship
Council® (FSC®), the leading international forest-certification organisation.
Our books carrying the FSC label are printed on FSC®-certified paper.
FSC is the only forest-certification scheme supported by the leading
environmental organisations, including Greenpeace.
Our paper procurement policy can be found at:
www.randomhouse.co.uk/environment

Printed and bound in Great Britain by CPI Group (UK) Ltd, Croydon, CR0 4YY

For Robert Pierpont

I believe that we should read only those books that bite and sting us. If a book we are reading does not rouse us with a blow to the head, then why read it?
—Nathan Zuckerman, 1981, *Zuckerman Unbound*, quoting Franz Kafka, 1904, letter to Oskar Pollak

Contents

Roth
Unbound

Introduction

I was leaving a crowded birthday party, in December 2002, when the host stopped me at the door and said that if I stayed he would introduce me to Philip Roth, whose work he knew I admired. The party was in a jazz club downtown—the thoughtful host and honoree was the jazz critic Stanley Crouch—and Roth was seated at the bar, surrounded by people. With courage kindled by Stanley and a couple of beers, I went up to him and blurted out that I thought he was one of the great American novelists of the twentieth century. He smiled and said, "But it's the twenty-first century." Then he turned to Stanley, beside me, and said, "You bring me these women and they insult me!" We laughed and I said a few more things that I hoped were less embarrassing. And then I left. Roth has no recollection that this ever happened.

Almost two years later, I received an envelope in the mail with the name Philip Roth and a Connecticut address stamped in the upper-left-hand corner. Inside was a brief, typed letter on plain white paper, explaining the context of a photocopy also enclosed. Roth was writing in response to an article I had written in *The New Yorker* about the anthropologist Franz Boas, whose life's work touched on some of the issues raised in Roth's most recent book, *The Plot Against America*: the dangers posed by the American Right during the thirties and early forties and the battle against isolationism and bigotry, to state these issues very broadly and in terms that Roth did not use in the letter at all. The photocopy was of the front page of a long-forgotten newspaper called *In fact*—"edited by

George Seldes, a left-wing maverick of sorts," Roth explained—dated
November 17, 1941. Someone had sent it to him because it featured an
article about Charles Lindbergh, who, in Roth's counterhistorical novel,
is elected to the American presidency. Roth was sending it to me because it also featured an article by Boas, and he thought that it might
be of interest. He mentioned that his father used to get *In fact* and also
I. F. Stone's Weekly: "Papers to stoke the indignation."

Readers of this book will learn that Roth not infrequently sends this
sort of letter to people who have written something that piques his interest. I replied and he replied and we ended up meeting for coffee in
New York City. My nervousness fell away immediately. Roth is a brilliant talker, but he also loves to listen: he's as funny as you might think
from his books, but he makes people around him feel funny, too—he
may be the easiest laugher I've ever met. This turned out to be the first
of many such meetings and discussions.

I am a journalist by profession but an art historian by training—half
a lifetime ago, I wrote a dissertation in Italian Renaissance art history
and spent long hours in European archives, searching for a single line
that might add a scrap of knowledge or a shade of meaning to beloved
subjects that had already been thoroughly researched. The smallest
discovery was exciting: it felt like being in touch with history and with
the world's great artists; it felt like tugging back the curtain of time a
fraction of an inch. And so, despite the easy camaraderie that Roth has
inspired through roughly eight years of discussing books and politics
and a thousand other things, it was not lost on me for a moment that
being able to talk with Philip Roth about his work was an extraordinary
privilege. On this subject, at least, I tried to keep track of everything
he said.

I did not have this book in mind; I didn't have anything particular in
mind. I reviewed one of Roth's books for *The New Yorker* and eventually became one of several readers to whom he showed his new work
before publication. (The first time he asked me to read a manuscript, I
said, "I'd be honored." He replied, "Don't be honored, or you'll be no
good to me.") This book began, in 2011, as an essay that was meant to
be part of a collection on American subjects. But it kept growing, for
two reasons principally: Roth has written so many books; and he was
willing to talk with me about them, at length.

Roth Unbound is fundamentally an examination of Roth's development as a writer, considering his themes, his thoughts, and his language.
By necessity, it covers an enormous span, from his Newark childhood,
during the Second World War, and the wholly unexpected outrage that
greeted his early short stories, through the literary (and unliterary) explosion of *Portnoy's Complaint*; from the self-renewal of his experiences
in Prague in the seventies and the imaginative fulfillment of *The Ghost
Writer* to the series of masterworks published between the mid-eighties
and the year 2000—*The Counterlife, Operation Shylock, Sabbath's Theater, American Pastoral, The Human Stain*—and, finally, to his short, intense novels of the twenty-first century. Of course, this summary barely
touches on the high points of a career that has spanned more than fifty
years and many different phases. In 2006, when *The New York Times
Book Review* conducted a poll among contemporary writers, editors, and
critics to determine "the single best work of American fiction published
in the last twenty-five years," a Roth novel did not come in first only because the votes for his work were split among seven different books. Not
since Henry James, it seems to me, has an American novelist worked at
such a sustained pitch of concentration and achievement, book after
book after book. And then there are the subjects: Jews in America, Jews
in history, sex and love and sex without love, the need to find meaning in
one's life, the need to change one's life, parents and children, the trap of
self and the trap of conscience, American ideals, the American betrayal
of American ideals, the upheavals of the sixties, the Nixon presidency, the
Clinton era, Israel, the mysteries of identity, the human body in its
beauty, the human body in its corrupting illness, the ravages of old
age, the coming of death, the power and failings of memory. It's a wonder this book isn't a lot longer.

Roth finished *Nemesis* in the fall of 2009, and he soon realized, even
if the public did not, that it would be his last novel. A literary study like
this could only have been written since then, with the full arc of Roth's
work completed. But Roth's retirement is also a precondition for the
somewhat hybrid form this book has taken, because of his own considerable contributions to its pages: memories, observations, opinions, thoughts
and second thoughts, jokes, stories, even songs. Unless another source
is noted, all quotations in the following pages are derived from my conversations with him. (Likewise, the remarks of various friends come

from my interviews and conversations with them.) To put it simply, he had the time to talk about his work because he wasn't doing it anymore. And it was exciting to him to look back on a lifetime's production that even he had not yet had time to sum up, beyond citing his heavyweight hero, Joe Louis, on retiring: "I did all I could with what I had."

Roth has been extremely generous. He has answered many, many questions. He has let me prowl through the files in his attic in Connecticut. I have talked to him long enough, and through sufficiently different circumstances—in sickness and in health, literally—to hear changes in opinion, and I have tried to account for these changes, too, aware of the hazards of setting down a passing thought as the permanent record. And he has done all of this with the understanding that he would read not a single word in advance of publication. For one thing, he is beyond caring very much what people say anymore; he's had an earful. For another, he knows better than anyone that freedom is as essential to writing as to life. And so, while this book has benefited beyond measure from Roth's presence, I have kept him resolutely out of mind when it comes to my critical task.

I should add that, despite my middle name, I am not related to my celebrated subject. Once, it's true, when we were both at dinner with a group of friends, someone asked about a possible familial connection, and Roth turned to me with a look of mild horror and wary recognition: "Did I use to be married to you?!" Fortunately, a moment of reflection proved that this was not the case.

In *Zuckerman Unbound*, Roth makes a distinction between the unwritten world and the world that emerges from his typewriter—as opposed to the real and fictional worlds—and with a sense of weight rather more evenly distributed than is generally allowed. This book is about Roth's written world, but it has not been possible to write about that world without also delving into the unwritten one—the life that has so often served the work. Biography is important to some periods more than to others and is used primarily as illumination. Yet, as Roth said in an interview in *Le Nouvel Observateur* in 1981, "Art is life, too, you know. Solitude is life, meditation is life, pretending is life, supposition is life, contemplation is life, language is life." This book, then, is about the life of Philip Roth's art and, inevitably, the art of his life.

Defenders of the Faith

"**W**hat is being done to silence this man?" The question, posed by a prominent New York rabbi in a letter to the Anti-Defamation League of B'nai B'rith in 1959, conveyed the tone of a demand and continued with the hint of a solution: "Medieval Jews would have known what to do with him." The figure condemned to bloody justice was a little-known writer of short stories named Philip Roth, aged twenty-six. In Roth's retellings of his first public battle, he tends to recall himself as even younger, as though trying to convey the vulnerability he felt when he was invited by his elders at the League to meet and discuss the problem. Back in his high school days, Roth had wanted to become a lawyer for this very organization, protecting American Jews from legal bias and discrimination—as he told two of its officers over lunch at Ratner's, the Jewish restaurant on Second Avenue, where, he fondly recalls, "the waiter's thumb was always in the soup." He was clearly a serious young man, and the lunch turned out to be a friendly affair. There was no way that the League could have controlled what he wrote, of course, even had its members wished to try, which they did not. ("Free country, the U.S.A.," Roth cheerily noted in an account of the incident decades later.) During the next few years, however, he spoke about his work at meetings sponsored by several Jewish organizations, where he was freely able to defend what the rabbi's next letter, written directly to him, just as freely denounced as "such conceptions of Jews as ultimately led to the murder of six million in our time."

One of Roth's stories was about a thirteen-year-old Hebrew school student who threatens to jump from the roof of a synagogue unless the rabbi, the boy's mother, and everyone else gathered in the street below kneel down and declare their faith in Jesus Christ. But this story, titled "The Conversion of the Jews," was not the one that had outraged the rabbi. There was also a story titled "Epstein," about a sixtyish married Jewish man whose wages of sin for a brief affair are, progressively, a humiliating rash and a heart attack. This one was not mentioned by the rabbi, either, although another rabbi was reported by *The New York Times* to have complained about Roth's portrayal of a Jewish adulterer and other "lopsided schizophrenic personalities," all of whom happened to be Jews. But were there any major characters in Roth's stories who were not Jews? In the eerie fable "Eli, the Fanatic," the irate citizens who want to evict a home for Jewish refugee children from an elite suburban town are not the town's long-established Gentiles but its nouveau suburban Jews, who see the refugees as foreign, embarrassing, and a threat to their new American status—a threat precisely of the sort that the rabbis found in Roth.

The source of rabbinical wrath had appeared in *The New Yorker* in March 1959 and was titled "Defender of the Faith." More than Roth's other stories, it was intensely realistic and psychologically complex. (Roth today calls it "the first good thing I ever wrote.") Set in an army camp in Missouri during the final months of the Second World War, it follows the moral and emotional progress of a fair-minded Jewish sergeant—a recently returned combat hero, numbed by all the ruin he's seen—who is repeatedly cajoled by a Jewish draftee into granting favors on the basis of their religious bond. The claims of Jewish clannishness were always disturbing to Roth's proudly American heroes: the Hebrew student in "The Conversion of the Jews" first gets into trouble by asking the rabbi how he can "call the Jews 'The Chosen People' if the Declaration of Independence claimed all men to be created equal." "Defender of the Faith" deals head-on with this conflict of loyalties: the finagling young soldier, on the point of successfully evading service at the front, is finally punished by the sergeant, who, despite reserves of feeling for the younger man and the memories of family he has stirred, has him reassigned to face the same dangers as the other men. When the pair confront each other at the story's end ("There's no limit to your anti-Semitism," the furious young man cries, "is there?"), the sergeant explains that he is looking out not for a particular people but for "all of us." This is the faith that he unequivocally defends, without, however, losing sight of the other faith that he has relinquished for it.

It was the depiction of the weaselly, lying, nineteen-year-old Jewish soldier that caused the stir. Neither Roth's conclusions, nor the controlling intelligence of the sergeant, nor, certainly, the story's literary qualities had any impact on those who were outraged by the mere suggestion that such a person might exist. The most incendiary aspect of the story, however, was its publication in *The New Yorker*. Roth's earlier work had appeared in such prestigious but little-read journals as the newly founded *Paris Review* and the largely Jewish-read *Commentary*, which had been established by the American Jewish Committee after the war. In fact, "your story—in Hebrew—in an Israeli magazine or newspaper," the censorious rabbi wrote to Roth, "would have been judged exclusively from a literary point of view." Here, however, in America, in a magazine widely esteemed in Gentile society, Roth's best efforts amounted to nothing less than an act of "informing."

Roth was genuinely stunned by the reaction: blindsided. On the morning that *The New Yorker* came out, he recalls, he had walked from his apartment on East Tenth Street to the newsstand on Fourteenth Street "about six times," until the magazine finally appeared, and then he took it home and "read it over and over, and then I read it backwards and then I read it upside down—I wouldn't let it out of my hands." Letters started coming in just a couple of days later and soon turned into such a deluge that the editors developed a form letter to send in reply. The story was a clear departure for *The New Yorker*, which had previously published Jewish stories on the order of *The Education of H*Y*M*A*N K*A*P*L*A*N* by Leo Rosten, stories that Roth describes as being about "cute Jews." (Alfred Kazin began his first review of Roth's work with the statement "Several weeks ago I was awakened, while reading the *New Yorker*, by Philip Roth's 'Defender of the Faith.'") But beyond literary circles, the response was evidence of the rawness of Jewish nerves, just fourteen years after the end of the war—with losses still being absorbed and the word "Holocaust" not yet adopted to describe them—and of the inability of many Jews to accept Roth's revelation of what he called their "secret": "that the perils of human nature afflict the members of our minority."

The publication of five of Roth's stories in book form, together with a novella, *Goodbye, Columbus*, took place in May 1959, just two months after *The New Yorker* hit the stands. Roth later reported that the slender volume was considered, in some circles, "my *Mein Kampf*." The new novella, which gave the collection its title, fueled heightening charges of Jewish self-hatred and anti-Semitism through the same material that made it irresistibly comic: its broadly vaudevillian treatment of the working-class Jews of Newark ("*Shmutz* he lives in and I shouldn't worry," Aunt Gladys worries) and, especially, its relentless skewering of the country club Jews of nearby but worlds-away Short Hills—a postwar suburban species still new to literature. After a brief drive up from Newark, where Aunt Gladys and Uncle Max spend steamy summer nights sitting in a dingy alley seeking a breeze, Neil Klugman, age twenty-three, arrives among sprinkled lawns, air-cooled rooms, and streets named for the colleges the local progeny attend. Neil, a somewhat defensive graduate of the Newark branch of Rutgers University, and a junior league if wised-up Gatsby, is in pursuit of a girl—a Radcliffe girl named Brenda Patimkin, home for the summer—whose fascination is inextricably bound to the careless self-possession that money breeds.

Roth was not in any conscious way responding to Fitzgerald's book, and *Goodbye, Columbus* was a spontaneously written work—"with some of the virtues and all of the defects of spontaneity," Roth tells me, now that its defects seem all too clear to him. Still, at the time, *The Great Gatsby* was indeed fresh and important in his mind. During the midfifties, in graduate school, he had taken a course on the American Twenties, in which each of the students was assigned a particular year for a cultural report. Roth had drawn 1925: "the most terrific year," he says. "*The Great Gatsby, Manhattan Transfer*, the start of *The New Yorker*." The impact of Fitzgerald's book on him was in its "angle of social observation," he says, but early critics saw more than a bit of Fitzgerald's feckless Daisy in Brenda Patimkin, ruthlessly competitive yet angelic in tennis whites as she and a friend with a fake Katharine Hepburn accent play on into the soft summer night, while Neil waits impatiently for their first date to begin. The fact that Brenda owes her beauty to a nose job and her family fortune to Patimkin Kitchen and Bathroom Sinks in lowly Newark does not detract from her allure. To Neil, she is every bit as much "the king's daughter" as Daisy was to Gatsby—Roth simply (if unknowingly) took over Fitzgerald's chivalric phrase. A king's daughter is a princess, of course, and Roth has been widely accused of helping to establish the stereotype of the Jewish American Princess. In fact, the term did not arise until more than a decade later, in the early seventies, and probably had more to do with the exaggerations of the entire Patimkin household in the movie version, directed by Larry Peerce, that appeared about that time.

Roth's book is filled with implications about class and race. Smart as he is, Neil has a dead-end job as a librarian, and the only significant person in his life, aside from Brenda, is a little black boy who shows up regularly to look at art books. Instinctively, Neil protects the boy from both the racism of a colleague and the threat that his favorite book, filled with reproductions of Gauguin's Tahitian paradise, will be borrowed by an unpleasant old white man. (Roth shamelessly stacks the deck against this second Gauguin lover.) Yet if Roth's hero feels empathy with a poor black boy staring at pictures of unobtainable beauty—Neil himself sees Gauguin's Tahitians in terms of the Patimkins—and feels a similar connection with the Patimkins' black maid, it's clear that neither the boy nor the maid feels anything toward Neil in return. He is on his own in an uncertain and uncomfortable social space, starry-eyed about Patimkin bounty, yet proud and angry enough to want to heave a rock through the glass wall of the Harvard library after Brenda finally makes the hard choice between him and her family.

The real novelty of Roth's view of American Jewish life, circa 1959, was its absence of any sense of tragedy or oppression. ("Green lawns, white Jews," one of Roth's characters remarks about *Goodbye, Columbus* some thirty-five years later, in *Operation Shylock*: "The Jewish success story in its heyday, all new and thrilling and funny and fun.") True, Aunt Gladys sends off bundles for the "Poor Jews in Palestine," but this seems already an archaic gesture. The far more up-to-date Mr. Patimkin, surveying his lavatorial empire, comes to the rueful conclusion that his adored children—Ron, Brenda, and Julie—know no more about being Jewish than the *goyim*. Hurling themselves into the American dream, the Patimkins live a continuous daily round of sports (an extra place is

set at dinner not for Elijah but for Mickey Mantle) and of eating—
gargantuan meals, served by Carlota, the maid, that smother conversation in active digestion and extra helpings. As a result, Neil, as their
guest, concludes that "it would be just as well to record all that was said
in one swoop, rather than indicate the sentences lost in the passing of
food, the words gurgled into mouthfuls, the syntax chopped and forgotten in heapings, spillings, and gorgings." And he does so in the form of
a little play:

RON: Where's Carlota? Carlota!

MRS. P.: Carlota, give Ronald more.

CARLOTA (*calling*): More what?

RON: Everything.

MR. P.: Me too.

MRS. P.: They'll have to *roll* you on the links.

MR. P. (*pulling his shirt up and slapping his black, curved belly*): What are
    you talking about? Look at that?

RON (*yanking his T-shirt up*): Look at *this*.

BRENDA: (*to me*) Would you care to bare your middle?

ME (the choir boy again): No.

MRS. P.: That's right, Neil.

ME: Yes. Thank you.

CARLOTA (*over my shoulder, like an unsummoned spirit*): Would *you* like
    more?

ME: No.

MR. P.: He eats like a bird.

JULIE: Certain birds eat a lot.

BRENDA: Which ones?

MRS. P.: Let's not talk about animals at the dinner table.

The comedy is not particularly cruel, since most of the individual
portraits are rooted in affection: for the unpretentious, belly-slapping
Mr. Patimkin, who has sweated his way up from Newark poverty; for
lithe and clever Brenda, breaker of rules and reader of Mary McCarthy;
even for knuckleheaded Ron, a former college basketball star who
keeps his jockstrap suspended from the bathroom shower—a colossal,
lumpen, sentimental guy, more like a warmed-up version of Fitzgerald's

Tom Buchanan than any Jew any previous American writer had conceived. The Patimkins harbor no doubts about their right to what they have or about their standing in America. But what did America think of them?

Goodbye, Columbus won the National Book Award in 1960, a remarkable achievement for a first book of short stories by a twenty-seven-year-old writer. It also received substantial praise from the "four tigers of American Jewish literature," as Roth identifies Saul Bellow, Alfred Kazin, Irving Howe, and Leslie Fiedler, all of whom recognized a strong voice and a fresh perspective—the next development in the saga of Jews in America to which they themselves belonged. Roth's depiction of the Patimkins, in particular, was considered (in Howe's words) "ferociously exact," a real reflection of the spiritual vacuity (in Bellow's formulation) that had befallen an untold number of American middle-class Jews. Some thirteen to eighteen years older than Roth, these literary tigers were—unlike Roth—the children of immigrants, born into a generation that kept them closer to religious feeling, however fiercely they had rebelled against it. The fact that Bellow saw Roth's rather cheerful and healthy if dull-witted suburbia as another chapter of the Jewish historical tragedy says more about Bellow than it does about Roth. But Roth was grateful for the critical support, especially for Bellow's statement that a Jewish writer should not be expected to write "public relations releases" in the hope of reducing anti-Semitic feeling and, indeed, that the loss to "our sense of reality" wasn't worth the gain, if there was any gain at all. Bellow gave Roth a meaningful go-ahead, when—awards or no awards—more people than ever seemed intent on getting him to stop.

Goodbye, Columbus also won the Daroff Award of the Jewish Book Council of America, just a year after it was given (by a different group of judges) to Leon Uris's *Exodus*. Roth's book was not a widely popular choice. Uris himself spoke out about the new "school" of Jewish American writers, "who spend their time damning their fathers, hating their mothers, wringing their hands and wondering why they were born." Their work, he added, "makes me sick to my stomach." Roth read the Uris interview, published in the *New York Post*, when it was clipped and sent to him by another angrily accusing reader. All these accusations were quoted by Roth himself in two essays of the early sixties: "Some

New Jewish Stereotypes" (*American Judaism*, 1961) and "Writing About Jews" (*Commentary*, 1963), both republished in Roth's 1975 collection, *Reading Myself and Others*. These essays—and Roth did not frequently write essays—show how seriously he took the charges, how wounded he felt by them, and yet how certain he was that he was right. He noted that people read *Anna Karenina* without concluding that adultery was a Russian trait; *Madame Bovary* did not lead readers to condemn the morals of French provincial women en masse. He was writing literature, not sociology or—Bellow's helpful phrase—public relations. He was aspiring to the highest artistic goals, and he expected that if he explained himself, very carefully, people would come to understand.

In 1962, Roth, who was teaching at the University of Iowa, accepted an invitation to speak at Yeshiva University in New York, in a symposium titled "The Crisis of Conscience in Minority Writers of Fiction." His fellow speakers were Ralph Ellison, whose depiction of Negro family life in *Invisible Man* had brought charges of defamation from his own community, and Pietro di Donato, the author of a novel about Italian immigrants, *Christ in Concrete*, that had been a bestseller in the thirties. But it was clear from the start that Roth was the center of interest. As he describes the event in his autobiographical volume, *The Facts*, the tone was set by the moderator's opening question: "Mr. Roth, would you write the same stories you've written if you were living in Nazi Germany?"

The prolonged attacks that followed left him in something like a state of shock, barely able to reply coherently to the questions and statements that were hurled at the stage and overcome by the realization that "I was not just opposed but hated." In sympathy, Ellison took up his defense; Roth remembers Ellison stating, in regard to his own work, that he refused to be a cog in the machinery of civil rights. Nevertheless, upon leaving the stage, Roth was surrounded by a still unsated, fist-shaking crowd. He escaped them, at last, with his wife and his editor. And in the safety of the Stage Delicatessen, over a pastrami sandwich, he vowed, "I'll never write about Jews again."

Real Americans

He had not intended to write about them in the first place. Roth has often pointed out that he had the childhood of an all-American boy, growing up in Newark in the thirties and forties—he was born on March 19, 1933, just as Franklin Roosevelt took office—doing his homework and listening to the radio and playing baseball. His grandparents were part of the great wave of Jewish immigrants from Russia and Polish Galicia at the end of the nineteenth century; he was named after his mother's father, who died before he was born and who had converted his Hebrew name, Feivel, to Philip. Roth's paternal grandfather, Sender Roth—who had studied to be a rabbi in Galicia and ended up working in a Newark hat factory—died when Philip was very young, but both grandmothers were presences throughout his childhood. The family visited them every Sunday, leaving in the morning to see his father's mother, who lived with his aunt in a tenement in central Newark—they had a coal stove, Roth remembers, that they cooked on—and, after lunch, driving to see his mother's mother in a tiny apartment in neighboring Elizabeth. When gas was rationed during the war, the family walked to Elizabeth about once a month, a happy adventure, he recalls, that involved crossing a bridge over the railroad tracks and skirting the edge of a large and dreadful cemetery. Yet neither Philip nor his older brother, Sandy, ever really got to know the grandmothers well, since the *balabustas* spoke hardly any English and the boys spoke no Yiddish at all.

Still, Roth remembers that great affection passed between the generations, even without words. In a loving letter that he wrote to his maternal "grandma" from college when she was very ill—his mother would have translated and read it to her—he proudly told her that he had a part in a play (it was the Ragpicker in Giradoux's *The Madwoman of Chaillot*) and described it as "a very poor man, much like Grandpa must have been when he first saw America. And like you and Grandpa, this poor man wants the world to be good." (Roth finds this letter unbearably sentimental today; but it simply shows a well-meaning nineteen-year-old writing to his grandmother on her own terms.) Among these good and venerable relations, Roth also recalls the plainly frightening figure of his paternal grandmother's sister, a stern and massively bundled woman called Meema Gitcha. Her name was "too good not to use," he says with a laugh—it appeared decades later in *Operation Shylock*—although even now he isn't certain what it means.

Roth's parents, Herman and Bess Roth, were both New Jersey born and bred—"Americans from day one," as he puts it. But, like so many of their generation, they served as a kind of buffer for their own children between the old world and the new. The family attended synagogue only on the High Holy Days—and mostly, it seems, to please the elder generation. His mother kept a kosher kitchen, Roth explains, for much the same reason: how else could the grandmothers come to dinner at their house? (He recalls his mother lighting Sabbath candles, however, as an entirely private devotional gesture, moving her arms hypnotically around the flame as though in a trance—remembering her father, he believes—just like the mother in "The Conversion of the Jews." Roth imitates the gesture for me with great tenderness, although it seems he has forgotten that he ever put it in a story.) Philip was sent to Hebrew school, three afternoons a week for three long years, and was ever resentful at spending the precious hours after school in a stuffy room above the synagogue, when he could have been out in the air at center field. It might have been worse, though. Sandy had to go to Hebrew school for five years; the family strictures were gradually loosening.

He remembers clearly that he was eight, and playing outside, when the news of Pearl Harbor interrupted the broadcast of a Dodgers–Giants football game. The radio had been on in the Roths' apartment, and his parents called down from the window to get him to come upstairs, where they explained what had happened and what war meant for the country. This was the first real break in the pattern of his life, after which all his memories become more distinct. Through the duration of the war, he followed battle maps and wrote long letters to two of his cousins overseas, young men whose father—one of his father's older brothers—had died young, and who spent a lot of time around his house while they were growing up. Another cousin, dressed in his U.S. Navy uniform, taught him to shoot craps. He was hugely impressed by "the manliness of the guys who'd been in the war," particularly since he felt himself to be, he says, "a good little Jewish boy, a sissy": a kid more brains than brawn. (He is quick to add, however, that he did not appear this way to others.) The romance of manliness that runs through Roth's work may have its beginnings here, in the experiences of a wartime child.

Eager to do his part, the skinny kid went door-to-door collecting old papers and tin cans, which he brought to the collection center at his school. Gym class now included a section called "commando obstacle": climbing fences, jumping over ditches, being a soldier. He loved it. In his own account of these years in *The Facts*, Roth has wondered if later generations—post-Vietnam generations—can ever comprehend the absolutely unambiguous sense he gained, during that war and because of that victory, "of belonging to the greatest nation on earth." These were years of continual propaganda about freedom and democracy; and years of striving, both at war and at home, to make the slogans real. It was a time when American promise seemed boundless, with opportunities open to all hardworking boys.

Newark was a city filled with upward-striving immigrants—there were significant populations not only of Jews but of Italians, Irish, Germans, and African Americans up from the South—although each group maintained its own staked-out area. The Weequahic section, where the Roth family lived, was an almost wholly Jewish enclave in the southwest corner of the city. Fully developed only in the twenties and thirties, it was settled by first-generation American Jews eager to leave the crowded squalor of their parents' immigrant quarters in central Newark's Third Ward, where Herman Roth was born in 1901. (Bess Roth, née Finkel, was born three years later, in Elizabeth, and had grown up as the only Jewish child in an Irish Catholic milieu.) Weequahic was made

up of tidy wood-frame houses, many of which—the Roths' included—
were divided into three apartments. Locust trees had been planted all
along Summit Avenue, where Philip lived at No. 81, in a five-room
apartment on the second floor, until he was nine. There was a little
lawn out front with a patch of irises, which Roth can still picture his
father tending in his undershirt on weekends. (He also remembers the
year that the irises did not come up because his father—a novice gar-
dener, to be sure—had planted the bulbs upside down.) The situation
was much the same on nearby Leslie Street, where the family moved
when the rent went up. The only difference was that the new house was
across the street from a Catholic orphanage, part of a complex containing a church and a school and a small working farm, all enclosed by a
chain-link fence. Behind the fence, he could observe the orphans playing—he never spoke to any of them—and feel how lucky he was to
have a family.

Out on this edge of the city, there were still plenty of empty lots,
filled with tall weeds and wild apple trees and, admittedly, some debris
("People would junk stuff," Roth notes, "but there was not a lot of it"),
where the neighborhood kids played. The area had been farmland in
the not too distant past, and Roth recalls the old grandfather of an Italian family next door on Summit Avenue—one of the few non-Jewish
families around—going out in his suit and tie (which was all he ever
wore) into the overgrown lots and "finding wild onion and chives and
even baby potatoes that he would bring back to use in their soup."
It wasn't exactly bucolic, he says, "but it wasn't totally urban, either—
there was so much open space."

The population of the newly built schools was Jewish, too. In Newark, as in every major American city, the public schools were expected
to complete the work of assimilation and social transformation that
parents had begun. The Weequahic schools were remarkably efficient
at their task; by second grade, Roth says, most of the kids assumed they
were going to college. "There was nothing else the parents had to give
us," he explains, "not money, not status, not positions, so they made
sure they gave us an education." He was so excited when he started going to school—the Chancellor Avenue School, on the commercial street
running perpendicular to Summit Avenue—that he used to run there
every morning.

But the schools also inculcated values beyond discipline and grades. Roth recently showed me the eighth-grade graduation program from the Chancellor Avenue School—dated January 30, 1946—which had been sent to him by an old classmate, listing Roth as one of two authors of a play titled *Let Freedom Ring!* His friend and co-author, Dorothy Brand, had played Tolerance and Roth had played Prejudice (even then, it seems, he had a propensity for the morally darker role), both invisible to the others onstage. In their little drama, Tolerance proposed a series of visits to families of different ethnic backgrounds, and Prejudice piped up with a matching series of insulting (if childish) expectations— something like "Their heads are full of chop suey," Roth recalls, when a Chinese family was proposed—expectations that would promptly be disproved by the scene the pair visited: the Chinese family, for example, was discovered reading Confucius at the dinner table. At the end, the entire class sang the forties liberal anthem "The House I Live In," and Roth, as Prejudice, slunk off the stage. In 1946, in Weequahic, this denouement was a better expression of the local creed than anything taught in Hebrew school.

If there was a difficulty with the schools and the educational project into which parents poured their hope, it was that the better the process worked, the more it left the parents behind and strangely foreign to their children. Herman Roth had left school after eighth grade; he provided for his family by means of unremitting labor and a stubborn perseverance that affected his younger son, even in the throes of adolescence, with its mixture of heroism and pathos. Selling insurance policies for Metropolitan Life, Roth rose about as high in the company's ranks as a Jew was allowed to rise in the thirties and forties, in accord with unofficial but openly practiced quotas and traditions. Philip was hardly unaware of the limitations set upon his father's career. As for anti-Semitism, he knew about the larger hate-filled American figures such as Father Coughlin and Henry Ford—virtually no one in the neighborhood, he remembers, chose to own a Ford—and he had witnessed several attacks on Jewish kids by local toughs. As a result of one "postgame pogrom," after Weequahic High won an unlikely football victory against a more favored city team, one of his friends had to be hospitalized. In *The Facts*, Roth writes that he was twelve when he began to think about becoming a lawyer and working for an organization like the

Anti-Defamation League, "to oppose the injustices wreaked by the violent and the privileged."

Yet the boy's general experience of anti-Semitism was not of a brutal persecution flowing direct from its Gentile source—the kind of anti-Semitism that had shaped his grandparents' lives and still echoed in his parents' minds. More often, he saw the deformations that such persecution had wrought in the older generations of Jews around him: the care in following rules, the need to make a good impression, the fear of stepping out of line and implicating an entire people in one's disgrace. If his father's habit of talking to everyone and of "glad-handing" people was embarrassing to him as a child, as Roth recalls in conversation, he eventually recognized in this behavior not merely the ways of a salesman but the desire "to allay anti-Semitism and show everyone he was a nice and regular guy."

For all that Herman and Bess Roth appeared to be typical first-generation American Jews, however, part of a population that famously put a premium on its sons becoming doctors and lawyers, they were notably sanguine about both of their boys becoming artists. Sandy—Sanford Roth, born in 1927, five years older than Philip—took classes at the Art Students League while still in high school and, after a stint in the navy, studied to be a painter at Pratt Institute in Brooklyn rather than attend college. (In an interview on the Internet series Web of Stories, Roth recounts how he would wonderingly "debrief" his brother when he returned from life drawing class at the Art Students League, where he'd been sitting in a room with an actual naked woman—"of all things, drawing.") In some ways, Roth says, his parents were simply too unworldly to have pushed their sons in any professional direction. But he also points out that his mother's beloved brother, Mickey (born Emmanuel), was a painter—unmarried, unsalaried, classically bohemian—whose canvases had pride of place in the Roth household, right along with a framed copy of the Declaration of Independence issued by Metropolitan Life. When Sandy adjusted his goals later on and went into advertising, it was not because of parental pressure but because he had acquired a family of his own to support.

As in many families, the brothers tended to divide up their accomplishments, and Sandy was the handsome one, the neighborhood heartthrob. Philip got the brains and very possibly the charm (and certainly the will) to become his scrupulously fair and loving mother's secret favorite—or so it always appeared to him, he tells me, and he believes it may have appeared that way to his brother, too, while they were growing up. Skipping a half-year term, twice, to more advanced grades, he was a top student and the family entertainer, a budding stand-up comic with an array of accents and impressions—mostly derived from radio—that kept his parents in stitches. His earliest passion as a reader was for sea adventures, and by the time he was eleven he had decided on a pen name: Eric Duncan ("the hard c's got me"). He typed out the title page of a sea adventure of his own, *Storm Off Hatteras*, but didn't bother with the rest of the book. He was just testing the feeling of being a writer.

During the war years, he was mesmerized by radio news reports and by the politically charged dramas written by Norman Corwin, the poet laureate of radio. He recalls Corwin's most famous show, *On a Note of Triumph*, broadcast on V-E Day, as "one of the most thrilling experiences of my childhood." A lot of Corwin's impact, Roth says, came from the American place names resounding through his prose: "A kid from Texas barrels through with a grenade to show a Nazi where the limit is!" Roth is improvising, in a broadcaster baritone, to suggest what the experience was like: "A kid from Chattanooga . . . ," he starts in again. "The names would just wash over me, and I'd think, 'This is a great country.'" One of the reasons for this geographic infatuation, he says, is simply that "the places were so remote, then. The words were so magical: *Chattanooga*." It can't be irrelevant that the thrill of language first came to this richly colloquial writer in the form of voices, and that these voices included not only the dramatic flights of Norman Corwin's scripts but Jack Benny, Bob Hope, Fred Allen, and a host of others Roth still laughs about and quotes. The script for *On a Note of Triumph*, published later in 1945, was the first book that he ever bought.

He was only twelve when he entered high school, and although the books that were assigned in class held no interest at all—he remembers being bored by both *Silas Marner* and *Scaramouche*—he was consumed by books about baseball and by the sport itself. As Roth tells it, his high school years were a time of intensely boyish camaraderie. There were girls he liked, and he went on dates; during his last two years, he had a steady girlfriend named Betty Rogow, dark-haired and pretty. Sex was out of the question, of course—"It wouldn't have dawned on me"—although he assures me that there was plenty of rubbing and feeling and enough necking so that it often felt as if "your lips had fallen off." (There was, of course, also plenty of training in what Roth refers to as "mastering my small-muscle skills," or the masturbatory arts; for a while, he says, he was smitten with a cardboard toilet paper roll, its inside smeared with Vaseline.) But the guys were the same friends that he'd been with since grade school—multiplied by three, since he'd moved through three different classes. They played ball, they played blackjack, they went to the movies on Friday nights and spent an hour and a half walking home, falling down laughing, stopping for bagels and eating half a dozen each. (These bagels were not as large, he informs me, as most bagels are today.)

The movies themselves weren't important. Whatever was playing would do. When he was younger, Sandy had taken him to see the Andy Hardy series, and at twelve he was swept away by *State Fair*, with its Rodgers and Hammerstein score and its Iowa charms: "You fell in love with a certain picture of America." His autograph book from his eighth-grade graduation lists the movie's hit song, "It Might as Well Be Spring," as his personal favorite and identifies its source as "the best movie there is." The little album also proclaims his favorite writer as John Tunis (the author of numerous baseball novels), his future profession as "journalist," his future college as "Northwestern" ("I knew nothing about it," he tells me, "I just liked the name"), and his favorite saying as, "Don't step on the underdog"—all confirming that he was a very good boy not only in his own retrospective account but in the reality of 1946. Three years later, he and his friends lied about their ages to get into Newark's Little Theater to see the old art film *Ecstasy*, infamously featuring Hedy Lamarr's bare breasts, in a scene that lasted, he recalls, about three seconds and that had the Weequahic pack fervently whispering, as the moment approached, "This is it! This is it!"

Books, however, were important, and here, too, America was key to his interests. He became an avid reader of historical novels by Howard Fast, with titles like *Citizen Tom Paine*. Fast was a member of the Communist Party, and his books, Roth says now, "celebrated American history from a Marxist point of view, but I didn't know that; I couldn't ferret out any particular point of view." It was the dramatization and the personalization of American history that got him. On the other side of seriousness there was Damon Runyon, whom he discovered in the newspaper: "I loved it that his people talked in that crazy way," he says. Every week, he would bicycle over to the Weequahic branch library and fill his basket with books. And after Sandy enrolled in Pratt, in 1948, he'd come home on weekends and leave his more sophisticated paperbacks scattered around. Once, Sandy brought home an entire summer's revelatory reading list: Sinclair Lewis, Sherwood Anderson, Ernest Hemingway, George Orwell. Roth was entering that wonderful period, he says, when "everything matters, and there is no such thing as a bad book."

There wasn't enough money for him to go away to college. After the war, Herman Roth had attempted to evade corporate obstacles and enter a brand-new business, frozen foods, working nights and weekends while staying on full-time at Metropolitan Life. He borrowed the money necessary to get the enterprise going, with the result that the family's savings were wiped out when it failed, while Philip was in high school. He graduated at sixteen, in January 1950, and enrolled in the Newark branch of Rutgers for the following fall. In the meantime, he got a job as a stock clerk in the S. Klein department store in downtown Newark, which required a period of training in the Manhattan flagship store on Union Square, just around the corner from the great used-book shops of Fourth Avenue. "I'd eat lunch right there in the bookstores," he says. Cheap paperbacks: new joy. He remembers being under the spell of John Dos Passos: "the trains, the strikers, the factories—the contemporary world as fiction." It was an enthusiasm that briefly helped to determine his career plans when he was fired from S. Klein after just a few weeks for being "a wise guy."

He wanted to work in a factory. So he got a job in a garage door plant in Irvington, New Jersey, where he sat in a tiny room, sorting nails in giant kegs, from eight in the morning until five. The first lunch hour he found terrific: "There was a softball game, I loved that, the guys, the workers." It was Dos Passos. It was glamorous. It was another ideal of manly romance. After lunch, however, he went back to sorting nails. He says that at dinner that evening he told his parents that his day had been great and then asked, "Do I have to go back?" He didn't even bother to collect a paycheck. An unheroic job as a summer camp counselor carried him through until fall.

The Newark branch of Rutgers, where he spent his freshman year, was situated in a former brewery downtown. The place appealed to his "liberal democratic spirit" and, putting him among the city's non-Jewish students for the first time, provided something new and even exciting. Unlike Neil Klugman in *Goodbye Columbus,* however, he moved on quickly. Living in the family's five-room apartment under his father's watchful eye was painfully constricting. Friction had been building throughout high school: Herman Roth was nothing if not absolutely certain of the way things should be done. "You're doing it wrong!" was, Roth recalls, his father's battle cry. (His mother, once her younger son had grown up enough to impress her—and even intimidate her—was just as characteristically given to saying, "Darling, whatever you think is right.") The experience of his father teaching him to drive, was, Roth tells me, "like the Battle of Iwo Jima"; he finally went to a driving school to preserve the peace.

Now angry fights were breaking out over the hours he kept. His father's idea of a curfew seemed suitable to a high school boy, and he was a college man. He knew even then that his father, who had seen three of his five brothers die young, was frightened for him; but that didn't make it any easier—in fact, the sympathy may have made it harder. Once, when he got home after midnight, he found the front door locked and had to bang and bang to be let in (by his mother). He applied to transfer for his sophomore year and managed to win a scholarship to Bucknell University in rural Pennsylvania, a welcome seven hours' drive away. It was a blessing, he says, mostly because it kept him from having the kind of seriously wounding battle with his father that neither of them wanted.

He would have been happy to go almost anywhere. He had fixed on Bucknell because a high school friend had gone there, and had returned for Christmas break with an enviable air of independence and tales of a girlfriend. But this Baptist-founded college set among cornfields also fulfilled his increasing desire to experience "America": the non-immigrant, non-ethnic country of the movies and the books and, particularly, of his current literary idol, Thomas Wolfe. The lyric ambition of *Look Homeward, Angel* and of Wolfe's other books—Roth had read them all by the time he left for Bucknell—drew him away from the idea of law school and intensified his bond to literature: not so

much as beautiful writing, he says (although Wolfe offered that, too),
but as an expression of appetite, quest, and freedom. He still calls Wolfe
"half a genius." Writing about this first literary hero more than fifty years
later, in some unpublished notes about the writers who affected him in
youth, Roth recalls the powerful effect on him of Wolfe's "raw yearning
for an epic existence—an epic *American* existence." At Bucknell, he had
hopes of finding something like it. Small-town life, ivy-covered buildings, a library with a white steeple and a carillon bell. Fraternities (even if
he joined the only Jewish one and resigned after little more than a year).
Compulsory chapel attendance (even if he read Schopenhauer in his
pew). Roth may have had an all-American childhood, but he had come
to suspect that he had never known any real Americans in Newark.

⚭

The stories he wrote at Bucknell were about real Americans, and so he
saw no place in them for Jews at all. The elevated precincts of literature
were out of bounds for his family and the people he'd known, for the
immigrant city where he had grown up. Nor was there a place on Parnas-
sus for comedy, although he was just discovering how raucous and ram-
bunctious a performer he could be, and not only when he played Nathan
Detroit in his fraternity's ten-minute pocket version of *Guys and Dolls* on
frat night. He entertained the young professors who befriended him
with outrageous stories of hometown Jewish life, part neighborhood
lore and part routines remembered from the comics at Newark's Empire Burlesque. But this was not anything that he could imagine writing
down.

It wasn't possible to study modern American literature at Bucknell;
even the year-long English honors seminar began with *Beowulf* and
ended with T. S. Eliot and Virginia Woolf. ("I was interested in British
literature. That's what literature *was*.") The only glimpse he got of anything different was reading the plays of Eugene O'Neill in a class about
American theater, which was taught by one of his young professor
friends, Bob Maurer. By chance, however, Charlotte Maurer, Bob's
wife, had worked as William Shawn's secretary at *The New Yorker*, and
Roth got to know her when he and his girlfriend babysat for the couple's
young son. ("The only place you could screw in those days was on the
bed of the professors when you babysat.")

When he and his pals took over the campus literary magazine—
"It was a purge," he tells me, "a real Khrushchev move"—the Maurers
were their advisers, and they modeled it on *The New Yorker*, including an opening section based on "The Talk of the Town." ("We were
over in Sheboygan the other day . . . ," he brightly mimics the voice.)
The magazine, called *Et Cetera*, also had plenty of room for what he
now calls his "sensitive little stories," often about tragic youths whose
allegorical existence stood for "something like the life of the mind," as
he writes in *The Facts*. These stories may have reflected some of the
cultural and even spiritual displacement that the young author experienced at "football-clothes-car-date-acne-conscious" Bucknell, but
they reflected none of the highly unliterary exuberance that he also
felt.

Junior year, he came into his own. He was editor of *Et Cetera*; audi-
tioning for the drama society, he got the leading role that he wrote to
his grandmother about. He also received his first recognition "for literary acumen," as he puts it, when one of his professors, Willard Smith,
singled him out for a paper he had written on Thomas Mann's story
Mario and the Magician and asked him to lead a class. Smith's approval
carried weight: he was known to have been at Princeton in the era of
F. Scott Fitzgerald and Edmund Wilson, and he cut an impressive figure in the first Ivy League–style suits that Roth had ever seen. There
was also cause for jubilation on the personal front, when, after two years
in college, during which he'd had hardly more sexual experience than
at Weequahic High, he won a girlfriend and launched his babysitting
career.

Betty Powell—another Betty; it was the era for them—was not the
cheerleader type one might have expected. The most sophisticated girl
on campus, by Roth's account, she came from a navy family and had
spent part of her childhood in Japan after the war. Frail and blond, she
had since then suffered through her parents' divorce, and her father died
of cancer while she was in college. She smoked and drank martinis—
often, seductively, both at once—and her mixture of knowingness and
vulnerability seems to have been immensely appealing. And she played
very hard to get. Roth courted her assiduously, and he can still recall
her telling him, "Will you please stop *mooning* over me?" He found the
expression so enchanting—an early sign of the effect on him of women's

language—that he pursued her even harder. (The value of those babysitting jobs was proved the next year, when Betty was discovered in
Roth's off-campus room, hiding under the bed. The only reason the
landlady didn't throw him out, he believes, is that he had not yet paid
the month's rent.)

But it was also junior year when he got into the first real trouble of
his life. And it was the result of his writing. Specifically, a double-
spread satire, in *Et Cetera*, of the campus weekly newspaper—a beloved publication whose earnest mediocrity made it a perfect target for
the self-styled twenty-year-old "critical antagonist." His teachers in the
English Department had nothing but praise for his wit. ("They had a
little Jewish Swift on their hands," Roth says—"Swiftberg.") And he
himself was pleased: this wasn't one of his artificial stories but a re-
freshingly "reckless" response to something real. Shortly after publication, however, he was called in to see the dean of men. He remembers
being scared. Potentially, at any rate, this was not a trifling matter: it
was 1953, the Korean War was still on, and being expelled would have
meant not only disgrace but vulnerability to the draft. The dean made
it perfectly clear that Swift was not in the Bucknell spirit—the "-berg"
part, Roth thinks, didn't help—and Roth was also brought up before
the college's board of publications. Seeking advice and comfort, he
went to see Mildred Martin, the most revered of his English teachers,
who later recalled that he had shown up at her house nearly in tears.
Roth balks at the notion that he was anywhere near crying. But he remembers, with appreciation, the counsel she gave: "That's what you
have to expect"—he recites the words with conviction—"if you want to
be a satirist in this country."

He was not expelled, but he had discovered his gift for literary ir-
reverence, and, through his interest in *The New Yorker*, the stories of
J. D. Salinger, eight of which had appeared in the magazine by the spring
of 1953. Roth had read *The Catcher in the Rye* as soon as it came out,
two years earlier. Now, however, as a writer himself, he hunted down
everything by Salinger he could find, including stories published during
the forties in *Collier's* and *The Saturday Evening Post*. It was "the voice,
the intimacy," he explains, that struck him. "That isn't what you learned
when you studied literature. There was this sense of talking, of confess-
ing. It was indecorous. How was I to know about this from reading

Thomas Hardy?" And it was Salinger, he says, who is most responsible for the embarrassing "sensitivity" of his early stories.

Looking for journals that might publish his stories, he spent a lot of time during his senior year in the periodicals room of the Bucknell library. *"The Hudson Review, Kenyon Review, The Sewanee Review,"* he says, "I read them all, and more." He was riveted by his discovery of *Commentary*. "I had no idea what it was," he says, "but here were articles and stories about Jews of a kind I had never come across before—objective, forthright, descriptive." In its pages, he came upon a review of Saul Bellow's recently published novel, *The Adventures of Augie March*. The reviewer, Norman Podhoretz, judged the book an overall failure but offered praise for Bellow's attempt "to put blood into contemporary fiction" and to provide "a sense of what a real American idiom might look like." Roth went out and bought the book—it was, he tells me, only the second or third hardcover that he had bought in his life, aside from textbooks. "Books cost around five bucks—it was an investment." At first, he found the book more confusing than exciting: "I didn't know what to make of it. It was so *new*. It was a tremendous invasion into my academic training, and into everyone's academic training, which was the point."

He read Bellow's novel again during his first year of graduate school, at the University of Chicago—a wholly different intellectual environment. And his eyes were suddenly opened to the kind of literature a Jew might write about Jews: ebullient, modern, mindful. As an object lesson for a young writer, *Augie March* showed that "you could put everything into a book," Roth says, "including thinking—which flies right in the face of Hemingway, who was then the supreme master." Despite the book's astonishing freshness, Roth felt continuities with another, already less fashionable literary master, his old hero Thomas Wolfe. Bellow, too, had read Wolfe with fervor, Roth points out, and the correspondences are clear: "the gush of language, the epic sense of life, the outsized characters, the passion for American bigness." But his new literary hero, Roth says, was "a whole genius."

Bellow was the great liberator from traditional Jewish literary confines—"I am an American, Chicago born" are Augie's famous first words—and he was soon followed in Roth's reading by Bernard Malamud, whose work was not so obviously rebellious. Malamud's stories are set among the Jewish immigrant poor and steeped in old-world sadness, yet Malamud made new art out of the Yiddish syntax and inflections of these people's daily speech. It was a kind of speech, Roth later wrote—"a heap of broken verbal bones"—that had appeared of no use to any serious writer before. And, adding to the wonders of Malamud: "He had written a baseball book!" Recalling Malamud's *The Natural*, Roth nearly shouts in recollected wonder. "I didn't know you could write a grown-up book about baseball! Where did you get permission?" Yet the most important lesson that these two great writers taught him, he says, was that their stories of familial life in Chicago or Brooklyn were "as valid as Hemingway's Paris or Fitzgerald's Long Island" and that Jewish experience could be made into American literature.

Roth's own voice could be heard as soon as he started to write about the people he knew best. "The Conversion of the Jews" and "Epstein" were written during a year-long army stint that began in the fall of 1955, when he was twenty-two. After a year of graduate school in Chicago, he had decided to enlist, rather than wait to be drafted, but his service was curtailed because of a back injury acquired during basic training at Fort Dix. (He later wrote a story about such an injury, "Novotny's Pain.") This was not the army he had read about in Irwin Shaw's *The Young Lions* or Norman Mailer's *The Naked and the Dead*, books he had devoured in his appetite for wartime heroism. He was assigned to a desk job at Walter Reed Hospital, in Washington, D.C., writing up hospital news for public distribution. Luckily, the job came with a typewriter that he was allowed to use in his spare time.

It was in this period that he discovered music—specifically, chamber music, the other art that has concerned and consoled him throughout his life, engaging him while relieving him of words. He had never heard classical music at home. In Chicago, he went to Orchestra Hall a few times, but the big symphonic pieces, while impressive, seemed to him "clamorous," and he went mostly because he thought he should. Then, at the army base in Washington, free tickets were available for concerts at the Library of Congress, where the Budapest String Quartet was in residence. It seemed like a good enough idea: he went alone, in uniform ("You could pick up girls in your uniform"), and he found himself deeply, unaccountably, stirred. The great conversion experience, he recalls, was Mozart's Clarinet Quintet, played by the Budapest with a visiting clarinetist—he is humming now, and trying to summon the name of the clarinetist at a concert fifty-seven years ago—and, he says, "I was gone!" He went to more concerts, and continued writing, but his back pain became so excruciating that he had to be hospitalized. He was released from the army with an honorable discharge in the summer of 1956, badly injured without ever having seen a battle.

The stories he left the army with show a remarkable ear for the way ordinary people talk and a new willingness to trust it. "Epstein" reached back to a neighborhood scandal that his father had brought up at the dinner table. "The Conversion of the Jews" was based on a story told by Arthur Geffen, a young writer friend in Chicago, about a boy who threatened to jump from the roof of a synagogue while his rabbi pleaded with him from the street. Roth liked the image so much—the juxtaposed figures, child and rabbi, one above and one below—that, he relates in the Web of Stories interview, he told Geffen, "I'll give you five years to write the story, and if you don't, I will." He adds, "I did it anyway, the next year—but Arthur's still my friend today."

When Roth returned to Chicago to teach, after leaving the army, this story—still unpublished and rejected by "all the classy reviews"—met with the approval of no less a critic than Saul Bellow, who was a special guest at a class taught by another of Roth's writer buddies, Richard Stern. Stern had asked Roth's permission to give the story to the class, and Roth sat in on the session. He went out for coffee afterward with Bellow and Stern, but he was awestruck by the great writer, and Bellow—however "amused by me," Roth recalls—showed no sign whatever of wishing to pursue a friendship. Still, Roth knew that his work had made the author of *Augie March* laugh.

Goodbye, Columbus had its origins in a Chicago eatery, the University Tavern, around the same time, in 1957. Roth was with Richard Stern and carrying on about a New Jersey family of country club Jews, whose terrific red-haired daughter, Maxine, he had dated steadily, if often long-distance, after graduating from Bucknell—and particularly about the experience of living in the family's big suburban house for several weeks one summer. Roth remembers that Stern asked him what he planned to do with "this stuff" and that he didn't even understand the question. It was Stern who told him to go home and write it down. Despite all Roth thought that he'd learned about the range of permissible subjects, the upscale Jersey suburbs seemed an impossible leap. He didn't see why anyone would be interested. "It hadn't dawned on me," he said much later, "that it was *my* stuff." Skeptical, he agreed to give it a try. He wrote a part of it and showed it to Stern, who asked for more. He wrote another part; still more was requested. And then he finished the whole thing in no time at all.

Not Letting Go

The stories that accompanied *Goodbye, Columbus* filled out not only its length but its themes, so that the whole collection appeared to be about Jewish cultural adjustments (or maladjustments) to contemporary American life. At the time, Roth argued against the widespread notion of his book as a report on the assimilation of a particular people. Surely it wasn't only Jews who struggle, as his characters invariably do, to live a larger, freer life than that ordained for them by birth or circumstance? (This might even be considered a reasonable definition of "American.") In an interview in the *New York Post*, in 1960, Roth described his work as being about "people in trouble": a fairly universal concept. In the book's immediate aftermath, however, far from ceasing to write about Jews, he attempted to confront the largest historical troubles that modern Jews had known.

Casting about for a subject for his first novel, he came up with the idea of an American Jewish businessman who travels to Germany after the war, determined to kill a German, any German at all; he didn't get very far with it, he says, because he had never been to Germany, and the subject seemed beyond his scope. He would have liked to write about Anne Frank, but he had no idea how to approach the subject. He did complete a play, commissioned by a producer of the television program *Playhouse 90*, about Jacob Gens, the head of the Vilna ghetto during the war, a man considered by many to have been a Nazi collaborator and by others to have been a noble-minded dupe. In the early sixties, before Hannah Arendt brought the Jewish Councils to wide attention, Roth chose to explore the "terrible but very appealing moral dilemma" of a Jew who bartered with the Nazis, offering up hundreds of Jewish lives in the vain hope of saving many more. "He had some belief that he could make it less horrible," Roth explains, "but one could argue that was impossible. He knew the plan was a failure from the moment he undertook it." The network decided against producing the script. "It was not the time for a play about a Jew turning in other Jews," Roth agrees today. "It was too early." Back then, however, he strongly believed that it should have been produced. Even though, he adds, "I probably would have had to run to Argentina, like Eichmann."

There could hardly have been a work more different than *Letting Go*, the novel that Roth published in 1962, shortly after the Yeshiva confrontation, and which contained not a page that would incite or likely even interest his attackers. *Letting Go* is about moral dilemmas, but on a far less earthshaking scale, written under the influence not of Bellow or of Malamud but of Henry James, an old master who had become new again in university English departments during the fifties, with the first volume of Leon Edel's biography and any number of new editions and works of scholarship. Roth's novel is a self-consciously Jamesian story of two young men, both graduate students at the University of Iowa: Gabe Wallach, an aspiring novelist, and Paul Herz, a struggling scholar, are based on Roth and his friend Ted Solotaroff, who actually met in a class on Henry James. (Solotaroff recalled that they used to refer to Isabel Archer as a *shiksa*.) The book, heavily plotted and polished, marked a retreat from New Jersey kosher dinner tables into a refined and recognizable literary mode. To the novelist, still shy of thirty, it's clear why the retreat seemed more like an advance.

There was a great deal to grapple with: a complex web of relationships among serious-minded young characters who judge humankind—and particularly one another—by the moral standards of *The Portrait of a Lady* and (back on familiar territory) between them and their mystified parents. But *Letting Go* is very much a book of its era, and about its era, the late fifties, and so is principally about *not* letting go: of responsibilities, of social expectations, of the standard divisions between men and women and the mutual sense of exploitation those divisions incurred. Roth's boyish heroes are dragged relentlessly downward by adulthood, during the last American era when taking on immobilizing obligations, in one's early twenties—marriage, children, a job to support them—was an essential proof of being a man. And the social setup is no less debilitating for the women.

It is a weighty subject, and Roth produced a weighty, frequently absorbing but, at six-hundred-plus pages, overlong and—toward the end, especially—laborious book. The author sometimes seems as dutifully constrained by his responsibilities as his moralizing heroes. "I felt I had to put everything in," Roth says, looking back; "I was writing a big American novel." In his ambition, he was still as close to his old literary idol Thomas Wolfe as he was to Saul Bellow—master of inclusiveness—or to James. There's some remarkably unabashed mimicry of Wolfe in *Letting Go*, as when Paul Herz, at his father's funeral, embraces his long-estranged mother: "Now he closed his eyes and opened his arms and what he saw next was his life—he saw it for the sacrifice that it was. Isaac under the knife, Abraham wielding it. *Both!* While his mother kissed his neck and moaned his name, he saw his place in the world. Yes. And the world itself—without admiration, without pity. Yes! Oh yes!" Put *that* on a blind literary test and see who comes up with the name Philip Roth. What *Letting Go* shows, more than anything else, is a gifted writer trying different identities and searching for his own.

Reviews were decidedly mixed; at the time, Roth said they made him sick. Even the more favorable ones—"Mr. Roth has a phenomenal ear for colloquial dialogue," Orville Prescott noted in *The New York Times*—acknowledged the book's unshapely sprawl and depressive atmosphere. (About the depressiveness, Solotaroff later wrote that Roth was not inaccurate—it was a time of difficult marriages, financial strains, endless winters—but that he had "laid it on and laid it on.") Alfred Kazin called Roth a "born realist, observer, recorder, satirist," and was typically astute in identifying Roth's major concern as "people trying to live by unfulfillable notions of themselves"—a concern that plays out in his work to the very end. But ambivalent notices about "the kind of bad book that only a good writer could have written" and "the best bad book of the year" did not win many readers, and *Letting Go* was a commercial as well as a critical disappointment.

The book has some marvelous scenes, though, that extend Roth's already familiar strengths—a Thanksgiving shared by a group of elderly

Central Park West Jews, perfectly suspended between satire and poignancy—and, in passages that look out through the eyes of a seven-year-old girl, effects that he never attempted again. (The girl believes that her teacher is her mother in disguise, a notion that Roth reused with much greater impact in the opening of *Portnoy's Complaint* seven years later.) And the novel's rather dour tone is occasionally shattered by a pair of slapstick Jewish comics squabbling over a cache of stolen underwear—a glimpse of the Meister waiting to emerge from behind the Master—although Roth keeps their antics, and his energies, in check. The focus stays tight on his anxious, continually thwarted, painfully stifled young men: one is emotionally captive to a demanding, vulnerable, long-distance father, the other to a demanding, vulnerable, all-too-present wife, and both are trying to stand firm and bear up when they really want to run like hell.

Roth had experience with both situations. He had married in February 1959, just before the publication of "Defender of the Faith," when he was on the verge of everything: at twenty-five, he had a story about to be published in a national magazine, a contract for his first book, and unstinting encouragement from important editors. Just the year before, trusting at last that he could make it as a writer, he had put academia behind him and moved to New York, where he and Margaret Martinson Williams were married by a justice of the peace in Yonkers, in what appeared to be the sealing of his youthful triumph. Maggie was to all appearances Roth's American dream made flesh. The product of a small midwestern town, Protestant, blue-eyed, and very blond, she was the "pictorial embodiment," he later wrote, "of American Nordic rootedness," which is to say of everything that he'd left home to find: "a virtual ringer for the solid, energetic girl in the cheery movies about America's heartland, a friend of Andy Hardy's, a classmate of June Allyson's." But that was only part of the attraction. He had met her in Chicago and had eagerly pursued her, although, as he pointed out, there was no shortage of blondes in the area. Maggie's special charm seems to have been the cracks in the picture, intimations of an America that Andy Hardy had told him nothing about.

Roth had completed his M.A. at the University of Chicago before going into the army. After getting out, he returned to Chicago, in September 1956, thrilled at being hired to teach freshman composition—at twenty-three, he was the youngest member of the English department—while continuing his graduate studies and still having time, between teaching and learning, to write. It was his first real professional job, he found Chicago exhilarating, and he was determined, as he wrote in *The Facts*, "to exercise my freedom to its utmost." With his army separation pay, he had bought a suit at Brooks Brothers (three pieces, glen plaid) that he wore to teach his classes; with four hundred dollars that he saved up writing movie reviews for *The New Republic* (twenty-five dollars every two weeks), he acquired an eight-year-old car. Although he was wearing a steel-ribbed brace under the suit to help with continuing back pain, and he had hardly any money, he gave the impression of a young man who was going places. Still, he had a hard time getting Maggie to agree to a date when, that October, he cornered her in the doorway of a bookshop and told her everything that he'd managed to find out about her—she was from Michigan, she had worked as a waitress, she had two children—after having noticed her a couple of years before.

In *The Facts*, written some thirty years later, Roth did not use her real first name—he calls her Josie—partly out of respect for her children. But he recounts in detail how he wooed her, Othello-like, with the exotic narrative of his New Jersey past: Campbell's tomato soup simmering on the stove when he came home from school at lunchtime; neatly ironed pajamas when it was time for bed. Ironically, it was Maggie's accounts of her far less winning childhood and the dangers she had passed that roped him in. Four years older than Roth, she was the daughter of an alcoholic father who was in jail for petty theft throughout the years that Roth knew her. Smart enough to have got into the University of Chicago at seventeen, she was unfortunate enough to have had to leave school after less than a year, when she got pregnant, at eighteen; or, rather, she was smart enough to get Roth to believe this story—that Maggie had gone to college at all turned out to be one of her many, many lies. Indisputably, though, she was now a divorcée whose ex-husband had custody of their children. And she had recently left the waitressing job in the diner where Roth had noticed her for an office job at the same university where he was busy grading papers and reading Henry James.

She had lived outside books. She seemed to him to be, in the words of a character in *Letting Go*, "so much more adult and genuine, more in contact with life's realities," than he could hope to be. (And certainly more adult, it seemed, than the New Jersey girlfriend, Maxine Groffsky, whom he would eventually turn into Brenda Patimkin and with whom he now parted ways.) Even his time in the army had not provided anything like her experience. As Roth saw it later, looking back on himself as a literary-minded naïf, he had been determined to "capitalize the L in life." Long habituated to easily mastering whatever challenges came his way, he was looking for "something difficult and dangerous to happen to me." And he found it.

The union of Philip Roth and Maggie Williams may have been the most painfully destructive and lastingly influential literary marriage since Scott and Zelda. Early on, Roth created a loving portrait of Maggie in *Letting Go*, in the character of a blond waitress and mother of two named Martha Reganhart, who takes up with one of the story's tortured heroes. Martha is warmhearted, sexy, wry, and none too bookish but very smart. No one puts anything over on Martha, and if her housekeeping skills are questionable and her taste in clothes sometimes embarrassing to her more aesthetically refined lover, she is nevertheless the most lively and likable character in the book. There is no doubt that she loves her children—even if she can't protect them—and her little boy and girl are also lovingly drawn. (Roth had spent a good deal of time with Maggie's children by the time he was writing the book.) It's uncertain how long it took Roth to realize how "idealized"—his word today—this portrait was, and that the very trials he had admired Maggie for enduring had left her irreparably scarred.

They broke up several times during his second year of teaching in Chicago. After one such occasion, Roth went to a campus reading by Saul Bellow, accompanied by his new girlfriend, a beautiful and wealthy graduate student named Susan Glassman. Maggie was also in the audience, and, as Roth recounts the story, he went over to say hello while his date went off to speak with Bellow. (A furiously insulting note from Maggie about her replacement was waiting in Roth's mailbox when he got back home.) It is intriguing to imagine the turns the American novel might have taken had Susan Glassman not bedazzled Bellow that afternoon and gone on to become his third wife three years later. They were married for four years—Bellow had two more wives still to come—and, after a bitter divorce, Glassman became the model for a number of unpleasant women in Bellow's work. The larger question, though, is how Roth's work would have been affected if Glassman had remained with her date that afternoon and kept Maggie Williams from becoming Mrs. Philip Roth.

It's an idle game, but what gives it interest is Roth's response when I make the suggestion to him: What if he had married Susan Glassman instead of Maggie? To my surprise, he takes the problem by its other handle and explains that he could never have been married to Glass-man because she was so beautiful and rich and had gone to Radcliffe, and he would have been "completely defenseless" against her. "What would I have done, just kissed her feet all the time?" The answer seems to provide a glint of insight into Maggie's appeal, scars and all. At the beginning, at least, when what was broken in her seemed within his powers to repair, when the dark Jewish boy was also the white knight, her needs and her brokenness seem to have equalized their status, in his eyes, and provided him with a role that he could understand.

Roth presents himself as having been unable to escape Maggie: he was emotionally unequipped, in over his head. One of the reasons that he left Chicago in the spring of 1958 and headed for New York was to get away from her. He spent the summer, though, on his first trip to Europe, blissfully alone, taking in the literary sights of London and the prostitutes of Paris (also a first) and getting as far as Florence and Siena. In Paris, he received the *Paris Review* Aga Khan Prize for "Epstein," thanks to the backing of George Plimpton. The award was given at a party in the Bois de Boulogne—"All these Paris swells were there," Roth says; "George knew them all"—where he accepted his check from no less a figure than Prince Aly Khan, best known for having been married to Rita Hayworth.

There was a dinner afterward at a Left Bank restaurant, where his biggest thrill of the evening came from sitting next to Irwin Shaw. "He'd fought in the war, and he'd written *The Young Lions*," Roth says. "I was twenty-five, and he was a bestselling writer, and we hit it off, because he was a Brooklyn boy. Although he'd moved to Paris—he was a gourmand, he was a great skier—he was *still* a Brooklyn boy. He wasn't a literary writer I'd come to love, but he was a real writer. And here he was talking common talk, to me: funny, lively, energetic, twenty years my senior, and giving me encouragement. I was flying!" There was also a French girl he'd met at the Café Odéon the night before and had invited to the party. She arrived on a motorcycle with a great roar. "It was like a Jacques Tati movie," he recalls. "I invited Jacques Tati in drag to come to the Bois de Boulogne."

As a parting gesture of goodwill to Maggie, however, and to squelch the guilt of leaving, Roth had helped her get a summer job in New York at *Esquire*, for precisely the months that he was away—a whole, safe ocean away. Unfortunately, she decided that she, too, would stay. She was standing on the pier, waving, when he got back. He tried to keep his distance, his perspective, his new and independent life. He rented a two-room basement apartment on East Tenth Street, supporting himself on part of the modest sum he had earned for *Goodbye, Columbus*. He didn't have much to spare, but he didn't need it. He lived on a tiny budget, alone, except for a cat he acquired that fall and named Allegra, after the gorgeously feline ballerina Allegra Kent. But, as it happened, Maggie wasn't able to replace her summer job, or wasn't able to hold the job that she got to replace it. And when she ran out of money, she showed up on his doorstep. It was a cold morning. She had her suitcase and no-where else to go. He let her move in.

In *The Facts*, Roth offers sound reasons for his actions. There was a chance that she would stabilize herself if she got a new start in life; there was a chance that she would hurt herself if she didn't. Above all, he says, he had been trained by his parents to seek solutions when a person needed help—even if that person had borrowed his spare type-writer and hocked it, claiming it had been stolen. (He found the pawn ticket in her pocket.) Even if that person claimed that his resistance to marriage must be a sign of his "latent homosexuality." (Very latent.) Even if her presence turned his apartment into what he called "a psy-chiatric ward with café curtains." Yet the reader's faith in his reasoning becomes troubled when, detailing events that led up to their wedding some three months after she moved in, he falls back on the tortuously passive locution "She turned up pregnant."

There had been a few encounters in the dark, he admits, unemotional and nearly anonymous. Still, at first, he suspected she was lying. She broke the news when he returned from a trip to Boston, where he had been checking the galleys for the publication of *Goodbye, Columbus*.

She appeared to be jealous of the book—she'd been telling people that she was his editor—and afraid that with success he'd rise beyond her reach. But she submitted a urine sample to the local pharmacy for testing, and the result was positive. (Roth himself went to get the result and remembers being so stunned that he said to the pharmacist, "Positive that she isn't pregnant? Or positive that she is?") Now she was threatening to leave the baby on his parents' doorstep if he didn't marry her. This he found all too believable. And so, barely able to support himself, at twenty-five, he made a harsh and desperate but perhaps predictable counteroffer: he would marry her if she had an abortion right away. Which she did, or claimed to do, with three hundred dollars from his precipitously reduced bank account. She returned from the procedure in pain and no little anguish at what he'd forced her to endure, which may provide a small part of an explanation for why, in the most inexplicable turn of all, he kept his part of the bargain. They were married on February 22, 1959. They had the same wedding anniversary as his parents.

Roth asks himself the question point-blank, in *The Facts*: "Why didn't I pick up *then* and run away, a free man? How could I *still* have stayed with her?" Instead of answering, however, he veers off toward the safely exalted ground of literature, and lays the blame on his having been a fledgling novelist in thrall to a bold if diabolical imagination: "The wanton scenes she improvised! The sheer hyperbole of what she imagined! The self-certainty unleashed by her own deceit!" In stripping him of his youthful certainties and his illusions, Maggie was nothing less than "the greatest creative-writing teacher of them all," he concludes, the force that shook him free of the tiresome innocence of his early stories and the elegant probity of Henry James. How could he leave all that behind?

Roth may not have known exactly why he stayed, and even today he isn't proud of the weakness that he feels his manipulability betrayed. He had been an embarrassingly good Jewish boy: "frightened of appearing heartless," subject to "an overpowering, half-insane responsibility," as he wrote in *The Facts*—or, in blunter language, "a sucker." This isn't a later rationale: these phrases reflect the same trapped and rueful sense of moral responsibility that pervades *Letting Go*. He still wonders how much of this conception of manly dutifulness he derived from his father—a man dedicated to fixing other people's problems, other people's lives. "That's what I learned from my marriage," Roth tells me today: "that I couldn't fix everything."

Of course, the marriage had dimensions that no later judgment or attempt at psychosexual diagnosis can comprehend. Not long after the wedding, Maggie converted to Judaism, an act that her new husband discouraged as "pointless" and self-abnegating, although he agreed to a second ceremony, at a Manhattan synagogue, with his parents present. (Roth enjoys repeating the advice that Maggie got from her grandmother—whom he liked—about marrying a Jewish man: "They're short, ugly little fellas, but they're good to their wives and children.") Maggie was with him through the early rabbinical attacks; she was with him through the writing of *Letting Go*. He helped her win her children back from her first husband, and, for part of the time that he taught at the University of Iowa in the early sixties, he was a dedicated live-in father to her ten-year-old daughter, Holly. He was also dedicated—as a tutor, as an older friend—to her twelve-year-old son, David, who went to boarding school but stayed with them on holidays and sometimes through the summers.

Roth became especially close to Holly, a bright but much neglected child, who, he recalls, could not even tell time when she came into his life. One afternoon in January 1962, halfway through his second year in Iowa, after a particularly nasty "conflagration" with Maggie, he announced that he was leaving for good. Maggie threatened to kill herself, but he'd heard that before, and he left. Still, once out on the street, he says, he began to worry that she might be going through with it, and he went back—not because of Maggie, he insists, but because he couldn't bear the thought that Holly "would get home from school and find her dead mother," or, at least, an unholy mess. Indeed, Maggie had taken a mixture of pills and whiskey and passed out. He got her to the bathroom, where she vomited, and it was while she was still a little groggy that she told him, "I wasn't pregnant in New York."

The story got worse. To obtain a positive result on the pregnancy test, she had used a urine sample that she'd bought from a pregnant woman among the down-and-out in Tompkins Square Park, a few blocks from Roth's apartment. There had been no abortion: she had gone to the movies instead. She'd seen Susan Hayward in *I Want to Live!* a couple of times and then come home crying about the pain and humiliation. All this she confessed, saying that she wanted to come clean to him before she died. Of course, there was the possibility that she was simply trying especially hard to hurt him and that the confession itself was a lie.

After that, he says, he slept in a separate room and told himself that he was staying on "to take care of Holly." He also began having an affair with one of his students, a twenty-two-year-old aspiring writer. (She puts in an appearance a few years later as Karen Oakes, a bicycling coed with strawberry braids, in *My Life as a Man*, where the affair is the cause of the suicide attempt/confession and not a result of it. Is this significant? In his fiction, Roth tends to find self-incrimination far more interesting than innocence.) He was only twenty-nine himself, and romance soon won out over demi-parental obligation, when, later that spring, he asked his student-love to run away with him. As he reports the story now, she had the good sense to decline.

He backed out of his plans to spend the summer with Maggie and her children in a rented house in Wellfleet, Massachusetts; leaving the house there to them, he stayed at his friend William Styron's house in Connecticut while the Styrons were away. He was greatly taken with a quotation by Flaubert that he found typed on an index card thumbtacked to the wall behind Styron's desk, a line that he has cited in his work and still quotes with approval: "Be regular and orderly in your life like a bourgeois, so that you may be violent and original in your work." When, that September, he started a new teaching job at Princeton, he and Maggie and Holly moved into their new house together, in a lastditch attempt at a regular and orderly life. It wasn't easy. Roth recalls that he and Maggie could fight about anything—how to pronounce the word "orange," for example, Michigan style or Newark style—and that poor Holly would look back and forth at them as though she were watching a tennis match. He thinks that Maggie even became jealous of his rapport with Holly. That's the only explanation for her telling him, out of the blue, that if he ever tried to seduce her daughter, she would kill him in his sleep with a kitchen knife. (There is a possibility that Maggie's father had molested her. Roth says that she once told him this had happened, but she was speaking in anger and never repeated the charge; he still doesn't know if it's true.) That night, he says, he hid all the knives before he went to bed.

Letting Go, published in the spring of 1962, was dedicated "to Maggie." By the end of the year, however, Roth had returned to New York from Princeton alone, in order to escape her yet again. Geographic distance seemed to be his only reliable strategy. She soon followed him to New York, but this time the separation stuck. Holly went off to spend a year at boarding school and then returned to live with her mother. Roth kept up with Holly by letter and then through occasional dates together, at least for a while, even when he and Maggie were at loggerheads. He recalls taking Holly to a Broadway show and being served by Maggie with a legal summons right there in his seat.

Still, he got away from her—physically, if not emotionally, and certainly not financially. She rejected all his efforts to divorce, and she seemed to have the legal system on her side in her quest to bleed him dry. He was far from free. But he was just turning thirty. He had everything before him. And being the kind of novelist that he is, he was now able to spend all his waking hours trying to imagine how Maggie had become what she was—desperate, infuriating, frightening, tragic—in his next book.

A Jewish Patient
Begins His Analysis

When *She Was Good* took five years to appear, accounting for the single longest gap in Roth's productivity—from 1962 to 1967—during the fifty-plus years of his career. For some time he couldn't write at all, being "imaginatively paralyzed," as he puts it, by his marital troubles. But he says that even without these troubles he might well have been confused about what to do, after the critical letdown of *Letting Go*. He finally began writing a book that he intended to call *The Jewboy*, about his early years, written in a semi-mythological, Malamud-like ("Malamuddy," he says with a laugh and the emphasis on "muddy") vein. "But I didn't know how to control a non-realistic book," he says, explaining why he left it unfinished. "If anything goes, anything goes. How do you control it?"

And he had Maggie too much on the brain, particularly the trick of the urine specimen. "I was haunted by that," he says. "Just haunted by it," he repeats, shaking his head: "It had taken me out of my young life, taken my strength, my promise, my industry . . . my everything—and that's what it had been about." Next, he wrote a play designed specifically to include the story of the phony pregnancy. The title was *The Nice Jewish Boy*, and although he completed it, and it was rehearsed at the American Place Theatre, in 1964, with the leading role played by a not yet discovered Dustin Hoffman, he decided that it was no good and called off a scheduled staged reading. "I had a live grenade in my hand," Roth says of Maggie's deception and what it meant to him. "But I didn't know how to use it."

In life, he was moving on: dating, making a new circle of friends, visiting Israel for the first time, teaching at Stony Brook and then at the University of Pennsylvania. He enjoyed teaching, but it was also an economic necessity. Roth had won a Houghton Mifflin Literary Fellowship for *Goodbye, Columbus*, a prize that brought his full payment for the book to seventy-five hundred dollars. For his next book, he followed William Styron's advice and moved to Random House, where he earned more money; but even so, his twenty-thousand-dollar advance for *Letting Go* had to be parceled out over the three years that it took him to complete the book. Roth recalls that his publisher, Bennett Cerf, was very kind to him when he was getting his footing in New York, after leaving Maggie, and invited him to glamorous evenings where he met Truman Capote, Frank Sinatra, Claudette Colbert, and, as excitingly, Martin Gabel, the former radio star who had narrated *On a Note of Triumph*.

In late 1964, Roth very briefly dated Jackie Kennedy. They met at a party and talked a long time ("she was smart"), but he was too intimidated—and, he adds, he lacked the proper wardrobe—to keep the relationship going. Invited to be her escort at a second dinner party, he went out and bought a new suit and a pair of black shoes. ("I was nervous. I'm left handed and they serve from the right. What if I dropped something on her?") Taking her home from the dinner, in her long black limo with the Secret Service guy up front—he had expected to hail a cab—he remembers thinking, "Am I supposed to kiss her? I know all about Lee Harvey Oswald, am I supposed to kiss her? What about the Cuban missile crisis, am I supposed to kiss her?" And he remembers her asking, when they got to her building on Fifth Avenue, "Do you want to come upstairs? Oh, of course you do"—the only sign she gave, he says, that she knew exactly who she was. Upstairs, she told him the children were asleep, prompting more inner turmoil on his part: "You mean the little boy who salutes like this and the little girl who calls her pony Macaroni?" When he finally kissed her, it was like kissing the face on a billboard. There wasn't much more to their acquaintance than that, he says—they saw each other only two or three times—although he "would have loved it if she could have been the corespondent in Maggie's lawsuit."

By this time he had met (at Bennett Cerf's) the woman who became his girlfriend for the next several years, Ann Mudge. She was a beauty

who was in quiet rebellion against a wealthy, conservative background—
and Roth, at eighty, looks back on her as one of the loves of his life. A
calm and gentle woman, Ann was the antithesis of Maggie and in some
ways the antidote to her. All the two women had in common, Roth
notes in *The Facts* (where Ann is called May), was their Protestant
blondness and their adversarial relation to the privileged world that
their looks seemed to represent. For Ann, despite her wealth, had suffered an emotionally harsh upbringing and, like Maggie, bore "the scars
of wounds inflicted" by it. She had left college without graduating; in
New York, she had done some modeling and some interior decorating—
not the most fulfilling work that she felt she could do. Once again,
there was a healing role that he could play—he soon encouraged her to
return to school—even as she helped him to heal his own wounds and
regain his equanimity.

But healing takes time, and what he needed to write about in these
years was Maggie. In 1965, he began a novel meant to include the purchased urine sample, but he found that he still couldn't bear to con-
template the marriage. Instead, he decided to use the stories that Maggie
had told him about her upbringing, along with his own experiences
of the people he'd met and the places he'd seen during visits to her
family: to examine Maggie's roots in the thirties, Maggie growing
up in the forties, and, especially, Maggie coming to young woman-
hood in the early fifties. Unable to confront the full force of the
woman as he'd known her, he determined to write about the girl he
hadn't known. But even after he settled down to work, the book went
through many, many versions. Cartons of manuscripts piled up, and
he feared for a while that he would never be able to get through the
story. He wrote a good deal of it while staying at the upstate New
York writers' colony, Yaddo, and his deep loyalty to the place originates
with the fact that *When She Was Good* was finally finished there, "after years of misery."

When She Was Good is a work as harsh and plain as the world that
Roth depicts. The book contains few jokes, no Jews, none of the easy
banter of *Goodbye, Columbus* or any other sign that it was written by
the author he had promised to be. This self-suppression marked a pains-
taking adaptation of style to subject. Roth was no longer standing outside the "Americans" he'd been observing since leaving home; he was

burrowing within them, even if only to discover a resistance to admitting depths. The principal male character, raised in the upright town that Roth calls Liberty Center, in an unspecified midwestern state, can't come any closer to cursing, even in his thoughts, than "that g.d. bed" or, about a girl he likes—a high school cheerleader—that she is "built, as the saying goes, like a brick s. house." The cheerleader herself is subject to rumors about whether she will "'spread,' as the saying goes, on the very first date." It's a world of clichés, repression, and petty scandal, and Roth adheres unblinkingly to its limitations—for better and worse, in a remarkable if sometimes costly literary feat. Roth says today that the book "might have been written by Sherwood Anderson," and takes satisfaction in having pulled it off. At the time, several critics assumed it to be a willed display of authorial range, seizing on a geographical (and emotional) realm too far from Roth's experience for him to get a proper grip. But *When She Was Good* is an obsessive work, deeply personal if strictly disciplined, about the destruction of the soul of the woman he felt had nearly destroyed him.

Roth's heroine, Lucy Nelson, is an ambitious small-town girl who dreams of a bigger, better life but goes terribly wrong along the way. An alcoholic father, a weak and ineffectual mother, a blundering boy who impregnates her at eighteen and, worse, marries her: all are responsible, as she sees it, for the shabbiness and disappointment of her life. And, in part, she's right. Despite the harshness of Lucy's judgments and her growing debasement, this is a sensitive account, powered by Roth's attempt to understand "the suffering," as he puts it now, "behind the anger." The hazards and constrictions of a young woman's life, circa 1950, are presented with chilling, Dreiserian reality: an eight-page seduction, part wheedling and part bullying, in which Lucy's boyfriend talks her into the backseat of his car and gets her pregnant; the condescending rebuff of the college-town doctor whom she begs to give her an abortion. In the broader view, Roth lets us see the disparity between the flawed human beings who surround Lucy and the monsters she imagines them to be, although the damage inflicted on her is so severe that the difference hardly matters.

Increasingly isolated, resentful, raging, Lucy is an incubus but also a product, a character of immense but curdled strengths. Reviews of the book often depended on what the critic thought of her, and the range extended from "one of those great literary portraits, like Emma Bovary or Becky Sharp" (Josh Greenfield, *The Village Voice*) to "hysterical" and "a full-blown bitch" (Wilfrid Sheed, *The New York Times Book Review*). The darker view reflects the consensus of virtually all the book's other characters; by the end, even Lucy's two-year-old son can't bear her. Although female critics at the time raised no objections to Lucy's portrayal (both Doris Grumbach and Maureen Howard found her all too real), Roth's reputation among feminists fell so low during the next couple of decades that her story was swept up in a kind of retroactive anger. In an interview with Roth in *The Paris Review* in 1984, Hermione Lee explained that "the feminist attack" on his work was based, in part, on the fact "that the female characters are unsympathetically treated, for instance that Lucy Nelson in *When She Was Good* is hostilely presented." Roth, responding somewhat defensively, contended that Lucy could be seen as "a case of premature feminist rage," and the claim is not without its merits. In a reconsideration of the book in *The Huffington Post* in 2010, Karen Stabiner set out all her feminist credentials while daring to declare that Lucy Nelson is "a fledgling and tragically failed feminist," and wagered that if readers came to *When She Was Good* without knowing who had written it they would assume that the author was a woman.

It's a dangerous thing to give birth to a writer—Roth likes to quote Czesław Miłosz, saying that "when a writer is born into a family, the family is finished"—and dangerous sometimes even to be a friend. (See the stories that Henry James and Edith Wharton wrote about each other.) But, *pace* Saul Bellow, there are special risks to one's eternal good name in marrying one. With Lucy reduced to a state of permanent outrage, *When She Was Good* concludes in a spectacular act of exorcism. After driving everyone away, Lucy wanders off on a freezing winter's night, more than half-deranged: "Farewell, farewell, philanderers and frauds, cowards and weaklings, cheaters and liars. Fathers and husbands, farewell!" Her body is discovered three nights later, under layers of ice and snow. It is a brazenly melodramatic stroke, compounded by the grisly irony that the discovery is made by a high school couple who have parked in the local lovers' lane, where Lucy first got into trouble, and who hit the frozen body with the shovel they are using to dig out the car. By this point in the story, her death is a huge relief—for the reader and, apparently, for the author. The book comes as close as a realistic novel can to driving a stake through its heroine's heart.

The reality of escaping Maggie was much harder. In early 1963, Roth obtained a legal separation, but only on condition that he provide her with a weekly sum of one hundred and fifty dollars, amounting to roughly half his annual income—an arrangement that was to continue until she chose to remarry or, more likely, given her preferences, for the rest of his life. Their marriage was childless and had lasted less than four years. She was thirty-three and able-bodied. He was twenty-nine, and his two published books had earned more praise than money. (Roth remembers that the judge who awarded the alimony asked how long it took him to write a book and that he replied, "Two or three years." The judge responded, "Can't you write any faster?") Even undivided his income was meager, and he was already borrowing money to pay for psychoanalysis, which he felt he urgently needed to control the resentment and rage that were now his.

Roth's psychiatrist, Dr. Hans Kleinschmidt, was a German-born Jew who had fled the Nazis in 1933, completed medical school in Italy, gone to Jerusalem in 1939, and, finally, immigrated to the United States in 1946. His field of special study was creativity, and he was known for treating artists and writers; Roth half jokes that his National Book Award got him a break on the rates. Roth began seeing him in the fall of 1962, traveling to New York from Princeton several times a week, and continued for about five years, a term that included significant gaps when he went off to Yaddo or spent summers away from the city. The psychiatrist may be credited with helping him make the final break from Maggie. Following a particularly horrendous fight, Roth recalls, he called Kleinschmidt and said that he had to see him that evening. After the session, Roth checked into a New York hotel—a room on an air shaft, at an "academic rate"—and never went home again except to collect his clothes. But Maggie remained the focus of his time in therapy; just talking out his fury at the deception of the urine sample required many months. His goal, he says, was to become "someone who would never be tricked like that again."

The doctor-patient relationship was not always smooth, however, since Kleinschmidt tended to invoke broad Freudian constructs (the "phallic threatening mother," the weak father), and Roth was certain that these abstractions did not apply to his family. "Why do you resist me?" Roth croons in a heavy German accent, mimicking his psychiatrist. Then, playing himself, several decibels louder: "Why do you resist *me!*" Yet it seems possible, at the time, some doubt was introduced— that the psychiatrist was able to rouse feelings of anger in Roth toward his mother and to draw up memories that justified them. The anger served a purpose, in both an emotional and a literary sense, as Roth makes clear in the later books *Portnoy's Complaint* and *My Life as a Man*. It wasn't long before Roth came to believe that this anger was unwarranted and wholly unfair, but by then the feelings and memories had done their work.

And while Roth admired Kleinschmidt in many ways, he had proof that the good doctor could be stunningly wrong. In the fall of 1967, Roth was experiencing a strange sense of weakness—"a general malaise," he says, "the feeling that something was wrong, sometimes nausea." One evening, he went off to a party at the 21 Club for the publication of William Styron's novel *The Confessions of Nat Turner*. Once there, he began to feel worse and became so dizzy that he could hardly stand. The next day, at his session, the psychiatrist assured him that he was suffering from envy. Roth protested that he thought Styron's book a masterpiece (he still does), that Styron was a friend and he wished him well, and then he asked—his trump card—why had he felt sick even before the party? "Because you were anticipating the envy," was the reply. Later that day, Roth felt so ill that he went to a hospital, where a doctor pressed down on his abdomen—"I shot up toward the ceiling in pain!"— and discovered that his appendix had ruptured and his stomach was filled with pus. He required immediate surgery. Two of Roth's uncles, his father's brothers, had died of peritonitis from a burst appendix, and Herman Roth had almost died of it, too, in 1944. For Roth, it was touch and go; he was in the hospital for a month. But in the end he felt that he had not only cheated death but saved his good opinion of himself.

He also discovered, around the same time, that Kleinschmidt had written him up in a psychoanalytic journal, *American Imago*, in an article titled "The Angry Act: The Role of Aggression in Creativity." His name was omitted, his profession slightly altered, but there he was, psychically naked, in his psychiatrist's baleful view: a man who suffered "castration anxiety vis-à-vis a phallic mother figure," who as a child had fantasized "that his teachers were really his mother in disguise," and who recalled a particularly awful occasion when he was eleven and his request for a bathing suit with a jockstrap was dismissed by his mother, in the presence of a saleslady, with the words "You don't need one. You have such a little one that it makes no difference." Furious with the psychiatrist, Roth, already down to just one or two sessions a week, thought of ending the analysis entirely. But he was getting too much from it, and in more ways than he had expected when he began.

These were the years when he was unable to write and finally produced the novel about Maggie's life (and death) that seems to have functioned as an imaginative adjunct to analysis. The analytic process, however, was also bringing new ideas to the fore: ideas about freedom, about breaking the constraints of good-Jewish-boyism that had bound him to the wheel of his marriage, and about breaking the constraints of literary propriety that had shaped both *Letting Go* and *When She Was Good*. Most critics yawned over *When She Was Good* when it was published, in 1967, and Roth's reputation seemed to be going downhill with everything else. But they snapped to attention when, that same year, excerpts from the raucous psychoanalytic whatever-it-was that he had in progress began to appear: "A Jewish Patient Begins His Analysis" in *Esquire*, in April; the instantly notorious "Whacking Off" in the unlikely intellectual bastion of *Partisan Review*, in August; and "The Jewish Blues," just one month later, in Ted Solotaroff's bold new publication, *New American Review*. We were not in the Midwest anymore.

By the spring of 1968, when a fourth chapter of the new work appeared, it was clear that something big was on the way. Roth was deeply involved with Ann Mudge by now, he was engaged in the anti-war movement—Mudge herself counseled draft-age men on their rights at a church in the Village—and he was writing at an unprecedented level of energy. Although the new book was still incomplete, signs of its impending success had already inspired Maggie to take him to court to demand more money, not for the first time. And then, one morning as he sat down to work, he received a telephone call from Holly, telling him that Maggie was dead.

He thought at first that it was a trick meant to catch him in a nasty response that Maggie could use against him in court. That sort of deliverance, after all, happened only in fiction. As it turned out, the circumstances of her death were far more banal than the frozen tomb he had invented: a car crash, in Central Park. No one else was hurt. For the sake of her children, he agreed to organize the funeral. It was a Jewish service, as Holly said she'd wanted, and Roth found himself selecting the appropriate psalms alongside one of the rabbis who had accused him, not many years before, of being a danger to the Jews. A few days after the funeral, he left New York for Yaddo, where in an excited rush of twelve- to fourteen-hour days he completed the book that would show the rabbi what he could really do to endanger the Jews when he put his mind to it.

A Jewish Joke

Portnoy's Complaint (pôrt'-noiz kəm-plānt') *n.* [after Alexander Portnoy (1933–)] A disorder in which strongly-felt ethical and altruistic impulses are perpetually warring with extreme sexual longings, often of a perverse nature.

Portnoy's Complaint was one of the signal subversive acts of a subversive age. The excitement surrounding its publication was so high that even before its appearance, in February 1969, *Life* magazine pronounced it "a major event in American culture." Along with rock concerts and protest marches—with which it seemed to have more in common than with other books—it spoke to the generation-wide rejection of long unquestioned and nonsensical rules, to the repudiation of powerful authorities, and to the larger struggle for personal and political freedom. The downfall of LBJ, the end of the war, the demise of hypocrisy! The final extinction of the fifties! And all by way of thirteen-year-old Alexander Portnoy, overcosseted Jewish son, obsessively masturbating behind the bathroom door ("My wang was all I really had that I could call my own") or wherever and however the undeniable need happened to strike. On a bus beside a dozing girl, into an apple core, into the family's uncooked liver dinner—the giddy exposure of masturbatory compulsion gave the novel its absolute stamp of the late-arriving Sixties, its obscene zest, and, of course, its notoriety. If Holden Caulfield ever behaved like this, he didn't tell us about it.

The subject of a wretchedly good Jewish boy's attempts to squirm out of the ethical straitjacket of his childhood was not so distant from that of some of Roth's earlier stories, or of *Letting Go*. By struggling to defeat his overdeveloped conscience and become a bad Jewish boy, however, Portnoy turned the tragic destiny of his earlier counterparts into comedy; and by failing miserably at being bad—by paying the price in mental anguish for every insistently outrageous deed—he made the comedy emotionally complex and painfully funny. Even grown to manhood, Portnoy remains "marked like a road map from head to toe with my repressions," incapable of unrepented pleasures. Yet in the ballistic force of the writing Roth himself achieved the freedom that his hapless hero could not win; the book's shameless, taboo-squelching language was liberating for both the author and his readers. In his Web of Stories interview, Roth explained the process of writing the book in terms of a private revolution: "I was overthrowing my literary education," he says. "I was overthrowing my first three books." And if, at the farthest extreme, he was overthrowing the "literary seriousness that had accompanied my education and that had launched me into writing in the first place," he was also finding a way to reclaim it.

The Portnoys had their origins as wildly exaggerated relatives who lived upstairs from Roth's own sane and solid family, in a manuscript that he abandoned when he hit on psychoanalysis as a way to tell the story. The premise of a marathon, book-length psychiatric session, following years of his own psychiatric sessions, was what finally allowed him, in his mid-thirties, to let go. The premise itself meant that nothing should be hidden. ("You want to hear everything," Portnoy tells his psychiatrist, Dr. Spielvogel, "okay, I'm telling everything.") Chronology was moot. ("I suddenly remember how my mother taught me to piss standing up! Listen, this may well be the piece of information we've been waiting for.") Digressions, diversions, excursions, were all permissible—were, in fact, the way to go. ("The only book I knew that operated through digression was *Tristram Shandy*," Roth notes, "but I wouldn't call that an influence.") It was this unprecedented permission that allowed him to blow the lid off Henry James and midwestern truculence and every gentle, Gentile characteristic that he had associated with the great American plains of Literature.

The public permissiveness of the era also played a role: politics, theater, sex, the political and sexual theater of New York. Even while he was toiling away on *When She Was Good*, Roth was performing dinner table routines for his New York Jewish friends, as he'd once performed radio routines for his parents and Newark routines for his teachers at Bucknell. These new routines were a literal sounding board for the antics of *Portnoy*, and he had found an ideal audience. These were people who had emerged from a background not unlike his own, who were as conversant with Lenny Bruce and The Fugs as with Freud and Kafka, and who could appreciate the mixture of reality and farce in his shtick about Jewish families. (Roth recalls that he once chased Jules Feiffer, in a manic two-person improvisation, all around the Upper West Side apartment of his publishing friends Jason and Barbara Epstein.)

In a milder era, Roth's conversational style had yielded *Goodbye, Columbus*; now it dawned on him that he could use this "uninhibited playacting" in his writing, too. Not since Henry Miller adapted his joyously filthy letters home from Paris in order to blast his way out of literary rectitude and into *Tropic of Cancer* had a writer plumbed such an essentially low-down mode—stand-up comedy with an improvisatory streak—to reinvigorate literature itself. Picking up once again with the material of the unfinished *Jewboy*, he turned his attention to the formation of the other half of the tormented couple that had made up his marriage. Tracing the chronic guilt that had got him stuck there and the fury that had laid him out on the couch, he dived into the swamps of the Jewish joke and splashed around.

And so thirty-three-year-old Alexander Portnoy recounts for the doctor, as calmly as he can, a recent evening in the company of his parents:

Doctor, these people are incredible! These people are unbelievable! These two are the outstanding producers and packagers of guilt in our time! They render it from me like fat from a chicken! "Call, Alex. Visit, Alex. Alex, keep us informed. Don't go away without telling us, please, not again. Last time you went away you didn't tell us, your father was ready to phone the police. You know how many times a day he called and got no answer? Take a guess, how many?" "Mother," I inform her, from between my teeth, "if I'm dead they'll smell the body in seventy-two hours, I assure you!" "Don't *talk* like that! God *forbid*!" she cries. Oh, and now she's got the beauty, the one guaranteed to do the job. Yet how could I expect otherwise? Can I ask the impossible of my own mother? "Alex, to pick up a phone is such a simple thing—how much longer will we be around to bother you anyway?"

The quietly beleaguered father, the manipulating gorgon of a mother, and the tortured son who (barely) survives to tell the story: Roth's trio was the newest development in the pained tradition of Jewish comedy. Jews had always been the Jewish joke's primary instigators and best audience. Scholars and psychologists (including Freud) have noted the Jewish propensity for self-lacerating humor, arising as an outlet for inevitable aggression and frustration. (Who else, after all, could the Jews take it out on?) And then, to limit criticism to one's persecutors reveals resentment and marks the victim. Also relevant is the will to self-protection: the same will that inspired African Americans to invent the rhyming insult game "the dozens"—if you said the awful thing first, it wouldn't hurt so much when it came out of other people's mouths, and a little laugh might even distract them from killing you. Among the varied subjects of the Jewish jokes that Freud catalogued in *Jokes and Their Relation to the Unconscious* (1905) are an aversion to taking baths (especially among Galicians), the deceptions of marriage brokers regarding their human merchandise (at times involving humps), and the gall of the scheming *Schnorrer* taking money from the rich man. But there is no sign of the Jewish mother.

A couple of decades later, at the end of the twenties, the most famous Jewish mother in the culture, Al Jolson's in *The Jazz Singer*, was a gentle, sweetly loving figure, the kind of household saint that led Irving Howe to describe the Jewish mother in immigrant America as "an object of sentimental veneration." The comic turns of Fanny Brice—in a vaudeville routine called "Mrs. Cohen at the Beach"—and Gertrude Berg brought in the meddling tone recognizable in Neil Klugman's Aunt Gladys, with her Borscht Belt syntax and her need to feed. ("You leave over sometimes I show your Uncle Max your plate it's a shame.") But Gladys, like her forebears, has no malignity and no real power. She is not Neil's mother, of course. And the new prototype—overbearing, powerful, wreaking psychic havoc—was just being born.

The "Jewish mother" did not emerge alone but had something in common with other monstrous "mother" types that were prevalent in the American imagination at the time: the domineering, parasitical "mom" of Philip Wylie's bestselling *Generation of Vipers* of the early forties ("She plays bridge with the stupid voracity of a hammerhead shark"), the supposedly cold and unloving "refrigerator mothers" whom psychologists blamed throughout the fifties for children's autism, even the recklessly driven stage mother of the hit Broadway show *Gypsy* of 1959. But historians of these things—Joyce Antler, Lawrence J. Epstein—date the emergence of the stereotypically Jewish mother, tellingly, to theatrical comedy: specifically, to a Nichols and May routine, performed on Broadway in 1960, in which Mike Nichols played a rocket scientist being reproved for failing to call his mother during take-off. ("It's always something!" the mother—an improvising Elaine May—replies.)

The joke was not without a basis in reality: Nichols later explained that his inspiration had come from a phone call from his own mother. Likewise, Roth cites among his inspirations for Sophie Portnoy, the transcendent Jewish mother, three stories submitted by three different Jewish graduate students to a class he was teaching at Iowa, all revolving around a Jewish son's inability to evade the watchful gaze of his omnipresent mother, and his envy of the Gentile boys for the parental indifference that allows them to sneak off to sexual adventures. In a 1974 essay, published in *Reading Myself and Others*, Roth explained that he had immediately identified the situation as "an authentic bit of American-Jewish mythology." But it was a while before he understood just how to give it life: by grounding it in "the recognizable, the verifiable, the historical"—that is, in the kitchens (and bathrooms) of Newark.

There were reasons for the Jewish mother's fraught overcautiousness, of course, in the long, historical uncertainty that her children would escape unbloodied from the most ordinary day under the boot of the Russians or the Poles or the Germans. The word "Holocaust" never appears in *Portnoy's Complaint*. It was not in common use during the years when Alexander Portnoy—or Philip Roth—was growing up. Yet it might be said to inform everything that Sophie Portnoy does. Alex himself connects the comic and the tragic as the intertwining threads of his own Jewish fate:

Doctor Spielvogel, this is my life, my only life, and I'm living it in the middle of a Jewish joke! I am the son in the Jewish joke—*only it ain't no joke!* Please, who crippled us like this? Who made us so morbid and hysterical and weak? Why, why are they screaming still, "Watch out! Don't do it! Alex—*no!*" and why, alone on my bed in New York, why am I still hopelessly beating my meat? Doctor, what do you call this sickness I have? Is this the Jewish suffering I used to hear so much about? Is this what has come down to me from the pogroms and the persecution? from the mockery and abuse bestowed by the *goyim* over these two thousand lovely years? Oh my secrets, my shame, my palpitations, my flushes, my sweats! The way I respond to the simple vicissitudes of human life! Doctor, I can't stand any more being frightened like this over nothing! Bless me with manhood! Make me brave! Make me strong! Make me *whole!* Enough being a nice Jewish boy, publicly pleasing my parents while privately pulling my putz! Enough!

But this is Alex speaking as an adult (however adult he has managed to be). As a boy he admits no excuses—and certainly none that make a special case out of the Jews. When his sensible older sister, Hannah, tries to quell his adolescent rage and defend their parents, she only upsets him further by invoking the Nazis. "I suppose the Nazis are an excuse," he cries, "for everything that happens in this house!" To which she replies, "Maybe, maybe they are." It's hard not to read their exchange as quietly central to all the paranoid hilarity. "Do you know," Hannah asks, "where you would be now if you had been born in Europe instead of America?" He doesn't have an answer, so she tells him: "Dead. Gassed, or shot, or incinerated, or butchered, or buried alive."

But Alexander Portnoy *was* born in America, the land of brotherhood and the dignity of man. He even wrote a radio play about Tolerance and Prejudice—taken from Roth's own eighth-grade graduation pageant—called *Let Freedom Ring!* Against this democratic dazzle, his parents' endless fears and admonitions appear not strategic and judicious but infuriating and ridiculous, and his parents themselves so distant from his safe American life that they "might as well have had plates in their lips and rings through their noses and painted themselves blue for all the human sense they made!" The perception of this cultural chasm was not new. In 1964, four years after the Nichols and

May routine, Dan Greenburg's bestseller, *How to Be a Jewish Mother*, emphasized such important techniques of the suddenly renowned maternal figure as "Making Guilt Work" and "How to Administer the Third Helping." The same year, *The New York Times* called the heroine of Bruce Jay Friedman's novel *A Mother's Kisses* "the most unforgettable mother since Medea."

She was in the air, so to speak, the best joke that postwar, comfortable, assimilated Jews could share about their distance from their living past. (In 1989, Woody Allen actually sent her into the air, like a huge and hectoring balloon, in *New York Stories*.) By the time *Portnoy* appeared, the *Times* could refer to Sophie's excesses as "new whines out of all the old battles." But Roth's book was the apotheosis of the subject, the killer punch. No other mother had overseen her son so scrupulously at both ends of the alimentary canal. Threatening him with a bread knife when he refuses to eat, she is equally threatening outside the bathroom door: "Now this time don't flush. Do you hear me, Alex? I have to see what's in that bowl!" The reason for the Americanized generation's desperate need to get away, if not to get revenge, is expressed by her son in screaming capital letters, should anyone have missed the point: "BECAUSE WE CAN'T TAKE ANY MORE! BECAUSE YOU FUCKING JEWISH MOTHERS ARE JUST TOO FUCKING MUCH TO BEAR!"

Small wonder that the tremendous affection Portnoy also feels for his parents tended to be overlooked in the hubbub that greeted the book, although it is as strong as his rage and as necessary to his psychic tension. ("Doctor, what should I rid myself of, tell me, the hatred . . . or the love?") There are so many things he remembers about his childhood with "a rapturous, biting sense of loss": coming home on a winter afternoon to the smell of tomato soup simmering on the stove, summers in a furnished room on the Jersey Shore, his parents' determination to spare him the harshness of their own lives. But filial tenderness was easily overshadowed by the anger and the masturbation and the golden-haired sexual conquests who taught the country a new Yiddish word, *shiksa*: a non-immigrant, non-Jewish, all-American girl, needing to prove nothing to anyone in the country that produced her.

The *shiksa* was the last and most thrilling taboo, combining sex and familial repudiation with the most powerful of Portnoyan desires: to be

American. ("What I'm saying, Doctor, is that I don't seem to stick my dick up these girls, as much as I stick it up their backgrounds—as though through fucking I will discover America.") So there is Kay Campbell ("like the soup") from Davenport, Iowa, who, amazingly, lives on a street called Elm Street and has a mother named Mary; there is Sarah Abbott Maulsby from New Canaan, Connecticut, who is inspired to her first act of fellatio by hearing the Budapest String Quartet play (what else?) Mozart's Clarinet Quintet. The Portnoyan manifest destiny, deeply patriotic, is "to seduce a girl from each of the forty-eight states." (In regard to Alaskans and Hawaiians—"Eskimos and Orientals"—he remains indifferent.) But no matter how much baseball Alexander Portnoy played as a kid or how many *shiksas* he conquers, no matter that he was valedictorian of Weequahic High or even editor of the *Columbia Law Review,* he cannot shake the suspicion that being Jewish—being Portnoy rather than Smith or Jones—means he will never be a real American.

Enough reason for an uproar among the Jews? For good measure, Roth threw in a little extraneous nastiness about the "fat, pompous, impatient fraud" who is the elder Portnoys' revered rabbi. "Don't you understand," fourteen-year-old Alex harangues his mother, "the synagogue is how he earns his living, *and that's all there is to it.*" The finale of the book brings Portnoy to Israel, where he attempts to force himself upon a nearly six-foot-tall red-haired ex-military Sabra—"spread your chops, blood of my blood, unlock your fortressy thighs, open wide that messianic Jewish hole"—only to fall back and admit that the main effect on him of being in the Promised Land is that he cannot get it up. ("Im-po-tent in Is-rael, da da daaah": it's a giddy discovery, which he sings to the tune of "Lullaby in Birdland.") Roth had discovered that a little opposition really got his juices flowing.

But the rabbis hardly registered in the overwhelming response to *Portnoy's Complaint.* A private letter to the Anti-Defamation League may have had some force in response to a short story, or even to the twelve thousand hardcover copies that *Goodbye, Columbus* sold. *Portnoy's Complaint,* however, sold two hundred and ten thousand copies during its first ten weeks and more than four hundred thousand by the end of the year, beating out *The Godfather* for the number one bestselling novel of 1969. Obviously, many Jews (as well as non-Jews) relished the book, and at least one rabbi publicly acclaimed it as a noble document reflecting mankind's unquenchable yearning for a moral life. (And who better to represent that yearning, he nobly noted, than a Jew?) But Roth's treatment of the equally unquenchable sexual yearnings that make havoc of that moral life was a lot more difficult for some Jewish readers to accept than Mafia murders seemed to be for Mario Puzo–reading Italians. When had so much dirty Jewish laundry ever been displayed before so many Gentiles, people who had never required as much as a soiled hanky to justify Jew-hating crimes?

Not merely outrage but open fear was evident in reactions like that of the Berlin-born Hebrew scholar Gershom Scholem, who had left Germany for Palestine in the twenties and now warned, in the Israeli newspaper *Haaretz*, that Roth had written "the book for which all anti-Semites have been praying," a work potentially more disastrous even than *The Protocols of the Elders of Zion*, and that "the Jewish people are going to pay a price." At home, a series of furious articles in *Commentary* included what Roth still calls "a complete and devastating attack on all my work" by his onetime supporter Irving Howe. In an article titled "Philip Roth Reconsidered," published in 1972, Howe dismissed *Portnoy's Complaint* as little more than "an assemblage of gags" and claimed that Roth had written nothing since *Goodbye, Columbus* to equal its literary interest, then went on to spend pages revoking his praise of that earlier work.

The Patimkins, in particular, whom ten years earlier Howe had found "ferociously exact," he now considered mere "lampoon or caricature." Roth, depriving his characters of the historical context that might have made them understandable—"the fearful self-consciousness which the events of the mid–20th century thrust upon the Patimkins of this world"—had chosen, instead, to elicit disdain by putting their vulgarity on "blazing display." Marie Syrkin, also writing in *Commentary*, added to Howe's charges, claiming that Portnoy's *shiksa* fixation plainly resurrected the stereotype of Jewish racial defiler that had been a prominent feature of Nazi propaganda and had come "straight out of the Goebbels-Streicher script." Roth barely touched on the subject of the Holocaust, but few of his Jewish critics now saw his work in terms of anything else.

And the uproar among the Unchosen readers of the book? And

among those Jews who found comparisons to Joseph Goebbels and Julius Streicher somewhat far-fetched? Readers who were not frightened or shamed by *Portnoy's Complaint* were thrilled by its support for various private overthrowings of their own. In 1969, you didn't have to be Jewish (or a man) to empathize with Portnoy's (unspoken) rebuke of his mother: "Where did you get the idea that the most wonderful thing I could be in life was *obedient*? A little *gentleman*? Of all the aspirations for a creature of lusts and desires!" Or with his argument that, at thirty-three, his unmarried status reflects not an affliction ("So what's the crime? Sexual freedom? In this day and age?") but a willingness to face the truth about marital bonds:

> I simply cannot, I simply *will* not, enter into a contract to sleep with just one woman for the rest of my days. Imagine it: suppose I were to go ahead and marry A, with her sweet tits and so on, what will happen when B appears, whose are even sweeter—or, at any rate, newer? . . . How can I give up what I have never even had, for a girl, who delicious and provocative as once she may have been, will inevitably grow as familiar to me as a loaf of bread? For love? What love? Is that what binds all those couples we know together—the ones who even bother to let themselves be bound? Isn't it something more like weakness? Isn't it rather convenience and apathy and guilt? Isn't it rather fear and exhaustion and inertia, gutlessness plain and simple, far far more than that "love" that the marriage counselors and the songwriters and the psychotherapists are forever dreaming about? Please, let us not bullshit one another about "love" and its duration.

Neither the social contract nor the marriage contract was about to be torn up, but by the late sixties, with some help from Roth, both were the worse for wear.

Portnoy's Complaint made Roth a rich man. In May 1968, he was in debt for eight thousand dollars: "I had been sitting in my room like in Solzhenitsyn's cell," he says, "doling out this money to Maggie and being angry." Suddenly, in June, Maggie was dead, his book was finished, and a messenger had delivered a publisher's check for a quarter of a million dollars. (*Life* magazine: "What's the tip on a quarter of a million?") He paid off his debts, he bought a car, he moved to a nice apartment on the East Side, and he took Ann Mudge on a first-class trip to

Europe, sailing on the *France*. He hadn't bought any clothes in years, so he had several suits made at one of the poshest tailors in London—Kilgour, French & Stanbury, on Savile Row. The experience wasn't as unfamiliar as he'd expected. "It was like the Temple B'nai Jeshurun in there," he assures me. "The cloth was like the Torah ark, and there was the silence and the light coming through the dirty windows, and all the tailors were Jews." He had more bespoke suits made elsewhere. He propositioned the first attractive journalist who was sent to interview him. He hired a call girl, while Ann was off somewhere, for an hour in a London hotel. "I was dizzy," he remembers, "dizzy with success and freedom and money."

He broke up with Ann as soon as they got back to New York that fall. Because he believed what he had written about marriage, because he had been so badly burned by Maggie, and because, after more than four years together, they had reached the point where marriage and children were the next expected step. ("She didn't say, 'Marry me,' she didn't have to say it, it was there in every moment.") Life was too full of possibilities. Yet he was not the sexual madman that many people took him to be. "The book came out in February 1969, and I went up to Yaddo in March and stayed for several months," he says in reply to a question about life after *Portnoy*. "That was my freedom."

True, but not the entire story. In December 1968, at a dinner party, he met a beautiful young woman named Barbara Sproul—a graduate student in the history of religion, twelve years his junior but "a grown-up" and "somebody who knows her mind," he says—who quickly became his next romance. Sproul visited him at Yaddo in mid-March and again in late March. In mid-April, when Roth realized that he could not face returning to New York, Sproul found a house for them to rent together a couple of miles outside Woodstock, just across the valley from a cabin that she already rented for herself. He had hardly taken a break between one long-term love affair and the next. Once again, he was living a determinedly regular and orderly life—although no one wanted to believe it.

He was a celebrity, and he became even more famous when the movie version of *Goodbye, Columbus* was released, just two months after the publication of *Portnoy*. What a doubleheader for the Jews! The movie was a huge success, and Roth believes that Ali MacGraw was marvelous as Brenda Patimkin, but that the mother—Mrs. Patimkin, played by Nan Martin—was shrill and overdone. Indeed, Vincent Canby's review in *The New York Times*, while highly favorable, took uneasy account of the difference between Roth's "lightly sketched" subsidiary characters and the movie's "overstuffed, blintz-shaped caricatures." The scene of a wedding reception, in particular, was singled out as an example of "gross moviemaking," and Roth unhappily recalls its "big chopped-liver sculpture, and people stuffing their faces, which I certainly didn't have." While still rather appreciating the film, as the best that has been made from his work, he notes, "A little shrillness goes a long way. As does a little Jewish vulgarity."

He was not merely famous, however, but notorious. The impact of the book, far beyond the sheltering walls of literature, is almost impossible to believe now. On April 1, 1969, the *Times* ran an editorial titled "Beyond the (Garbage) Pale," which shared the page with equally authoritative statements on the Lindsay administration's hospital reorganization bill and federal cuts in welfare spending. The editorial's general concern was the plummeting of "standards of public decency" in unnamed works of theater and film. But it reserved special rancor for "one current best-seller hailed as a 'masterpiece,' which, wallowing in a self-indulgent public psychoanalysis, drowns its literary merits in revolting sex excesses." (It seems almost too pat that Eisenhower's funeral procession was the headline story of the day.) According to the *Times*, the courts had let down the American people by refusing to outlaw such "descents into degeneracy," and the critics had suspended their judgment—indeed, the evidence was in plain sight on the other side of the page, which featured an enormous ad for the same bestseller, with quotes heralding "an American masterwork" (*Life*), "the most important book of my generation" (*The Washington Post*), "an autobiography of America" (*The Village Voice*), and—from *The New York Times*—"a brilliantly vivid reading experience" that was also "potentially monumental in effect."

On television, Jacqueline Susann, author of the scarcely stainless *Valley of the Dolls*, said on *The Tonight Show* that she would like to meet Philip Roth but wouldn't want to shake his hand. Roth himself refused to appear on television, not wishing to make himself more recognizable than he already was: the book jacket had an author photograph on its back. People continually accosted him in the street, apparently convinced that they knew him intimately. ("Hey, Portnoy, leave it alone!") This was why he left the city to hide out at Yaddo, pursued by competing rumors that he was dating Barbra Streisand and that he had been committed to a hospital for the insane.

Unlike so many symbols of its era, *Portnoy's Complaint* has survived: it shows signs of becoming a classic rather than a relic. There was a twenty-fifth-anniversary edition, with a new introduction by Roth; a few years later, in 1997, Louis Menand, in *The New Yorker*, wrote, "Portnoy is forever." And it remains remarkably controversial in an era when John Updike's once scandalizing *Couples* has slipped into the realm of the comfortably historic, and Norman Mailer's *Why Are We in Vietnam?*—another deliberately provocative and well-received sixties novel about the new America—has faded from sight. In 2009, on its fortieth anniversary, *Portnoy* was awarded an unofficial, retrospective Booker Prize, at the Cheltenham Literary Festival, for the best novel of 1969. A dissenting judge on the jury, the English classicist Mary Beard, complained about the choice in a *Times Literary Supplement* blog, deriding the book as "literary torture" and a "repetitive, blokeish sexual fantasy." She was met with a hail of reactions, pro and con, ranging from a heated defense of "the can't-put-it-down vigour of Roth's writing" to derisory comments about his "ethnic stereotypes" and the calmly universalizing assertion that "any man who's grown up in an ethnic-immigrant household in America has his entire life story etched out in the pages of that book." One person who hadn't read it reported the decision to buy a copy right away: "There must be something about the book if it provokes such a range of comments."

Looking back, Roth wonders what might have happened had he not written *Portnoy's Complaint*. He believes that it still determines his reputation, as a writer and as a man, in a diminishing as well as in a positive way. (In February 2013, *Town & Country* put Roth on its list of "Top 40 Bachelors"—at the age of seventy-nine—with a single comment: "The recently retired Pulitzer Prize winner has rarely met a shiksa he didn't like.") To Roth, the most important scene—"the pumping heart of the book"—was almost entirely overlooked and has nothing to do with masturbation. It is a seemingly peripheral scene that involves Alex's Uncle Hymie getting rid of the *shiksa* cheerleader his son adores:

the determined father secretly tells the girl that his son has an incurable disease and is under doctor's orders never to marry, then slips her some cash in case she didn't fully understand. When the son finds out, he and his father have a furious, physically violent face-off, in which the boy is wrestled to the floor and cruelly subdued. A few years later, when the son is killed in the war, the only consolation people can think to offer is that he didn't leave behind a *shiksa* wife or *goyische* children. Roth's point was the insularity and brutality of Jewish family life in those years: the whole-life demands, the mortal ruin that repaid transgression.

Roth admits that he never actually saw such physical violence, although his father used to tell the story of *his* father having beaten up an older son to "save him" from marrying what Herman Roth called "a worldly woman." The phrase, Roth explains, referred to an older woman, possibly a divorcée—not a *shiksa*—but he heard many stories about Jewish parents paying off Christian girls or sitting shivah for children who had married outside the faith, exactly as if those children were dead. This was the cultural background against which *Portnoy's Complaint* was written, and Roth now suspects it was the aspect of the book that Jews found most upsetting, in its revelation of "Jewish rage, and in particular Jewish rage against the Gentiles." It is also the cultural background from which the author came, although he has been tireless in stating that such brutality was entirely foreign to his family. For one thing, his parents had never objected to his dating—or marrying— anyone because she was not Jewish. For another, they were emphatically (how many times has he had to say this?) not the Portnoys.

"A novel in the guise of a confession," Roth wrote in 1974, in an essay titled "Imagining Jews," "was received and judged by any number of readers as a confession in the guise of a novel." The casually unliterary, first-person naturalness of Roth's voice led many readers to imagine that Portnoy's story was his own, despite his avowal that this naturalness was a hard-won technical achievement, something like the acting style of Marlon Brando. (Previous books in the "Jewish son" tradition may have helped to cloud the issue: the jacket of *How to Be a Jewish Mother* featured two photographs of the author, Dan Greenburg, being spoon-fed by his mother, one as a toddler and the other at what looked to be age thirty.) It's true that the Portnoys have certain points of resemblance to

Roth's father and mother, as revealed in his later nonfiction: Jack Portnoy, like Herman Roth, is a hardworking insurance salesman without a high school education but with a substantial moralizing streak. Sophie Portnoy has Bess Roth's aptitude for the housewifely arts and makes the same tomato soup when her son comes home for lunch. *Portnoy* also exploits some of the same incidents as Dr. Kleinschmidt's article, including Sophie's reply to eleven-year-old Alex's request for a bathing suit with a jockstrap: "For *your* little thing?" Despite the cozy happiness that Roth recalls of his early years, it isn't difficult to fathom why, in *The Facts*, he admits that his favorite word from childhood onward was "away."

But the Portnoys were not his parents. They had begun as neighboring relations, after all, and became parents only with the psychoanalytic setting: "You don't lie on the couch and talk about your neighbors for five years," Roth remarks. And it was his father, anyway, who drove him crazy; his father, not his mother, who was difficult and domineering, if also heartrendingly well-meaning. It was his father's interference that he'd had to escape, all the way to Bucknell and Chicago. His mother was a reticent being by comparison, the family's peacekeeper when the males went head-to-head. A lady, a meticulous writer of thank-you notes, a passionate admirer of Eleanor Roosevelt: a woman about whom Roth's only real-life criticism is that she was at times "a little too *comme il faut*." Roth has been explaining and defending her now for decades, and I am somewhat surprised one day when he mentions that his brother, Sandy, probably saw things differently.

It is the summer of 2009, shortly after Sandy's death, and Roth is musing about how differently the boys perceived their mother. Roth worshipped his big brother in his youth and maintained a steady relationship with him throughout their lives, but he believes that Sandy had probably disliked their mother ever since he came home from school, age five, to find her playing with a new baby. It's also possible that she behaved differently with her firstborn: stricter, maybe, more frightened and hovering. In any case, Sandy, who failed to have the artistic career he wanted, blamed their mother for making him too closed and careful, too intimidated to succeed as an artist, and he continued blaming her, Roth says, until the day he died. It was Sandy's relationship with their mother that Roth used as a model for *Portnoy*. If Roth himself felt any youthful ambivalence about her, any trace of anger that psychoanalysis may have stirred, it is long forgotten. He says that there is not a day that he doesn't think of his mother or of something she said that seems to him wonderful. Not that she said anything exceptional. "It was just ordinary mothering," he says, "quite wonderful enough."

Shortly before *Portnoy's Complaint* was to be released, Roth warned his parents that they might be bothered by reporters. This was beyond their comprehension, and his mother wept because she feared that he was deluded about the effect the book was going to have, and would be disappointed. Both his parents had always been proud of his work and couldn't understand the charges it had drawn. When his father told the story of a neighbor that Roth turned into "Epstein," about an aging adulterer who is caught more or less with his pants down, Roth says that he told it with the same wry sympathy that he himself tried to capture on the page. Who could think that this ordinary human stuff was racial calumny? Or anti-Semitic?

Yet, as the tidal wave of reaction to *Portnoy* began to swell, Roth felt the need to get his parents out of harm's way. He sent them on a cruise, first to London, where he had a friend look after them and show them around. (The friend happened to be Delmore Schwartz's ex-wife, Gertrude Buckman, who found Herman Roth almost impossible to handle. "My father," Roth cries rather proudly, "outdid Delmore Schwartz!") After that, he sent them on their first visit to Israel. They were gone for a month, so, as he'd planned, they missed some of the early firestorm over the book. His father had taken along a supply of copies, though, and later recounted how on the ship he kept asking people, "You want an autographed copy of my son's book?" Then he would go to his cabin, get a copy of *Portnoy's Complaint*, and sign it himself: "From Philip Roth's father, Herman Roth."

Drilling for Inspiration

Roth's ultimate answer to all the accusations against him was his faith in America. In the bluntly titled essay "Writing About Jews," published in *Commentary* in 1963, he replied to the question of whether he would write as he did if he were in Nazi Germany by pointing out that he was emphatically *not* writing there, and that legal barriers to persecution were strong in the United States. And should those barriers ever seem to be weakening, he went on, the actions needed to strengthen them would certainly not include his critics' demands for "putting on a good face"—that is, for pretending that Jewish lives were subject to none of the failings that mark the lives of other people. Jews who insisted on this sort of falseness and repression were choosing to live as victims in a country that had finally freed them from that role. As he saw it, the undue tolerance of persecution that history had bred among the Jews—"the adaptability, the patience, the resignation, the silence, the self-denial"—must end now, in America, where the only proper response to the threat of a restriction of liberties was, "No, I refuse." Unlike his detractors, he didn't doubt his rights or his place here. As a free-speaking Jew and a man head over heels in love with American ideals, Roth could reasonably defend his work as part of the great national project of liberation.

By 1969, however, he was less sure about the country's ideals. Richard Nixon was in the office once held by Franklin Roosevelt; the goals of the Vietnam War had replaced those of the Second World War; the

progress of what Roth called the "demythologizing decade" was propel-
ling him, like so many others, into unprecedented political opposition.
In March 1970, with some of his *Portnoy* money and his new girlfriend,
Barbara Sproul, he traveled to Cambodia. It wasn't a political trip, initially; Sproul had suggested it to celebrate his birthday and to help him
escape from the still oppressive post-*Portnoy* fame. They went first to
Greece, and the trip also included Bangkok and Rangoon. Sproul was
completing a doctorate in religion, comparing the creation myths of different cultures, and her interests ranged wide. Roth had been asked by
an editor at *Look* magazine to keep his eye out for an interesting subject, and at first he thought he'd found it in Bangkok, where he was as-
tonished to see—"whatever one had heard"—that "every ounce of female
flesh was for sale."

Most astonishing were "all these tiny Thai girls with their pimps
waiting at the airport for the GIs to arrive for R and R," he recalls today.
"The guys would hire a girl for maybe fifty bucks for five days, sign up
for the week. And you'd see them leaving, too, back at the airport, it
looked like they'd fallen in love, the girls madly kissing them goodbye
and calling out, 'Bye-bye, GI, I love you! I'll visit you in Ronkonkoma' or
wherever . . . and then they'd just wait there until the next plane came
in." He took notes, too, on kickboxing matches and on a local band of
AWOL GIs who "looked like a cross between Hendrix and the crew of
Captain Ahab's ship." It was, he says, in a phrase of the time, "a rock-and-
roll war."

They arrived in Cambodia, to see the temples at Angkor Wat, just
weeks before U.S. air strikes on the country began. (Or, rather, before
airstrikes that the government was forced to acknowledge began; secret
bombings had been going on since 1965.) Roth took the time to visit a
few settlements along an enormous lake some miles to the south, and
there he knew that he'd found his subject. On his return home, he
wrote an article, titled "Cambodia: A Modest Proposal," that appeared
in *Look* in October 1970 and has been republished in *Reading Myself
and Others*. Half satire—the tribute to Swift is clear—and half tragedy,
it begins with a simple description of what he'd seen among the clusters
of bamboo huts set on stilts in the soft mud: "The possessions of each
household appeared to consist of a sampan, fishing nets, straw baskets
for fish and rice, and a water jug." And then Roth explains that it would

make far more political sense to drop shoes, vaccines, bags of rice, re-frigerators, and air conditioners, rather than bombs, on the helpless population. He acknowledges that there are serious risks to this alter-native program; somebody is bound to be hit on the head. So he is pro-posing "specially demarcated air-conditioner drop zones," to prevent the casualties that our compassionate government surely wished to avoid. ("I am categorically opposed to the crushing of any child anywhere under an air conditioner, *even a Communist child*.")

He had turned to political satire, he said, because of a single word: "Nixon." He was proud to say that his devout New Deal Democratic family had considered Nixon a crook some twenty years before the rest of the country caught on. When, in a single week in April 1971, the president granted leniency to Lieutenant William Calley, one day after Calley's conviction for the murder of twenty-two Vietnamese civilians at My Lai, and then released an anti-abortion statement proclaiming his "personal belief in the sanctity of human life," Roth could not resist writing an op-ed piece, which *The New York Times* rejected as "taste-less." Barbara Sproul, living with him in Woodstock at the time, tells me that she remembers him banging away on the typewriter and saying over and over, "Tasteless, I'll show them tasteless!" In a mere three months, he had completed the full-length anti-Nixon satire, *Our Gang*.

Published in the fall of 1971, and featuring epigraphs from Swift and Orwell, the book betrayed serious moral rage behind its twisted tales of Trick E. (Tricky) Dixon, who campaigns to bring the vote to the unborn, while defending Lieutenant Calley from charges made by "Mon-day Morning My Lai Quarterbacks." When a concerned citizen wonders if one of the women killed by Calley may have been pregnant—which would make him guilty of the serious crime of abortion—Tricky points out that you can't expect "an officer rounding up unarmed civilians" to distinguish between a Vietnamese woman who is pregnant and one who is merely stout. "Now if the pregnant ones would wear maternity clothes, of course, that would be a great help to our boys. But in that they don't, in that all of them seem to go around all day in their paja-mas . . ." He promises the American people that he has a secret time-table for the complete withdrawal of the Vietnamese people from Vietnam.

Tricky is eventually murdered and found stuffed into a plastic bag, and large numbers of citizens turn out to be eager to confess to the crime. The president of Random House, Robert L. Bernstein, was reluctant to publish the book, at first, not for political reasons but because of what Roth himself now calls questions of "taste and discretion," particularly on the subject of assassination (in whatever bizarre form), and despite the fact that Tricky is back on his feet in the last chapter, planning his comeback, from Hell. Roth tells me that he and Bernstein had "a very reasonable discussion," however, in which Roth elaborated on the place of satire in a civilized society and mentioned Swift—"You always pull out Swift," he adds, "when you're doing something disgusting." The publisher ultimately agreed that bringing out the book was the right thing to do.

In *The New York Times Book Review*, Dwight Macdonald called *Our Gang* "far-fetched, unfair, tasteless, disturbing, logical, coarse and very funny"—"in short, a masterpiece." He said that he laughed out loud sixteen times. Needless to say, he mentioned Swift. The review put the book on the bestseller list, where it remained (albeit in the lower reaches) for four months. Even today, it delivers some knockout laughs, although not nearly as many as Macdonald got. The problem with *Our Gang*, though, isn't that it's dated—we are unlikely ever to be rid of the kind of deadly political obfuscation that Roth mocks—but that there is a lot of space between those laughs, and the jokes themselves are too often suited to a frat night skit: overextended and strained. In part, this is because Roth, without any real characters to explore—his cast also includes the likes of Lyin' B. Johnson and Chief Heehaw of the FBI—was out of his element, which was writing novels about people with sometimes overscaled but always recognizable emotions. And also, in part, because he was struggling to exaggerate a reality so grimly absurd, it outdid satire.

NIXON: What if anything do you know about the Roth book . . .

HALDEMAN: Oh, a fair amount.

NIXON: Who is responsible? The Roth thing I notice it's reviewed in *Newsweek*, which might indicate that they might be very much behind that.

HALDEMAN: Yeah, because they gave it a review way out of proportion to the book. We got advances of it and our people were very disturbed about it. It's a judgment call. I read it, or skimmed through it. It's a ridiculous book. And it's sickening, and it's—

NIXON: What's it about?

HALDEMAN: It's about the president of the United States.

NIXON: I know that! I know that. What's the theme?

HALDEMAN: Trick E. Dixon. And the theme is that, uh, he's tied to the abortion thing. The thing that inspired the book was your statement on abortion, and so he's decided that—and then he juxtaposes that with your defense of Calley, as he puts it, who shot a woman who had a child in her. A pregnant woman. And he relates that you're defending a guy who kills a woman with an unborn child in her . . . Balances out. It's sick, you know, perverted kind of thing . . . It ends up with you being assassinated—or with Trick E. Dixon being assassinated, and then he goes to hell and in hell he starts politically organizing down there.

NIXON: Did *The New York Times* review it favorably too?

HALDEMAN: I didn't see the *Times* review, so I don't know that.

NIXON: How big is the circulation?

HALDEMAN: The book? It isn't showing up on the sales lists yet. There's no indication of it. But Philip Roth is a very big author, so he's got—

NIXON: What is he? What is he?

HALDEMAN: He wrote *Goodbye, Columbus*, which became a very big movie, which got him some notoriety. But then his big thing is *Portnoy's Complaint*, which is the most obscene, pornographic book of all time.

NIXON: That's what I mean . . .

HALDEMAN: This book is apparently obscene in a different kind of sense. And it's very cute. The minister in it is Billy Cupcake instead of Billy Graham. And the attorney general is John Malicious instead of John Mitchell. And you know he's done this play on names all the way through it. But it's—at least to me it seems a very childish book. I never read *Portnoy's Complaint*, but I understand it was a well-written book but just sickeningly filthy . . .

NIXON: Roth is of course a Jew.

HALDEMAN: Oh yes . . . He's brilliant in a sick way.

NIXON: Oh, I know—

HALDEMAN: Everything he's written has been sick . . .

NIXON: A lot of this can be turned to our advantage . . . I think the anti-Semitic thing can be, I hate to say it, but it can be very helpful to us. I mean you hear a singer even as brilliant as Richard Tucker and he's a Jew.

HALDEMAN: Is he?

NIXON: . . . He's pushy . . .

HALDEMAN: There are a lot more anti-Semites than there are Jews, and
the anti-Semites are with us generally and the Jews sure aren't.

This conversation was not invented by Roth—imagine the howls of
outrage if it had been—and it touches on subjects that he never approached in *Our Gang*. It is a transcription (with some omissions where
other subjects were briefly taken up or the voices are inaudible) from
the Nixon tapes, recording a conversation between the president and
his chief of staff, H. R. Haldeman, held on the morning of November 3,
1971, in the Executive Office Building of the United States.

Roth had written *Our Gang* hurriedly, while other subjects were on
his mind and on his desk. Following several bombings in America by
the radical anti-war group the Weather Underground, he began a novel
about a teenage girl who blows up a building. He completed fifty or
sixty pages, but he couldn't get a story to coalesce around the character
or imagine what would happen after the bombing, so he put the manuscript away. He was also having trouble with a novel that he was trying
to shape—again—around his marriage and the purchased urine sample that Maggie had used to trick him into it. He had tried to find a
place for the tormenting scene even in *Portnoy*. Although it had not
worked in anything he'd written—"too lurid and dark," he says today—it
would not let him go.

The hero of this unruly novel keeps above his desk the maxim by
Flaubert that Roth had found above Styron's desk: "Be regular and orderly in your life like a bourgeois, so that you may be violent and original in your work." It's true that the life Roth had settled into with
Barbara Sproul in Woodstock showed no trace of the violent and original books that he was brewing or, even less, the uproar over *Portnoy* he
had fled. Sproul worked on her dissertation while he wrote. He loved
living in the countryside and walked for miles every day. (Sproul remembers that she had just about convinced him that no one cared who
he was when, as they were walking on a quiet country road, a man
stuck his head out of a car window and yelled, "It's Portnoy!") Although
there weren't many people around, Roth became good friends with the
painter Philip Guston, a co-refugee from Manhattan twenty years Roth's

senior, who—according to an essay that Roth wrote about him years later—was in the act of "an artistic about-face" very like Roth's own (it involved farce and dread and a rejection of complexity), since he was "bored and disgusted by the skills that had gained him renown." In place of the unmourned New York literary world, there was teaching, which Roth has always loved. "That's the one place where I could be serious about books," he says today, rather wistfully. "Everywhere else, you bring up a book and people start talking about movies."

Roth had begun teaching a literature class at the University of Pennsylvania in 1965, but he stopped in the aftermath of *Portnoy*, because, he says, "I just didn't want to be visible." In 1971 he began again, teaching a course in Kafka. He still had his New York apartment, and he and Sproul would travel from Woodstock to the city on Monday; he'd leave for Philadelphia on Tuesday morning and return to New York late Tuesday night. Sproul taught an introductory philosophy course at Hunter College during the week, and they would drive back to the country after her last class. The sheer amount of effort involved—he certainly didn't need the money anymore—suggests how important the experience was to him.

Sproul is a woman of large intellectual appetite and accomplishment; she went on to become director of the Program in Religion at Hunter (she was brought up a Unitarian and has never been religious herself), but she did not consider herself especially literary. She remembers Roth going over every class with her as he made his notes and worked out his thoughts. She happily read her way through a long reading list that he provided—a kind of life reading list—and also kept up with the weekly assignments for his classes. She often read his copies of the books, and she was perplexed, at first, by the underlining. She recalls bringing one mysterious passage to Roth to ask why he had marked it—she had an ingrained sense that reading was meant to convey information—and her surprise and delight when he replied, "because it's beautiful."

Even now, there is nothing that Roth loves talking about more than books: plots, characters, language, even particular old paperback editions. None of his passion for these things has faded. There are works he regularly rereads: Hemingway's *A Farewell to Arms*, Thomas Mann's *Mario and the Magician*. (He says that if he were dying and were allowed to read just one more thing, it would be *Mario*.) He's been known to give copies of whatever he's reading to his friends, to get the talk going. Returning to teaching, in 1971, he found his students at Penn wonderfully responsive. "They had the freedom that the sixties had given them, but they still had their brains," is how he puts it. "I just had to light the fuse and step back." Through the mid-seventies, he taught books from all over the literary map: *Madame Bovary* and *Cancer Ward*, works by Céline, Genet, Mishima. One year, he taught a class just in Colette and Chekhov, another year it was his twin idols Kafka and Bellow: "the hunger artist and the artist of abundance, of superabundance," he says. "I wanted to show them the pendulum, the swing of fiction."

Back at his writing desk, he was on an escapade meant to take him as far from both *Portnoy* and the darkly nagging marriage theme as he could get. He loved baseball almost as much as he loved books; it was tied to his childhood, and it was one of the uncorruptedly mythic things still going on in the country. If Malamud had written about it, why couldn't he? Just about a two-hour drive from Woodstock is the Baseball Hall of Fame, in Cooperstown, where he went to read through the library and listen to the tape recordings of old players, taking down a lot of what he heard. He was, he says, in bliss. The book that he came up with, *The Great American Novel*, is a sprawling, cheerful, wearying, sometimes funny, ultimately headache-inducing farce, a book that at least one male, sports-loving writer I know—Scott Raab of *Esquire*—considers an overlooked masterpiece, but that seems to many a giddy mess.

Perhaps he loved the subject too much. There appears to be nothing that Roth did not happily throw into the epic of a Second World War–era baseball team of misfits—a one-legged catcher, a one-armed outfielder, a midget with the jersey number ½—to whom he gave some of the godlike names he had learned on his trip through the temples of Asia. (A decade earlier, at the Iowa Writers' Workshop, Roth was on a softball team made up of novelists who played against a team made up entirely of poets—Mark Strand at first base, Donald Justice as shortstop—in a league that many people might consider almost equal misfits, although Roth is very proud of his home-run record and swears that the poets were tough.) The heroic pitcher at the center of Roth's tale, Gil Gamesh, was bullied as a child for being Babylonian ("Go back to where you belong, ya' dirty bab!") and is ultimately revealed to be a Communist spy. Ernest Hemingway puts in an appearance, sailfishing and arguing about the Great American Novel with an eighty-seven-year-old sportscaster he accuses of stealing his style. ("If I have a message," "Hem" declares, "I send it Western Union.") Meanwhile—enough not being nearly enough—a seagull swoops down on Hemingway crying, "*Nevermore!*" The midget players multiply, and the sportswriter, Word Smith, gives us his baseball-inflected take on *Moby-Dick*. To borrow the criticism of one of Mr. Smith's readers, it's "wildly excessive" and "just a little desperate."

Desperate for what? To follow up on *Portnoy?* To escape from *Portnoy?* To reestablish writing as a practice unaligned with personal torment? Roth completed the manuscript during a stay at Yaddo, and the very next day he had an even more outlandish idea for a book: What if a man turned into a breast? It came partly from Kafka, of course, but also from the distinct sense that his *Portnoy* readers—even the ones who loved the book, or maybe especially those—viewed him as a "walking prick." When they came up to him in the street, that's what they saw, it seemed to him, that's whom they were congratulating. It was disheartening, it was infuriating, and the inherent shame and self-disgust in the idea may cast a darker light on his baseball team of freaks and outcasts. But here was a way both of expressing what had happened to him and of turning it around. "It was like Henry Higgins," Roth traces his line of thought today: "Why can't a woman be more like a man? But in reverse."

So a new protagonist, David Kepesh, professor of literature at Stony Brook—who has recently completed five years of psychotherapy to help him get over a Grand Guignol marriage, and who finally has a lovely girlfriend and any number of reasons to think he is coming into the clear—wakes up one morning to find that he has turned into a giant breast: six feet long, a hundred and fifty-five pounds, with an acutely sensitive five-inch rosy nipple. It's a wonderful setup. And there's some pungency in Kepesh's anger at Gogol and Kafka for getting him into it. "Many other literature professors teach 'The Nose' and 'Metamorphosis,'" his doctor argues. "But maybe," Kepesh answers, "not with so much conviction."

Unfortunately, Roth has nowhere to take it from there. Aside from some hints of deeper content in Kepesh's pre-transformation waning of desire for his perfect girlfriend, and a father strong and loving enough to behave as though nothing untoward had taken place, the book suffers from the same absence of real characters and feelings as *Our Gang* and *The Great American Novel*. Roth, unlike Kafka, is not an abstract artist. His satire is most potent when—as with the Patimkins or Mrs. Portnoy—it is channeled through or obstructed by some warmth or contending emotion. The fact that the giant breast becomes obsessed with sex, and in a notably unmetamorphosed way ("Doctor, I want to fuck her! With my nipple!"), seems more a reaching into the old grab bag than a development of the book's invention. *The Breast* is a very brief book—Roth wrote it in a few weeks—but it ends in exhaustion, with another writer doing the work, as Roth quotes in full Rilke's poem on an archaic torso of Apollo, concluding, "You must change your life." Roth had certainly changed Kepesh's life and had also changed his own. But changing his work was harder.

None of these books of the early seventies—conscientiously grotesque, surreal, and often overwrought—did his reputation much good. "I wasn't trying to alienate the huge audience I'd won with *Portnoy*," he tells me, "but I didn't mind if I did." Pause. "And I guess I did." Some critics took the books as a reflection of the anarchic and somewhat surreal times. But they were also a reflection of Roth's post-*Portnoy* uncertainty and confusion. *The Breast* and *The Great American Novel* were published in reverse order of their writing, in 1972 and 1973, respectively. Roth had changed publishers, leaving Random House for Holt, Rinehart & Winston in order to work with the editor Aaron Asher, who was a close and much admired friend. It was Asher who thought *The Breast* seemed more nearly related to *Portnoy* and *Our Gang* and that this trajectory made more sense. What Asher was really waiting for, Roth says, was the big book he had promised next.

In April 1972, Roth, completing his transformation from a city boy, bought an eighteenth-century farmhouse in northwestern Connecticut and soon moved in there with Barbara Sproul. Forty acres, a small apple orchard, a few giant maples fronting the house, and a studio looking out over open fields: a setting for Chekhov rather than for any scene remotely associable with the Portnoys, or with the tormented book that he was finally able to complete there. *My Life as a Man* is the long-delayed work about his marriage. The difficulties he had in writing the story, the false starts, are carefully described by Roth's stand-in writer-hero, Peter Tarnopol. And the evidence of these difficulties takes the ingenious form of two stories that Tarnopol himself has written, placed at the beginning of the book, using different voices and familial details— third person, first person, a brother here, a sister there—in the hope of sparking his imagination and getting the book done. Roth's hero is well aware that others may not find the subject of his dreadful marriage as compelling as he does. His older sister writes to him, "Why don't you plug up the well and drill for inspiration elsewhere? Do yourself a favor (if those words mean anything to you) and FORGET IT. Move on!" But he does not have a choice: "Obsessed, I was as incapable of not writing about what was killing me as I was of altering or understanding it." Killing him still, though by the time *My Life as a Man* was published, in 1974, Maggie had been dead for six years.

No matter. As Tarnopol's psychiatrist points out—the same Dr. Spielvogel who honed his listening skills on Alexander Portnoy—one may be released from a trap and yet still not be free. The only hope the writer has is to write everything down, in order to understand and, eventually, to overcome. So here is the story of Maggie—called Maureen Tarnopol in this book—borrowing his typewriter and his finding the pawn ticket for it in her pocket. Here is her lie about being pregnant, and here, at last, is the urine sample that she bought, the abortion that she did not have, and the Susan Hayward movie that she saw instead. Here is the alimony that he paid without an end in sight. And here is the psychiatrist who blamed Tarnopol's "phallic threatening mother" for his susceptibility to such a marriage, arousing in him a blaze of anger toward his real and painfully perplexed mother, made more intense by memories of her occasional insults to his boyish pride—signs of nothing more, Tarnopol says he realizes now, than that she was not perfect. He is certain that the doctor's characterization of his mother was entirely wrong, even if it was necessary, in psychiatric terms, to "deplete the fund of maternal veneration" that Maggie—or rather, Maureen—had been able to draw on. So here, rather discreetly placed some two hundred and twenty pages in, is both an explanation and an indirect apology for Sophie Portnoy.

My Life as a Man is perhaps most powerful today as a depiction of the force and the fallacies of psychoanalysis in America, at the height of its influence. In conversation, Roth looks back on his own analysis as having been, in many ways, a kind of "brainwashing." "Like the North Koreans," he only half jokes, "the psychiatrist would torture you and torture you with his false interpretations, and when he stopped you were so grateful that you just accepted them." Freud was undoubtedly a genius, but the idea of translating his ideas into this kind of therapy was "outlandish," because it "stamped everyone with the same story." The story is about responsibility and guilt—guilt for your suffering, guilt even for your unconscious fantasies, which are the same unconscious fantasies that everyone is assumed to have. Roth mentions the female patients whom Freud accused of fantasizing the childhood abuse that they had actually suffered. The real problem with Freud, Roth concludes, is that "he wasn't a good novelist. He didn't pay enough attention to individual difference, to the details."

Tarnopol's new anger at his mother may serve a psychiatric purpose, but it does nothing to abate the old anger at his wife, which erupts in a hideous explosion. In one of the final scenes between the miserable pair, Maureen's promise to talk about divorce turns out to be just another trick; she has come to his apartment, instead, to read him a story she has written about him. "Two can play," she tells him, "at this kind of slander." And when she refuses to leave, throwing herself to the floor and grabbing on to a chair, he smacks the crap out of her. Literally and disgustingly: blood and shit are soon everywhere, all over the room. The smell is awful. And still, he admits he's having a good time, threatening to kill her even as he knows he won't. It's a shockingly violent scene, considering that this is Roth and not Norman Mailer. ("By the way," Roth says to me one day, without my having asked, "I never did that.") Afterward, Tarnopol, being a Roth protagonist and ever a good boy beneath the bad, helps her telephone her lawyer; he's in even bigger trouble than before. The book has a sudden denouement, when Maureen, like her real-life counterpart, dies in a car crash. But even that fate is not enough to satisfy Tarnopol. "Why isn't there a devil and damnation?" the unmerry widower rails at her ghost. "Oh, if I were Dante," he swears, weighing one more literary option, "I'd go about writing this another way!"

For obvious reasons, this book marked the start of Roth's big trouble with women, in the literary sense. Even Peter Tarnopol, examining his output, worries that he is "turning art into a chamberpot for hatred," semi-quoting his idol, Flaubert. A couple of years after the book was published, in December 1976, a cover story by Vivian Gornick in *The Village Voice* featured photographs of Roth, Bellow, Mailer, and Henry Miller—"like big Wanted posters," Roth recalls—under the headline "Why Do These Men Hate Women?" Gornick, a frontline feminist and an impassioned critic, was not calling them bad writers (except, sometimes, and with adequate quotations, Mailer) and was far from immune to the power and beauty of their finer work. She was almost over the top in her admiration for the stories of *Goodbye, Columbus* ("brilliant and deeply moving . . . filled with character, wisdom, and a luminous sense of the quest for a moral, feeling life . . . everything Tolstoy said a book should be") and warmly sympathetic toward *Portnoy's Complaint* ("a work so full of wonderful human dishevelment, a work so clearly *about* panic rather than driven by it, that we could not but laugh and anguish together with the dubious Portnoy"). If it were not for *My Life as a Man*, Roth would clearly not have made her list. As Gornick puts it, not without reason, the problems with the women in *Portnoy* were Portnoy's problems; the problems with the women—or, as she might better have said, the woman—in *My Life as a Man* were the author's. She was not the only critic to classify the book as therapy rather than fiction.

My Life as a Man is a work of tremendous humor, colloquial verve, and formal playfulness, with Tarnopol's two "short stories"—which introduce his own fictional protagonist, Nathan Zuckerman—set against a longer "factual" section titled "My True Story." Yet there is something uneasy and impacted at its core: a sense of confinement, and—despite the technical displays—a lack of freedom. Roth at last returns to a cast of living, breathing characters but keeps them at the perimeter of the central marriage, in the form of ricocheting voices. There is Tarnopol's sister, Joan, a wholly self-created woman (through electrolysis as well as education), who is happy in her marriage, her children, and her skin. (She is safe from any attempts by her brother to include her in his writing, she tells him, because "you can't make pleasure credible. And a working marriage that works is about as congenial to your talent and interests as the subject of outer space.") There is the rather wise if wrongheaded psychiatrist, Dr. Spielvogel, always available for emergency advice and consistently amenable. ("If you are incarcerated," he assures Tarnopol after the beating, "I will try my best to get someone to take over your hours.") And there is a Brenda Patimkin redux named Sharon Shatzky, young and bold and gaily sensual, whose virtues—"character, intelligence, and imagination"—Tarnopol does not realize until too late, after he has thrown her over for Maureen.

Maureen. What does it mean for a writer to put someone he considers a psychopath at the center of a novel? The problem with *My Life as a Man* is not that Maureen is deluded, scheming, and sometimes vicious but that her husband's day-and-night obsession with her delusions, her schemes, and her viciousness sucks the air out of the book, thins its texture, and makes it slack with repetition. The reader sometimes feels as Tarnopol does while writing, "trying to punch my way out of a paper bag." Maureen is a villain, but she's not uninteresting: she apparently scratched her way out of a bleak and intolerant white-trash family, she has a flashy former husband, a bit of glamour still, and she can be a witty as well as a fierce opponent. Speaking from the dead—where Tarnopol has dispatched his stories for her to read—she retitles his book *My Martyrdom as a Man*, which is not at all unapt. (It's typical of Roth to give the enemy the best lines.) She is in forward motion, however frenzied. Tarnopol, on the other hand, seems merely a dullish Portnoy, complaining of his Gentile wife instead of his Jewish mother, *"I can't take any more."* No matter how he tries to transform this story into art, he admits, there is "emblazoned across the face of the narrative, in blood: HOW COULD SHE? TO ME!" Tarnopol, all too clearly, is spinning his wheels. And despite the book's formal inventiveness and its gleaming comic bits, so was Roth.

In the mid-seventies, the worrying question asked about Maureen was not the usual one asked about a character in a novel: Is she credible? (In fact, some thought she failed that basic test; Morris Dickstein, in *The New York Times Book Review*, wrote that Maureen "might as well be a creature from Mars.") The looming question now was: Is she representative? Is she merely a woman or is she Woman? Gornick, for one, had no doubt about the answer. The force of her conviction even led her to misrepresent Tarnopol's beating of Maureen, already ugly enough, as the scene in which "the wife is being beaten to death," and to deduce from this that "Roth is clearly saying this repellent creature—and all those who resemble her—*deserves* to die." There's quite a jump between those little dashes. Gornick can be a close and astute reader; the misrepresentation suggests that her anger with the scene, perhaps with the entire book, short-circuited her critical faculties. The vituperativeness of the rest of her comments ("dehumanizing vileness"; "disintegrating moral intelligence"; "unacknowledged misogyny" that "leaks like a slow, inky poison") seems as extreme as her praise of Roth's earlier work. (Gornick's judgment has grown even more extreme with the years. In an essay in *The Men in My Life*, of 2008, she theorizes that both Roth and Bellow displace a Jewish anger against Gentiles onto women, and sweepingly condemns Roth's post-*Portnoy* body of work: "In all the books to follow over the next thirty years, the women are monstrous because for Philip Roth women are monstrous.") There were other critics, including Dickstein, who thought *My Life as a Man* showed problems with women, although Dickstein went on to suggest that Roth's quarrel was with people in general. But the word "misogyny" stuck.

Roth's hero had been at pains to make it clear that he did not hate women. He just hated the woman he had married. And with good reason. When his harshest critic of all, Dr. Spielvogel, accuses him of "reducing all women to masturbatory sexual objects"—there is no criticism that Roth himself does not anticipate—Tarnopol offers an anguished refutation, invoking in his defense a series of tender love affairs and explaining that, had Maureen been merely an "object" to him, he would never have married her. "Don't you see," he cries, "it isn't that women mean too little to me—what's caused the trouble is that they mean so much. The testing ground, not for potency, but *virtue!* Believe me, if I'd listened to my prick instead of to my upper organs, I would never have gotten into this mess to begin with!"

It's clear why critics were able to label the novel "therapy" without knowing much of Roth's private life. Tarnopol's cry is identical to Roth's own later explanation, in *The Facts*, of the moral and emotional ties behind his real-life marriage. There will be skeptics here, too, of course. Maggie Martinson Williams Roth had no more chance to present her point of view than do her fictional stand-ins. It is easy to imagine a silent woman as a woman maligned—a victim of what Maureen Tarnopol calls "this kind of slander"—and one searches for an objective scrap about Maggie's life and temperament, something to juxtapose to Roth's disturbing portraits. An interview with her son, David Williams, was published in the *St. Louis Jewish Light* in 1975, when he was twenty-seven, working in St. Louis as a trucker but hoping to switch to anti-poverty work. Approached by a reporter who had figured out his relation to the famous writer, Williams agreeably submitted to a number of questions. The answers, however, are not redeeming. "Mother was not only a very sexy-looking woman and an intelligent person," he said. "She was also very destructive. She tried to destroy everyone in her path." Even so, he says, "Philip would defend Mother to me when I criticized her."

As for "Philip," whom Williams had not seen in many years, he recalled that he had helped him get into a good boarding school and had helped to prepare him for it. Tutoring him in literature, Philip had selected books that he "literally forced me to read"—he mentions *The Red Badge of Courage* and *Fail-Safe*—and had discussed them with him at the kitchen table, "until he was satisfied that I comprehended the author's real reason for writing the book." He also "arranged to have me tutored in math and grammar," Williams continued, "but Philip himself was my main tutor." There were other subjects, too: "On masturbation," Williams says, "Philip quoted this Harvard dude who said that 98 percent of everyone masturbates and the other two percent lie." Williams acknowledged that he had been a pretty wild kid—"that's the only way I knew how to survive"—and "I've got to say that if it were not for the positive influence Philip had on my life at that time, I might be in jail today."

Yet, in some ways, Roth was not writing about a single woman. Even in this very hyperbolic novel, in which Tarnopol admits that any generalization he makes might well be viewed as "an unfortunate consequence of my own horrific marriage," he cannot help noting that his experiences were related to a wider social malaise. The expectation for fulfillment in marriage and only in marriage that had characterized American women of the fifties—the era of the Tarnopols' (and the Roths') wedding vows—was based on notions of "female dependence, defenselessness, and vulnerability," and abetted by the equally distorting "myth of male inviolability." No surprise that the result, for many women, was resentment. Maureen Tarnopol enjoyed her husband's literary success but also despised him for it. "Vicariousness was her nemesis: what she got through men was all she got." *My Life as a Man* is marked by its own resentment and sexual biliousness, but—as with *When She Was Good*— the author's underlying arguments are far from inimical to women, or to feminism. Tarnopol's case against what he calls "the Prince Charming phenomenon" makes him sound remarkably like Vivian Gornick.

There is still a final turn of the marital screw. The epigraph to *My Life as a Man* is a line from Maureen Tarnopol's diary, which is discovered, at a late stage in the novel, by her stunned and exhausted husband: "I could be his Muse, if only he'd let me." She, who did everything she could to thwart him? To get in his way? The diary also contains a more detailed and confident statement of her literary value to him. "If it weren't for me he'd still be hiding behind his Flaubert and wouldn't know what real life was like if he fell over it," she writes. "What did he ever think he was going to write *about*, knowing and believing nothing but what he read in books?" It's a line of thinking that Roth picks up fourteen years later, when, in *The Facts*, he suggests that he stayed with Maggie as long as he did because she was "the greatest creative-writing teacher of them all, specialist par excellence in the aesthetics of extremist fiction." Coming from him, the statement seems emotionally evasive and too clever by half, yet in a twisted way, made all too clear in this savage, funny, part-brilliant, part-strangled book, it is also very possibly true.

Kafka's Children

"**Y**ou must change your life." Roth had been traveling, teaching, reading—doing everything he could to renew himself. Although he kept his apartment in New York, he was rarely there. He was no longer interested in what people called a social life. He was working steadily. None of the books he'd written since *Portnoy* had approached its success—*My Life as a Man* was a particularly dismal flop—and while this record wasn't anything to be happy about, it was not the core of the problem. He knew very well who he wasn't, even if that happened to be what thousands of people thought he was. "I am not a bum or a lecher or a gigolo," Peter Tarnopol says to his psychiatrist, "or some kind of walking penis"—a message that had so far failed to reach Roth's audience. But even the audience didn't really matter. Finding out who he was, getting outside himself, understanding what was meaningful to him and doing something about it, in his life and his work: these were the somewhat blurry aims that came into focus almost as soon as he arrived in Prague.

"I wanted to see Kafka's city," he says, "and accidentally I found something more important." He was taking a trip, again with Barbara Sproul, as a reward for completing a long bout of work. Their plan was to see "the beautiful cities," so they went to Venice (where he'd been before) and Vienna (where he went to Freud's house and many museums) and then hired a car to drive them to Prague. It was the spring of 1972, almost four years since Soviet tanks had crushed the democratic hopes of the liberation movement known as the Prague Spring. During his first few hours of walking the city, Roth was captivated by its shabby, worn-down beauty, the big castle across the river, and the quiet, often empty streets. ("The only other tourists were a Bulgarian trade delegation.") It was clear that "people were not happy," he says, but he could tell at once that "there was something here for me."

He was not unaware of Czech political woes or their literary ramifications. Barbara Sproul was an active member of Amnesty International—"part of the vaguely missionary spirit that also drove her religious interests," Roth says now—and, when not touring the city, she was visiting the families of people who had been jailed. Sproul tells me that it was lucky for her that the sexist Czech authorities did not take her seriously—"they thought I was just the bimbo." Every day, "government agents would set off after Philip," and she would be free for a few hours to follow her rounds. (By the mid-seventies, Sproul was Amnesty International's Czech coordinator.) For Roth, a meeting with the editorial board of his Czech publishing house began to suggest at least a part of his own purpose there. At its conclusion, an editor who spoke fluent English asked him to join her for lunch. And the first thing she told him was that the other people he'd just met were "swine," mere government lackeys who had been hired or promoted after the Soviet crackdown, when the original board members were fired. She offered to introduce him to the "real" literary Prague.

They began by having dinner with his Czech translators, Rudolf and Luba Pilar, who were completing their work on *Portnoy's Complaint*—even though the book was unpublishable in Czechoslovakia at the time. Many books, they explained, and many writers were unpublishable in Czechoslovakia. For the time being, *Portnoy* would appear in *samizdat*—a typed manuscript passed around in as many carbon copies as could be made. Despite the political and social hardships of their hosts' situation, Roth recalls the evening as "hilarious." The Pilars had been having special trouble with the book's obscenities, and they spent a lot of time re-translating their Czech translations of the dirtiest bits into their own English, to determine if they'd got them right. (Barbara Sproul recalls one choice example, rendered as "He licked her pan.") Hilarious, but also fascinating, upsetting, and exciting.

Roth had always thrived on moral engagement, as a man and as a writer. From the boy in "The Conversion of the Jews" who challenges his rabbi on the subject of "The Chosen People," and the heroes of *Letting Go* struggling with their sense of responsibility for others, to Alexander Portnoy locked in his internal struggle to be free of ethical imperatives, and even the vein-popping outrages of Trick E. Dixon: it's the moral battle that these immensely varied works have in common. One might say that the moral battle was essential to Roth's sense of being Jewish—the factor that made him declare, many times, that he was grateful to have been born a Jew. Historical weight, unjust opposition, burdens of conscience, looming threats of exposure and disaster, difficult claims of loyalty. What a subject for a writer to be born to! In truth, the heyday of the subject was more his parents' era—*there* was some no-nonsense anti-Semitism—but even his father, after a lifetime on the bottom rungs of Metropolitan Life, had been promoted, in the fifties, to district manager of a swath of southern New Jersey, where he ran an office of some fifty people. God bless America. Yet here, as far from Newark as Roth could get, he found another living moral subject, complete with historical weight, threats of exposure, and difficult claims of loyalty. In Prague, he felt at home.

The first trip was brief, but when he returned to New York he plunged into the subject: Czech history, Czech literature, Czech film. His friend Robert Silvers, the co-editor of *The New York Review of Books*, put him in touch with the Czech émigré journalist and film critic Antonín Liehm, who was teaching a course in Czech culture at Staten Island Community College. Roth took the ferry out there every week and got to know not only Liehm and his wife, Mira, a film historian, but various film directors who visited the class. He took the ferry back one day with Ivan Passer, after the class watched *Intimate Lighting*—"If Chekhov could have written and directed a movie, it would have been *Intimate Lighting*," Roth says now—and he and Passer went on to dinner and what became a long, close friendship. (Passer later got Roth to write a screenplay of *When She Was Good*, hoping to direct it, but the project came to nothing.) He read whatever novels he could find in translation, and his life was more and more about things Czech: he often went to dinner at one of the Czech places over in Yorkville, where he met an ever-widening group of people. His fortieth birthday party, in March 1973, thrown for him by Barbara Sproul, was held at one of these restaurants, and photographs show a mix of guests from all phases of his life: the Liehms and other new Czech friends; Mildred Martin and Bob and Charlotte Maurer from Bucknell (Roth kept up with the teachers he admired throughout their lives); a visiting contingent of Chicago friends; New York editors; and, at the center of it all, his beaming parents.

It was at this time that he wrote an extraordinary experiment of a story, which suggested the stirring of fresh impulses in his work. "'I Always Wanted You to Admire My Fasting'; or, Looking at Kafka," was published in *American Review* in 1973 and republished two years later in *Reading Myself and Others*. Completed after he taught a Kafka class at the University of Pennsylvania the previous fall, and dedicated to "the students of English 275," this quietly radical work begins not as a story but as an essay, with Roth contemplating a photograph of Kafka taken in 1924, at the age of forty—exactly Roth's age at the time, he notes, although it was the final year of Kafka's life. Kafka died "too soon for the holocaust," Roth writes, introducing the no longer new if not yet capitalized historical term into his prose. "Skulls chiseled like this one were shoveled by the thousands from the ovens; had he lived, his would have been among them, along with the skulls of his three younger sisters."

His life had been grim. In a few insightful if professorial pages, Roth traces Kafka's troubles with his overbearing father, his difficulties with women, and the events of the year in which he finally succumbed to tuberculosis. Had he lived on, Roth notes, it is almost impossible to imagine Kafka—"so fascinated by entrapment"—immigrating to Palestine with his friend Max Brod or in any way escaping the most horrible of fates. And then Roth himself opens the trap and sets him free. Essay cedes to fiction, and suddenly it is 1942, and the fifty-nine-year-old Czech Jewish émigré to America, Dr. Franz Kafka, is the Hebrew teacher of nine-year-old Philip Roth, who, to the delight of the rest of his class, has dubbed the peculiar old man—with his German accent, his cough, his faintly sour breath—Dr. Kishka. But little Philip is not unkind. In fact, learning that his teacher lives alone, in a single room, he is fired by "redemptive fantasies of heroism" about those he has learned to call, in quotes, "the Jews of Europe." He decides to intercede by talking to his parents: "I must save him. If not me, who?"

And so Dr. Kafka is invited to the Roths' for dinner, along with Philip's Aunt Rhoda, a lively spinster with theatrical ambitions, whom Kafka is intended, Philip realizes with horror, "to *marry*." To Philip's amazement, Kafka takes Aunt Rhoda out on several dates, and she is so enlivened by his interest that she gets a leading role in the Newark Y's production of *Three Sisters*. (In a fantasy within a fantasy—Roth today says he's sure that "Kafka must have read Chekhov"—Kafka opens Rhoda's eyes to the beauty of Chekhov's play, reading it aloud to her all the way through. As we learned at the start of the essay, Kafka had lost three sisters.) Of course, even with the literary saint enmeshed— like the mythic Portnoys—in the details of Newark domesticity, there is only so far that Roth can take Kafka in this world. The romance fails because of an undetermined problem of a sexual nature or, as Philip's father concedes, because Dr. Kafka is "*meshugeh*."

The story ends with a pair of painful transformations. Philip has become a college junior, staying on at school during summer vacation to write stories, but also because he cannot bear going home anymore. He cannot stop fighting with his father, and crying over the fights, because he is being crushed not by paternal criticism but by an overbearing and unbearable love. To his own dismay, both his parents—"they, who together cleared all obstructions from my path"—seem "now to be my final obstruction!" His mother, hurt and confused, continues to write letters, in one of which she encloses a local newspaper obituary, on which she has written: "Remember poor Kafka, Aunt Rhoda's beau?" He reads: "a refugee from the Nazis," "a Hebrew teacher," "70 years old," "no survivors." And no books, he adds. "No *Trial*, no *Castle*, no Diaries." Only a few "*meshugeneh*" letters to Aunt Rhoda, maybe still preserved with her collection of Broadway playbills. ("*Meshugeh*" versus "*meshugeneh*": there are very few people left in the world who can calibrate the difference, and Roth is not among them.)

The fate of Kafka the survivor isn't a matter only of the exchange between fact and fiction, or between life and art, although these subjects will be crucial to Roth's later work. The chill here comes with the confusion of power between life and art, between fact and fiction. At the story's end, and about its end, Roth sensibly asks, "How could it be otherwise?" Kafka's heroes do not reach the Castle, or escape the judgment of the Court. Kafka's hunger artist, from whom Roth takes his title—the ultimate ascetic, who makes starvation an art—dies and is forgotten. Kafka himself had requested that his manuscripts be destroyed, unread. "No," Roth concludes, "it simply is not in the cards for Kafka ever to become *the* Kafka." His literary survival and magnitude are the impossible fate, which Kafka himself would have been the last to believe.

This brilliant hybrid of a story was completed just before Roth's second trip to Prague, with Barbara Sproul, in the spring of 1973. This time, he went prepared with a list of writers who had likewise been alerted about him. His closest contact and general guide there was the English-speaking Ivan Klíma—child survivor of the Terezín concentration camp, novelist and playwright, whose works had been banned and his passport confiscated by the Soviet-backed regime. Another immediate ally was Milan Kundera, who spoke little English yet impressed Roth as an intensely magnetic figure: "a combination of a prizefighter and a panther." Roth had read two of Kundera's books—*Laughable Loves* and *The Joke*—in their tiny English editions, and he and Kundera were soon having long conversations, three or four hours at a time, via the translating services of Kundera's wife, Vera. "By the time it was over Vera looked like she'd had sex with both of us," Roth remembers with a laugh, "pale, her hair all over her face, and very excited from the conversation." Kundera's books, too, were banned in his homeland, as were the works of other writers and translators Roth met—Ludvík Vaculík, Miroslav Holub, Rita Klímová. Sproul remembers that a number of Czech writers were infatuated with the subject of American cowboys and Indians and, in particular, that Vaculík challenged Roth to see who could list more Indian tribes. Roth quickly fell behind and was caught out improvising tribes like "the Kreplach."

Sproul also recalls the feeling of "responsibility" these trips gave both of them—"as Americans, we had all this privilege, all this power, and what were we doing with it?" Cut off from foreign royalty payments and denied any form of intellectual work, the best of literary Prague, true heirs of Kafka, were sweeping streets or working at other menial jobs to earn a living. On leaving the city this time, Roth asked Klíma, "What do you people need?" (One can hear the echo of young Philip in Roth's Kafka story: "If not me, who?") And the answer came simple and clear: "Money."

Roth asked for a list of fifteen writers who needed help, and back in New York he hatched a plan. Setting up a bank account he called the Ad Hoc Czech Fund, he drafted fifteen writer friends to contribute a hundred dollars a month, matching each of them to a writer in Prague. "It made it more personal if they had a name rather than a fund," Roth explains. On that principle, he set up Arthur Schlesinger with a historian and Arthur Miller with a playwright; other writers he enlisted included John Updike, Alison Lurie, John Cheever, William Styron, and John Hersey. On the Czech side, Roth notes, Klíma was on the list the first year but took himself off the next, when his situation improved. (Roth had also arranged an academic appointment for Klíma at Bucknell, the sort of honor that could get him out of Czechoslovakia. But Klíma declined, "because of solidarity, and because he didn't want to have it easier than the others," Roth says, adding, "He's a saint.") Kundera, always "a lone wolf," in Roth's description, was never part of the plan.

Of course, the intended recipients' mail was routinely opened, so the Ad Hoc funders couldn't just send them checks. "I took the money over to a downmarket travel agency in Yorkville," Roth explains today. "I was looking for one that was really grubby, less likely to be infiltrated by the government, and I found one with papers piled up in the windows, really slovenly, and this guy behind the counter who looked like the fat headwaiter in *Casablanca*." These places specialized in getting money to family members behind the Iron Curtain. "I'd give him the money and he'd send off fifteen coupons—*Tuzek* coupons—that were redeemable in Prague banks, in hard currency." Roth was careful to vary the actual amounts—sometimes he sent off two or three small coupons per month—as well as the times he sent them, to keep from arousing suspicion and allow even blacklisted writers to cash them in. Klíma made sure that all the coupons had been received, and he would write discreetly either to his sister in the United States or to Roth. "It was a hole in the fabric," Roth acknowledges, "and it worked."

He had another idea for helping out, with far wider consequences: getting these writers read. This was impossible in Czechoslovakia. But it might be made to happen in America and looked to be a good thing all around: good for the writers' sense of being heard, maybe even good for their political protection—international fame had undoubtedly helped Solzhenitsyn—and good for American readers. Back in New

York, he took this argument and a list of works he admired to an editor at Penguin Books. The result was a series, Writers from the Other Europe, which began publication in 1974 and continued until the Velvet Revolution and its concomitant freedoms, seventeen volumes later, in 1989. These books had all been published in English, and the translations were not new; but "each book had been brought out, singly, by a different publishing house, as a good deed," Roth says, "and it died." Not only was he bringing books together but, as general editor of the series, he was continually reading new candidates, selecting cover art, and outfitting each volume with an introduction by an esteemed, attention-getting writer. Roth himself wrote the introduction for one of the first volumes, Kundera's *Laughable Loves*—at the time, virtually no one in the United States knew who Kundera was—and others were introduced by the likes of John Updike, Angela Carter, and Joseph Brodsky. "I wanted to send them into the world with a flourish," Roth says, lightly waving his hand. "It was my own little Hogarth Press."

Roth was attracted not only by the terrible predicament of these writers or the politics of their books. Eastern European writers "revealed a whole side of literature that is muted in the American tradition," he says, a side that he still values highly. Call it a detached relation to realism. (Roth rightly objects to the term "surrealism" in regard to these books.) "The richness of the screwball strain" is another way he puts it. Although he says that he did not really wish to pursue this in his own work, it could be argued that he had been pursuing it, on his own, ever since *Portnoy's Complaint*. "American realism is a powerful source," Roth tells me, "and I love it—it's given us Bellow and Updike—but it's only one literary given." These writers from "the other Europe" were giving him something else, an angled and sometimes inverted vision that had to do with their descent from Kafka, even when, as in the case of Kundera, Roth also found traces of his other presiding literary god, Chekhov.

Kundera's *Laughable Loves* is not a political book but, rather, a collection of stories that focus on "the private world of erotic possibilities," in the words of Roth's introduction. It contains one story—"Let the Old Dead Make Room for the Young Dead"—that Roth found strikingly "Chekhovian" in its tenderness, its concern for passing time, and its sheer quality. Roth notes that Kundera has a sense of humor often lacking in the erotic specialists of other traditions, such as, say, Mailer and

Mishima. (The sexual humor in Roth's own work goes unmentioned.) He points out that even in Kundera's most political book, *The Joke*, the young protagonist, sentenced to years of labor in a coal mine for a harmless joke, takes a purely sexual (if comically foiled) revenge, attempting to seduce his political betrayer's wife. Sexual revenge is the only possible kind, Roth implies, for a man who is "otherwise wholly assailable." (A world away, in Newark, one hears Alexander Portnoy's cry: "My wang was all I really had that I could call my own.") For Roth, it is important that Kundera, even in his bleakest work, remains "fundamentally *amused* by the uses to which a man will think to put his sexual member, or the uses to which his member will put him"—and, more, that this amusement prevents him from even approaching the sexual mysticism or the ideology of orgasm that characterizes so many other male writers on sex (*pace* Mailer and Mishima). Satire, amusement, self-amusement, eros, vulnerability, "a striking air of candor that borders somehow on impropriety": these are some of the qualities that Roth was finding in Kundera and his colleagues. Small wonder that he felt a sense of kinship—of discovering long-lost brothers.

On his next trip to Prague, in 1974, Ivan Klíma introduced him to another talented dissident (and self-declared heir of Kafka), Václav Havel. Havel's plays had been banned by the regime and his passport confiscated, but he had managed to keep out of further trouble. Roth was already familiar with his work. Ironically, Havel's absurdist dramas with their political overtones had become part of New York's Off-Broadway theater scene—*The Memorandum* was performed during Joseph Papp's first season at The Public Theater, in 1968. Havel had traveled to New York to see it and stayed on for several weeks; he returned to Prague the summer that the Soviet tanks rolled in. *The Memorandum* won an Obie Award for Best Foreign Play—Havel got another Obie in 1970—but, of course, he could not travel to collect them. Klíma, Havel, and Roth met over lunch, with Klíma serving as translator. Havel had come in from his home in the countryside, where he had been keeping a low profile and trying to write—"but he was still stewing," Roth says, knowingly. "Just because you live in the country doesn't mean you can stop stewing."

In fact, Havel had come to Prague to show Klíma a letter he'd been composing, addressed to the general secretary of the Czechoslovak

Communist Party, Gustáv Husák. Roth remembers Klíma's reaction very well: "You are going to get in a lot of trouble." (As, indeed, he did, when the thirty-three-page letter was published in English in the British journal *Encounter*—once backed by the CIA, and still assertively anti-Soviet—the following year. "So far, you and your government have chosen the easy way out for yourselves," Havel wrote, "and the most dangerous road for society.") Roth also remembers Havel's intelligence and wit, which came across even in translation. At one point Havel spoke a little English, and Roth still enjoys—and has employed in his writing—one of his mistaken idioms. "Things had got so bad" for someone, Havel said, that "he committed suitcase." Roth didn't laugh, because the subject was too serious and the malapropism seemed rather brilliant: "When you leave here for good," he says, "it makes perfect sense to say that you commit suitcase."

Roth was also introduced that spring to Kafka's niece Vera Saudková, the daughter of Kafka's youngest and favorite sister, Ottla, who died at Auschwitz. (Kafka's two other sisters died either in the Łódź ghetto, where they were sent from Prague, or in the Chełmno death camp.) A woman in her early fifties, Saudková was born three years before her uncle's death. A letter from Kafka to Max Brod compared little Vera's delight when he praised her attempts to walk, even after she had plumped down on her bottom, to his own delight with Brod's praise of his recent novel (which happened to be *The Castle*). Roth was enchanted just to be in her presence.

She still had Kafka's writing desk in her possession, and she let him sit at it. She showed him a drawer full of family photographs, some of which were familiar, but many of which had not been published. He was particularly struck by a photograph of Kafka's father as a very old man, being pushed in a wheelchair, especially when Saudková told him that this most famously intimidating of fathers "had taken Kafka's death brutally, and had never recovered." Holding the photograph, Roth found his mind humming with Kafka's famous lines about his father, beginning, "Sometimes I imagine the map of the world spread out and you stretched diagonally across it"—more than thirty years later, Roth recites the lines from memory as he tells this story. And all the while he was staring at the image of "this aged father," he says, "to whom grief and defeat had happened, as they do to all."

Roth visited Saudková several times. She had once worked at what Roth calls "an ill-named Prague publishing house, Freedom House," but lost her job, like everyone associated with socialist liberalism, when the Russians came in. Eager to provide help and, possibly, get her out of Czechoslovakia, Roth asked her during one of his visits if she might care to marry him. The proposal was strictly a matter of politics and friendship. (Roth had in mind W. H. Auden's marriage to Erika Mann in 1935, which gave the bride British citizenship.) Saudková thanked him but declined. Prague was her city, she'd had her whole life there, and her two teenage sons were growing up there; despite the difficulties, she didn't want to leave. ("Or else," Roth remarks, deadpan, "she was waiting for an offer from John Updike.")

As the series title Writers from the Other Europe suggests, Roth was eager to present writers from beyond Czechoslovakia. In 1974, he traveled from Prague to Budapest, and Hungarian writers were soon added to the series. Polish writers were introduced through the counsel of a Polish-born friend in New York, Joanna Rostropowicz Clark, and Roth considers the Yugoslav novelist Danilo Kiš (A Tomb for Boris Davidovich) one of the finest writers, along with Kundera, whom the series made known. Although the original focus was on living writers, for evident political reasons, it eventually widened to include the quicksilver Polish Jewish genius Bruno Schulz, who was murdered by a Nazi soldier in 1942, and whose work was almost completely unknown; and Tadeusz Borowski, a Polish writer of perfectly matter-of-fact and entirely harrowing concentration camp stories, who had been a member of the Warsaw underground and had lived through Auschwitz before he committed suicide, at twenty-eight, in 1951. Roth was accomplishing many things with this series of books. Not least, however, he was opening himself to the question that Alexander Portnoy had refused to hear: Where would you be now if you had been born in Europe instead of America?

By the mid-seventies, he was traveling back and forth so regularly that he began to draw attention. In Prague, he was used to being followed. But one day, when he was being trailed by his "usual" plainclothesman, he was suddenly approached by two uniformed police. "They said I had to go with them," he recalls, "but they didn't touch me. I showed them my passport, but they didn't seem to care. We were standing near a trolley stop, so I yelled out to the people waiting there, in English and French, my name, and that I was an American citizen, and they should tell someone at the embassy if I was arrested." And then, when both of the officers walked off to consult with the plainclothesman, Roth seized his chance and jumped onto a trolley. "I rode for ten minutes, and then I hopped off and took a trolley in another direction," he says. "When I thought I knew where I was, I got off and went to a phone kiosk and called Ivan Klíma—and he said, 'Philip, they're just trying to scare you.' Well, they did." But the incident wasn't over. "That night they arrested Ivan. They took him down to the police station, but he knew how to be questioned. They asked him, 'Why does Philip Roth come back to Prague year after year?' And he had the perfect answer. 'Don't you read his books?' he asked them. 'He comes for the girls.'"

And Then He Sends Me Claire

The Czech financial transfers fell apart when, after a few successful years, Roth was convinced by his friend Jerzy Kosinski, then the president of PEN, to let PEN take over the arrangements. "Because it would be tax-deductible," Roth explains now, with chagrin. "I said to Jerzy, it doesn't matter, nobody cares, but finally I gave in." He had already written a long, unsigned report for PEN, sent to all its members, offering information about Czech dissident writers and precise details about the covert methods that the government used—in violation of international copyright laws—to confiscate their foreign royalties. But the committee handling the transfers now complained about restricting the money to Czechoslovakia, claiming that PEN was "playing into the State Department's hands" by "doing this anti-Communist thing," Roth recalls, shaking his head. Their point: Why shouldn't money also go to writers victimized by fascist governments that the United States upholds? "So the whole thing ended," he says. "I've always known all my life, if you want to do anything, do it yourself and keep it small." And, he adds, "I was sick about it. I had as little to do with PEN after that as I could."

In 1977, the Czech government refused to grant him a visa. He was persona non grata and, although his interest in the writers there never flagged, he was unable to return to Prague until 1990, after the Velvet Revolution, when Václav Havel had been elected president, and Ivan Klíma met him at the airport. But there was no going back to the life he'd led before his experiences in Prague. During the late seventies, Roth began making regular trips to Paris, where Milan Kundera, now a good friend, had managed to relocate, and by the early eighties he was also regularly visiting Israel, where he was drawn by the kind of moral fervor he had known in Prague. More immediately, though, the task of remaking his life was continuing through a romance he had begun with the English actress Claire Bloom. They had met before on a few occasions, when one or both had been tied to other people. When they ran into each other on a New York street in 1975, Roth's relationship with Barbara Sproul had ended—although they remained (and remain) friends—and Bloom had gone through a second divorce. Bloom found Roth, she has said, unusually handsome and intellectually daunting. He was equally impressed with her, and for good reason.

Bloom was the granddaughter of Eastern European Jews who settled in London; in a memoir she wrote in 1996, *Leaving a Doll's House*, she recalls her family's Yiddish-accented wonder when the press dubbed her "the English Rose." Extraordinarily precocious, she had made her professional acting debut at fifteen, played Ophelia to Paul Scofield's Hamlet at seventeen, and become a star with the movie *Limelight*, opposite Charlie Chaplin, at twenty-one. (Roth says he fell in love with her on-screen when he saw *Limelight* in a Newark movie house in 1952.) She was now forty-four—two years older than Roth—and, he still recalls, "astonishingly beautiful." She lived in London with her teenage daughter and was in New York only on a brief visit. But she returned a few months later, in February 1976, and they saw each other every night; he was taken not just with her beauty but with everything about her. "The avidness with which we talked!" he recalls—"about our pasts, about our work, about difficulties, about books." She had more nineteenth-century English novels in her head than anyone he'd known "outside a college English department." And he was fascinated by her life as an actress, which he felt had many similarities with (and equally interesting differences from) his own imaginative work. Within a year the pair had decided to live together, spending half their time at his Connecticut farmhouse, the other half at her house in London. Love had given him another world, just when he needed it most.

It was an exciting world, by any standards. His earliest London experience with Bloom was a three-week visit in the late summer of 1976, staying in her house on the edge of Chelsea; he recalls that her daughter was away for all but the last couple of days of his stay. Bloom was rehearsing a play based on Henry James's *The Turn of the Screw*, directed by Harold Pinter, and Roth walked her to rehearsal at a church in South Kensington every morning—"I was so delighted to be with her"—and then picked her up when the rehearsal was over. In this coming and going, he had frequent occasion to talk with Pinter, and he and Bloom were soon a foursome at dinner with Pinter and his soon-to-be wife, Antonia Fraser. When, the following year, he rented a writing studio in Notting Hill, not far from the home that Pinter and Fraser shared, he frequently met one or both of them for lunch at a neighborhood restaurant. Roth is a great admirer of Pinter's work and can talk with gusto and precision about the "social edge" that distinguishes his plays from Beckett's. The friendship was important to him throughout his early years in London.

He also renewed his friendship with the British poet and critic Al Alvarez, whom he had met on a long-ago visit and who introduced him to his Hampstead neighbors David Cornwell (otherwise known as John le Carré) and Alfred Brendel—the first great musician Roth had met, he says, except for a brush with Toscanini at a party back in the fifties. In London, he went to hear Brendel play whenever he could. And dinner at the Brendels' might include Isaiah Berlin and Noel Annan. So who wanted to stay home? "I socialized in London fifty times more than I ever did in New York," he says today. "At the beginning, I didn't get the idea. I wanted to read at night. Then I realized that reading at night was for the country."

And, as if London were determined to make up for Prague, he got to spend time there with another of Kafka's nieces, Marianne Steiner, a daughter of Kafka's middle sister, Valerie. Then in her sixties, Steiner had been eleven when her uncle died, and shared memories of the Prague that they had known together. Her family had escaped the Nazis in 1939, returned to Prague after the war, and then escaped the Communists in 1948. She had inherited a number of Kafka's major manuscripts (*The Castle*, *The Metamorphosis*, *Amerika*) from Max Brod, who had taken them with him to safety in Palestine in 1939. It was Brod whose decision to ignore Kafka's instructions and to publish rather than burn the manuscripts had upended fate and made Kafka into "*the*

Kafka." (Brod died in Tel Aviv in 1968. Twenty years later, when his heirs sold the manuscript of *The Trial* to the state-run German Literature Archive for nearly two million dollars—it outbid libraries in England and Israel—the German book dealer who brokered the purchase was quoted in *The New York Times*, saying, "This is perhaps the most important work in 20th-century German literature, and Germany had to have it." Roth responded with an angry letter to the paper, pointing out the "lurid Kafkaesque irony" of both the statement and the purchase.) Steiner left her manuscripts to the Bodleian Library in Oxford, in the country that had saved her family, twice.

And there were the bookshops. Almost the first thing Roth did when he arrived in London was to check out the bookshops on Fulham Road, near Bloom's house. As ever, he was feeding an enormous literary appetite. He still relates with palpable excitement his discovery, in a London bookshop, of the works of Robert Musil, which he found stunning (and curiously Bellow-like) in the way they "incorporated mind into the fabric of the prose. Not behind it, as in *The Magic Mountain*, where the characters have philosophical discussions," he says, "but within the fabric of the prose itself." London publishers offered an array of books that he had never encountered before: there was Curzio Malaparte (whose work he found in Bloom's own library) and a number of followers of Freud, including the "entertaining but screwy" Georg Groddeck, and Sándor Ferenczi, one of whose contributions to analytic theory, Roth notes, was to have the patient sit in his lap. ("That would have cut my analysis in half.")

But he was searching specifically for books by Eastern European writers. It was in a London bookshop that he came across the mordant comedies of Witold Gombrowicz—a homosexual Polish aristocrat who had spent much of his adult life in poverty in Buenos Aires, a satirist, a rule breaker, and, for Roth, an immediate confrere. He quickly added Gombrowicz's novel *Ferdydurke* to the series, and he negotiated with the publisher to append an essay that Gombrowicz himself had written on the book. The subject of immaturity, a Gombrowicz specialty—championed over what passes for maturity and frustratingly misunderstood by critics—formed a particular tie with Roth's own literary past. (In the essay, Gombrowicz, whose first story collection was titled *Memoirs of a Time of Immaturity*, wrote, "Consequently the critics exclaimed joyfully: 'Look at him! He isn't mature!'" After which, he added, "Immaturity—what a compromising, disagreeable word!—became my war cry.") And although Gombrowicz was not the only modern novelist to give a protagonist his own name, the fact that he was willing to "put himself at the center of the chaos," Roth says, was more than a little exciting to him. Finally, there was simply "his devilishness, like the devilishness in Pinter, that I liked."

Roth was also writing. In the summer of 1976, he was near completing a new novel, *The Professor of Desire*, conceived as the story of David Kepesh's life before he turned into a giant breast, in which the professor who taught Kafka with a bit too much conviction went to visit the scene of the original crime, Prague. But it's a sign of Roth's love for Bloom that, while in London, he spent a great deal of time working not on the novel but on a gift for her: an adaptation, for television, of a Chekhov short story, "The Name-Day Party," with a leading role for Bloom as a wealthy married woman who cannot bear the social lies that she and her husband tell. "There's a line I loved," Roth says now. "'Why do I smile and lie?' That's Chekhov's ability to do it in six words." (Although there was some interest from producers, the project didn't go forward, which Roth still considers a pity: "Claire would have been brilliant in it.") From Kafka to Chekhov, the pendulum of his own fiction was swinging, as Roth—yielding to domestic happiness, sharing his life (as Chekhov did) with a successful actress—continued to work changes in himself.

The Professor of Desire was published in 1977 by Farrar, Straus and Giroux. In yet another change, Roth had again followed Aaron Asher to a new publisher, although this time he stayed—even after Asher moved on—for fourteen years. The book, dedicated to Bloom, is about transitions, and is a transitional book. Very different from the boisterous sexual joke of Kepesh's debut, it is a gently Chekhovian sexual tragedy, with a force that builds out of unlikely beginnings. The early sections, detailing the Catskills childhood and post-adolescent sexual high jinks of a good Jewish boy obsessed with "the detonation of my seed"—young Kepesh, loose in London, enjoys threesomes and a little light whipping—seem rehashed and formulaic; Roth had done this kind of thing much better before. And the book gets worse before it gets better. Kepesh's marriage to a femme fatale with a mysterious Hong Kong past is simply silly: the femme herself seems like a forced attempt to vary the equally familiar theme of a destructive wife, and a parody of Hemingway's famed seductress Lady Brett, with lines like "I'd say half the girls who fly out of Rangoon on that crate that goes to Mandalay are generally from Shaker Heights." (Leave it to Roth, though, to have Kepesh tell her, a few pages after this remark, that there's a heroine in a book called *The Sun Also Rises*, named Brett, who reminds him of her.) Lacking the grim power of Lucy Nelson or Maureen Tarnopol, Helen Kepesh is too slight a figure to account for the situation in which her ex-husband finds himself halfway through the book, but there he is: impotent, barely capable of smiling much less of having sex or feeling love, pouring out his guts to his psychiatrist, and howling, "I want somebody!" into the bathroom mirror.

Kepesh tells his story in his own fluent and sardonic voice—Roth's gift for the first-person intimate remains uncanny—which lacks the hysterical edge (for the most part) of Alexander Portnoy's, even as Kepesh laments the same painful division between body and soul, or sex and love, or freedom and responsibility, or necessary physical gratification and equally necessary but incompatible happiness. A devoted professor of literature, Kepesh is able to approach the problem analytically and with the aid of many literary references: the book contains passing insights about writers from Melville to Colette, while Kafka and Chekhov loom as large as any of the major characters. On the model of Kafka's "A Report to an Academy," in which a speaker recounts "the life I formerly led as an ape," Kepesh ultimately writes a report to his own Academy—"Honored Members of Literature 341"—about "the life I formerly led as a human being." His goal is to make the students understand his personal qualifications for teaching a course in the literature of ungovernable erotic desire.

The course is intended, in part, to help him explain his history to himself. But he also has a pedagogical motive. Kepesh wants his students to read novels about sexual desire because, having experienced it themselves, they will be less likely to consign these books to the academic netherworld of "narrative devices, metaphorical motifs, and mythical archetypes"—or even of the old standbys "structure," "form," and "symbols." There's at least a chance that they will connect this literature to their own lives. (At the time, Roth informed a French interviewer,

Alain Finkielkraut, that, as a teacher, he forbade the use of this kind of jargon "on pain of expulsion.") Because books are not, as the hated formulation of the day would have it, "non-referential." Books are entirely referential, and what they refer to is life. Kepesh admired Kafka when he read him in college, but it is only later, when the impotence sets in, that Kafka's "obstructed, thwarted K.'s banging their heads against invisible walls" take on greater meaning. He wonders if *The Castle* isn't linked to Kafka's own erotic problems. Kepesh himself is so horribly obstructed—so "Kafkafied," in one of his usages—that for a long time he cannot even work on his book about Chekhov.

And then he is saved. Sex, love, and finally—what more proof could he need?—completing the book. On romantic disillusionment in Chekhov. (Did you expect happily ever after? With Chekhov? With Roth?) He reads Chekhov stories every night, "listening for the anguished cry of the trapped and miserable socialized being, the well-bred wives who during dinner with the guests wonder 'Why do I smile and lie?'" Chekhov, for Kepesh, reveals "the humiliations and failures" of people who seek a way out of restrictions and conventions—out of boredom and stifling despair—people who keep struggling toward a freer life, even though they inevitably fail. Kepesh's Chekhov seems hardly less oppressive than Kepesh's Kafka. Yet he has found a way back to life through the Russian writer and, more important, through a young woman who has given him the confidence to write again. "I'd thought the god of women, who doles them out to you, had looked down on me and said, 'Impossible to please—the hell with him,'" he tells her, bringing her hand to his lips. "And then he sends me Claire."

Claire Ovington, the heroine of *The Professor of Desire*, got her first name well before Bloom entered Roth's life; she is the same girl for whom Kepesh's desire is fading before he turns into the Breast. (The metamorphosis, oddly enough, works to restore his appetite. There may be a warning here to be careful what you wish for.) Roth says that he simply liked "the open sound" of "Claire." A twenty-five-year-old schoolteacher, tall and blond, orderly and kind, Claire has used orderliness and kindness to help her survive a difficult childhood and construct a life beyond it. "As tender within as without," with the scrubbed beauty of an Amish woman and—this is Kepesh, remember—magnificent breasts, Claire is a healer of the wounds inflicted by Maggie/Lucy/

Maureen/Helen. She is based, in a general way, on Barbara Sproul; a "beautiful cities" trip is also on Kepesh and Claire's agenda.

Roth and Sproul were together for six years. It was her desire to have children, Sproul explains—she was then nearing thirty—that caused them to part. "She wanted something I couldn't give her," Roth agrees, although he notes that they continued to tend "our baby, Czechoslovakia," together. There was certainly some sadness at the time of the breakup, but there were no hard feelings—or, considering the circumstances, very few. (Sproul invited him to her wedding, in 1978; he didn't go.) "He's a professor, he's a priest of literature," she says today, "and I always knew that he was married to his books."

Kepesh and Claire get twelve pages of happiness before the ebbing and the chafing and the fear, for him, set in. He loves her; he knows that she is the best thing that has happened to him. The fact that she dislikes having semen in her mouth is not important, surely. ("As if such a thing matters! As if Claire is withholding anything that *matters*!") One need not admonish Kepesh for stupidity, ingratitude, callowness, or a lunatic and suicidal loss of all perspective: he does this himself, even as memories of a more audacious lover—belonging to his former life, as a different human being—fill his head. This other woman is hardly more than a stick figure, with no existence beyond the sexual, and can be seen as both a failure of the book and part of its point. And if Claire seems an uncommonly unflawed creature, that, too, is part of the harsh and rueful point. This is the exchange he is unwillingly willing to make.

Reviews were generally favorable, but hesitations were expressed even by the enthusiastic. In *The New York Times Book Review*, Vance Bourjaily called the book "an erudite examination of the troglodyte within us," but criticized Roth for making too much of the obvious fact that couples have more sex at the start of a relationship than later on. That's just the way it is—"a sad, small, universal, necessary joke." But it's part of a novelist's endeavor to render such universal jokes with freshness, surprise, and, when necessary, indignation—the way they hit us before we come to terms, before we know the experience is universal or a joke or anything we may call small. Kepesh struggles to dismiss his sexual restlessness. He is willing to accept, sexually, "a warm plateau" ("I am no longer a little bit of a beast, she is no longer a little bit of a tramp"), but he fears the inevitable, precipitous descent into the cold. Nothing in the book's superficially charged-up early sex scenes is as disturbing as this calmly measured juxtaposition of love and desire. Everything good on one side of the scale; sex on the other side, pressing it down.

Sexual desire in its absolutism and its folly is a momentous subject, but was it enough of a subject anymore for Roth? In Prague, Kepesh tours a number of Kafka landmarks: his school, the site of his father's business, the tiny house that his youngest sister rented for him one winter. (In a Kafkaesque dream, he is taken to visit Kafka's whore, now nearly eighty: ten American dollars to find out what they did together, five more to inspect her anatomy, for literary purposes. Given his field of interest, it's tax-deductible.) Near the end of the day, he confronts his guide, a man who was also once a literature professor but who lost his job when the tanks rolled in; his wife, formerly a research scientist, now works as a typist in a meat-packing plant. When asked how he gets through each day, the man has a simple reply: "Kafka, of course." And when, in turn, he asks Kepesh about his interest in Kafka, Kepesh speaks of his former impotence, equating it with the man's plight—the body's intransigence felt to him, he explains, like "some unyielding, authoritarian regime." Kepesh speaks with modesty ("Of course, measured against what you—") and even wins the man's sympathy, but the argument seems tainted with self-inflation and does not so easily win the reader.

Roth seems to be struggling to import the larger meanings of his recent European experiences into the narrow frame and focus of an unreconstructedly Portnoyan hero's life. The result is to make Kepesh appear petulant and small, if eager to outgrow his petulance and smallness. Visiting Kafka's grave in the little Jewish cemetery outside town, he places a pebble from the gravel walk atop the tombstone—a pebble, too, atop the facing tomb of Max Brod—an act of traditional Jewish homage that he admits he has never performed at the graves of his own grandparents. But this cemetery contains not only the literary great and well remembered. Looking around, Kepesh is surprised to discover plaques all along one wall inscribed to the memory of the Jewish citizens of Prague who were exterminated in Terezín, Auschwitz, Bergen-Belsen, and Dachau, and to realize that there are not pebbles enough for them all.

The Professor of Desire comes to rich and startling life in its final scene, with the arrival of Kepesh's garrulous, well-meaning father (a typically scene-stealing Herman Roth) at Kepesh and Claire's idyllic country house in the Catskills. The only character to possess a voice that easily breaks through the buzz of Kepesh's thoughts, Mr. Kepesh is accompanied by another old Jewish man with a remarkable voice, a friend he introduces as "a victim of the Nazis" and a survivor of the camps. And as candles burn low during dinner on a perfect summer night, and Bach drifts softly from the record player, the survivor tells his story in a few calmly reflective paragraphs. When he is done, and the old men have gone to bed, Kepesh remarks to Claire that the entire evening—the unexpected tale of a ruined world, the music, their love, their fear of losing each other—is the stuff of a Chekhov story and might be called "The Life I Formerly Led." That night, he holds Claire tighter than ever before. Because he knows it will not last.

The Life I Formerly Led was a contender for the title of this book. And Roth's hero, in the end, is being drawn back helplessly to that former life. But in which direction was Roth going? *The Professor of Desire* mixes outgrown themes with energetic, imaginatively charged new signs and scenes, and with a muted tenderness that is like nothing in his work before. It is neither a book one would want to be without nor a fulfilled achievement. After the trio of facile satires and the literary plunge into the marital abyss, it was certainly encouraging. Yet Roth had not had an important success since *Portnoy's Complaint* eight years earlier. And *Goodbye, Columbus* ten years before that. Two celebrated books in eighteen years. For all his fame and his evident talent, it was not a sterling record. In 1977, Roth's literary future was, at best, uncertain. Could he free himself from his old and wearing preoccupations? Would he ever find a way to turn the worlds of love and ruin into a story of his own?

The Madness of Art

"Little Beauty" the nurses called her—a silent, dark, emaciated girl—and so, one morning, ready to talk, she told them that the surname was Bellette. Amy she got from an American book she had sobbed over as a child, *Little Women*. She had decided, during her long silence, to finish growing up in America now that there was nobody left to live with in Amsterdam. After Belsen she figured it might be best to put an ocean the size of the Atlantic between herself and what she needed to forget.

She learned of her father's survival while waiting to get her teeth examined by the Lonoffs' family dentist in Stockbridge. She had been three years with foster families in England, and almost a year as a freshman at Athene College, when she picked an old copy of *Time* out of the pile in the waiting room and, just turning pages, saw a photograph of a Jewish businessman named Otto Frank . . . She cried for a very long time. But when she went to dinner in the dormitory, she pretended that nothing catastrophic had once again happened to Otto Frank's Anne.

The Ghost Writer, published in 1979, is a novel so seamless that it appears to have been conceived and poured out whole. In fact, it had been brewing for a long time and had grown out of disparate ideas. Roth had wanted to write about Anne Frank since the early years of his career: to change her history, to have her survive, and to bring her to America, as he had brought Kafka in his story of 1973. The subject of the martyred Jewish girl, however, was much harder to approach. The risks of hagiography on the one hand and tastelessness on the other were all too clear. And what would be the dramatic point? More recently, after several visits to Prague, he'd begun to write about an American novelist who is struggling with the circus-like success that his culture offers—a huge, Portnoyan success—and then, on a trip to Czechoslovakia, becomes involved in the lives of writers with genuine struggles: the story that eventually became *The Prague Orgy*. He wrote a long draft, beginning with the young writer starting out and continuing with his success, but he realized that he was compressing the material too much. He had enough for several books.

The first of the books, then, was about a young writer coming to grips with the demands of his vocation, through a visit to an older writer who has been his idol. It was a somewhat Jamesian scheme: just the master and the student, more or less, and lessons learned. The older writer would be a figure rather like Malamud, whose work had meant so much to Roth and whom he had visited many times since they met, through a mutual friend, in 1961. Malamud was a master of unassuming tragedies lit by an almost equally painful if compensatory comedy; Roth later compared his "parables of frustration" to Samuel Beckett's. Off the page, however, he was a reserved and even taciturn figure, with a starchy demeanor that reminded Roth of an insurance agent, one of his father's colleagues at Metropolitan Life. He recalls Malamud asking his wife to make him half an egg for breakfast. No indulgences. Hardly any laughter, not much by way of conversation: all of his energies taken up, it seemed to Roth, by "responsibility to his art." This was an unwavering, all-suffering responsibility—impressive in the man but insufficient for the requirements of a flesh-and-blood fictional character. Malamud was small in stature, and Roth gave his master writer the more imposing physical presence of his friend Philip Guston, whose artistic drive was similarly all-consuming. But there was something still lacking, something he had to add to make this figure dramatically compelling, and more human.

And then Roth recalled that once, while he was visiting the Malamuds at their house in Vermont in the mid-sixties, a girl had been there, a Bennington student, who was doing some sort of clerical work for Malamud. Roth did not meet her, and he didn't know if she was there for that day only or for a longer time. He caught just a glimpse of her, "sitting on the floor in the other room, going through his papers," he says now. "The image was like a Vermeer—a woman alone, engaged in something, with a pretty profile." It was entirely unthinkable that the rather dour man he knew had any romantic or even personal involvement with the girl. But with this flash of memory, Roth found a way to complicate the character, and his disparate ideas for a book began to come together.

In *The Ghost Writer*, Nathan Zuckerman, aged twenty-three, arrives at the country home of the great writer E. I. Lonoff, takes the measure of the place—the books, the piano, the solitude, the big maple trees, the snowy fields—and promptly decides: "This is how I will live." Most important to this decision is Lonoff himself: his full-souled devotion to the literary calling, his modesty, and, not least, his admiration for Zuckerman's own work, which consists at the time of just four published stories. Zuckerman has sent these stories to the older man, seeking not merely the approval of a master but the blessing of a father. Because Zuckerman is troubled. For the past five weeks he has not been on speaking terms with his own beloved father. Their argument, which is all he can think about, is the result of his latest story, still unpublished, which he sent to his parents for their usual approval. And which, for the first time in his life, he has not received.

Zuckerman's story—think of "Epstein," think of "Defender of the Faith"—is based on a dispute over money that took place within the extended Zuckerman family. It has so upset his father that he has tried to talk Nathan out of publishing it. ("Your story, as far as Gentiles are concerned, is about one thing and one thing only," he says: "Kikes and their love of money.") Failing that, Mr. Zuckerman has sent the story to Newark's most revered Jewish leader, one Judge Wapter, who in turn has written Nathan a lengthy letter, asking him to consider a series of questions, beginning with: "If you had been living in Nazi Germany in the thirties, would you have written such a story?" The judge concludes by advising Nathan to see the current Broadway production of *The Diary of Anne Frank*—he and Mrs. Wapter were there on opening night. It's an experience that might teach him something about the Jews.

Lapidary, without a word to spare, *The Ghost Writer* is not much longer than *Goodbye, Columbus*. The action takes place during a period of some eighteen hours, in the Lonoffs' house, where Nathan spies a mysterious girl sitting on the floor in an adjacent room, going through Lonoff's manuscripts. (She looks to him like a Velázquez *infanta* rather than a Vermeer.) She is a refugee, it turns out—from where, it is not clear—and speaks with a strange and fetching accent. With heavy snow starting to come down, both of the young guests spend the night. It's a setup as simple as that of a mystery novel, yet this slender book has historic reach as well as dramatic depth. From the opening paragraph, one feels a new calm and lucid power in the writing:

> It was the last daylight hour of a December afternoon more than twenty years ago—I was twenty-three, writing and publishing my first short stories, and like many a *Bildungsroman* hero before me, already contemplating my own massive *Bildungsroman*—when I arrived at his hideaway to meet the great man. The clapboard farmhouse was at the end of an unpaved road twelve hundred feet up in the Berkshires, yet the figure who emerged from the study to bestow a ceremonious greeting wore a gabardine suit, a knitted blue tie clipped to a white shirt by an unadorned silver clasp, and well-brushed ministerial black shoes that made me think of him stepping down from a shoeshine stand rather than from the high altar of art.

It is a book of memory, then: we are looking back a long way. The year is 1956. Lonoff, we soon learn, died five years later, in 1961. Zuckerman's own fortunes after this visit are unknown. The snow and the fading light and the closely attentive prose give the atmosphere, throughout, a Chekhovian glow that has its precedent in the final scene of *The Professor of Desire*. But where that book ended, Roth is just beginning.

At least part of this breakthrough must be credited to a new protagonist, Nathan Zuckerman. Although Roth has the reputation of a confessional writer, no one is more aware of the importance, for literary freedom, of self-disguise. In an obituary essay on Malamud, published in *The New York Times Book Review* in 1986 and republished in Roth's 2001 collection, *Shop Talk*, Roth points to the contrast between that tightly constrained man and his richly unconstrained art and invokes a German term from Heine, *Maskenfreiheit*: "the freedom conferred by masks." One might more accurately refer to Nathan Zuckerman as a new mask. For, although a character of the same name appears in *My Life as a Man*, the new Zuckerman is entirely different from that maritally entrapped and often enraged figure, as he is different from Peter Tarnopol and David Kepesh, who have also been maritally entrapped and enraged—just like Philip Roth.

True, this Zuckerman has many biographical similarities with Roth. Born in 1933 in Newark to a doting Jewish family, Zuckerman went to college, spent some time in the army, and is now an aspiring writer. The facts that his father is a chiropodist rather than an insurance salesman, that he has a younger brother rather than an older one, and that he went to the University of Chicago as an undergraduate make no real difference. The fact that he moved to New York rather than return to Chicago when he got out of the army, and so never crossed paths with Maggie—or Maureen, or Lucy, or any of the various other names she has borne—is more pertinent. Up until recently, Nathan had a pretty girlfriend, but she smashed all the dishes and threw him out when he confessed (rather nobly, he'd thought) to his susceptibility to her equally pretty friends. A bit disheartened, he went off to a writers' colony, where he easily recovered during the weeks before he arrived, in December 1956, at Lonoff's door. Not maritally entrapped, or about to be entrapped. Not enraged, except perhaps by Judge Wapter. And fully able, at twenty-three—the age at which Roth cornered Maggie in the doorway of a Chicago bookshop—to carry on with being twenty-three, a writer, and free. What *Maskenfreiheit*!

But if Nathan Zuckerman allowed Roth to return to the time of his most disastrous decision and take another path—up a snowy hill to a writer's country house—he was not without a struggle of his own. It first appeared, in less than fatal form, with his job as a door-to-door magazine salesman, potentially distracted by lascivious housewives ("Either get laid," says his boss, "or sell *Silver Screen*") who are never lascivious enough: "I of necessity," Zuckerman concludes, "chose perfection in the work rather than the life." The choice becomes tougher, however, when the work becomes Art and he is confronted, at the Lonoffs', with the master whose only, self-confessed purpose and pleasure in life is to sit at his desk all day, every day, and "turn sentences around." And confronted, too, with the angry voice of Lonoff's lonely, worn-out wife: "*Not* living is what he makes his beautiful fiction *out* of!"

Art versus Life: Nathan, at the youthful crossroads, is befuddled. It's not just that he might have gone the other way if one of those housewives had given him the chance. He might never have approached Lonoff at all had he succeeded in getting through to Lonoff's worldly counterpart, Felix Abravanel—Roth's marvelous portrait of the artist as a writer whose outsized life includes "beautiful wives, beautiful mistresses, alimony the size of the national debt, polar expeditions, warfront reportage, famous friends," and so forth. Abravanel is a mocking mix of Mailer and Bellow, with the emphasis falling squarely on Bellow in Roth's telling of Abravanel's visit to a Chicago classroom where a story by Zuckerman is being read, just as Bellow once attended a Chicago class in which Roth's "The Conversion of the Jews" was discussed. Bellow admired Roth's story, but, as Roth remembers it, he certainly wasn't interested in pursuing an acquaintance. And Abravanel admires Zuckerman's story, while making it clear, in his cashmere sports coat and his self-involvement and his devastating, condescending charm, that he is not in the habit of offering help to younger writers, much less in the market for a twenty-something son. (One of the most beautifully Jamesian phrases in this James-haunted book is Roth's assessment of Abravanel's charm, "like a moat so oceanic that you could not even see the great turreted and buttressed thing it had been dug to protect.") Although Roth and Bellow had developed a friendly rapport by the time of *The Ghost Writer*, it was widely rumored that the portrait of Abravanel did not bring them any closer.

Fathers versus Art: an even bigger problem or, at least, a more immediate one. And the choice, for Nathan, is unbearable. In his *Paris Review* interview, published a few years after the book appeared, Roth described the subject of *The Ghost Writer* as "the difficulties of telling a Jewish story." ("In what tone? To whom should it be told? To what end? Should it be told at all?") Even back in 1971, in an article he wrote for *The New York Times*, he had recognized that it would have been "asking the impossible" of many Jews to react to his early stories without anger and fear, "only five thousand days after Buchenwald and Auschwitz." But in this book he brings the problem home. Nathan is haunted by the image of his bewildered father, standing alone on a darkening street corner after Nathan has refused to repudiate his story, "thinking himself and all of Jewry gratuitously disgraced and jeopardized by my inexplicable betrayal." Still, he can't back down.

That night, in the makeshift bedroom of Lonoff's study, he sits in his undershorts at the great man's desk. Beside the desk, on index cards pinned to a bulletin board, are two quotations, one ascribed to Robert Schumann, about Chopin, and one by Henry James: "We work in the dark—we do what we can—we give what we have. Our doubt is our passion and our passion is our task. The rest is the madness of art." The final phrase confuses him. Isn't it art that is sanity, against the madness of everything else? Yet these are the words that hang over Lonoff's head every day while he turns his sentences around. Nathan pulls out a pad and begins to write, first a reading list from the books on Lonoff's shelves, then an account of the remarkable day, featuring Lonoff's praise of Nathan's own distinctive literary voice—"I don't mean style," Lonoff said, "I mean voice"—and, inevitably, a letter to his father about his art and his voice and his family bonds that will explain everything. But he cannot finish it because he cannot find the right words.

And also because he is distracted by the voices of Lonoff and the mysterious young woman arguing in the room overhead. By the simple act of standing on Lonoff's desk, with his ear to the ceiling—and a volume of Henry James under his feet, for literary support—he learns that the two have been lovers. He is astounded. The great ascetic! (Roth was as astounded as everyone else when Malamud's biography, published in 2007—twenty-eight years after *The Ghost Writer* and twenty-one years after Malamud's death—revealed that Malamud had indeed had a serious love affair with a nineteen-year-old student, in the early sixties. "People started asking me," Roth says, "how did you know?") Nathan is upset, however, mostly because the unimaginable scene has exposed the limits of his imagination. If only he could invent something equally presumptuous!

Enter Anne Frank. She has gone by the name of Amy Bellette since waking up in a British Army field hospital. She hadn't meant to conceal her identity—there was no reason to, since no one knew who she was. She simply wanted to forget. As a foster child, she had gone to England (where she burned the number off her arm while ironing a blouse), and then, through Lonoff's sponsorship, she had come to America, to the Berkshires and Athene College, where Lonoff still teaches two classes a year. He vouches for her exceptional prose style. She told him who she really was only years after she arrived—after she went to see *The Diary of Anne Frank* on Broadway, in 1955, and couldn't bear her secret anymore. Of course, he didn't believe her story, at first. Who would? Her greatest pain, however, was keeping the fact that she was still alive from her beloved father. The cost of telling him now was just too great. Because of her book and because of the lessons it taught. She went back and forth in her mind, continually: her father, her book, her father, her book. People went every day not only to see the play in New York, but, in Amsterdam, to the family's secret hideaway, as though it were a shrine. They pitied her, they cried for her, and not only for her. "I was the incarnation of the millions of unlived years robbed from the murdered Jews. It was too late to be alive now," she concludes. "I was a saint."

That Anne Frank was indeed a saint presented a tremendous problem for Roth. For a time, his desire to write about her was nearly outmatched by his fear of appearing "blasphemous," as he confided in a letter to his friend Jack Miles, a former Jesuit seminarian and a historian of religion who was then working as an editor at Doubleday. Roth had spent weeks wrestling with the issue, writing no more than a sentence or two a day, and he and Miles decided to reread the *Diary* simultaneously and exchange their thoughts. On December 2, 1977—nearly two years before the publication of *The Ghost Writer* (and nearly twenty years before the publication of Miles's Pulitzer Prize–winning book, *God: A Biography*)—Roth fulfilled his side of the agreement, writing Miles a seven-page, closely typed letter, fiercely analytic yet deeply tender, detailing his ideas about the famous book and its author: a winning girl, a writer by nature, a Jewish European (as opposed to a European Jew) who dreamed of studying in Paris, an adolescent who adored her father and disliked her mother and who was already something of a genius, but not yet a saint. The diary answered her immediate needs: to confide the unsayable ("particularly about her mother"); to give way to occasional despair; and to write. She began to imagine that she would publish a book based on the diary only with the dawn of her understanding that "what began as a personal record has a historical dimension"—that is, when her sense of the experience had changed from "this is what I had to do, to this is what a Jewish family had to do, in order to survive the war."

The central question of Roth's letter is: What gave her book its vast appeal? In strictly literary terms, Roth compares Anne Frank's hold on readers with that of Huck Finn and Holden Caulfield: "Can you think of any other adolescents able to hold our interest?" Of course, her voice is not as stylized or as "distinctively 'adolescent'" as theirs, but then she is not an adult pretending to be an adolescent but a real one, and one whose attitude toward society was necessarily wholly different: "She is locked out and wants more than anything to be let back in: her dream is to go back to school." Then, too, she presents her terrible confinement as a kind of adventure story. (He quotes: "I am young and strong and am living a great adventure"—May 3, 1944.) The *Diary* has similarities with *Robinson Crusoe* in its "testing of civilized ingenuity," in the way it faces the problems of "how to get on with life, how to get on with the development of the self, under the pressures of confinement and in the shadow of death." And, there is her personality: not too perfect (Anne claimed that her more serene and submissive sister, Margot, was perfect), not too flawed, a girl with whom adolescents could identify yet whose "mercurial and spirited" nature made her everybody else's ideal daughter. "She was, in the simplest and most attractive sense of the word, alive. And that is what is so crushing, and so representative, about her death."

And what might have made the book less appealing? "Had she survived the war," Roth writes, "I wonder how many readers it would have had, if any." As "his" Anne surmises in *The Ghost Writer,* for her to be among the survivors rather than among the murdered six million would have drastically changed readers' perception of the book. Roth suggests to Miles that, rather like Lore Segal's autobiographical novel *Other People's Houses,* about her family's escape from Austria, *The Diary of a Young Girl* "might have run in sections in *The New Yorker*—and that would have been that." He wonders, too, whether people would have been so affected if she had continued writing in the camps. "There is something so strong about the way that it breaks off—I suppose it says something about the writing itself, or about how this girl seems to us to live most passionately through writing. The silence, the blankness, that follows the last page stands for the undescribable horror."

Finally, had Anne Frank been more overtly or stereotypically Jewish—
"a shtetl or ghetto child," Roth suggests, "with Isaac Singer's childhood"—
"I doubt that her diary would have meant so much to Christians, or for
that matter, even to Jews in great numbers." Her fate would have been
considered unjust but somehow understandable. The arrest of this particular girl, however, is "beyond understanding." Not just a Jewish tragedy
but an absurdist tragedy, something out of Kafka. ("Someone must have
traduced Anne F.," he writes, "for one morning, the police, etc. . . .")
Without her confinement, Roth went on, this girl—who had gone to a
Montessori school until the Nazis ordered her into the Jewish Lyceum,
whose "languages to be learned" are French and English, whose "'pet'
subject is Greek and Roman mythology"—would have had little reason
to think of herself as a Jew. Ironically, "she is far more Jewish to us than
she was to herself." And then Roth asks the question that is looming
over him: "What do you think would happen if I said aloud (that is, in
print) that the least Jewish of Jewish children is our Jewish saint?"

Anne Frank is the ghost of *The Ghost Writer*, but Nathan Zuckerman
is the ghost writer, creating a new story for her in her stead. In the morning light, it's a story that Nathan recognizes as the product of his own
fevered, fiction-making, father-obsessed brain. This sleight-of-hand solution to the problem of portraying Anne Frank is ingenious. The threats
of both blasphemy and kitsch are dissolved—this is not *really* Anne
Frank, after all. Yet Roth has it both ways. We are deeply drawn into
her postwar story, before Nathan's authorship is exposed, and cannot
readily step back. We can dismiss the specter of her presence, intellectually; emotionally, however, it is harder to shake. (This may be Roth's
greatest lesson from Kafka: the more fantastical the imaginative plan,
the more realistically detailed the execution.) Nathan's fantasy serves
his own purposes so well that he himself has a hard time letting it go.
The next morning at breakfast—where Lonoff requests half an egg—
Nathan begins to imagine that he will marry Anne and bring her to
meet his parents in New Jersey. ("'Married? But so fast? Nathan, is she
Jewish?'") When he introduces her to them, they will see at last what
he really is, more clearly than he could express in any letter:

> Anne, says my father—the Anne? Oh, how I have misunderstood my son.
> How mistaken we have been!

But Roth mines Anne Frank's story—both the real story and the ghosted one—for much more than the comedy of Nathan's predicament, despite the irresistible Jewish joke. Again and again, the searching questions of Roth's letter are dramatically transformed in the novel. He has things to say about the developing craft of the ambitious young writer ("Suddenly she's discovering reflection, suddenly there's portraiture") as well as about the nightmare that is her subject. "She's like some impassioned little sister of Kafka's," Nathan tells Amy Bellette, coming out of his dream, or trying to drag her in: "What he invented, she suffered." But it's the lessons of the *Diary* that are his central, worrying concern. For all the tears that have been shed for Anne Frank, has her book really taught anybody anything?

The question may seem naive. But Nathan, in the voice of his imaginary Anne, comes to an answer about the lessons of the book that accords, perhaps unsurprisingly, with Roth's defense of his stories years earlier. The *Diary* has touched so many people—and here Roth says "aloud" the most hazardous thing he felt he had to say—because there was nothing notably Jewish about this mostly secular, Dickens-reading, European family who just happened to be Jews. "A harmless Chanukah song" once a year, a few Hebrew words, a few candles, a few presents; there was hardly more to it than that. They were in no way foreign, strange, or embarrassing—and look what happened to them. They were entirely charming, in fact, especially, of course, Anne. And look what happened to her. What did it take to provoke what happened? "It took nothing—that was the horror. And that was the truth. And that was the power of her book." As Roth had once replied to the rabbis, it is impossible to control anti-Semitism through exemplary behavior, accomplishments, or charm. Because anti-Semitism originates not in the Jews but in the anti-Semites. Repression, pretension, "putting on a good face": all useless. Anne's diary offered a double lesson, really. For Gentiles, a lesson in common humanity, the nightmare made real because of how familiar Anne and her family seemed. And for Jews, the fact that this familiarity had not done a thing to save them.

The Ghost Writer has a formal, almost musical structure: four sections in which the themes intertwine as tightly as in a chamber quartet. The third section, the Anne Frank section, might be called the scherzo, or even *quasi una fantasia*, and required much rewriting. The first draft,

Roth says today, was "overdramatized, and lyric in the worst sense," since he was intimidated by the subject. He'd written it in the third person (Nathan telling Anne's story) but then decided to rewrite it in the first person—Anne telling her own story—in order to wash out the overstatement and the saintliness, or what he calls "all that UJA rhetoric." (The United Jewish Appeal was not known for its literary subtlety.) The girl who wrote the diary would never write in such an elevated tone about herself. Then he translated it back into the third person, now cleansed of the problems of tone. The result is natural and vivid and disconcertingly plausible; humor is continually shadowed by the sorrow of the source. Yet even Nathan finally suspects that this new fiction will not acquit him from the charges of anti-Semitism that his earlier story had brought. Rather, it will seem to his judges "a desecration even more vile than the one they had read."

And, to some, it did. "The *chutzpa* of it," John Leonard complained in *The New York Review of Books*, "appropriating the Ophelia of the death camps"—a jarringly snide phrase, unlike anything in the book— "for his dark, libidinal purposes, his angry punch line." In *The New York Times*, Robert Towers seemed not quite to register the degree of fantasy involved, although he reported feeling "slightly cheated, slightly offended," when it all dissolved at breakfast. Still, overall, the book won tremendous praise. It was published in its entirety, in two parts, in *The New Yorker*—like Roth's vision of a survivor's diary—in the summer of 1979, thanks to an enterprising editor there, Veronica Geng. ("She was determined to get me into the magazine," Roth says; this was his first appearance in its pages, then considered Updike country, since the story "Novotny's Pain" in 1962.) Roth lost out on the Pulitzer Prize only when the board ignored the jury's preference and gave the award to Norman Mailer's *The Executioner's Song*, a big book that played even trickier games with fact and fiction. But *The Ghost Writer* was the full success that had seemed out of Roth's reach for so long. Like *The Great Gatsby* or Willa Cather's *The Professor's House*, it is one of our literature's rare, inevitably brief, inscrutably musical, and nearly perfect books.

What had happened to make this possible? Was it simply the passage of time, or the long-term effects of psychotherapy, that had helped him to vanquish his old grievances and his old demons and move on?

All that Roth says about the internal combustion that produced *The Ghost Writer* is, "I think I found the right people," meaning, primarily, Lonoff and Anne Frank: "They just widened the scope of the contemplation." There is something uncanny in the way this widened scope fits within a story of such snowbound intimacy, like a construction snug on the outside that turns out to be vast within. It is clear how much Anne Frank meant to Roth; he walks a very fine line between history and imagination. Emanuel Isidore Lonoff—who may contain a touch of Isaac Bashevis Singer—also grows to be historically large. His famous stories, like Malamud's or Singer's, are built out of "everything humbling" that men like Nathan's father have labored to escape, and yet are "shamelessly conceived." The rejection of shame seems essential to a book that is finally about three Jewish writers differently placed in history. After the war, Nathan's Anne conceals her camp experiences in order to avoid being pitied. When someone tells her that she needn't be ashamed, she replies, "I'm not ashamed. That's the point." And Nathan—whose shamelessness as a writer needs no underlining—recalls that his discovery of Lonoff's stories filled him with the same sort of pride that was inspired in his parents "by the establishment in 1948 of a homeland in Palestine that would gather in the unmurdered remnant of European Jewry."

Yet this stoic pride is neither easily won nor perfectly maintained. Lonoff's serenity is unflappable, and Nathan seems hardly to understand the fears that motivate his parents. But he must understand, because he accords his Anne a final, tortured outburst, in which she recalls the experience of rediscovering her diary—her published, celebrated *Diary*—and how it opened the floodgates to feelings she believed that she had sealed away. This is not the sweetly optimistic Anne Frank whose most famous words—thanks to the Broadway version of the *Diary*, thanks to the movie version—are "In spite of everything I still believe that people are really good at heart." This is an Anne Frank who feels not only hatred but the shame that she had fervently denied, and a desire for revenge so intense that it provides her with a final reason to remain dead and thus allow the diary to live:

> The package came from Amsterdam, I opened it, and there it was: my past, myself, my name, *my face intact*—and all I wanted was revenge. It

wasn't for the dead—it had nothing to do with bringing back the dead or scourging the living. It wasn't corpses I was avenging—it was the mother-less, fatherless, sisterless, venge-filled, hate-filled, shame-filled, half-flayed, seething thing. It was myself. I wanted tears, I wanted their Christian tears to run like Jewish blood, for me.

A surviving Anne contains all the possibilities—as the living Anne contained all possibilities—represented by the pages that are blank.

༄

For a writer so nourished by the personal, the phrase "the right people" may also be viewed in a nearer sense. *The Ghost Writer* is dedicated to Milan Kundera, suggesting that Roth's new friendships in "the other Europe" also had widened the scope of his contemplation. And then there is Claire Bloom, with whom Roth was sharing his life when, in 1977, he began the book: a small, dark, beautiful Jewish woman who was born in Europe in 1931, a year and a half after Anne Frank.

Roth had been exploring the divide between European and American experiences of the war, and particularly between European and American childhoods, for a long time. In the early story "Eli, the Fanatic," a school of wraith-like refugee children proves too unsettling for the Jewish parents of an American suburb, whose own children are "safe in their beds." In *The Ghost Writer*, Nathan has an exchange with Amy Bellette, in which, wondering at her accent and probing at her identity, he asks if she has been through the war. He missed the war himself, he tells her:

> "And what did you have instead?" she asked me.
> "My childhood."

Bloom was eight and at a café in Cornwall, on vacation with her mother and brother, when a voice on the radio announced that England was at war. The three of them crouched in a ditch at the sound of an air-raid siren as they were returning to their cottage. A few months later, bombs blew half the roof off their house, in Bristol. In 1941, she went to America with her mother and brother—they stayed first with relatives in Florida, then in Forest Hills, Queens—but the little group returned to be with her father in London in late 1943. After being held up in Portugal for several months, they arrived on the very day the second London blitz began and remained for the duration of the war. On Roth's desk throughout the time he worked on *The Ghost Writer*, he kept a photograph of Anne Frank and another photograph—strikingly similar in appearance—of Bloom at about the same age.

Not that it was always paradise in the house that Roth shared with Bloom in London. Bloom has written, in *Leaving a Doll's House*, that her daughter, Anna, had already suffered greatly through her parents' divorce—Bloom's first husband and Anna's father was the actor Rod Steiger—and then through Bloom's disastrous second marriage to a man whom Anna loathed. More, the girl was "furious and justifiably hurt" when Bloom began to spend weeks in New York with Roth, complaining that "I had once again chosen a man over her." Roth initially worked hard (even by Bloom's account) to win the girl's favor—she was seventeen when he moved in, in 1977—and there was clearly enough love and excitement between the couple to carry them forward. But the family trio did not run smoothly. It was to ease and escape these tensions that Roth rented the small, one-room writing studio in Notting Hill—it had been passed on to him by his good friend Alison Lurie—which he outfitted exactly as he had his studio in Connecticut. There, looking out onto an English garden, he patiently wrote and rewrote the story of Anne Frank, alive and well across the ocean. As for Bloom, her professional activities that year included a recording, for Caedmon Records, of excerpts from Anne Frank's *Diary of a Young Girl*.

Bloom also made a very concrete contribution to Roth's book. It doesn't require an intimate of Roth's to note, as Bloom does in her memoir, that there was a great deal of Roth himself in E. I. Lonoff and the way he lived: the idyllic country house with the books, the maple trees, the solitude, and the long days devotedly spent "turning sentences around." The months that she spent with him in Connecticut every year were invariably quiet and could be lonely. She recounts with good humor a day when Roth, working on *The Ghost Writer*, came out of his studio to ask her to describe, for the sake of his portrait of Lonoff's long-suffering wife, Hope, what it was like to live with a writer in the country. As Bloom recalls, she didn't need to be asked twice: "We don't go anywhere! We don't do anything! We don't see anyone!" Her complaints fed directly into Hope Lonoff's plight—although Bloom's fictional counterpart, needless to say, does not spend the rest of each year in London or on the stage or making films. (Bloom actually played Hope Lonoff in a televised adaptation of *The Ghost Writer* in 1984.) Rather, like a Chekhov heroine, she merely longs to live in Boston someday.

Hope Lonoff knows, however, that the city's noise and distractions would make the move impossible for her husband, the man who has exchanged life for art. Nathan knows it, too. He observes how the house and the surrounding land protect the writer from the outside world, in a passage suggesting that it may have been simply the Connecticut landscape—Roth still speaks with awe about "its open spaces, its emptiness in winter"—that brought a new magic to Roth's work, even if the ultimate message was not new:

> There was still more wind than snow, but in Lonoff's orchard the light had all but seeped away, and the sound of what was on its way was menacing. Two dozen wild old apple trees stood as first barrier between the bleak unpaved road and the farmhouse. Next came a thick green growth of rhododendron, then a wide stone wall fallen in like a worn molar at the center, then some fifty feet of snow-crusted lawn, and finally, drawn up close to the house and protectively overhanging the shingles, three maples that looked from their size to be as old as New England. In back, the house gave way to unprotected fields, drifted over since the first December blizzards. From there the wooded hills began their impressive rise, undulating forest swells that just kept climbing into the next state. My guess was that it would take even the fiercest Hun the better part of a winter to cross the glacial waterfalls and wind-blasted woods of those mountain wilds before he was able to reach the open edge of Lonoff's hayfields, rush the rear storm door of the house, crash through into the study, and, with spiked bludgeon wheeling high in the air above the little Olivetti, cry out in a roaring voice to the writer tapping out his twenty-seventh draft, "You must change your life!"

Eating Only Words

Fame and fortune were not so rich as subjects. *Zuckerman Unbound*, which continued the writer's story, is a book about the consequences of a book—about the "counter-spell" that a work of fiction casts on its writer's reality. Another slender novella-like volume, published in 1981, it takes Nathan forward in time thirteen years, to the watershed moment in 1969 when he has become a huge success, owing to a distinctly *Portnoy*-like book titled *Carnovsky*. Six weeks after the scandalizing book has appeared, Nathan can't walk the New York streets without being accosted, he is getting mail addressed to "The Enemy of the Jews" (care of his publisher), and he has made a million bucks. He has also realized that success isn't all it's cracked up to be. But even Zuckerman admits that "being a poor misunderstood millionaire is not really a topic that intelligent people can discuss for very long," and he is right. *Zuckerman Unbound*, a lively but undernourished book, feels like a letdown after *The Ghost Writer*. In part, it's the letdown that comes with the writer's progress from youthful idealism to the marketplace. Anne Frank? Henry James? Zuckerman is called "the Jewish Charles Dickens" by a guy who is trying to get him to endorse pickled herring on a television commercial and who offers to get an actress to play Zuckerman's mother if she's unable to join him for the job.

It's a lonely book beneath the jokes, though, as Nathan is increasingly unbound from the people in his life. At thirty-six, he has obtained his third divorce. He spends most of his time alone in his new Upper

East Side apartment, worrying about who's calling and who isn't. He is obsessed with other people's obsession with his book. The most arresting example of the corrosive effects of fame, American style, however, is not Zuckerman, with his uncommon success, but someone with the far more common experience of failure: a highly unstable Jewish paranoiac motormouth from Newark named Alvin Pepler. This semi-brilliant one-time quiz show star has suffered a history of injustices, the latest of which, in his estimation, is the utterly arbitrary absence of talent that has kept him from writing a bestselling book like Zuckerman's.

Alvin Pepler is a glorious fool, attempting to impress Zuckerman with knowing a big-time producer who has "an option on the Six-Day War, for a musical." (The choice of a script writer, he assures him, is down to three: "You, Herman Wouk, and Harold Pinter.") But the furious resentment that erupts from beneath the flattery makes Pepler more than a comic butt. He is a troubling, if hilarious, figure, a personality so overbearing that he makes Zuckerman seem recessive; he fills the pages so completely that the absence of a plot is hardly noticed. (Pepler is implicated in an uncertain scheme to kidnap Zuckerman's mother. "Haven't you given her enough misery with that book?" the kidnapper argues.) Pepler is a promise of things to come in Roth's work: the manic, slightly dangerous doppelgänger. (Zuckerman, sizing him up as "The Jew You Can't Permit in the Parlor," realizes that this is exactly "how Johnny Carson America now thinks of me.") He is also the furious herald of contemporary, post-riot Newark, a racially torn ruin totally unlike the sentimentalized city of Zuckerman's bestseller. "What do you know about Newark, Mama's Boy! I read that fucking book!" he shouts. "Newark is junkies shitting in your hallway and everything burned to the ground!" But this was a reality that lay beyond Roth's current subject and a tragedy that he did not yet see as having anything like the moral weight of Communist Prague.

A Roth hero without a moral problem is inconceivable, and Zuckerman's lack of any serious moral difficulty in the first three-quarters of the book accounts for a sense of slackness, despite the popping comic rhythms—a sense of energies confined to the surface. The fact that Zuckerman has written a *Portnoy*-like book doesn't mean that he shares Portnoy's complaint. He may sometimes miss the wife he has just divorced, but he has no regrets about his marital failures and no major internal conflicts. He has an affair with a glamorous movie star, but it hardly registers—on him, or on us—because she's a lifeless figure, no more credible in her "gown of veils and beads and feathers" than Roth's earlier glamour girl, Helen Kepesh. The movie star does, however, give Roth a chance to slip in something of Bloom (if only in that she is reading Kierkegaard's *The Crisis in the Life of an Actress*, a book that Bloom had introduced Roth to), a bit of his friend Edna O'Brien in her Irish charm, and a bit of his brief experience of dating Jackie Kennedy. (There's the limo that pulls up when he has offered to take her home from a party, the utter confidence of her sequential lines, "Would you like to come up? Oh, of course you would," and a good-night kiss that's like "kissing a billboard.") Yet for all the sexual fame that Zuckerman has attained, he is not particularly concerned with sex. He lives in full relation only to his parents, and it is they who provide the serious moral consequences of the book.

If Roth spared Zuckerman the burden of his own marital history, he gave him a burden that Roth had never known, in a father who disapproves of his work. The elder Zuckerman, we learn, eventually forgave his son for the story that caused all the trouble in *The Ghost Writer*, and even developed some pride in his books. By the time *Carnovsky* appears, however—it is Zuckerman's fourth novel, as *Portnoy* was Roth's—Nathan is almost relieved to know that his father, who has suffered a series of strokes, won't be able to read it. (Zuckerman's mother is too gentle a soul to complain, even when people say to her, straight out, "I didn't know you were crazy like that, Selma." She merely needs to have her son assure her that "you are yourself and not Mrs. Carnovsky" and that his childhood was "very nearly heaven.") But, alas, a neighbor, coming regularly to the nursing home, has obligingly read the offending book to the old man, as a result of which he has a sudden, massive heart attack. He is rushed to a hospital, where, lying on his deathbed with the entire family gathered around, Mr. Zuckerman looks into the eyes of his elder son and pronounces his last word on earth: "Bastard."

At first, Nathan wonders if the writer in him has made him hear things. Maybe his father merely said "faster." Or "better." Or "vaster." Who knows why? Hearing "bastard" was just a writer's wishful thinking: "Better scene, stronger medicine, a final repudiation by Father." He notes approvingly that Kafka once wrote, "We should read only those books that bite and sting us. If a book we are reading does not rouse us with a blow to the head, then why read it?" And what more rousing blow to the head than this? For Nathan, the unwritten world is an uncertain place, and reality has become an elusive, exotic phenomenon—he can refer to it only in French, quoting Flaubert pining for "*le vrai*." But the demands of art may have finally taken him too far.

Nothing was wrong with his hearing. His brother, Henry, lets him know with certainty: "*Of course* he said 'Bastard.'" And more: "You killed him, Nathan," Henry cries, furious and weeping. "He'd seen what you had done to him and Mother in that book!" To make his conundrum worse, Nathan admits that he knew what his father would feel, even while he was writing the book, "but he'd written it anyway." And now he no longer has a father, and his brother will not speak to him. Except for his half-crushed mother, he has lost his closest human ties. It's a harrowing ending for a comedy, and so credibly related to Roth's own experience that one interviewer, walking into the trap, asked Roth to discuss the deathbed scene in relation to the death of his own father. Roth pounced, replying that "the best person to ask about the autobiographical relevance of the climactic death of the father in 'Zuckerman Unbound'" would be none other than his father, Herman Roth, then alive and prospering in Elizabeth, New Jersey. (And, he might have added, still handing out self-signed copies of Roth's books.) Roth concluded helpfully, "I'll give you his phone number."

In the spring of 1981, just as *Zuckerman Unbound* was released, to lukewarm reviews—in *The New York Times*, Anatole Broyard found it "reasonably funny, reasonably sad, reasonably interesting"—Bess Roth died suddenly of a heart attack. Roth was in London at the time. He had talked to his mother that morning; it was a Sunday, and he called his parents every Sunday morning. She had been in good spirits if not in the best health, and he had told her teasingly that he expected to take her on a mile-long walk with him in the Connecticut countryside that summer, when his parents came for their usual visit. In fact, she died at dinnertime, after taking a long and tiring walk with his father. Writing about her death a few years later (in *Patrimony*), Roth speculated rather touchingly that she might well "have gone off that afternoon hoping to begin to prepare herself for our summer stroll." The words convey not guilt but his desire to be a presence in her final acts—to have provided her with some happy anticipation. He got the news that night and flew back the next day. But he had missed his chance to be with her at the end, and it remained a vivid loss.

∞

"When he is sick, every man wants his mother" are the first words of *The Anatomy Lesson*, published in 1983. And Nathan Zuckerman was now very sick. Just the year before, Roth himself had received a diagnosis of "significant" coronary artery disease. He was forty-nine years old and had no history—or symptoms—of heart problems. The blockages were found on a routine exam. He had experienced a number of physical troubles over the years: the back injury that still flared up from time to time; the appendicitis that had almost killed him in his thirties; and, more recently, a long bout of neck and shoulder pain that had never been successfully diagnosed. Such experiences had forced him into an acute awareness of his body and how to care for it. He was thin, he exercised regularly, he didn't smoke. But because his doctors insisted that surgery was too dangerous, and the medication they prescribed caused impotence as an immediate side effect, he decided to try a less effective medication, work even harder at keeping himself fit, and take his chances. He told almost no one about the diagnosis, aside from Bloom and his brother and the executors of his will. But he began to say to friends that he did not expect to live long.

The Anatomy Lesson is about pain. Pain and writing. Pain and not writing. Real physical pain that has taken over your life and that has no explanation and no apparent remedy. Also about the pain of having written a book that killed your father and made your innocent mother's life a hell, until she—Mrs. Zuckerman, that is—died, too, just a year after Zuckerman's father, in 1970. It is now 1973, the Watergate hearings are on TV, and Nixon is the only other man in the country in as much trouble as Zuckerman. Four years have passed since his father's curse, and he hasn't written a thing. Three years since his mother's death. For a year and a half now, he has had excruciating pain in his neck and shoulders and arms, starting behind his right ear and branching downward from the scapula like a menorah held upside down. The pain is so bad that he cannot sit at a desk, or carry groceries, or think about anything much except the pain. He's made the round of doctors. One of the orthopedists says that it is the result of twenty years of hammering away at a manual portable typewriter—his beloved Olivetti—but his new IBM Selectric doesn't help. An osteopath says that he's been warping his spinal column ever since he learned to write, left-handed and twisting around to keep from smearing the ink, when he was seven years old. A psychiatrist, whom he walks out on, says it is clearly a result of guilt—from that book. Holding any physical position that allows him to write is excruciating (and dictation is impossible; he needs to see his sentences). The pain abates somewhat when he stops trying to write, but the simple fact is that without writing Zuckerman has no reason to exist.

The Anatomy Lesson begins as a comedy, and even as it grows dark and devastatingly sad, you can't stop laughing. The conclusion of the opening sentence, about how a sick man wants his mother, is "if she's not around, other women must do." In his illness, Zuckerman has four women, arriving and departing in shifts, bringing him food and servicing him sexually or saving time by doing both at once. This is the first of the Zuckerman books to show him sexually engaged, although he is far from active in the process, lying on his back on the floor on a plastic mat, with a thesaurus carefully placed beneath his head for support and relief. (The thesaurus makes an especially dispiriting contrast with the volume of Henry James that he placed beneath his feet back at the Lonoffs', in the heedless youth of his own volume one.) He is hardly more capable of motion than Roth's earlier unmanned hero, the six-foot breast. Yet he's been reduced so far that sex, at the start of the book, is all he has. Another cause for ironic despair: the pain has erased the crucial distinction that Zuckerman has been struggling to make, since the publication of his book, between his sex-obsessed hero and himself.

Sometimes he thinks that the pain is a result of the loss of his mother, even though she didn't have the impact on him that his forceful father had, and his memories of her have become principally—in a lovely phrase—"a breast, then a lap, then a fading voice calling after him, 'Be careful.'" Selma Zuckerman lived quietly and died that way, of a brain tumor, misdiagnosed until it offered an unmistakable manifestation, in her own single parting word:

> Her first time in the hospital, the doctors diagnosed a minor stroke, nothing to leave her seriously impaired; four months later, when they admitted her again, she was able to recognize her neurologist when he came by the room, but when he asked if she would write her name for him on a piece

of paper, she took the pen from his hand and instead of "Selma" wrote the word "Holocaust," perfectly spelled.

This incident takes place in 1970 in Miami Beach, the word "Holocaust" inscribed by a woman who almost certainly never spoke it aloud, and whose previous writings consisted of thank-you notes, recipe cards, and knitting instructions. "But she had a tumor in her head the size of a lemon, and it seemed to have forced out everything except the one word," Zuckerman notes. "It must have been there all the time without their even knowing."

This inventive little parable was not invented. Roth tells me that he heard the story from his longtime editor and friend Aaron Asher. It had happened during the hospitalization of Asher's mother, a European Jew who had immigrated to America in the late thirties—unlike the fictional Mrs. Zuckerman, who had grown up safe and unthreatened in New Jersey. But the moral of the tale applies to both women; in fact, that *is* the moral of the tale. Roth, when questioned about this scene in an interview in the London *Times* after the book's release in England, explained that for American Jews the Holocaust is "simply there, hidden, submerged, emerging, disappearing, unforgotten." Without this word, he said—that is, without the event it represents—"there would be no Nathan Zuckerman, not in Zuckerman's fix," nor would there be a "father and his deathbed curse." If one could somehow obliterate this history, "none of these Zuckerman books would exist." Nathan takes the piece of paper from the doctor, folds it up, and puts it in his wallet. When the interviewer asked Roth why Nathan doesn't throw it away, he replied, "Who can? Who has?"

Yet Zuckerman does not believe that he has anything to write about. His parents are gone, Newark is gone. Even his wives are gone. Not that any of these things appeal to him as subject matter anymore; not that any of them seem important. He has been trying to write, instead, about the life of one of his girlfriends, an acerbic Polish émigrée who stops by to drink his wine and have a little sex and complain about the fact that he considers her a "subject," which he does, although without success. As he explains this literary failure to himself:

> You don't want to represent her Warsaw—it's what her Warsaw represents that you want: suffering that isn't semi-comical, the world of massive

historical pain instead of this pain in the neck. War, destruction, anti-Semitism, totalitarianism, literature on which the fate of a culture hinges, writing at the very heart of the upheaval, a martyrdom more to the point—some point, *any* point—than bearing the cocktail-party chitchat as a guest on Dick Cavett. Chained to self-consciousness. Chained to retrospection. Chained to my dwarf drama till I die.

Tempting as it is to impute these feelings to the author, it should be noted that Roth, in his *Paris Review* interview, in 1984, made exactly the opposite point, deriding the presumed literary advantages of writers in the kind of oppressive system that he had seen up close in Czechoslovakia: "That system doesn't make masterpieces; it makes coronaries, ulcers, and asthma, it makes alcoholics, it makes depressives, it makes bitterness and desperation and insanity." He expressed no doubt about his preference for "our extensive, lively, national literature," even with its trivializing problems. But this rational and hard-won view, voiced by a fifty-year-old writer with real experience of both systems, lacks the exasperated comedy, the wild solipsism, and the sheer self-satire that are the essence of Zuckerman. Roth's enduringly provocative creature—a protagonist, after all, as well as a writer—has never been to Warsaw (or to Prague), doesn't know what he is talking about, is hopped up on pain medication, and is increasingly delusional as he works himself into a tailspin.

The Anatomy Lesson won high critical praise. In *The New York Times*, Christopher Lehmann-Haupt called it a "rich, satisfyingly complex conclusion" to the Zuckerman trilogy, and John Updike, in a detailed review in *The New Yorker*, called it "a ferocious, heartfelt book" in which "the central howl unrolls with a meditated savagery both fascinating and repellent, self-indulgent yet somehow sterling, adamant, pure in the style of high modernism." Yet the book was also criticized, even by its admirers—like Updike, with his "self-indulgent"—for what Lehmann-Haupt termed Zuckerman's "endless self-absorption and scab-picking." The outstanding evidence of these unpleasant traits was generally found in Zuckerman's unrelenting rage against a literary critic who has attacked his work. ("Someone said that a friend had seen him walking in Cambridge with a cane. From kidney stones? Hooray.") When Zuckerman isn't focused on his pain or his harem, it is this critic—whose offending article he has nearly memorized, as in school he memorized "Annabel Lee"—who occupies his thoughts.

Although Roth gave this eminent Jewish critic the name Milton Appel, his real-world identity as Irving Howe was, in the words of William Gass, "hidden like a lamppost in the living room." Biographically, Appel was virtually identical with Howe: the son of impoverished Yiddish-speaking parents and a member of the old *Partisan Review* group, Appel had lavishly praised Zuckerman's *Goodbye, Columbus*–like first book, finding his portrait of materialistic American Jews almost too documentarily exact. But he had turned against Zuckerman after *Carnovsky*, claiming to find the very same figures an offensive caricature, "twisted out of human recognition" by Zuckerman's hostility to Jews. According to Zuckerman, Appel's attack upon his career "made Macduff's assault upon Macbeth look almost lackadaisical." Appel did not merely decapitate him—"a head wasn't enough for Appel"—but tore him "limb from limb."

There may be other aspects of Roth's relation to Howe that were less recognizable. Appel has edited an anthology of Yiddish fiction— very like Howe's landmark 1954 anthology, *A Treasury of Yiddish Stories* (co-edited with Eliezer Greenberg)—that Zuckerman, in his early twenties, had found exhilarating, as a rebellious act and a stand against "the snobbish condescension of those famous departments of English literature from whose impeccable Christian ranks the literary Jew, with his mongrelized speech and caterwauling inflections, had until just yesterday been pointedly excluded." Zuckerman had even been inspired to attempt to learn Yiddish, if only for about six weeks. During Roth's first year in Chicago, in 1954, he too spent a number of weeks bent over a Yiddish grammar book and English–Yiddish dictionary, bought second-hand, equally inspired if no more tenacious than his hero. Roth, learning Yiddish?

Clearly, the critic's attack had been a terrific blow because he was so important to the writer. Zuckerman frequently rereads one of Appel's old *Partisan Review* essays, about the inevitable conflict between coarse-grained old-style Jewish fathers and their bookish American sons, to console himself for his fights with his own father. But if there is any instigating reality behind Roth's depiction of a father repudiating his son because of what he has written, it came not from Herman Roth but from Irving Howe.

Still, Zuckerman's tirades about Appel were intensely annoying to many critics, particularly since the Howe connection made the anger seem not merely Zuckerman's but Roth's. (Roth was not known for silently enduring critical malfeasance. Nearly a decade earlier, in 1974, he had excoriated Lehmann-Haupt, not because of a bad review—the *Times* critic loved *Portnoy's Complaint*—but because of what Roth described, in *The New York Review of Books*, as a lack of "any critical standards, criteria, or position that it is possible to take seriously," a prose style "no longer even acceptable in high school book reports," and a general level of consideration that was "an insult to the community of American writers." Heckling the reigning *Times* critic would become something of a Roth specialty.) Even Updike was now advising that, by the age of fifty—Updike was fifty-one, a year older than Roth—"a writer should have settled his old scores." Others complained of Roth's vengefulness and even of "blood on the page."

In conversation, Roth defends himself by pointing out that "I was depicting a writer—and what is more characteristic than rage against a critic?" What is more characteristic of any artist? The painter Philip Guston, Roth reports, "was enraged for life by Hilton Kramer." Updike, in his own series of books about a writer, Henry Bech, giddily abandoned his superior indifference to critics. In the satire *Bech Noir*, written in 1998, Updike's seventy-four-year-old alter ego murders four of the offending creatures, whose decades-old attacks he remembers word for word. ("The thought of him dead," Updike writes of one critic, "filled Bech with creamy ease.") The striking fact about Roth's equally satirical hero is that he is not nearly as successful against his foes.

Zuckerman's deathless fury has been reignited by Appel's suggestion that he write an op-ed essay for the *Times* in support of Israel, since 1973 was the year not only of Watergate but of the Yom Kippur War. Appel, deeply worried about Israel's future, feels that Zuckerman can reach people beyond his own more limited sphere. "And what kinds of people are they?" Zuckerman shoots back, having telephoned Appel precisely to release his rage and so perhaps to ease his pain. "People like me who don't like Jews? Or people like Goebbels who gas them?" The great surprise of the scene is that Appel, whom we have been prepared to think a curmudgeon, turns out to be reasonable, intelligent, and willing to put all differences aside for the larger cause. Zuckerman, on the other hand, is irrational, insulting, and—while extremely funny—barely capable of recognizing the existence of a cause larger than himself. The figure being mocked by the author is not Appel but Zuckerman, who, slamming down the phone, is in even more pain than before.

For those who are wondering, Roth and Howe never had such a conversation, although Howe had indeed suggested that Roth write something about Israel, in 1973, just a year after his critical attack, and Roth had responded by writing Howe a letter that was less than cheerfully compliant. In the late seventies, in an interview in *The New York Times Book Review*, Roth was still lamenting the critic's original change of heart. ("He was a real reader.") He couldn't know that, in the same years, Howe was thinking about writing a "fresh and affirmative" new essay on Roth's work—in the words of Howe's biographer, Gerald Sorin, based on information originating with Howe's wife. (Sorin wonders if Roth's Kafka story, with its loving Jewish family, played a part in Howe's desire to recant his charges. In any case, Howe never wrote the essay.) In 1983, the year of *The Anatomy Lesson*, the two men spoke briefly—with perfect civility, Roth emphasizes—as members of a jury at the American Academy of Arts and Letters; a few years later, Roth asked Howe to write an introduction to one of his Writers from the Other Europe volumes (George Konrád's *The Case Worker*). They never discussed their earlier conflict. Yet Roth reports, with unmistakable satisfaction, that a mutual friend, Bernard Avishai, told him that when Howe was dying, in the early nineties, he said to Avishai, "I was wrong about your friend Roth."

As for Updike, he noted in his review that it was unfair to complain about the book's "frenzied solipsism"—however much it irked—since "frenzied solipsism" is what the book is all about. At bottom, indeed, this is the essence of Nathan's illness, as Nathan himself comes to see it: the source of the pain. It's the pain of being a writer. Sick of everything about his vocation—the hours and years alone, the use of people as material, the long habit of "starving myself of experience and eating only words"—Nathan is sick of himself. But, of course, it isn't only writers who get caught in the trap of the self; there's something here for everyone. And, as Nathan shows, the tighter the lid of the self is fastened—and Nathan's lid is screwed down very tight—the more crazily exhilarating is the prospect of release.

Seeking escape from his pain with the aid of Percodan and vodka and a little pot, he decides to apply to medical school and become a doctor. It was Nathan Zuckerman, after all, who heard the roaring voice of the Hun battering across the snowy fields to tell E. I. Lonoff, tapping out a twenty-seventh draft, that he must change his life. Lonoff was deaf to the voice, but Zuckerman will heed it. He will give up writing. He will help other people. ("Other people. Somebody should have told me about them a long time ago.") He's spent enough time in doctors' waiting rooms; how hard could it be?

Nathan flies to Chicago to consult an old college friend about medical school, while continuing to self-medicate and self-obsess. And *The Anatomy Lesson* hurtles inward with him at breathtaking speed. On the plane, flying at even higher personal altitudes, he convinces the man in the adjacent seat that he's a professional pornographer named Milton Appel. (As a career alternative, it makes a good deal more sense than medical school.) The irrationality of his plan is something that Nathan is forced to confront when he sees his friend, who is now an anesthesiologist at the university hospital and the kind of solid and beneficent presence that Nathan longs to be. It's a relief to have this calmly authoritative voice challenge Nathan's brilliant lunacy; it's a relief to feel the book crack open to admit any other meaningful voice. But there's no stopping Nathan's trajectory toward implosion—even as the voices from outside multiply, and it starts to snow.

The most stirring voice turns out to be, not surprisingly, an elderly Jewish man of the sort who often walks away with Roth's books—although this one, Mr. Freytag, is a far more fragile figure than the various incarnations of Herman Roth. The father of Nathan's friend and a recent widower, he cannot get over the loss of his wife. From the moment Nathan lays eyes on him, we enter a world that is part Marx Brothers and part Beckett:

> On the front steps, in fur hat, storm coat, and buckled black galoshes, an old man was trying to sweep away the snow. It was falling heavily now, and as soon as he got to the bottom step, he had to start again at the top. There were four steps and the old man kept going up and down them with his broom.

For Nathan, downing his third Percodan of the day and emptying his Tiffany flask, snow recalls childhood and coming home from school.

Snow means being protected, loved, and obedient—all the lost feelings that preceded the onset of audacity, doubt, and pain. Snow, which returns the reader to the lyric world of *The Ghost Writer*, is also the reason that Nathan is visiting Mr. Freytag: he has come to take him to visit his wife's grave before the storm buries her a second time.

In the old man's empty house and then in a long black rented hearse-like limo, the sorrowing widower and the motherless son carry on a quiet duet about the woman each has lost, the old man supplying the keening lines and Nathan the steady refrain:

> "A woman who for herself wanted *nothing*."
> "Mine too." . . .
> "She was my *memory*."
> "Mine too."

Then through the cemetery gates, to a Jewish burial ground backed by a sinisterly smoking building—it's only a factory, but the oncoming storm gives it the look of something much worse—where the two men walk out on the whitening path together. And where all hell breaks loose, as the old man launches into a tirade about his delinquent grandson, and Nathan's mind gives way completely. Furiously attacking "the last of the fathers demanding to be pleased," he struggles in his stupor to get his hands around the old man's throat—"Freytag! Forbidder! Now I murder *you*!"—sliding after him through a world obliterated by whirling snow, and finally keels over headfirst onto a tombstone.

The scene is a phantasmagorical tour de force, the underlying tragedy entirely unimpeded by the slapstick. It gives way to a sudden and equally disturbing calm: a quiet and exacting coda in which Zuckerman, waking in the hospital, is unable to speak a word. He has fractured his jaw; a doctor comes to wire it shut. In an interview in *The Nation* in 1985, Roth was asked about the curiously metaphorical state in which his hero finds himself, and he began by shrugging off the question: "He breaks his jaw falling on a tombstone in a Jewish cemetery, after overdosing on painkillers and booze. What's so metaphorical about that? Happens all the time." But on reconsideration, he admitted that he had been thinking of the rabbi who, back in the fifties, had written to the Anti-Defamation League of B'nai B'rith, demanding, "What is being done to silence this man?" He'd remembered that line while he was finishing the book. "And that's why I broke Zuckerman's jaw," Roth concluded. "I did it for the rabbi."

Nathan can no longer talk; but, more important, he no longer feels the need. Wandering through the hospital in his robe and slippers, trailing the doctors on their rounds like a kind of mascot, he needs only to listen and to look—at suffering such as he has never seen or heard before. The surgeries. The cancers. ("You look green, Doctor," a doctor tells him, laughing. "Maybe you're better off sticking to books.") The resurgent hopes that are quickly followed by death. The pain. "And always the enemy was wicked and real," he thinks. He is humbled and abashed, perhaps even ennobled. Yet that doesn't mean that he can escape his own particular and solitary fate: his "future as a man apart," as he puts it, or—in a brilliant double entendre, which closes the book with the precision of a jeweler's clasp—"the corpus that was his."

∞

The Prague Orgy brings Nathan, at last, to the story that Roth originally wanted to tell: a wealthy and celebrated American writer, the beneficiary of all that the rather tawdry system offers, comes face-to-face with the poverty and persecution of his Czech contemporaries. But Nathan has not come to Prague to help the writers. In a new Jamesian turn, he is trying to get hold of a manuscript, the unpublished stories of a Czech Jew who wrote in Yiddish and was killed under the Nazis, and who is said to have been (here James verges on Borges) the Yiddish Flaubert. As in *The Aspern Papers*, the manuscript is in the possession of a woman who doesn't wish to give it up. But this woman, named Olga, is unlike anyone in Henry James: "All the great international figures come to Prague to see our oppression, but none of them will ever fuck me," she complains. *"What will save Czechoslovakia would be to fuck Olga."*

Roth's knowledge of the city had deepened since *The Professor of Desire*. He's not a tourist anymore. Prague is a great deal more than Kafka. The Czech writers whom Nathan meets in his bugged hotel room or in their squalid quarters are sardonic, desperate, and full of stories. ("They, silenced, are all mouth," Nathan thinks, "I am only ears—and plans.") Roth draws on his personal experiences: Ivan

Klíma's explanation to the police that Roth came to Prague "for the girls" is the same one prepared by a Czech ally in case Zuckerman gets into trouble. And Roth attended parties of just the sort that give the book its title—if not quite the orgies that the participants liked to pretend, flouting their reputation for "virtuous political suffering," then wild enough. As the persistent Olga points out, "To be fucked is the only freedom left in this country." It should be noted that Zuckerman, to her frustration, keeps his pants on throughout.

Roth also knew from experience the often voiced sensation that half the citizens of Prague were employed in spying on the other half. He was used to being followed, much of the time, by the obvious plain-clothesmen, but it took him a while to realize that he was also being followed by an acquaintance, the well-known double agent Jiří Mucha—the son of the famous Art Nouveau painter Alphonse Mucha and the host of the city's biggest parties. Roth recalls that when they ran into each other on the far side of town one day, where Roth had gone—really, for once—to see a girl, he automatically exclaimed, "How strange to see you here!" And Mucha replied, "Not strange at all!" The fiction takes the relationship between spy and spied-upon one madcap step further: when a government-sanctioned hack is threatened with dismissal because his reports on a dissident writer are so ill-observed that they are useless, the dissident offers to write the reports himself. "I know what I do all day better than you," he tells him. "And I can be rid of your company, you shitface." The lesson, lost on no one, is that a good writer and a good spy require similar gifts.

Roth's accounts of life in Prague are piquant—like Olga, the city has a striking cynical pathos—although they amount to hardly more than a series of vignettes. *The Prague Orgy* is the briefest of the Zuckerman tales; it was published not independently but as an epilogue when the books were released in a single volume, *Zuckerman Bound*, in 1985. Although it was the initial impetus for these hundreds of pages, it came off merely as an afterthought, earning hardly any critical attention at all. Roth says that he sometimes wonders if he should have put the Prague section at the start of the Zuckerman volumes, where it might have had an impact and would have set the story of Zuckerman's fame in a different light. "Conrad might have done it that way, set it on a freighter where he runs into someone telling him a story about Prague, before his own story begins." But, even aside from the freighter, he says, "That's not for me." It may be significant that *The Prague Orgy* takes place in 1976, the last year that Roth was allowed into Czechoslovakia. By the time he got around to writing it, he'd been out of touch with the city for nine years, and his interests had moved elsewhere.

The most affecting part of Roth's account of Prague required hardly any experience at all, since it explains how the city evoked "the Jewish Atlantis" of Zuckerman's childhood, when, during the worst years of the war, he collected nickels for the Jewish National Fund, to help establish a Jewish homeland in Palestine. It wasn't Palestine, however, but Prague, with its old-time streetcars and blackened bridges and barren shops and medieval streets, that Zuckerman envisioned as the sort of place the Jews would buy with all those nickels: "a broken city, a city so worn and grim that nobody else would even put in a bid." It's a city where stories are always being told, on park benches and on line at the grocery, a city where everywhere people are telling "anxious tales of harassment and flight, stories of fantastic endurance and pitiful collapse." Because stories—jokes, too—are "the form their resistance has taken," just as they are "the national industry of the Jewish homeland." Stories are what the Jewish people had, like the people in Prague today, "instead of life"; stories are what the people themselves become, "in lieu of being permitted to be anything else." Small wonder that Roth can't pry his storytelling and his Jewishness apart.

It is ironic but hardly unexpected that when the American Jewish would-be savior of the works of the Yiddish Flaubert finally gets his hands on the stories, he cannot read a word of them. Even the triumph of obtaining them turns immediately to defeat when the Czech police seize the manuscript and force Zuckerman, ignominiously, to leave the country. "Another assault upon a world of significance degenerating into a personal fiasco," he notes. Exit Zuckerman as a serious person, with accomplishments and sufferings that are serious, too. "No, one's story isn't a skin to be shed—it's inescapable, one's body and blood," he reflects. "You go on pumping it out till you die, the story veined with the themes of your life." If Roth seemed to be admitting the limitations that his critics had been chiding him for, he was also refusing to give ground.

This is not the first time that Zuckerman has been thrown back upon himself, after all, in the pages of *Zuckerman Bound*. Bound indeed. Restrained, tied up, cramped, forced into ever deeper recesses of the self. Until, at last, there is a liberating explosion in Roth's work, in which bits and pieces of Zuckerman—alive, for the most part, and fairly well—are scattered from chapter to chapter, life to life, fate to fate. Roth thought of calling this explosion *The Metamorphosis*, but the title was already taken. Instead, he went with *The Counterlife*.

Cain to Your Abel,
Esau to Your Jacob

"You in England? The Jersey boy with the dirty mouth who writes the books Jews love to hate—how do you survive there? How can you stand the silence?" Nathan Zuckerman is visiting Israel when he is asked this series of questions by an old friend, an Israeli journalist who is shocked to hear that Nathan has moved to London. In terms of decorum—just for starters—Nathan is assured that Israel could not be more different from England. In this still new and much contested country, "it's enough to live," his Israeli friend explains; "you don't have to do anything else and you go to bed exhausted." Even in the outright matter of decibels, he adds, "Have you ever noticed that Jews shout? Even one ear is more than you need." England and Israel in the late seventies are the immediately juxtaposed worlds of *The Counterlife*, which presents itself as a book about places—the chapter titles include "Gloucestershire" and "Judea"—although it is really about the ways that places affect people. As a novelist, Roth is more psychologist than poet, and by the mid-eighties he had put in decades as a kind of Kafka Domesticus, examining the traps that people build to live in. *The Counterlife*, published at the end of 1986, is an exhilarating culmination of the theme: a book about transformation, about what happens when people finally break free.

Roth knew what that felt like. By the time he was writing *The Counterlife*, he was deep into his London life with Bloom—he usually remained in London through the winter months and returned to

Connecticut in summer, when Bloom would come and go, depending on her professional commitments and her desire to be in London with her daughter. Roth, who tells me that he imagined E. I. Lonoff as the kind of wholly isolated man that he inevitably would have become had he stayed in Connecticut year-round, gives Bloom full credit for his deliverance from that fate. "Claire came along to take me out of that," he says. "I don't know whether it's right to say she saved me, but she certainly changed things." He adds with a smile, "You must change your life." The most exciting of the changes, aside from the feeling that he had finally shed his identity as the author of *Portnoy's Complaint*, was entering Bloom's theatrical world.

Now he was not only writing about Chekhov or teaching Chekhov but getting his hands into the work, adapting a translation of *The Cherry Orchard* for a production at the Chichester Festival, in which Bloom played Madame Ranevskaya. He also wrote two more television plays for Bloom, one based on the Russian Jewish writer Eugenia Ginzburg's memoir of her years in the Gulag, the other about the Dominica-born Welsh-Creole novelist Jean Rhys: two fascinatingly ethnic choices for "the English Rose," about which Roth was extremely enthusiastic, although neither was produced. Roth, who speaks of his talent in terms of "the ability to perform, to dramatize," loved being part of the process by which Bloom developed a role. Whether attending rehearsals—as he did for *The Cherry Orchard*—or going over lines, he was "as capable of getting worked up over her performances," he reports, "as over my own writing." He proudly recalls giving Bloom a key to her celebrated performance as Lady Marchmain in the 1981 British television film *Brideshead Revisited*: remembering a letter in which Chekhov tells his actress-wife (the original Madame Ranevskaya) that finding "a certain smile" will unlock a difficult role, Roth suggested that Bloom assume the enigmatic smile of their friend Antonia Fraser—Harold Pinter's aristocratic wife, who also bore the honorific "Lady." For him, this was a world of experiences to be relished: in her memoir, Bloom writes of Roth visiting her during the *Brideshead* filming, at Castle Howard, and joking about "this nice Jewish couple" staying in the enormous baroque palace. "Try not to feel the curtain fabric," he told her, "and don't ask how much per yard."

If all this new life fed into the intensity of *The Counterlife*, so did

Roth's feeling during much of the eighties that he was living on borrowed time, because of his heart condition and the questionably adequate medication. Also adding to the intensity, he admits, was the fact that he was having a secret affair. As he describes it, the woman was thirty when he met her—Roth was not quite fifty—unhappily married, and the mother of a small child. She was English, an Oxford graduate, and initially called to interview him for the BBC. She was also exceptionally eloquent; he seems to have been smitten as much by the felicities of her speech as by her looks. (It was through her, he says, that he learned about "upper-middle-class English life.") Their relationship took place entirely within the narrow confines of his writing studio, except for a few walks on Hampstead Heath and a couple of "accidental" meetings at concerts, occasions that they felt somehow gave them the license to go out to dinner together afterward. ("It wasn't exactly rational," he says with a shrug.) Is it any more rational to ask why the affair took place at all? Is it ever?

In the Bloom household, the tensions between Roth and Bloom's daughter, Anna—or between Roth and Bloom over her behavior with Anna—had become extremely wearing for all. In 1978, Anna, who was eighteen and a student at London's Guildhall School of Music, left the house and moved into a residence hall, at Bloom's request, in response to Roth's request. The move prompted an emotional crisis that was still painful to Bloom nearly twenty years later, when she wrote about it in her memoir. But Anna returned home for good a few months later, and the three of them resumed exactly where they had left off. Bloom, caught in what she describes as a "no-win situation," and "attempting to make up for what I had failed to do in the past," acknowledged that her behavior with her daughter over the years "made Philip feel as though he was an intruder in our closed circle." The fact that he found another circle to include him may or may not require such an explanation. In any case, Roth now says that he was "elated" by the affair. But nothing was more elating than the book that this counterlife was helping him to write.

As it begins, Henry Zuckerman, Nathan's brother and a successful New Jersey dentist and family man, has learned that he has a potentially fatal heart condition. Since the only effective medication renders him impotent, and since the high point of Henry's life is having sex with his dental assistant, he talks his doctor into performing risky multiple bypass surgery, and dies. Or else: Henry survives the surgery, but his brush with death has made the limitations of his life all too clear, and, in search of greater meaning, he leaves his family to join a settler community on Israel's West Bank—or, in the settlers' terms, Judea—where Nathan tracks him down in order to talk some secular sense into him and perhaps get him to return to his wife and children. Or maybe: It is really Nathan who has the heart problem and a passionate affair that makes him decide to risk the surgery, and Nathan who dies. His long-estranged brother, Henry, sneaking into Nathan's Manhattan apartment after the funeral, finds the manuscript of Nathan's latest novel, which contains the wholly fictionalized account of Henry's heart trouble, as well as details of a not-so-fictional affair that he once had the bad sense to confess to Nathan, and the entirely insane adventure in Judea—the same chapters we have just read. Betrayed and infuriated by his brother's writing—again!—Henry destroys the chapters. Or else—why not?—Nathan, impotent from the medication, has found the love of his life in a young Englishwoman whose verbal flair is so endearing that the erotics of speech almost make up for the more conventional kind. But, seeking greater meaning in his life, he wants to marry her and become, for the first time, at forty-five, a father. Nathan has the operation, he survives, and he moves with his new and pregnant wife to London, where the anti-Semitism of English society makes him so argumentative that one night she simply walks out of the book.

Such a summary makes *The Counterlife* sound coyly postmodern, but there is nothing random or left to chance in its reversals and revisions. The book is a masterwork of craft and wit: its narratives flash and twine with the same jeweler's precision that Roth had brought to the final chapters of *The Anatomy Lesson*, but here the workmanship is extended to three hundred and seventy-one pages. Its themes—the human need for transformation, the human need for meaning, the Jew in history, the power of lust, the power of language, the power of landscape, the volatility of identity—are as compellingly embodied as Roth's insidious gift for talk and countertalk can make them. "If you seriously want to renew your life, there's no way around taking a serious risk," Nathan says, steeling his future wife for the possible outcome of his surgery. His words apply as well to Roth pouring his forces into a novel of complex ideas rendered in an equally complex form, a book not quite like anything that anyone had written before.

Roth speaks of *The Counterlife* as the turning point of his career, the book that "changed everything." Almost a quarter century after its publication, much of what he says boils down to the matter of size. "It was an aesthetic discovery, how to enlarge, how to amplify, how to be free," he explains to me one day. "I didn't know how to do it. I knew how to condense." When he is reminded of the ample size of *Letting Go*, he laughs dismissively, and when asked what he has learned about writing in the intervening years, he replies simply, "Everything." As for postmodernism, he had absolutely no desire to write a postmodern book. In *The Anatomy Lesson*, Nathan Zuckerman is interviewed by some university students on the debilitating subject of "the future of his kind of fiction in the post-modernist era of John Barth and Thomas Pynchon"— a dismal future, presumably, reflected in questions like "Do you feel yourself part of a rearguard action, in the service of a declining tradition?" Roth, however, remains as placidly uninterested in literary trends (although postmodern writers have been his friends) as he is in any kind of literary theory. "John Barth was a very nice man," he says, "but give me John Updike."

So how did the structure of the book come about? "I wrote one section and then I thought, 'What if the opposite happened?'" he says. "I generally spend a lot of time in the 'what if' stage." There's plenty of precedent for these practices in his 1974 book, *My Life as a Man*, in which two different opening autobiographies turn out to be the fictional works of a narrator who titles the next section "My True Story." And as Roth sees it, he was veritably pushed into questioning the boundaries of fiction by the public's assumption that *Portnoy's Complaint* was a personal confession. It would be hard to mistake *The Counterlife* for a confession, since it is not consistently written from a first-person point of view, or even from a single point of view. Yet Roth now brought the same vocal immediacy that had made *Portnoy* so persuasive—his confiding, close-up, artfully artless style—to a book in which dead characters return to life. (Roth likes to say that he had to kill Zuckerman "just to make people stop saying that I write only about my own experience.") It's a testament to the power of words on the page, to our eager susceptibility as readers, and to Roth's skills not as a postmodernist but as a fervent realist that our emotions are engaged even when the fiction is tauntingly exposed.

Despite the hall-of-mirrors intricacy, Roth wrote *The Counterlife* in exactly the way that he writes everything: spontaneously, with one incident providing inspiration for the next. There was no initial plan and no outline—he'd last used an outline, he tells me, with *Letting Go* ("and you see where that got me"). He doesn't produce more than a page or two a day—sometimes, agonizingly, less—but he works his way through several drafts.

"The first draft is really a floor under my feet," he says, addressing a recent class at Columbia taught by a friend, Benjamin Taylor, and speaking, despite his retirement, in a somewhat poignant present tense: "What I want to do is to get the story down and know what happens." Then the language begins to develop, and the story inevitably becomes more complex. "The book really comes to life in the rewriting," he says, and he does a lot of it. When he's taken it as far as he can go, he gives the manuscript to a few close readers: "people who I know are on my side, but who will speak candidly." He has relied on this practice since the beginning, with his Chicago friends Ted Solotaroff and Richard Stern; the writers Alison Lurie, Joel Conarroe, Hermione Lee, and Judith Thurman are among those he enlisted later on. (He never uses more than four readers for a single book—"any more would drive you crazy"—and he likes to vary the people, depending on the book.) Aside from the specific points these readers make, Roth says, "they give me back the subject in a way I haven't seen it." He holds himself to a mantra during the initial writing: "What it's about is none of your business"— meaning that he isn't interested in "themes." His job is simply to make the book persuasive. "I don't mean to be falsely naive," he tells me after the class: "By the third draft I have a good picture of what my concerns are." Still, it's helpful and sometimes surprising to have these readers tell him "what the book is 'about.'"

He had no doubt that *The Counterlife* would be "about" Israel, at least in part. Roth had visited the country for the first time in 1963, when he was invited to participate in a symposium about Jewish writers, in Tel Aviv, and had traveled around on his own for a few weeks. "This was before Israel was defensive and belligerent and everyone was asking why you didn't come to live there," he tells me. "This was before the wars." Writing at the end of the sixties, he set the final chapter of *Portnoy's Complaint* in Israel—the pre-1967 Israel of his memories, where the only artillery is metaphorical and refers to the power of the sun. But he now finds this section to be weak, "not fired by imagination." His imagination was deeply fired, however, when he returned in the early eighties, to what seemed a very different country. "It wasn't Israel as California anymore," he says. "It was Israel as the Middle East, and all that people could talk about was politics."

He went back regularly after that and tried to experience every aspect of the country. He toured Jerusalem with Aharon Appelfeld. He visited several West Bank settlements with a leader of the settler movement, Elyakim Haetzni. ("My liberal Israeli friends would not have found him delightful," he says, "but I was just interested in listening." Indeed, Roth reports that the novelist Amos Elon was furious with him for visiting the settlements, no matter the purpose—"What if I had gone to visit Joe McCarthy in America?" Elon asked—and argued that Roth's mere presence would be taken for approval. This did not stop Roth from returning, although he kept his profile very low.) He went into the Negev with a leading Israeli scholar of Bedouin culture, Clinton Bailey, to dine in a tent—"or, rather, a lean-to," he says, "a tent sounds too romantic"—with Bedouins. And everywhere, he took notes, while responding to "the dilemmas, the contradictions, the moral choices," and "especially to the moral anguish of Israelis on the Left." As a writer, his feelings were not so different from those he had experienced in the seventies in Prague—another place with "conflicts and antagonism right on the surface," he tells me—or, for that matter, in the sixties in New York. "I knew," he concludes, just as he did about Prague, "that there was something here for me."

Israel was the moral and historical subject that Roth had been looking for: not somebody else's Warsaw or his childhood Atlantis or totalitarian Prague but the land the Jews had truly bought a part of with their nickels and their lives. And it was credibly *his* subject, both in terms of what he called, in a video interview for the Hebrew University in Jerusalem, "a natural allegiance, by no means as dense with meaning as my allegiance to America, but dense with sentiment," and in terms of a familiar opposition to his life as an American Jew. In *The Counterlife*, contemporary Israelis replace the dwindling generation of European Jews on the other side of the historical scale, as continuing victims of the violence that Roth had eluded in America, the country that gave him, like Nathan Zuckerman, a childhood in place of an annihilating war.

"Jews," Nathan reflects in a startlingly incisive throwaway line, "are to history what Eskimos are to snow." And modern Jews had willfully remade their history. When it came to counterlives, Israel was a nation-wide inspiration. "Who better than the Jews who went to Palestine to show this theme?" Roth asks in conversation. "They changed their language, they changed their names, they became farmers, they even changed the shape of their bodies, developed muscles—the goal was to change their identity entirely." In *The Counterlife*, Nathan, visiting his brother in a West Bank settlement, contemplates the influence of the land itself on Henry, a gun-toting refugee from the peace and safety of New Jersey:

> As for the larger landscape, you could see, particularly in this light, how someone might get the impression that it had been created in only seven days, unlike England, say, whose countryside appeared to be the creation of a God who'd had four or five chances to come back to perfect it and smooth it out, to tame and retame it until it was utterly habitable by every last man and beast. Judea was something that had been left just as it had been made; this could have passed for a piece of the moon to which the Jews had been sadistically exiled by their worst enemies rather than the place they passionately maintained was theirs and no one else's from time immemorial. What he finds in this landscape, I thought, is a correlative for the sense of himself he would now prefer to effect, the harsh and rugged pioneer with that pistol in his pocket.

Still, Nathan cannot help wondering if the most truly Jewish thing about his brother—"our father's best son"—is not that he has moved to Israel, or is learning Hebrew, or has found his people or his God, but that he felt impelled to do all these morally irreproachable things in order to justify leaving his wife.

As a subject, Israel also seems to have offered a strangely welcome note of danger. ("You envy me," an Israeli friend scolds Nathan, "you think, 'Craziness and dangerousness—that sounds like fun!'") *The Counterlife* is crowded with characters who voice their conflicting and often peculiar views about Israel, while Nathan plays the role of Diaspora straight man. An American-born Alvin Pepler–style intrusive fan and nutcase, who comes upon Nathan near the Wailing Wall, turns out to be a hijacker, on an El Al flight, no less. (Unlike Pepler, he gets a fully developed plot.) The leader of a one-man movement, described in a tract titled "Forget Remembering!," he is dedicated to the dismantling of Jerusalem's Holocaust memorial and to the general goal that Jews forget the Holocaust entirely. Everyone else is sick of hearing about it, after all; who knows what further retribution lies in store? "No more masochism to make Jews crazy—no more sadism to stoke goy hate!" he yells. How did he come up with such a manic idea? "Every idea I ever had," he tells Nathan admiringly, "I got from reading your books!"

At the other extreme, in Judea, Nathan meets the leader of the settlers, whose physical and mental qualities are conjoined with true Dickensian authority: "His face had the sardonic mobility that comes of peering nobly down upon self-deceiving mankind from the high elevation of Hard Truth." Roth, careful not to stack the deck, presents the man as thoroughly paranoid but not a monster; he recites his hard political line while proudly showing off "the treasured leatherbound masterpieces collected in Berlin by his grandfather, a celebrated philologist gassed at Auschwitz." (Roth's writing rarely draws attention to itself. The startling thud of "Auschwitz" at the end of this phrase is rendered through both sound and sense: the lulling rhythm of the old masterpieces and the grandfather, the sudden hiss of "gassed.") One of Nathan's liberal Israeli friends is worried, in fact, that Nathan will put this "lying, fanatical, right-wing son of a bitch" into a novel, fearing the influence that such a character might have on the American opinion that determines American financial aid that, in turn, determines Israel's ability to fight its foes. Although Nathan is quick to note that "Congress does not depend upon prose narrative to figure out how to divvy up the take," it is clear that the stakes are extraordinarily high. Here, the consequences even of stories can be life and death. And Nathan is at risk, once again, of being "the dangerous, potentially destructive Jewish writer poised to misrepresent and ruin everything." One might almost imagine that Roth missed the rabbis.

Yet Roth felt that he didn't know enough about Israel to set an entire book there. Nor did he feel that he understood the English well enough to set an entire book *there*, even after he'd been living in London half the year for some eight years. In his *Paris Review* interview, published shortly before he started *The Counterlife*, Roth explained to Hermione Lee that it had taken Isaac Bashevis Singer about twenty years to get Poland sufficiently out of his system, and America sufficiently into it, to begin writing about his famous upper Broadway cafeterias. "If you don't know the fantasy life of a country," Roth said, "it's hard to write fiction about it that isn't just description of the decor, human and otherwise." He confessed that he didn't really know "what means what" to the English and that his perceptions were especially clouded by speaking the same language, more or less—"I believe I know what's being said, you see, even if I don't." But his biggest problem in writing about England was that "I don't hate anything here." This lack of antagonism made it pleasant to reside there as a person but difficult as a writer, since "a writer *has* to be driven crazy to help him to *see*. A writer needs his poisons." Or, at least, this writer did. "The antidote to his poisons," Roth acknowledged, "is often a book."

By setting England in contrast to Israel, though, he could write about both, with a bit of New York fitted in between to bridge the gap. His horizons were expanding; Zuckerman's role was diminishing. In a work about changing places, the dual focus on the pair of Jersey-born brothers—one headed for England, one for Israel—became central to the story even before Roth quite realized the importance of the relationship between them. Two very different men, who had been the measure of each other all their lives, each defining himself as what the other was not: the original counterlives. Henry the good son, the family man, the defender of the norm; Nathan the renegade, the family-destroying writer, the gossip column womanizer, the star. "Cain to your Abel," as Nathan says to Henry. "Esau to your Jacob." From Nathan to Henry flows love and rue and more or less benign condescension. On Henry's part, there is love and rue and a festering resentment that ultimately erupts into rage.

The subject at hand, one more time but with culminating force, is Art versus Life, morally speaking. The confrontation begins at Nathan's funeral, where Henry silently endures a eulogy celebrating his brother's art and "reckless comedy." (As though recklessness were a good thing, as though art were the be-all and end-all.) It continues with Henry discovering the manuscript of Nathan's latest book—*The Counterlife*, lacking only the chapter in which Henry discovers it—and realizing just how reckless Nathan has been: here is Henry's real name, his wife's name, his children's names. Appalled at what he finds, Henry is also appalled at himself for stealing the pages from his dead brother's desk.

Driving home to New Jersey from Manhattan, he is still thinking about his brother as he stops at a Howard Johnson's to dump the pages in the trash:

> He was a Zulu, he thought, a pure cannibal, murdering people, eating people, without ever quite having to pay the price. Then something putrid was stinging his nostrils and it was Henry who was leaning over and violently beginning to retch, Henry vomiting as though *he* had broken the primal taboo and eaten human flesh—Henry, like a cannibal who out of respect for his victim, to gain whatever history and power is there, eats the brain and learns that raw it tastes like poison.

It's a realm of emotion that Henry has never entered before: "quaking before the savagery of what he'd finally done and had wanted to do most of his life, to his brother's lawless, mocking brain." It's a realm that Roth had never fully entered, either. The new worlds he had approached were making him see things in a different way. It's a wretched finale for the Zuckerman family, with two parents dead and two brothers cannibalizing each other's brains. Divorce, heart disease, pistols, the deadly politics of the Middle East: still, there's nothing more devastating in Roth's world than art.

Nathan and Henry Zuckerman were conceived as counterlives, and there is no autobiographical basis for their deadly opposition, any more than there was for Nathan's dying, cursing father. ("Better scene, stronger medicine.") Sandy Roth was the older brother, an advertising man, not a dentist, and most important, he was a loving presence in Philip's life, quickly on the scene, especially in Philip's older years, whenever he was needed. Yet Roth's memories undoubtedly played some part in Henry's and Nathan's personal divisions: chafing constraint versus determined liberty, the conventional career versus the unconventional art. If there was a grain of sand in the Roth brothers' relationship, it did have to do with art: Philip's success versus Sandy's unfulfilled hopes— Sandy began painting again only after his retirement. Roth now says that Sandy rarely mentioned his books, not out of a Henry-like resentment but out of a feeling that he didn't have the language to discuss them. (Henry declines to speak at Nathan's funeral, because he believes that "Nathan had got the monopoly on words.") There was a time in their young manhood, Roth writes in *The Facts*, when his "disdain" for the "advertising man's point of view" must have been as clear to Sandy as Sandy's uneasiness around intellectual types—whom he suspected of mere pretension—was to him. Philip loves classical music; Sandy hated it, Philip tells me, "because he felt they were trying to put something over on him." There is nothing very important in these fraternal differences, except in the way that the novelist put them to use.

A memory is a living fact. The writer seizes it only to pass it on to the imagination—"the butcher, imagination," in Roth's words, "pitiless, brutal and cruel"—which then enacts a process that, according to Roth, is even more gruesome than that of Henry eating Nathan's brain: "It clubs the fact over the head, quickly it slits the throat, and then, with its bare hands, it pulls out the guts." Only then does the imagination return the fact to the mind, in "a dripping mass of eviscerated factuality." Roth was explaining the art of writing fiction, on accepting the National Book Critics Circle Award for *The Counterlife*, in April 1988. Speaking about the imagination, and sounding rather like Henry, he assured the audience, "You wouldn't want it as a friend."

Several facts of Roth's experiences as a Jew in London—a Jew who looked like a Jew and, increasingly, felt like a Jew—were processed for *The Counterlife*. (He grew an assertively rabbinical beard in these years, quite deliberately, as much as to say, "Bring it on.") There was the way that Israel was denounced, almost as a matter of course, at literary and liberal-minded dinner parties, where Roth heard Israelis loosely compared to Nazis. There was the way that people in public places lowered their voices when they said the very word "Jew," as though it were a kind of curse. (Roth's immediate response, he says, was to yell "Shit!" as loudly as he could.) There were insulting clichés on television, and a newspaper cartoon he particularly remembers, showing Menachem Begin standing atop a pile of bodies with a "What, me worry?" gesture. Back in the late sixties, when he took his very blond girlfriend, Ann Mudge, to dine at the Connaught, a dowager at a nearby table had complained loudly of a bad smell while staring pointedly at him. Amazingly, there was another incident in a restaurant years later, when he was dining with Claire Bloom—she also tells the story in her book—and a woman at an adjacent table began to talk, loudly, about having bought a ring from "a little Jew" who had "naturally" cheated her. (In each instance, Roth got up and told the woman off.) Added together, such experiences suggested a connection between Israel and London that became a central vision of the book. The extremism of the Israeli settlers—who seemed half-mad to a secular American Jew—is a result of the kind of anti-Semitism that the same American Jew encounters, to his shock, in London. Roth had located something in England to hate, a most productive poison.

It wasn't as though he hadn't known about anti-Semitism at home. There had been no secrets during his childhood about the outspoken hatred of American giants such as Henry Ford, Charles Lindbergh, and Father Coughlin, whose weekly radio show used to make Roth's father apoplectic. There had been his father's personal handicap in climbing the corporate ladder, the attacks on Jewish kids by boys yelling "Kikes!" that Philip himself had witnessed, and a college fraternity system that he later described as "tightly segregated." But this was distant thunder, part of a nearly historic past and nothing like the personal anti-Semitism that he experienced as an adult—"to my face" and "against my flesh," he says—in London.

A couple of these experiences went directly into the book: the fashionable dinner party remarks about Israel and "appalling Zionism," the woman in the restaurant complaining of the smell. No need to slit the throats of these facts to spill their guts. What Roth did not know and never claimed to know, however, was how widespread or systemic these noxious currents were. His English friends insisted that he was being overly sensitive, making too much of the remarks of a few hotheads or plainly crazy people, and that anti-Semitism was not a problem in England. Roth felt vindicated—if not, in this instance, happily so—when Martin Amis, reviewing *The Counterlife* in *The Atlantic Monthly* and "writing in my capacity as an Englishman," stated that Roth had got it right, exposing "a phenomenon that is really there" and that remained "something like a dirty habit of privilege," although he believed it was in retreat.

In *The Counterlife*, Roth makes the problem much worse for Nathan (of course) by bringing anti-Semitism into the heart of his new family. Nathan's lovely, pregnant wife is as fragrantly English as Portnoy's blondes were sturdily American. Languid, "deliciously civilized," and able to quote John Donne with ease, Maria Freshfield grew up amid the mists and meadows and decaying gentlefolk of Gloucester-shire. (Roth lifted the name "Freshfield" from Milton's "Lycidas," and if he got the line slightly wrong—it reads, "Tomorrow to fresh woods," not fresh fields—he's in good company; it's been called one of the most of-ten misquoted lines in English poetry.) Roth's heroine was based on his secret English lover at the time, although, for understandable reasons, he claimed that she was based on a lover from the years before he had met Bloom, the American but Oxford-educated writer Janet Hobhouse. He shifted the locale of the affair to his New York apartment, appropri-ate to his time with Hobhouse, but preserved the real woman's ensnar-ing seductiveness of speech—"those gently inflected English ups and downs." Nathan has barely a word to say about his lover's face or legs or breasts, but he's willing to risk surgery and put his life on the line for "a finely calibrated relative clause." Maria is the ideal English maiden, and she comes equipped with a viciously anti-Semitic sister and a mother no less biased, if better controlled.

The crisis arrives in the final chapter, titled "Christendom," which opens with a Christmas caroling service in a West End church. Na-than, attending the service with Maria's family, starts out by feeling like a spy, "Jewishly" suspicious of the Disneyland manger and the notion of resurrection. And he ends up being utterly stunned by a "hymn of hate" that is spewed at him by his sister-in-law: "It must be terribly worrying whether you're going suddenly to forget yourself, bare your teeth, and cut loose with the ethnic squawk." She concludes with a warning that he'd better not "stand in the way of a christening" for his and Maria's as yet unborn child.

In short, London—that is, "Christendom"—makes Nathan Zucker-man more of a Jew in eight short weeks than he had ever been before:

> A Jew without Jews, without Judaism, without Zionism, without Jewish-ness, without a temple or an army or even a pistol, a Jew clearly without a home, just the object itself, like a glass or an apple.

And a Jew with a sudden, imperative plan to have his future son circumcised, although he had dismissed the idea in Israel just days ear-lier. Now, however, it seems a necessary acknowledgment of his history, a repudiation of the demands of Christendom, and a sign of the differ-ence he knows that he will never be allowed to forget.

But what if Nathan has made it all up? The mother's intolerance, the sister's anti-Semitic tirade—what if nothing unpleasant happened at that carol service? What if the service didn't even happen in England but in some long-ago time, with another Christian wife, in New York? What if the fiction is really fiction? Maria, sneaking into Nathan's apartment shortly after Henry leaves, reads the final chapter of *The Counterlife*—all that Henry has left behind—and is shocked to find her family grossly maligned. The conclusion is obvious: Nathan was brought up "ringed round by all that Jewish paranoia," and "there was something in him that twisted everything." The hatred was not her sister's but his own. Or, as she comes to think by the time she writes her farewell letter to him, being a Jew had simply become too easy, and a life without horrible difficulties "is inimical to the writer you are. You actually *like* to take things hard. You can't weave your stories otherwise." He needed her family to be anti-Semitic so that he could write the hate-filled book that she is now escaping in disgust. But the book ends with something like a hymn of love, from Nathan to Maria, imploring her to return, and to recognize that all the life they can ever have is in these pages.

The Counterlife was widely greeted as a great success. In *The New York Times Book Review*, William Gass compared it to Haydn's *Surprise* Symphony and wrote, "I hope it felt, as Mr. Roth wrote it, like a triumph, because that is certainly how it reads to me." Martin Amis called it the fulfillment of Roth's early promise, although he believed the achievement had less to do with structural ingenuity than with the suitably immense and contentious subject of Israel. There were objections to the book's religious content, but for the first time in Roth's career, they did not come from Jews. John Updike, in *The New Yorker*, offered a mixture of celebration and irritation, pronouncing the book a "performance to cap performances," albeit of themes he had wearied of several books before. Zuckerman's trouble with the carol service seemed to hit a particularly painful nerve. ("Christmas carols! Christianity at its absolute sweetest!!") (Yes, those are two exclamation points.) And Updike reached near Rothian levels of comic dismay in comparing Zuckerman's paean to circumcision with "a richly nuanced plea, in a novel by a Kikuyu, in favor of tribal scars and clitoridectomy, or an old Chinese poem hymning the symbolic beauty of bound feet."

It isn't entirely surprising to find these criticisms from the creator of Harry (Rabbit) Angstrom, a character for whom an implicitly mystic faith and an explicitly uncircumcised penis are life's primary motivating forces. Rabbit's story had extended by this time over a sequence of three books; the most recent, *Rabbit Is Rich*, published in 1981, had won all the major American literary prizes and had established Rabbit as an emblematic American mid-twentieth-century man. A onetime high school athlete, a car salesman, a father, a WASP, a close reader of nothing deeper than *Consumer Reports*, Rabbit is a man as mired in ordinary life as Zuckerman is not, and as Zuckerman imagines that he longs to be. Updike seems to agree that the root of the self-conscious singularity that makes Zuckerman less than representative—less of a Rabbit-like lens for seeing the wider culture—is that he is a writer.

"Who *cares* what it's like to be a writer?" Updike asks, speaking up for Henry the dentist, the kind of plain-guy hero Updike much preferred, and urging Roth to rid himself of Nathan. Of course, Updike had also written books with a Jewish writer-hero, Henry Bech. (Why a *Jewish* writer? In order to be as different from Updike himself as possible, Updike said, and because "a Jewish writer is almost as inevitable as an Italian gangster.") Bech is far less three-dimensional than Rabbit—or, for that matter, than Zuckerman—but whether this is because he is a writer is impossible to say. Oddly, Bech's attitude toward Christendom is harsher than anything Zuckerman comes up with: "Being among the goyim frightened Bech, in truth," Updike wrote in *Bech Is Back*, in 1982; "their collective chill was the chill of devils." Bech, too, spends time in London but has no distressing experiences there. (Does this make Bech less paranoid? Updike less paranoid? Or just less likely to be picked out and insulted in restaurants?) Unlike Martin Amis, Updike concludes that Roth's account of British anti-Semitism is "too bald and savage" and, as he notes that Maria observes, is really a testament to Nathan's inner violence and aggression. It's hard to know whether one is delving deeper or just going around and around to point out that Maria's observations about Nathan's inner violence were written by Nathan and, ultimately, by Roth.

Mary McCarthy also praised the book's early sections and, particularly, its Israel chapter, but she, too, halted at the gates of "Christendom." Roth had great respect for McCarthy's opinion. ("She was a heroine to me," he says today. "She had a terrific critical sharpness; she could be dead wrong, but she was never unclear.") Her name appears twice in *Goodbye, Columbus*, and McCarthy's on-the-couch short story, "Ghostly Father, I Confess," published in 1942, is an interesting psychiatric predecessor to *Portnoy*. Roth recalls having met her at Elizabeth Hardwick's years before; he had seen her a couple of times more recently in Paris, where she lived, and had sent her an early copy of *The Counterlife*. As one would expect, McCarthy states her objections straight out: "I bridle at your picture of Christianity," she writes. (Both her letter and Roth's response appear in *Shop Talk*.) Although she neither believes in God nor considers herself a Christian in anything but upbringing, McCarthy is "irritated and offended" by his London scenes. "There's more to Christmas, that is, to the idea of the Incarnation, than Jew-hatred," she informs him, and as for Christmas caroling, outsiders should try to get the general idea, "as I hope I would try to get the idea of the Wailing Wall, repellent as it is to me, if I were taken to it." She closes by mentioning that she had last seen a mutual friend, Leon Botstein, at a Christmas carol sing in New York.

Thanking her graciously, Roth reminds her that Zuckerman behaves very well at the carol service—no differently from the way she would behave at the Wailing Wall—and he disputes any implication that the Incarnation is presented as being exclusively about Jew-hatred. Zuckerman is well aware, Roth writes, that his thoughts in church "are determined by his Jewishness and nothing more." Moreover, Roth explains that he wrote the London scenes in relation to the scenes in the West Bank settlement and in reaction to the skepticism that Zuckerman feels there; if not for this desired contrast, he would not have written the scene in the church at all. Roth's explanation to McCarthy seems a remarkable change from his literary past—a maturation? a softening? He concludes by telling her that he balanced the book this way because he did not want all of Zuckerman's skepticism to be "focused on Jewish ritual and none of it on Christian. That would have had all the wrong implications and made him seem what he is not, and that is a self-hating Jew."

You Mustn't Forget Anything

By the mid-eighties, life in London was beginning to pall. Roth's English lover had broken off their affair; unlike Maria Freshfield, the real woman chose to remain with her husband, although she telephoned Roth, after *The Counterlife* appeared, to say that she was displeased not with her portrait but with being unable to take proper credit for it. On another front, Roth's friendship with Harold Pinter had deteriorated badly in the wake of Pinter's political radicalization over U.S. actions in Nicaragua. Roth, hardly a supporter of Ronald Reagan, tells stories of Pinter yelling in his face, "*Your* president, Ronald Reagan," and continuing with a string of accusations. "I told him, 'I don't want to argue about Reagan, I don't represent him,'" Roth explains, but Pinter was unrelenting, and Roth is not one to back down when he feels he's attacked unjustly. (Nor, it's clear, was Pinter.) However much Roth may have loathed certain American policies, he says now, "I didn't agree with him that America was the scourge of the world." To Roth, Pinter's anti-Americanism "wasn't even a matter of politics; it became a theology." There were shouting matches between the men, at dinner at the Pinters' home and even in restaurants. Roth remembers an evening when he and Pinter were "on our feet, arguing chin to chin," and he could see Alfred Brendel, seated nearby, holding his hands together tightly, as though in fear that "we were going to start throwing punches and someone might land on his hands."

And he was missing home. In *The Counterlife*, Zuckerman defends

America to the Israeli settlers, who maintain that a Jew has no business making a home anywhere but Israel; among the homogeneous English, too, he longs for melting-pot America. He even gives a bit of a patriotic lecture: "I could not think of any historical society that had achieved the level of tolerance institutionalized in America or that had placed pluralism smack at the center of its publicly advertised dream of itself." It was a dream Roth was eager to believe in again. In terms of his work, he was feeling caught between worlds: unable to write about the "opaque" world of the reticent English and drifting further away from his American base. "I just felt lost," he says. Most of all, he missed the language: "the jumpy beat of American English," as Zuckerman puts it, out of which Roth had built his novels, and beside which British English had turned out to be as useful to him, he says, as Latvian. He began having regular Sunday breakfasts with another American-born friend, the painter R. B. Kitaj, at an American-style diner on Fulham Road called Tootsies, where he tried to abate his growing longing for American food, talk, and people.

But he had troubles far greater than homesickness during this period. A harrowing range of illnesses and bungled treatments and medical chain reactions might reasonably have accounted for years of literary silence. The fact that Roth continued writing during the late eighties is evidence both of an unrelenting work ethic, for which he credits his father, and of the fact that writing was the essential condition of his life. In the fall of 1986, while staying alone in Connecticut, he had a recurrence of intense back pain, which left him barely able to sit, stand, or drive, even to the nearest supermarket; Sandy came from his home in Chicago to help him get through it. At the end of the year, he suffered a knee injury in the London pool where he swam nearly every morning, for the sake of his back as well as his heart. The injury led to knee surgery in March 1987 in New York, but a misdiagnosis of the problem and a now disapproved procedure resulted in increased pain. The ameliorating drugs that were prescribed included the sleeping aid Halcion, an innocuous-looking pill so potentially dangerous that it would soon be taken off the market in several countries. In Roth, it brought on a panoply of horrific side effects: hallucinations, panic attacks, and ultimately a suicidal depression that went on for four tortured months before the symptoms were traced to their source. Then he had to go cold turkey to get off the Halcion. Just two years later, in the summer of 1989, his heart condition caught up with him, and he underwent emergency quintuple bypass surgery, the same dangerous procedure that he had given to both Zuckerman brothers in *The Counterlife*. As he told an interviewer at the time, the experience was of absolutely no use to him, because he had already put it in a book.

The Facts, written in the wake of the Halcion devastation, is for most of its length a plainspoken, fairly dry autobiography. Roth has called it a sequel to *The Counterlife*; he has even called it "*my* counterlife*"—that is, his life untransformed by fiction. In the opening pages, he explains that he began writing the book "as a spontaneous therapeutic response" to the drug's near obliteration of his sense of self, which had left him in an alarming state of uncertainty about "why I do what I do, why I live where I live, why I share my life with the one I do." *The Facts*, then, is an act of psychic reconstruction, focusing on the crucial fact of "what I do," as Roth retraces the steps that led him to the signal moment when "the manic side of my imagination took off" and "I became my own writer." If he could figure out how he got there once, he could get there again. The book covers just the first thirty-five or so years of his life—Roth was then fifty-five—and the imaginative takeoff to which it leads is the writing of *Portnoy's Complaint*.

This loss of self was especially fraught for a writer who drew so deeply on the personal. While many victims of such a nightmare might have turned to their childhood to get their bearings, it is telling that for Roth the personal self and the writing self had become virtually indistinguishable. ("Memories of the past," he reminds us, "are not memories of facts but memories of your imaginings of the facts." To some degree, we all make up our histories.) But there was another reason that he had decided to retrace his childhood: an "eruption of parental longing," also brought on by the depression. Although well into middle age, Roth reported himself in need of "a palliative for the loss of a mother who still, in my mind, seems to have died inexplicably," and in equal need of a way "to hearten me as I come closer and closer and closer to an eighty-six-year-old father viewing the end of life as a thing as near to his face as the mirror he shaves in."

Closer and closer and closer. The tenderness in Roth's treatment of Jewish men of his father's generation had been one of the steadiest aspects of his work since *Letting Go*, not excluding the extremely hard-working, well-meaning, and permanently constipated Jack Portnoy. This recurring type gave even lesser books (such as *The Professor of Desire*) some of their most highly charged and touching moments. Now Roth was expressing his love directly, with an unconflicted open-ness that he explains he was unable to feel during his teenage years, when he lived in his father's house and was shaped (and countershaped) by his father's iron will. "After nearly forty years of living far from home," he writes, "I'm equipped at last to be the most loving of sons."

At the other emotional extreme, he is still inflamed about his mar-riage to Maggie (whom he calls Josie; he changed the names of all the women in his life after the manuscript was completed). He also covers his Bucknell years and the assault at the Yeshiva University symposium in 1962; he pays tribute to the turbulent sixties and to the New York Jewish friends in whose company he performed the mixture of report-ing and Dada that turned into *Portnoy*. But *The Facts* basically divides into the immortally juxtaposed forces of good and evil: his parents and Maggie, who are not unrelated in the virtues and vices that they repre-sent. For Maggie was "blighted at the core by irresponsible parenting," and Roth stumbled into her trap—a total innocent—precisely because the world that his parents had built was so fundamentally decent that he was unable even to conceive that, in marrying, any evil could befall him.

All of which Nathan Zuckerman jeers right off the page. The narra-tive of *The Facts* is framed by two letters. One, from Roth to Zuck-erman, at the opening, asks for a candid evaluation of the text; after all, Roth isn't used to writing without some Zuckerman-like intermedi-ary. Zuckerman's reply comes in a much longer letter at the close, and is immediately notable for the color and amped-up energy of a voice that seems to be more Roth's than Roth's, so to speak: the voice of the novel-ist, at last. Which is very much part of Zuckerman's point. "I am your permission," he tells Roth, "your indiscretion, the key to disclosure." Without Zuckerman—or some other mask—Roth is kind, discreet, and far from exciting. Also, far from truthful. "Where's the anger?" Zuck-erman rails at him. Where are the familiar and vivifying grievances, the criticism, the satire, the disgust? "You've begun to make where you came from look like a serene, desirable, pastoral haven," he charges, "when, I suspect, it was more like a detention house." It is simply not credible that this arcadian childhood led Roth to write *Portnoy's Complaint*.

Or, to marry Maggie—"a woman who had a sign on her saying STAY AWAY KEEP OUT" and who was not something that merely happened to him but something that he *"made happen."* Zuckerman insists that she ought to be honored in the book with her real name, as Roth's only full-scale antagonist and the person most responsible for making him the writer that he is. When Roth calls her his "greatest creative-writing teacher" earlier in the book, he's just trying to be interesting; but it's also the truth. He still hasn't given her enough credit. She's the heroine of his life, the heroine he was looking for: "the psychopath through whose agency you achieved the freedom from being a pleasing, analytic, lovingly manipulative good boy who would never have been much of a writer." Without her, there would have been no consuming anger, without the anger no psychiatrist, and no *Portnoy's Complaint* or any of the real and literary results of that book. In short, he owed her everything.

The letter also reveals that Nathan's wife returned to him after their quarrel, in *The Counterlife*, and—rather a long time later, it seems—is still pregnant. Maria, too, has read the manuscript and is intensely worried for the Zuckerman family's future, on the irrefutable evidence that Roth is "still on that Jewish stuff." Nathan is worried, too, but his chief concern is to avoid extinction and make Roth understand how much the books require his presence. He doesn't have to work so hard to convince the reader. The plainest fact of *The Facts* is that Roth without Zuckerman is "what you get in practically *any* artist without his imagination." The implicit lesson of *The Facts* is that the only way to reach the truth is through fiction. Hence Zuckerman's candid advice about Roth's text: "Don't publish."

But publish he did, in 1988, the same year that he was changing his life again. After eleven years spent half in London, he returned to America full-time, living alternately in the Connecticut farmhouse and in New York, where, with Bloom, he settled into an Upper West Side apartment on West Seventy-seventh Street, with a view of the skyscrapers of midtown. He also acquired a writing studio two blocks away, on West Seventy-ninth—which, given the professional concentration in the area, he calls Writer's Block. "I used to walk around sometimes and say, 'I'm home,'" he says. "I'd just stand on a street corner and smile."

One of the joys of coming home was teaching again. He was appointed Distinguished Professor of Literature at Hunter College, a highly regarded branch of the City University of New York. There were more adults among the students at Hunter than in the standard liberal arts college, and their range of experience made the classes very rewarding for the distinguished professor. "They were intense, demanding, talkative," he says of the students. "I could really make contact with them, and they could make contact with the books." He taught one course a year for three years, the contents varying according to his interests: Eastern European writers, American writers. One year, he taught what he unofficially called a Holocaust course, with readings that included Tadeusz Borowski's *This Way for the Gas, Ladies and Gentlemen* (published in the Writers from the Other Europe series) and Gitta Sereny's *Into That Darkness*, about Treblinka. He had the students make drawings of the camp layout, according to Sereny's precise descriptions, "to really know how impossible it was to escape."

And he taught several books by Primo Levi, who had become personally important to Roth in these years. A great admirer of Levi's work, Roth met the Italian writer in the spring of 1986, when Levi was visiting London. In the hour or so they spent together—Levi spoke exacting English—they formed a bond that both could feel. That summer, Roth suggested to *The New York Times* that he do a long interview with Levi, on the American release of his latest book, *The Monkey's Wrench*. Roth flew to Turin with Claire Bloom and spent several days in Levi's company, forming a kind of friendship by immersion, and one that went remarkably deep.

Levi, who was thirteen years older than Roth, was not the first camp survivor Roth had met (both Ivan Klíma and Aharon Appelfeld had been in concentration camps as children), nor was he the first writer Roth had met whom he frankly considered to be a genius (that was Bellow). But Levi was both a survivor and a genius, as well as a lively and unpretentious man. After many hours of talk together, Roth "distilled" a conversation that ranged from the attributes that had enabled Levi to survive Auschwitz (Roth proposed that Levi's systematic intellect had something to do with it; Levi countered that it was nothing but luck) to his ability to combine a nearly thirty-year career as a chemist and the manager of a paint factory with his work as a writer. Roth's appreciation for Levi's factory career seems touched with a romanticism that Roth sometimes brings to work outside the solitariness of writing, a sort of semicomic yet genuinely heartsore, Chekhovian longing. "His work answered the need for other people," Roth says of Levi today. "I would give my right arm for that kind of connection while I'm writing." One thinks of Zuckerman's desire to be a doctor (or a pornographer) and of Roth's pleasure in the classroom.

At Roth's request, Levi showed him and Bloom around the factory, although he had retired from it a dozen years earlier—Levi was then sixty-seven—and took them on a tour, too, of his native Turin. (Levi's scrupulous biographer, Ian Thomson, depicts Levi taking Roth into the cathedral to view the Shroud of Turin, but in this instance Thomson seems to have slipped. Roth says that this never happened, nor could it possibly have happened: "He knew I'd just turn around and walk out.") When Roth and Levi parted, they wept and embraced—"which was not characteristic of either of us, really," Roth says—and Levi said, "I don't know which is the older brother, and which is the younger brother."

By the time Roth left Turin, he felt that he'd made a friend for life. There were letters back and forth, with Roth encouraging Levi and his wife, Lucia, to visit the United States, promising a series of speaking engagements, introductions to congenial people, and, in general, a wonderful time. Roth had been proposing such a trip even before he left Turin. Although Levi had undertaken an American book tour just a year earlier, his answer was always the same: "It's too late." Roth believes that Levi meant, in part, that literary fame had come too late, but also that he could not escape caretaking duties for his ninety-one-year-old mother, now paralyzed by a stroke, who lived with the Levis in the same apartment where Levi was born. "At least, he thought he could not go away for more than a few days," Roth says. "I don't really know the situation. He was the most devoted Jewish son you ever met."

Levi was a secular Jew, connected to the Jews of Turin by a sense of history rather than by religion. The Turinese Jews are Sephardic, with a lineage that can be traced back hundreds of years—to Avignon, to Spain. "Of course, that was interesting to him," Roth tells me. And he speaks of the contrast with the Eastern European Jews of his own background: "We don't know how far back we go. If we, too, knew where we came from and how far back we went and who the people were, we, too, would be interested, as Jews. But we stop, we stop, and all the witnesses to our past were destroyed."

Roth was in London when he heard of Levi's death, in April 1987, just seven months after the time they'd spent together. "I was dumbstruck," he says: "The effect was staggering—it hit me like the assassinations of the sixties." Roth spent that afternoon at the home of the Italian journalist Gaia Servadio, the mutual friend who had introduced him to Levi, consoling each other. Levi had died in a fall from the third-floor landing into the stairwell of his apartment building, and his death has commonly been deemed a suicide. Roth, without claiming any special knowledge, thinks that this verdict is probably correct. He points out that Levi was extremely depressed by his domestic situation, and that he'd recently had prostate surgery, which had doubtless left him at least temporarily incontinent, as such surgery generally does. "He was a meticulous man," Roth says. "He couldn't stand it." Roth also blames the fact that Levi had left his factory job to write full-time, confining himself to the family apartment. Many people consider Levi's memories of Auschwitz to be the "real" cause of his death—the headline in *Corriere della Sera* was CRUSHED BY THE PHANTOM OF THE CAMP—but Roth believes that if these memories played any role, it was because Levi had returned to the subject in *The Drowned and the Saved*, the meditative work that he completed shortly before his death. Roth assigned the book to the students in his course. "It's a masterpiece of grief," he says now, "and of thinking about grief, and to think of him thinking about this every day . . ."

Roth himself was not quite back to writing fiction yet. The novelistic amplitude that he'd discovered in *The Counterlife* required more strength than he could summon in the post-Halcion late eighties, a period that he now characterizes as "an in-between time." Only in hindsight was it clear to him that he was "fighting my way toward a big book." Still trying to regain his equilibrium, in early 1988 he traveled to Israel to interview his friend Aharon Appelfeld, a living lesson in how to overcome horrific damage. Appelfeld had escaped from a concentration camp at the age of eight and had spent three years hiding from the Nazis in Ukrainian forests, yet he was now an admired Israeli novelist and a husband and father, living a steady, productive life. While Roth was in Jerusalem, he saw a notice in a newspaper about the trial of John Demjanjuk, the Ukrainian-born Cleveland autoworker who stood accused of having been an infamously brutal camp guard, known as Ivan the Terrible, at Treblinka. Roth attended sessions of the trial and took careful notes, although he had no idea how he might use them. Back in the States, he took still more notes, now about his father's disintegrating health: a brain tumor was diagnosed just as Roth and Bloom were moving to New York. Being with his father, paying close attention to him—as he hadn't been able to do with his mother—was Roth's way of dealing with the impending loss. Yet, while these grave and difficult subjects were weighing on his mind, waiting for the imaginative process to begin, he completed a little book of remarkably high spirits and high risks.

Deception, published in 1990, is an offshoot of *The Counterlife*. It even presents itself as a notebook for *The Counterlife*, recording conversations between the author and several women with whom he has had affairs—a Czech émigrée, a former student, a close friend now stricken with cancer—but focusing on the unhappily married English mistress who became the novel's Maria Freshfield. The affair between these two is happening in the present, and most of their easy-flowing talk seems to be taking place postcoitally (or, when it's particularly inspirational, pre-re-coitally), even though the book, which is written entirely in dialogue, contains almost no mention of body parts or physical acts. The atmosphere, the characters, and the metaphysical puzzle of a plot emerge from the sparest materials a novelist can use. No exposition, very little description, not even any "he said, she said" to clarify who is speaking: just the voices. ("I'm an écouteur," the protagonist says, "a talk fetishist.") *Deception* might be called a play rather than a novel—one critic referred to Pinter's *Betrayal*, on a similar subject, while another, noting the scarcity even of stage directions, called it a radio play. Roth has said that he was feeling his way back to fiction in the conversations between Zuckerman and Maria in the later pages of *The Facts*, and the reader can sense the connection with those pages, not only in the lovers' playfulness but in Roth's evident delight at the rekindling of his imagination.

Imagination—undermining reality, amplifying reality—is as much the book's subject as adultery. The principal love affair takes place in the small Notting Hill studio of a writer called Philip, who has written novels about a fictional writer called Zuckerman. The conversations range widely, from the woman's marital dissatisfactions and Philip's adventures in Prague to British anti-Americanism. (At a dinner in "London's highest literary circles," an unnamed Englishman has been railing at Philip about the horrors supported by "'*your* president.'") This Philip is married, however, a detail that creates a problem when the "notebook" is discovered by his wife. In tears, she accuses him of going off to his studio every day not just to write but to meet women. And he attempts to calm her by explaining that these "women" are fictional characters, that the conversations are exercises for a novel, and that the English mistress who "sounds so fucking well born" (in his wife's words) is based on a woman he had an affair with in New York, before he ever met his wife. As for calling the protagonist "Philip," he explains, this is nothing more than a literary strategy, a method of self-implication that gets his creative juices flowing. Initially, at least, she isn't convinced:

> "You love her more than you ever loved me!"
> "*Because she doesn't exist.* If you didn't exist I'd love you like that too."

The logic is irresistible. And then she is put in the position of seeming not only a jealous wife but a literary philistine if she insists that everything she has read is "real." The wife doesn't know what to believe, and neither do we—although we both have our suspicions of being masterfully played.

Roth and Claire Bloom were not actually married when this book was written, and many readers who rejected the literary argument for Philip's calling himself "Philip," and assumed that the book was autobiographical, also assumed that the beautiful English actress (who sounded so fucking well born) was his model for the mistress, not the wife. Bloom herself did not see it this way when Roth showed her the manuscript—as he showed her all his manuscripts—a few weeks after he finished it. The reason was obvious. Not only was the husband in the manuscript named Philip; the wife was named Claire. Roth went out immediately after giving it to her and called his good friend Judith Thurman, who had already read it and had strongly advised him to cut the name "Claire." Now he asked her, "What should I do?" Thurman tells me that she remembers her response quite clearly: "Meet me on Fifty-seventh Street with a credit card." They didn't find anything at Tiffany's, but at Bulgari he purchased a spectacular gold-and-emerald snake ring, just in case Bloom reacted the way that any woman in the situation would react.

In her memoir, Bloom recounts her fury and their confrontation over what seemed to her an outrageous insult. But after Roth's apparently brief and entirely unsuccessful attempt at a literary justification (it involved "the richness of the texture"), they made their peace. He agreed to delete her name; Bloom accepted the jewelry. Still, in some ways Roth had won this bizarre literary game of betrayal in plain sight: Bloom writes that Maria Freshfield, in *The Counterlife*—and, by extension, the woman in *Deception*—was based on "the beautiful, gifted novelist Janet Hobhouse, with whom Philip, the year before we met, had had a brief and intense relationship." She doesn't say what her conclusion was about the other women—fact or fiction—and since she was the only person with a reason to care about the distinction, why should we? The words the women are made of remain the same. Yet the question of intent—whether we believe his authorial excuses, whether the women are *meant* to be real—makes the book feel like one of Escher's impossible constructions. On how many levels does *Deception* deceive?

To help us make up our minds, toward the end of the book, Philip receives a phone call from his mistress, some years after their affair has ended. He has moved back to America. She has read his recently published novel, clearly *The Counterlife*, in which she figures as a major character—"I don't think Freshfield was at all a good name for me"— and she is torn between being upset because he has stolen her words and being miffed because she isn't receiving credit for them. She, too, refuses to swallow any of the "highbrow nonsense" that he offers about the deeper realities of fiction:

> "As I made you up, you *never* existed."
> "Then who was that in your studio with my legs over your shoulders?"

She threatens to get even by writing a book of her own, about him— odd that Roth didn't give this plan to the wife; here reality outdistanced even *his* imagination—and he replies that he may write another book about her, incorporating the very scene we happen to be reading. It's ingenious, but it can also be maddening, depending on one's appetite for ingenuity and the lively music of Roth's crossing voices. This vocal tirelessness reminded Updike, for one, of Bach. "You see Roth as a musician in this book," he said of *Deception*, in a comment in *Maclean's*: "It's tempting to see his work as variations on what seem to some people not enough themes. But you have to admire the way he sticks to his themes and, like Bach, does one more turn through his obsessions."

Some of these obsessions—British anti-Semitism, for example— were already too outworn to be brought to anything resembling life. He made up for this somewhat with the freshness of his jubilation at being back among the Jews of New York—"the real obstreperous Zion"—with their unapologetic forcefulness, their elbows on the table, their impudence. *Deception* is also notable for the emergence of what, if it is not another obsession, is certainly Roth's recognition of a new and significant opposition. Here, in the midst of so many female voices—the mistress's voice is particularly witty and intelligent, more so than Maria's in *The Counterlife*—there appears out of nowhere a little courtroom scene in which the writer-protagonist is in the dock. Instead of a rabbi or a judge demanding to know whether he would have written his books in Nazi Germany, however, a female prosecutor is charging him with "sexism, misogyny, woman abuse, slander of women, denigration of women, defamation of women, and ruthless seduction." The questions to be answered now are: "Why did you portray Mrs. Portnoy as a hysteric? Why did you portray Lucy Nelson as a psychopath? Why did you portray Maureen Tarnopol as a liar and a cheat?" And, ultimately, "Why do you depict women as shrews, if not to malign them?" His crimes, he is warned, carry severe penalties.

It should be clear by now that Roth, when attacked, prefers to goad rather than retreat: to make mischief, to get adrenaline flowing. He is a great explainer, though, and "Philip" makes a pass at defending himself through a question of his own: "Why do you, may I ask, take the depiction of one woman as a depiction of all women?" He makes a vague attempt to distinguish politics from literature, an attempt that is quickly dismissed. He gets off a couple of good jokes, as when he points out that Shakespeare also depicted a shrew, and the prosecutor upbraids him for comparing himself to Shakespeare: "Next you will be comparing yourself to Margaret Atwood and Alice Walker!" But the satire, which inevitably ends with the defendant sexually provoking the non-plussed prosecutor ("Help, help, he's exploiting me, he's degrading me"), seems a throwback to the comic book silliness of Roth's old Nixon jokes, or even the Bucknell satire that got him hauled before the dean of men. Kid stuff, as gleefully taunting as he could make it: he even addresses the prosecutor as "girl."

The adrenaline was flowing now. Fay Weldon, a writer known for her feminist convictions, gave *Deception* a nearly rapturous review in *The New York Times Book Review*, calling it a "swift, elegant, disturbing novel" and placing Roth alongside Thomas Pynchon at the forefront of contemporary writing. It was "O.K. by me," she said, that Roth was "rather old-fashioned about women," particularly in a novel about seduction that uses language so seductively. ("And there we are, writer and reader both," she wrote, "fulfilled in post-coital languor.") Yet she concluded by skewering the finale of the trial scene and by quoting it—or the parts of it that seemed "over the edge" of the literary—"as my revenge, on behalf of all those women whom Roth in his novels has indeed exploited, degraded and defamed." In the daily *Times*, Christopher Lehmann-Haupt wondered if Roth, seeking to emulate the heroic rebelliousness of the Eastern European writers he admired, hadn't "turned a woman into his longed-for totalitarian state." And in the *London Review of Books*, Julian Symons started right in by characterizing Roth as a writer whose "women are hardly more than receptacles for semen, emotional punching-bags or ministering angels." Case closed.

The cover of the book probably didn't help. Simon and Schuster, Roth's new publisher, made news when it bought Roth away from Farrar, Straus and Giroux with a $1.8 million contract—negotiated by Roth's new agent, Andrew Wylie—for three books, beginning with *Deception*. Roth is openly grateful to the editors he has worked with over the years—Joe Fox, Aaron Asher, and Veronica Geng are names that he mentions often—and one reason for making the move was that his editor at the time, David Rieff, was leaving for a career in journalism. (Roth tells me that he read the whole of *The Counterlife* aloud to Rieff one long night, when he had the feeling that something was wrong with the book, "and whenever the sentence was weak, one or the other of us rang the gong, so to speak.") But it was also true that, in his late fifties, he felt pressed to earn more money. His books had always sold respectably, but even the most critically acclaimed novels he had published in the past decade or so—*The Ghost Writer, The Counterlife*—had hardly been bestsellers. Roth recalls virtually begging Roger Straus to increase his advances so that he wouldn't have to change publishers, and Straus's reply: "You don't earn it back." But Simon and Schuster had a plan for making Roth a more commercial author: the cover of *Deception* was an artfully blurry photograph of a couple in bed, the man's hand holding the woman just above the odalisque curve of her hip, registering somewhere between a romance novel and soft porn.

The publisher was openly attempting to recover the scandalous momentum of Roth's earlier years: "to get across the sexiness of the book," a Simon and Schuster official told the *Times*, "and link it to 'Portnoy's Complaint.'" Roth—who had been fleeing the *Portnoy* image for years—hated the cover but felt that he "had to yield to the publisher," something that, he says, he never did again. (Roth moved on to another publisher, Houghton Mifflin, after this contract was up, and he remained there.) In any case, the cover and the accompanying ad campaign failed to have the desired effect. *Deception* was not a commercial success. But even before it appeared, Roth was working on another book.

Herman Roth died in October 1989 at eighty-eight, not quite three months after Roth underwent emergency bypass surgery. Roth hid the fact that he was having surgery from his ailing father, telling him that he'd be out of touch for a few days, attending a conference at Yale. In the new book, Roth describes the old man, who learned the truth a few days later, as both angry and near tears because he had not been told about the surgery and had been unable to help, crying, "I should have been there!" And Roth explains that he felt much the same way during his weeks of convalescence, praying—to his father—"Don't die until I get my strength back. Don't die until I can do it right." Roth had only recently been allowed to start driving again when, one night in late October, he was awakened by a phone call. He hurried to the New Jersey hospital where his father had been taken to the emergency room. Roth had been writing about his father since the brain tumor was diagnosed; he completed *Patrimony* in the months immediately after his father's death.

It's difficult to imagine two works by a single writer that are more different—never mind two works written back to back—than the clever, evasive, cloud-borne *Deception* and *Patrimony*, a work of nonfiction (it's subtitled *A True Story*) that is earnest, straightforward, and unsparingly emotional. No fancy writing, no formal games. Here is the level, un-adorned voice familiar from the early sections of *The Facts*—Roth with-out a mask—given weight and urgency by the life that the author feels compelled to record and preserve. Readers had been getting fictional-ized glimpses of Herman Roth for years. ("It's virtually impossible for me to keep him out of a book I write," Roth told an interviewer on French TV; "I have to lock all the doors and put the furniture up against them to keep him out.") Now, at last, we had a full-length portrait from life, intensely loving but never sentimental.

The retired insurance man with an eighth-grade education, who made a life for his family out of sheer dutifulness and what Roth calls "spirited decency," was also stubborn, obsessive, crude, and unwittingly cruel in his compulsion to correct other people—a man whose admoni-tions became so ruthless in his later years that Roth's mother thought about divorcing him. (That revelation is almost as much of a shock to the reader as it must have been to Roth.) For Roth, who details his youthful yearning to replace his shamefully undereducated father with someone more dignified, his father now appeared to be the source not only of his personal strength but of his strength as a writer. "He taught me the vernacular. He *was* the vernacular, unpoetic and expressive and point-blank, with all the vernacular's glaring limitations and all its durable force."

As autobiography, *Patrimony* scatters light on some of Roth's earlier works. Here is Herman Roth's account of his father beating one of Her-man's brothers, to keep him from marrying "a worldly woman," adapted in *Portnoy*; here is a boyhood friend named Lenny Lonoff. More impor-tant, this unflinching book inaugurates the subjects of illness and death, which take on hurricane force in Roth's later work. Yet very little surpasses the poignancy of a scene in which Herman Roth bargains with a surgeon for "another couple of years" and then, within minutes, expands the request to "just another three or four years." Roth, sitting by his father's side, recognizes his overwhelming desire—tempered only by the fear of seeming greedy and calling down a worse fate—to out-and-out demand "another eighty-six years!" There is, too, the excru-ciating frankness with which Roth observes his father on a bright summer day, surrounded by his family, yet "utterly isolated within a body that had become a terrifying escape-proof enclosure, the holding pen in a slaughterhouse."

On a happier note, *Patrimony* anticipates Roth's future books because Herman Roth's story is so much a story about America: "All the time I'm thinking that the real work, the invisible, huge job that he did all his life, that that whole generation of Jews did, was making themselves American. The *best* citizens."

Although the sophisticated writer hardly resembles the insurance salesman, there are many instances in which Roth seems also to be writing about himself: stories of Herman Roth's zest, his discipline, his doggedness, "the hypnotic hold that the mundane destiny of an ordinary immigrant family seemed still to have on him," as it does on the author of this book. "You mustn't forget anything—that's the inscription on his coat of arms," Roth writes about the father he has resurrected with such meticulous care, thought by thought, year by year. "To be alive, to him, is to be made of memory."

Although he suffered nightmares about his father for some time afterward, Roth's heart surgery renewed his hold on life. "I was so happy," he says. "I was free of this time bomb that had been ticking in my chest." He was suddenly much stronger, and everything seemed possible, including marriage. In April 1990, after more than fourteen years together, Roth and Bloom were married in the Upper West Side apartment of their friend Barbara Epstein, the co-editor of *The New York Review of Books*—the same apartment where Roth had chased Jules Feiffer around in a mad pre-*Portnoy* improvisation years before. Not all the omens were encouraging. It was Bloom who proposed marriage, and it took him three weeks to respond; his previous experience with divorce led him to insist on a prenuptial agreement, which she agreed to sign only two days before the wedding; unbeknownst to Bloom, he'd been having an affair for years with a married Connecticut neighbor; and he had written *Deception*. Yet it seemed that he loved her, they were imaginatively well matched, and he wanted the marriage to work. Or it was the beginning of the end.

Professionally, he was undoubtedly regaining his strength. *Patrimony*, published in 1991, received superlative reviews, even from critics who'd had trouble with his other recent work. In *The New York Times*,

Michiko Kakutani noted approvingly that the book "eschews the defensive mirror games the author likes to play with fact and fiction" and offered, instead, "a new directness and tenderness of emotion"; she called it "one of Mr. Roth's most powerful books yet." Contrary to his custom, Roth went on a nationwide reading tour and was particularly happy to appear at Bucknell, at a reading held in honor of (and in the presence of) his beloved teacher Mildred Martin, whom he had visited almost every spring for years. ("She was the fairest person I've ever known," Roth says of Martin today. "She had wit, and she was dead serious about educating us.") And he began working on a book that he felt certain was the best he'd ever done: a kind of capstone to the period that had begun with *Portnoy*, his ultimate book about the Jews.

A Holiday About Snow

peration Shylock is the product of Roth's renewed vigor after the Halcion-induced breakdown and quintuple bypass surgery. With the concerns that had been running through his work for years brought to a global scale and a furious pitch, the book reads as though the author had resolved, after so narrowly cheating death—twice—to get absolutely everything in. And to get in everybody Jewish who would fit: Shylock, Freud, the Israeli spy Jonathan Pollard, the murdered American tourist Leon Klinghoffer, Irving Berlin. There are not one but two Philip Roths in the book. (Roth meant it when he wrote that being "implicated" heated things up for him.) One of them has written all Roth's books, is married to a woman named Claire, and is slowly recovering from the mentally disruptive effects of Halcion. Yet this is not a book about Philip Roth. There is no father, no mother, and scant mention of Newark. Even "Claire" exists only to warn her husband, sensibly and protectively, about exposing himself to a danger he cannot resist: tracking down and confronting the other Philip Roth, an impostor who is using his name and fame to propagate a theory that he calls Diasporism—billed as "The Only Solution to the Jewish Problem"—in lectures and interviews that he is giving in Jerusalem. One fictional Roth arrives there to overtake the other in January 1988, in time for the trial of John Demjanjuk and for the stirrings of the first *intifada*. These are not background events for a personal drama; they are the reasons the personal drama takes place.

Roth, the author of so many convincing masks, is clearly captivated by the mysteries of identity. ("My guess is that you've written metamorphoses of yourself so many times," Nathan Zuckerman tells him in *The Facts*, "you no longer have any idea what *you* are.") An early title for *Operation Shylock* was *Duality*. The book carries an epigraph from Genesis, about Jacob wrestling with the angel, and another by Kierkegaard: "The whole content of my being shrieks in contradiction against itself." If Israel runs away with the story once again, Roth was able this time to track the turbulence of *its* identity through an entire turbulent book. The Demjanjuk trial was the germinating seed, nationally and personally. It had been going on for more than a year when the real Philip Roth walked into the courtroom, in January 1988, just as he does in the novel. Indeed, the details of the proceedings contained in the novel have a journalistic accuracy that derives from the fact that Roth attended the trial compulsively, day after day. "Twenty feet in front of me sat a man accused of being one of the worst human beings who ever walked the earth," he explains to me, "and all around me the survivors, wanting his blood. Here was history."

But whose history, exactly? Demjanjuk's lawyers argued a straight-out case of mistaken identity, and offered in evidence their client's spotless record as a hardworking immigrant and model American citizen, a churchgoing family man admired by his neighbors. His accusers, they said—traumatized, elderly, with memories eroded by the decades—had mistaken him for someone to whom he merely bore a physical resemblance; someone, furthermore, who other survivors reported had been killed in a camp uprising at the end of the war. The protagonist called Philip Roth is riveted—as the real Philip Roth was riveted—by the mere proximity of such a figure. ("There he was. *There he was.*") In *Operation Shylock*, Roth imagines, in an extraordinary Nietzschean outburst, what it must have felt like to be this murderous peasant youth, having the time of his life at Treblinka: "What a job! A sensational blowout every day! One continuous party! Blood! Vodka! Women! Death! Power! And the screams! Those unending screams! And all of it *work*, good, hard work." The sixty-eight-year-old man in the dock hadn't smashed open a skull in nearly fifty years; no wonder he appeared so benign. But is the contrast so strange?

> You've really only lived sequentially the two seemingly antipodal, mutually excluding lives that the Nazis, with no strain to speak of, managed to

enjoy simultaneously—so what, in the end, is the big deal? The Germans have proved definitively to all the world that to maintain two radically divergent personalities, one very nice and one not so nice, is no longer the prerogative of psychopaths only.

Unless, of course, they had the wrong man. Not a demon but someone perfectly innocent. Because after all the months and all the witnesses, no one seemed able to tell for sure.

Operation Shylock is subtitled *A Confession*, and a preface presents the entire book as a factual account of events that culminated, in the late eighties, with Roth's agreeing to work as a spy for Israel's foreign intelligence service, the Mossad. Many names throughout the text are marked with a tiny circle, to indicate that they have been changed. Other, well-known names serve to anchor the account in reality. Aharon Appelfeld, for instance, whom Roth had traveled to Jerusalem to interview, is accurately described, and Roth quotes extensively from the published interview itself. This careful regard for provable data accords with an initial brusquely factual tone that functions like the runway under the wheels of a 747 gathering speed.

The doppelgänger in Jerusalem turns out to be a longtime Chicago private eye who is dying of cancer, and who is accompanied by a luscious blonde named Wanda Jane ("Jinx") Possesski. A former nurse, Jinx is also an officially recovering anti-Semite, thanks to a ten-step program that this phony Roth has developed, Anti-Semites Anonymous. While chasing the pair around the city, the book's "real" Roth is recruited by a Palestinian friend, who may or may not be a double agent, to meet with Yasir Arafat in Tunis. He is also recruited by an ancient Mossad spymaster named Smilesburger (no little circle marks the name; clearly, it is already an alias) for a mission designed to reveal the identity of Israelis who are secretly funneling money to the PLO. No wonder he worries that he may still be feeling the hallucinatory effects of Halcion.

In all these twists and turns, Roth—the author—has never seemed more of an *écouteur*, or talk fetishist: every permutation of a position in the Israeli spectrum, it seems, is given a voice. The book is a compendium of speeches, propositions, and diatribes, offering equally passionate and conflicting "solutions" to the problems of a Jewish state surrounded by enemies. The whole thing is vastly implausible on anything but the deepest level, where it is often moving and profound. (What is more implausible than Jewish history in the twentieth century?) Roth was steering his immense and chattering cargo toward what he saw as a kind of Jewish *Finnegans Wake*: hallucinatory, folkloric, dense (but never incomprehensible), and aimed at the heart of the Jewish dream.

Roth, as an expert on crackpot solutions to Israel's problems, demonstrates just how intractable those problems are. In *The Counterlife*, there is the Jewish hijacker who demands that Jews forget the Holocaust, so that Gentiles can forget the guilt that is the only explanation for their continuing vilification of Israel. ("Otherwise," he warns, "they will annihilate the State of Israel *in order to annihilate its Jewish conscience!*") *Operation Shylock* centers on the false Philip Roth's even more staggering plan, Diasporism, which calls for Israeli Jews of European heritage to return, en masse, to their countries of origin—to Poland, Ukraine, Romania, Lithuania, Germany—where they will be greeted with joy by the Christian citizens, who have missed them. (The secondary program he has developed, Anti-Semites Anonymous, is meant to deal with any snags in the Christian reactions.) After this second exodus is accomplished, Israel will be able to shrink to its original 1948 borders, and its tiny remaining non-European Jewish population will live peacefully in the larger Arab surround. As a result—and here is the point, the same nagging, terrifying point—a second Holocaust will be averted in the Middle East.

Diasporism is Zionism in reverse. (Roth evidently took the word "Diasporism" from a little book called *First Diasporist Manifesto*, by his friend the painter R. B. Kitaj, but there is not a trace of Roth's invented meaning among Kitaj's vague theories.) As such, it is no more incredible, Philip the Diasporist insists, than Theodore Herzl's plan to establish a Jewish state in the desert, which had appeared equally mad in his time. The former private eye who looks remarkably like Philip Roth (and looks more and more like him as the book proceeds, even to the way he wears down the heels of his shoes) is devoting his life to preaching the cause. And for a while, it appears that his most important convert (aside from Lech Wałęsa, with whom he has met in Gdansk) is the famous author himself. Easily mistaken for his double, Roth-the-protagonist begins to imitate his double imitating him and to give Diasporist speeches of his own. Freely adding little twists (he is having tremendous fun, or is he still feeling the Halcion?), he explains how he got the idea from the greatest Diasporist of them all, Irving Berlin:

> The radio was playing 'Easter Parade' and I thought, But this is Jewish genius on a par with the Ten Commandments. God gave Moses the Ten Commandments and then He gave to Irving Berlin 'Easter Parade' and 'White Christmas.' The two holidays that celebrate the divinity of Christ—the divinity that's the very heart of the Jewish rejection of Christianity—and what does Irving Berlin brilliantly do? He de-Christs them both! Easter he turns into a fashion show and Christmas into a holiday about snow. Gone is the gore and the murder of Christ—down with the crucifix and up with the bonnet! *He turns their religion into schlock.* But nicely! Nicely! So nicely the goyim don't even know what hit 'em. They love it. *Everybody* loves it.

His point, though it may be difficult to discern at first, is that there have been more effective ways of "defusing the enmity of centuries" than the bloodshed that Israel currently endures and employs. "I took more pride," he says, "in 'Easter Parade' than in the victory of the Six Day War, found more security in 'White Christmas' than in the Israeli nuclear reactor." Which brings us back to the dangers at hand. If the Israelis ever reach a point where they feel impelled to drop a nuclear bomb, he concludes, "they will have saved their state by destroying their people." Because "they will never survive morally after that; and if they don't, why survive as Jews at all?"

The novelist is mistaken for the Diasporist not only because of the similarity in looks but because of the reputation of his books. To any Palestinians who happened to be readers of modern American literature, there was no disparity between Philip Roth's renowned hostility to Jews and his purported plan to move them out of Israel. Both were commendable positions, possibly even helpful ones. And so our protagonist is approached, in a crowded Jerusalem marketplace, by a Palestinian recruiter for the PLO (unless he is really working for Israel) who also happens to be an old friend from the University of Chicago. This learned, elegant, American-schooled, and totally enraged Palestinian is called George Ziad (the name, we see, has been changed). Roth—I mean the man who actually wrote this book—tells me that he adapted the name from that of a Palestinian who took him into Palestinian areas in the West Bank, and to visit an Israeli military court in Ramallah (where Ziad takes the fictional Roth), in order to show him a dirtier side of Israeli justice than was being broadcast in the Demjanjuk trial. Roth insists that Edward Said, the eminent Palestinian and Columbia professor, never entered his mind, although reviewers often mentioned him, and *The New Yorker*, despite its meticulous fact-checking department, consistently misspelled the character's name George Zaid.

Whatever his origins, and whoever he is working for, this Palestinian intellectual gets some of the strongest moral and political rhetoric in the book. After years of living in Boston and disavowing any connection with his past, he has given up everything, including a job he loved, teaching literature, and brought his wife and son to a dusty West Bank outpost, where, attempting to repossess his father's land, he has succeeded only in repossessing his father's anger. His daily life is a series of roadblocks and humiliations. Twenty years of the occupation, forty years of the Jewish state, have "corroded everything moderate in him" and made him wholly subject to "the great disabling fantasy of revenge." And for some fourteen pages he spills out his opinions, his grievances, his memories, and his fury on the subject of Israel:

> *This state has no moral identity.* It has *forfeited* its moral identity, if it ever had any to begin with. By relentlessly institutionalizing the Holocaust it has even forfeited its claim to the Holocaust! The state of Israel has drawn the last of its moral credit out of the bank of the dead six million—this is what they have done by breaking the hands of Arab children on the orders of their illustrious minister of defense.

This from the author who was outraged by the anti-Israel talk at London dinner parties. Roth has not changed his position (if, as a novelist, he can be said to have any positions at all). He has created a character.

The only brake on Ziad's rage comes from his wife. A pencil-quick, unforgettable sketch of female pragmatism and anguished motherhood, Anna Ziad regrets the life that her family has left behind in Boston and is choking over what she considers to be her husband's destructive loyalties. "Why aren't you loyal," she cries to him, "to your *intellect?* Why aren't you loyal to *literature?*" Valuing her son's future far above the "childish, stupid ethnic mythologies" she sees on every side, she argues: "Isn't it 'life' when you read books and listen to music and choose your friends because of their qualities and not because they share your roots? Roots! A concept for *cavemen* to live by!"

An intense, migraine-afflicted, morally complex Palestinian woman: it is hard to imagine a stranger skin for Roth to inhabit, even for a few pages. Was there a model? Had she any basis in reality? (Does it matter?) Roth replies to my questions in the negative, saying that he had simply tried "to reverse the stereotype, a process that usually leads you toward reality." In fact, the most lauded modern Arabic novel of the Palestinian struggle, Elias Khoury's *Gate of the Sun*, which drew on hundreds of oral histories and was published a few years after *Operation Shylock*, features a heroine—a warrior's wife and a mother—of similar pragmatic and protective strengths.

And the Israeli countervoice? There are several, with deep attachments to the state, who speak out of a hard-won sense of *realpolitik* that passes for a saddened wisdom. The question of a national moral identity is fully played out between a father and son: the latter, a twenty-two-year-old army lieutenant, is so sick of the violence he has seen, and of the monstrous reflection of himself that he sees in the eyes of Palestinian women and children, that he is ready to go off to study at NYU. ("Nine tenths of their misery," he says of the Palestinians, "they owe to the idiocy of their own political leaders. *I know that.* But still I look at my own government and I want to vomit.") The father, a camp survivor who is now a Haifa manufacturer, argues that the morally esteemed British and French and Canadians would act exactly as the Israelis act if they were faced with the threats the Israelis face. "A state does not act out of moral ideology, a state acts out of self-interest," he lectures his son. "A state acts to preserve its existence." When the idealistic young man protests that it might be better, then, to be stateless, the father replies wearily, "We tried it." He hardly needs to add, "It didn't work out."

If this is the only argument made in support of the contemporary Israeli state, the moral feeling for the people who have historically defined the state is intense. Looking around during the Demjanjuk trial, Roth-the-protagonist notes that the greatest mystery isn't that a monster managed to live an ordinary life but rather, as he imagines telling the monster, that "those who cleaned the corpses out for you, your accusers here, could ever pursue anything resembling the run-of-the-mill after what was done to them by the likes of you—that *they* can manage run-of-the-mill lives, *that's* what's unbelievable!"

Of course, not everybody managed it. Aharon Appelfeld, already a familiar sort of Rothian alter ego—"hiding as a child from his murderers in the Ukrainian woods while I was still on a Newark playground playing fly-catcher's-up"—has a doppelgänger of his own. He is a sad and wistful figure called Cousin Apter, a tiny "unborn adult" who has emerged less than intact from even greater childhood horrors than Appelfeld's. The permanently childish Apter, Roth explains to me, is "what might have happened to Aharon if he hadn't escaped into the woods."

Does all this suggest that the Holocaust is the bedrock reason, and reason enough, for loyalty to Israel? It is the Israeli spymaster, Smilesburger, who denounces any attempt to "hide behind Appelfeld" as a morally comfortable way of supporting Israel. After all, he asks, "what justification is Mr. Appelfeld from Csernowitz, Bukovina, for the theft from them of Haifa and Jaffa?" Projecting a future Palestinian victory and a very different war-crimes trial in Jerusalem, the spymaster points out that all supporters of Israel will be accused of facilitating "the imperialist, colonialist theft that *was* the state of Israel." Whatever the fine distinctions in their reasoning, Smilesburger and Philip Roth will be hanged side by side. Millennial claims on the land? A millennial history of murderous anti-Semitism? Standing with one's tribe? The Holocaust? Being condemned, as a Jew born where and when he was, in whichever way he turned? No, the only explanation that Smilesburger plans to give for his position, to any such future court, is: "I do what I do because I do what I do."

These are the graver aspects of *Operation Shylock*. The book is crowded not only with arguments about political morality but with jokes, shtick, absurdities, impossibilities, the escapades of people with American cartoon names (Jinx, Smilesburger) or Yiddish cartoon names (Moishe Pipik, Meema Gitcha), and with outright belly laughs. It is a wildly and distractingly antic book, though, precisely because it deals with grave and hazardous subjects. Wild, distracting, and antic are Roth's ways of avoiding pomposity, sentimentality, and didacticism.

Even more than in 1959, and especially now that he was dealing openly with the Holocaust and the moral foundations of Israel, Roth was the anti–Leon Uris. He knew the risks that he was taking in this nervy, jabbering, structurally pinwheeling book: at one point, Roth-the-protagonist worries that the story is "too freakishly plotted" and that the careering sequence of events leaves "nowhere for intelligence to establish a foothold and develop a perspective." Is one voice right and the other wrong? For whom does the author speak? With Roth, this is simply the wrong question. His goal is to speak for them all.

The character Philip Roth does arrive at some conclusions. Coming down from his "Easter Parade" high, he dismisses Diasporism as "thinly camouflaged anti-Zionist crap." He takes up the offer to work as an Israeli spy—going to Athens and then to another, unnamed European city on a dangerous mission, although he does so mostly for the excitement it will add to the book. This information brings us full circle, back to the straight-faced statements of the preface and to the book's subtitle, A Confession. But the account of this adventure, we are told, which made up the original final chapter of the book—it was titled "Operation Shylock," the code name of the mission—had to be deleted because of the threat it posed to Israeli security and to other agents in the field. Instead of the dynamic conclusion toward which the story has been building, we get an epilogue, set nearly five years later, that depicts a meeting between the protagonist and his Mossad handler, over plates of chopped herring at an Upper West Side eatery, in which Roth is threatened and cajoled—"Call it fiction instead. Append a note: 'I made this up'"—and finally paid off, with a great quantity of cash, for omitting the ending of his book. This is now the ending of the book—except for an appended "Note to the Reader" that begins, "This book is a work of fiction." With the sole exceptions of the excerpts from the Appelfeld interview and some "verbatim minutes" of the Demjanjuk trial, any resemblance to living people or actual events "is entirely coincidental." The note concludes, "This confession is false."

The flesh-and-blood Roth was so delighted by the giddy pleasures of this fact-and-fiction game that he continued to talk up the spy story in an unblinkingly ingenuous interview with The New York Times, on the book's release, in 1993. ("I added the note to the reader as I was asked to do. I'm just a good Mossadnik.") This was his full-out return to fiction, and he was expecting a big reaction: he was very happy with the book. ("I felt like I was dancing as a writer," he tells me, about the experience of writing it.) He seemed to be happy, period. Bloom had just turned sixty-two, and he gave a big party for her in Connecticut. He himself was turning sixty; there was a party for that, too, given by his former doctor and closest Connecticut friend, C. H. Huvelle. An early review of the book by Paul Gray, in *Time* magazine, was ecstatic ("Roth has not riffed with quite this comic abandon since *Portnoy's Complaint*"), and *Time* began to put together a cover story. It was canceled, however, when less enthusiastic reviews began to come in.

The most influential critics tore into the book, in great part, for not being a more traditional novel. In *The New York Times*, Michiko Kakutani noted that the sheer amount of talk ("and talk and talk and talk"), however brilliant, threw the book off balance and undermined the plot; "one somehow expects a novel to be more shapely and selective." She found that Roth was prevented from engaging with outside issues by an all too familiar "solipsism, repetitiveness and obsessive self-interest." And, not surprisingly—given her praise of *Patrimony* for its lack of "defensive mirror games"—she had no patience for "the author's tiresome games with mirrors." In the *Times Book Review*, D. M. Thomas was generally positive, but his praise was buried amid plot details and qualified by a complaint that the subordinate characters lacked independent life. Toughest of all was John Updike in *The New Yorker*, offering broad praise ("as painstakingly written as it is elaborately developed") but hitting hard at the same frustrations the others had expressed: "The characters turn out to be talking heads, faces attached to tirades," the book was "an orgy of argumentation," and it didn't seem to matter to Roth whether the arguments were good or bad, heartfelt or perverse or frivolous. The structure, too, was dubious: like *Deception*, it seemed to have been assembled out of monologues and interviews. Some readers already felt that Roth's recent books contained too much Roth, Updike charged—Updike was clearly among them—but *Operation Shylock* contained too much of everything. Roth, as an author, had become exhausting.

This had to hurt. Whatever Roth thought about the capacities of professional reviewers, he had an unflagging respect for Updike's opinion. They had developed a friendly acquaintance over the years, starting when they were young and full of plans and arguing about the Vietnam War. (Roth tells me that one of their arguments, somewhat transmogrified, made it into *Rabbit Redux*, with Updike—a defender of the war—in the role of the politically conservative Rabbit, and Roth's views emerging from a black revolutionary character called Skeeter.) Roth and Bloom had gone to dinner at the Updikes' house, near Boston, when Bloom was performing there. (Roth was mightily impressed by the layout of the house, with separate rooms for Updike's various projects—novels, poetry, reviews—and a typewriter in each one.) Roth didn't write reviews, but he telephoned Updike whenever he admired something, and Updike—who Roth says generally stayed aloof—would occasionally write him a note. In assessing his generation of writers, Roth often says that Updike had the greatest natural gift of all of them.

There was some consolation, a few months later, in a strongly positive (if not very influentially placed) review by Janis Freedman Bellow, in the Boston University alumni magazine, *Bostonia*, defending Roth against the charges of solipsism and emphasizing his engagement with his subject. The author was Saul Bellow's fifth and final wife; a graduate student when she met her future husband, she had recently completed a doctorate in French literature at the University of Chicago. She was outraged by the negative reviews of *Operation Shylock*, and Bellow had encouraged her to write a review of her own. Bellow also felt the book had been "unfairly manhandled by the press," as he told the *Chicago Tribune* the following spring, mentioning that he was teaching it in a course at Boston University, on "living writers I find especially interesting." Also consoling, *Operation Shylock* won the PEN/Faulkner Award that spring for the best novel of the year.

In responding to accusations of solipsism, Roth has often tried to explain the meaning that the use of his name in his books had for him at the time. For years, he'd been fascinated by European novelists (Genet, Céline, Gombrowicz) who, casting themselves as characters in their fiction, reveled in pointing a finger not at the sins of fictional others but at themselves—a method Roth describes as "I'm in the broiler, watch me broil." (As far back as *The Professor of Desire*, in the Prague-inflected seventies, an angry young writer makes a case against "that holy of holies" Chekhov: "Why is the brute never Anton but some other slob?") When he began writing *Deception*, a novel about adultery, he thought it would be enlivening for everyone—for him, for readers—if the leading character was not a randomly named protagonist but him. He explains, "If I say that *I* am the one putting my hand on the girl, that *I* am cheating . . . there's something at stake."

It seems clear, too, that in the post-Halcion years of questioning identity, drawing on real names gave him an extra charge. The names of the women in *The Facts* were changed before publication to protect their privacy—and "because I didn't want to read them in reviews," Roth adds—but it was important to writing the book that the real names were in place. In the case of *Operation Shylock*, a spinning dreidel of identities, Roth reports that all the "doubles" books he read before he started writing—*Dr. Jekyll and Mr. Hyde*, *The Secret Sharer*—left him feeling that the modern reader could be drawn in further if, again, the doubled figure was Roth himself. He sees the current memoir craze as the "vulgarized version of a real modernist need." Which he sums up as: "You must be Raskolnikov. I am Pipik."

In December 1992, a few months before *Operation Shylock* was published, Roth began to experience a recurrence of back pain. He was on a reading tour for *Patrimony*, visiting universities and cultural centers around the country; he took to wearing a back brace during the ninety-minute readings and to downing a couple of shots of vodka afterward to ease the pain. He recalls that sometimes it got so bad that, between cities, he had to lie down on the airport floor. Despite the mood of happiness at his sixtieth birthday party, that March, several photographs show him clutching his back. It was becoming clear by then that *Operation Shylock* was not going to be the big critical and commercial success that he had hoped for. But even that disappointment was overshadowed by the pain, although the pain may have made the disappointment harder to bear. By May, when he received an honorary degree from Amherst, he was barely able to drive home. That summer, he had to stop working on the new book that he had begun, because he could neither sit nor stand at his desk with any comfort. After months without substantive relief, and unable to work, he began to plummet emotionally. He recalls that it was only his fear of the snapping turtles and the water snakes in his pond in Connecticut that kept him from throwing himself in.

It isn't a joke, or a metaphor. In the summer of 1993, a suicidal depression began to close in on him, as deep and frightening as the

Halcion-fueled breakdown five years earlier. He feared that the physical pain would never go away. In his own words, from a private account he wrote later, he was experiencing "the most unimaginable form of dread I had ever known, there waiting for you when you opened your eyes in the morning, there when you tried unsuccessfully to get to sleep at night." It felt as though "a trap door opens within you," the account goes on. "And you are utterly defenseless in another world—you are dropped into the nether region of your worst dead-of-night fears." He was then living in Connecticut, as he always did in summertime. Bloom, in her memoir, writes that he seemed "afraid of being alone with me" and that, very soon, he did not want her there at all. Sandy came to stay for a while, and the brothers returned together to Sandy's home in Chicago for about ten days. When the suicidal thoughts did not abate, Roth called his doctor, who arranged to have him admitted to a psychiatric hospital, Silver Hill, in New Canaan, Connecticut. He flew back east again right away.

He entered the hospital in early August and remained for seventeen days, then returned to the house. Bloom was away, at his request, but close friends came to stay with him. When he felt himself sinking again, in early September, he readmitted himself for another stay of approximately the same length. He was taking an anti-inflammatory drug for his back pain and medication for depression. By the time that he was released, for good, in late September, he was feeling not only better but revitalized, free of pain for the first time in three-quarters of a year. He now views the depression as having been an excruciating process of mental clarification, letting him see what he needed and wanted for the rest of his life. "It was dreadful to have lived through, yet it turned out to be a merciful affliction." He returned to New York directly from the hospital and, within hours, resumed work on the new novel. The following month, he filed for divorce.

He speaks of experiencing a sense of great relief. He had managed not to kill himself. The illness had been overwhelming; so was health. The anti-inflammatory medication kept his back pain at bay, and the other drugs were not needed for long. And he was free. Free of a woman who, as he says now, had seemed too often unsupportive through his months of pain and fear—Bloom herself writes, with regret, that her "panic" had made her appear "lacking in compassion"—and whose vulnerability (as Bloom also saw it) had become a burden; free of a companion who had become a living distraction from work that had never felt more pressing. In *The Counterlife*, Nathan Zuckerman observes that the most Jewish thing about his brother, Henry, is that he had to move to Israel and learn Hebrew and rediscover his God—all these morally irreproachable things—in order to justify leaving his wife. Roth's depression was no less harrowing and real for having provided a similar justification.

Bloom did not legally fight the prenup, in exchange for a comparatively modest settlement of a hundred thousand dollars. To judge from her memoir, it seems that both of them, at least intermittently, imagined that they would remain friends. Yet this period could not always have been as easy for Roth as he claims: for a while he thought of selling his beloved country house and building a new one nearby, just to get away from disturbing memories; he went as far as commissioning an architect and having a model built, although he eventually gave it up. He was living alone in the New York apartment, working in his studio every day, and at night either seeing friends for dinner or—the kind of detail he can't resist throwing in—glued to the O. J. Simpson trial. The new book was coming along with astonishing ease. He felt that the writing was energized by his return to life, even though the book was about grief, loss, and the art of dying.

Nobody Beloved Gets Out Alive

"It began because I was looking for a place to be buried," Roth explains about writing *Sabbath's Theater*, in his Web of Stories interview. He was nearing sixty and, he thought, "I'd better take care of that." The search was set off by the death of his friend and former lover Janet Hobhouse, in 1991. She was forty-two. Ovarian cancer. They had been lovers for a brief time in 1974, when she lived upstairs from him in an apartment building on East Eighty-first Street, in New York. (In *The Counterlife*, Maria lives upstairs from Nathan; he calls the elevator their "*deus ex machina*.") Hobhouse was beautiful and gifted, as Bloom wrote in her memoir; she was also married. Although she was born in New York, she had spent years in England, and Roth liked her accent. Beyond a few deliberate and deceptive touches, she wasn't Maria Freshfield, of course—she was the alibi for the woman who was Maria Freshfield—but she was undoubtedly the woman who talks about her chemotherapy in *Deception*. ("I may be bald but I'm not even forty. I really don't think I should die.")

Hobhouse wrote about Roth, too, in a memoir-like novel titled *The Furies*—it began as a memoir—in which Roth, renamed Jack, figures as a romantic artist-hero, all coiled energy and liquid black eyes. Hobhouse was clearly in love but not blindly so: she frankly assesses the contrast between the "extremeness" of her lover's fiction and the "old-maidish Prufrockery" of his cautious, self-protective ways. (This is a discrepancy that all of Roth's friends observe: the literary pirate who carries a bottle of Purell.) When she revealed that a psychiatrist had prescribed lithium for her, he backed away. She sensed his fear of getting entangled with another unbalanced woman, even if she didn't know his history. But she did not see the contrast between his work and his life as diminishing; to the contrary, she wrote that it made her love him more. This was how the work got done. "I admired his fasting."

Hobhouse died before *The Furies* was published. Much of the book revolves around her mother, a troubled woman who had committed suicide a few years earlier. Hobhouse had buried her in a Revolutionary-era cemetery in Cornwall, Connecticut, near Roth's home, with the understanding that she would be buried there, too. The sad task of getting this done fell to Roth, who also acquired the stone for her grave. Hence the idea of finding his own cemetery plot, an adventure that Roth has recounted to friends and interviewers alike, *con brio*. First, he imagined himself in the same bucolic country cemetery, "but I just thought I wouldn't be comfortable there," he says. "Aside from my friend, I thought, who would I talk to?" He dismissed several other nearby places for similar reasons, then went to look at the New Jersey cemetery where his parents are buried, but none of the adjacent plots were available. The cemetery warden walked him around, looking for a suitable location, but when Roth pointed toward a plot not far from his parents, the man—"a real comedian," Roth says—shook his head: "I don't like that for you, Mr. Roth. There's not enough legroom." By then the authorial impulse had kicked in. "It began to dawn on me," he says, "that someone who's looking for a grave to be buried in might be interesting—especially if he's going to commit suicide."

It is tempting to say that Roth drew Mickey Sabbath out of his depression, when only the fear of snapping turtles and water snakes kept him from throwing himself into his pond; and out of the powerful sense of life that swept over him when he managed not to do it—or, rather, the powerful sense of life that had kept him from doing it all along, no matter how awful his fear and despair. *Sabbath's Theater* is Roth's most emotionally intense book, a book that seems to be running a fever. It is also a masterpiece of twentieth-century American literature: coursing with life, dense with character and wisdom, it gives the deepest experiences we face—dying, remembering, holding on to each other—the startling impact of first knowledge, first incredulous awareness. Roth accomplishes this largely by avoiding expectations. *Sabbath's Theater* is deliberately abrasive and insanely funny—even more than in *Operation Shylock*, Roth shocks us into feelings that pieties could not induce. For all its laughs, the book is essentially a tragedy, and filled with tears. It brings us smack up against our most terrible losses and our utterly useless outrage at the fact of our extinction—at the fact that, as Mickey Sabbath says, "There's nothing on earth that keeps its promise."

Mickey Sabbath is not Zuckerman, not Kepesh, and not Philip Roth. In terms of simple biography, he is a few years older than these fellows and has had nothing like their academic backgrounds. Sabbath was a sailor in his youth: he shipped out as a merchant seaman at seventeen, directly after high school, in 1946, and what he remembers best about the ports and the towns and the experiences is the whores. ("Particularly fond of whores. The stewlike stink of those oniony parts. What has ever meant more to me?") Much of Sabbath's pungent history—"Bahia, where there was a church and a whorehouse for every day of the year"—Roth got from the sailor past and sexual lore of his expatriate painter friend in London, R. B. Kitaj. He had little feeling for Kitaj's painting, and Kitaj's frequent Jewish subject matter did not reflect the kind of Jewishness that was meaningful to Roth. ("He wanted to attach to Jews in a historical way, not in an everyday way," Roth says, reflectively; "historical suffering and battles, but not ironing pants.") Yet Roth listened devotedly to Kitaj's tales of his exotic travels and his visits, during his teens, to the best and the lowest brothels from Buenos Aires to Havana. (Mickey Sabbath: "To be back there, to be seventeen in Havana and ramming it in!")

Sabbath grew up in a town on the Jersey Shore, where the Roth family spent a few weeks every summer. But Sabbath spent his entire childhood there, a Jewish kid among the Italians and the Irish—it was the Irish who turned the common Jewish name Morris into Mickey. After the years at sea, he became a puppeteer, performing on the street and eventually running a little ninety-seat place of his own, on Avenue C: the Indecent Theater of Manhattan. Roth remembers that his mother's youngest, unmarried sister, his Aunt Honey—renamed Aunt Rhoda when Roth paired her off with his fictional Kafka, the Newark Hebrew teacher—worked for a WPA puppet theater and brought two marionettes as gifts for him and Sandy; they kept them at the back of their closet, and he loved to see them collapsed there whenever he opened the door. He also recalls that while writing this book he spent a good deal of time with avant-garde puppeteers, and swears that he saw an all-puppet version of Kafka's *The Trial*, performed by a visiting group from Prague, in Czech.

At sixty-four, Sabbath has retired from puppetry because his hands are crippled with arthritis, and he has been forced to retire from teaching, too, because of an unfortunate incident involving a female student, phone sex, and a tape recorder. (The entire filthy conversation runs along the bottom of the relevant pages, like footnotes.) But—despite being a shortish barrel of a man, with a straggly white beard and uncertain hygienic habits—he remains wholly dedicated to his alternate vocation as a whoremonger and dirty old man.

Mickey Sabbath suffers from no inhibitions, in part because he has rejected the bargain that most people make with civilization and its discontents. He has none of Alexander Portnoy's constricting ethical impulses. Yet if he is free of constraints—"freed from the desire to please"—it is because he has already lost so much: his older brother, shot down during the war; his mother, who never recovered from the loss; the wife of his youth, who disappeared somewhere along the way. And a beloved mistress, who has just died of cancer and who meant more to him than any other woman he had ever known. Sabbath can do whatever he wants, at whatever risk, because nothing more can be taken from him.

And so he has become a haunter of cemeteries. Inept at dealing with the living, Sabbath is assured and intimate with the dead. He talks fairly often with his mother's ghost. ("Do you know only what you knew when you were living, or do you now know everything, or is 'knowing' no longer an issue? What's the story?") He would prefer to be dead himself, but he cannot manage to commit suicide, no matter how carefully he plans or how often he tries. He manages to mess up every deadly scheme. There's the cemetery where his parents and his brother are buried, for example. He arrives there in perfect good faith, ready to resign himself to the adjoining plot, only to discover that his mother's older sister, who died just two years earlier, has taken his space. Did they forget all about him? Did they assume he was already dead, because of the way he lived? It's a bad blow:

King of the kingdom of the unillusioned, emperor of no expectations, crestfallen man-god of the double cross, Sabbath had *still* to learn that nothing but *nothing* will ever turn out—and this obtuseness was, in itself, a deep, deep shock. Why does life refuse me even the *grave* I want! Had I only marshaled my abhorrence in a good cause and killed myself two years ago, that spot next to Ma's would be mine.

And even if he could manage the logistics, get the time and place exactly right, there is always one more experience looming that he can't bear to miss. Sabbath is firmly attached even to the worst aspects of life, perhaps especially attached to those, because they are all that he has and because they show just how strong his attachment is:

> Yes, yes, yes, he felt uncontrollable tenderness for his own shit-filled life. And a laughable hunger for more. More defeat! More disappointment! More deceit! More loneliness! More arthritis! More missionaries! God willing, more cunt! More disastrous entanglement in everything.

The experience that's hardest to leave behind is, of course, sex.

Sabbath's Theater is a very cheerfully dirty-minded book, elevating the familiar theme of sex as freedom into sex as a protest against the grave itself. And Mickey Sabbath protests quite a lot. Aside from any number of determinedly outrageous acts—golden showers, graveside masturbation—the book contains rhapsodic odes to the morning hard-on ("No deceit in it. No simulation. No insincerity. All hail to that driving force!") and the clitoris ("The mother of the microchip, the triumph of evolution, right up with the retina and the tympanic membrane. I wouldn't mind growing one myself, in the middle of my forehead like Cyclops's eye"). "Shocking" sexual antics had already become something of a default mode in American fiction, and Roth, since the advent of Zuckerman, had confined his heroes to little more than fleeting cartoon lust. But Sabbath is serious about sex, and he has met his match: a short, dark-haired, middle-aged Croatian émigrée, a bit on the plump side, who runs an inn with her husband in New England and whose sexual appetite and contempt for rules surpass even Sabbath's. This prodigal's name is Drenka Balich, and the truly surprising aspect of her affair with Sabbath is not its every-which-way taboo-breaking sex but—so much harder to bring off—the depth and innocence of their love.

How many great love affairs have there been in recent fiction? This one lasts thirteen years. And then, at fifty-two, Drenka gets sick and dies, sending Sabbath on a downward spiral and starting the novel on its course. Like *Lolita*, Roth's book is a retrospective account of a transgressive passion—Sabbath and Drenka are both married, both dedicatedly promiscuous—although, in this case, the woman is anything but a nymphet:

> It was supposed to be otherwise, with the musculature everywhere losing its firmness, but even where her skin had gone papery at the low point of her neckline, even that palm-size diamond of minutely crosshatched flesh intensified not merely her enduring allure but his tender feeling for her as well. He was now six short years from seventy: what had him grasping at the broadening buttocks as though the tattooist Time had ornamented neither of them with its comical festoonery was his knowing inescapably that the game was just about over.

And it isn't only the sex, or the daring in the sex, or the defiance of convention in the sex. Drenka is practical, funny, and—an attribute as important as the others—an old-fashioned, loving mother. When she takes five hundred dollars from Sabbath for playing his whore, she buys a gift for her grown son. (The son is a state trooper, and Drenka owns a scanner that monitors police radio signals, so she can keep track of his whereabouts when he's on duty all night; her devotion is nearly worthy of Mrs. Portnoy.) Part of the thrill is in the contradiction: "A respectable woman who was enough of a warrior to challenge his audacity with hers," by which Sabbath means that Drenka is proud and pleased to have had sex with four men in a single day. But Drenka is also described (by Sabbath) as "plainly ecstatic to be living on earth," and as "a piece of human sunlight" (by her clueless, adoring husband). It would be a stretch to call Mickey Sabbath a hero, but Drenka Balich is undoubtedly a heroine, a worthy descendant of the great adulteresses of European literature.

Roth was initially inspired by a married Connecticut neighbor with whom he had begun an affair in the late seventies; the affair had continued right through his marriage and, finally, survived it, although not for long. The arrangement was never exclusive. Roth was away in London, after all, for half of every year, and he was not the only man with whom this "unashamedly polyamorous woman" (as he describes her to me) was adulterously involved—for him, in fact, this was the essence of her charm. He viewed her as a sensualist, a nonconformist, and a wholly free spirit; he wondered if this freedom had to do with the fact that she was not American. (She was not Croatian, however, but Scandinavian. Friends of Roth's who knew her at the time reinforce his claims: Judith Thurman talks about a woman who was "completely uninhibited"— virtually echoing Roth's book—and yet maternal, "the most caressing person I've ever known," although Thurman also thinks she probably exaggerated her sexual exploits to impress Roth.) It lasted up until the time that he was suddenly divorced and she was suddenly divorced, and they began "seeing each other regularly," Roth explains, "for more than just a few stolen hours of sex." The relationship collapsed, apparently under the weight of ordinariness, in 1995, the year that *Sabbath's Theater* was published.

Yet the character of Drenka, in all her sunlight, is drawn from imagination as much as memory. The great gift that Roth bestows on her is not beauty but an absolute, good-natured freedom, which is based in strength and radiates joy. An intoxicating earth mother, Drenka is absolved of sentimentality by raunchy sex and weight around the hips. It is easy to enjoy her, and impossible not to weep along with Sabbath at her deathbed. Although she does not live the way most women live, or might want to live, she enlarges the sense of female possibility, and that's what heroines are for.

And then there is the way Drenka speaks. For all the sexual animation of Roth's heroes and their famed excitement over breasts, they are also and increasingly voice men, suckers for a woman's words. (Even Alexander Portnoy rejects a flaxen-haired beauty because he can't bear her "cutesy-wootsy boarding school argot"; Nathan Zuckerman, of course, risked his life for "a finely calibrated relative clause.") "Phonetic seduction," Roth calls it here. Sabbath relishes both Drenka's "juicy" accent and, even more, her knack for turning clichés into little verbal artworks: "It takes two to tangle," "I've got to get quacking," "a bottomless piss." For Sabbath, these malapropisms have a cheering linguistic freshness— she calls another lover's erection "the rainbow," because it is long and has a curve—that reflects the lack of cliché in the way she thinks and lives. (Linguistic torture, on the other hand, is inflicted by the college girl who tells him that she feels "empowered" by knowing him—"that language which they all used and which made him want to cut their heads off"— and by his wife, who returns from AA meetings speaking interminably about "sharing": "What he loathed the way good people loathe *fuck* was *sharing*.") The morality of language, freedom from cant: or, as Sabbath puts it, the pleasure of words "freed from their daily duty to justify and to conceal." There is nothing Mickey Sabbath won't do with his body, but his sense of language remains unsullied.

Roth's own language takes on a new richness and beauty in *Sabbath's Theater*, a development that he attributes to the unprecedented freedom that he felt in writing it—"the freest experience of my life." He believes that he owes this literary freedom, in turn, to the unrestricted personal freedom of Mickey Sabbath: a far more unbridled protagonist even than Portnoy. The prose, cast in a deeply subjective third person, moves seamlessly in and out of Sabbath's thoughts, revving up to gale force while maintaining the confiding ease that Roth had long ago perfected. Despite a touch of almost biblical grandeur here and there, despite the mortal themes and the immortal longings and the musical swellings, *Sabbath's Theater* reads as naturally as *Goodbye, Columbus*.

As a strict linguistic moralist, however, Roth makes beauty pay its way. His style has always been hard to characterize beyond the energy and concentration, the uncanny capturing of voices, and a tendency toward exclamation points and capital letters when he is on a comic tear—when he grabs you by the collar and won't let you go. He is still unlikely to linger over a landscape. He distrusts extended description— the glinting observations of a surrounding world that give Updike's work its texture—and seems ever wary of the risks of pretentiousness or of diffusing the pressure of the voice. Even here, a note of lyric gorgeousness is apt to end with a blackened eye, as when Sabbath comes to stand at Drenka's grave, in an isolated country cemetery, in the dark of night, when her son or husband or other more properly accredited mourners are less likely to discover him:

> Five months after her death, a damp, warm April night with a full moon canonizing itself above the tree line, effortlessly floating—luminously blessed—toward the throne of God, Sabbath stretched out on the ground

that covered her coffin and said, "You filthy, wonderful Drenka cunt!
Marry me! Marry me!"

You didn't think you were going to get a whole sentence about the luminous moon, did you? This passage works almost as a formula for the
entire book: a mixture of the male hormone that Sabbath calls "prepos-
terone," crazy sorrow, and love.

It was possibly frightening and certainly strange to visit a cemetery
late at night, alone. And to render the atmosphere exactly, Roth began
to visit Janet Hobhouse's grave, late at night and alone. The Cornwall
cemetery happens to lie just at the edge of the town; in the book, Roth
moved it farther away and onto a hillside, partly for the scenic drama
but mostly in order to allow Sabbath to perform his peculiar rites of
mourning, which include (lovingly) ejaculating on Drenka's grave. (Sabbath is outraged when another man shows up—it's the rainbow!—and
delivers the same tribute.) Roth had visited Hobhouse's grave often in
the months after her death. Drenka's horrible cancer death clearly owes
much to that tragic example. But Roth's midnight visits, he tells me,
were not all tragedy. Prowling around the gravestones late one freezing
winter night, he says, he could distinctly hear Hobhouse's voice addressing him: "You're working on a book, aren't you?"

Sabbath's Theater makes no use of the tricks of time or the narrative
tumult that are key to *The Counterlife* and *Operation Shylock*, because
its central point is that time moves in only one direction and leads to
only one end. Sabbath's thoughts about death, his longing for people
who are gone, flow steady through its pages; the beauty is the result not
of adjectival elaboration but of close observation and imaginative precision. Here Sabbath, having exhausted all other possibilities, has a
eureka-simple inspiration for abolishing death:

> Turning life back like a clock in the fall. Just taking it down off the wall
> and winding it back and winding it back until your dead all appear like
> standard time.

And here he reads the tombstones in a cemetery he has gone to visit:

> Beloved wife Tillie. Beloved husband Bernard. Beloved husband and fa-
> ther Fred. Beloved husband and father Frank. My beloved wife our dear

mother Lena. Our dear father Marcus. On and on and on. Nobody beloved gets out alive.

Mickey Sabbath is a natural poet, yet he is also undeniably repellent to many people—in and out of the book—with his grizzled
eroticism and his glee in defilement. Certainly, part of Roth's intention
is to push us through these repellent qualities to a wider embrace of the
human animal. "Repellent" is a word that comes up often when he talks
about this book: "I wanted to let the repellent in," he says. Why? "Because we try so hard not to see it," he replies. "We just throw an ugly
name on it and look away." Roth says that he learned about the importance of admitting the repellent, in literature, from Henry Miller, and,
indeed, it's difficult to imagine Mickey Sabbath without the precedent
of *Tropic of Cancer*. Roth had read it sometime in the mid-fifties, in the
notorious Obelisk Press edition that travelers smuggled in from Paris
before the book became legal, in 1961, in the United States. In some
unpublished notes about his literary influences—the same notes in
which he looks back on Thomas Wolfe—Roth reports that he read
Miller as he had once read Wolfe, "swooningly," thrilled by his explora-
tion of "vast areas of unspeakable thought and unspoken-of conduct,"
and by his unashamed witness to "the impertinent minutiae of male
desire."

It might be said, of course, that this description applies equally to
Roth. And the freedom of *Portnoy's Complaint*, in this light, may owe as
much to Miller as to psychoanalysis. ("All the force in Henry Miller,"
Roth's notes continue, "all the anarchistic individualism seemed to be
generated and sustained by his phallus.") Roth is a far greater novelist
and comprehends far broader areas of thought and conduct. But Miller's lesson remains. Let the sexual in. Let the body in. It's there in *The
Ghost Writer*, when young Zuckerman announces that he intends personally to enlarge Isaac Babel's definition of the Jewish writer as a man
"with autumn in his heart and spectacles on his nose" to include "blood
in his penis." It's there in *Patrimony*, when Roth cleans up his father's
shit after the old man has had an accident, scraping it out from between
the wooden floorboards of the bathroom with a toothbrush. Let the repellent in. It's part of life. Not until *Sabbath's Theater* did Roth take up
the challenge in full, bringing a rigorous intellect and aching honesty to

the subject of the human body—compulsive, smelly, beautiful, ugly, riddled with cancer and love, corruptible only in death.

But the idea of the repellent is also, for Roth, associated with a train of political thought. The repellent gets in the way of "ideal plans," he wrote in the notes for several classes that he taught about his own books, at Bard College, in the late nineties. "If only we could get rid of the repellent Jews, or the repellent rich," the notes continue—and we are back in the historical catastrophes of the twentieth century: "If we can just slay the repellent, we will be pure." There is probably not another category that Roth holds up to such suspicious scrutiny as "the pure." But if Mickey Sabbath in some ways wins our admiration for not being "big on oughts," the friends whose lives he disrupts see things differently. And Roth—ever the moral pugilist—puts real weight behind the counterargument, in favor of the normal, the peaceful, and the pleasures of living by the oughts.

The chief defender of the upright is Sabbath's loyal friend Norman Cowan, a genuinely decent man—a kinder, less angry Henry Zuckerman—who offers Sabbath refuge in his Manhattan apartment, although Norman is struggling, even before Sabbath's one-man wrecking committee arrives, to maintain domestic peace. Norman is not a blind or limited person, not a simpleton. He sees all the dangers in the world that Sabbath sees. It is precisely *because* of these dangers that he has chosen to live a very different life and hold tight to "the portion of the ordinary I've been lucky enough to corral." (Sabbath is not unappreciative of the benefits of Norman's choices: "The repose when all is well. Somebody there while you wait for the biopsy report to come back from the lab.") But even princely Norman is pushed to the edge after Sabbath tries to seduce Norman's wife and raids his nineteen-year-old daughter's underwear drawer. Norman speaks for a lot of people when he angrily dismisses Sabbath as "a pathetic, outmoded old crank" and "the discredited male polemic's last gasp." Roth himself says that he wouldn't be able to tolerate Mickey Sabbath in person. For one thing, Sabbath is just too dirty. "If he were sitting right here," Roth says, gesturing at his nice white couch, "I'd throw him out."

Norman's seducible wife is more open to Sabbath's ways, however, and offers a more psychologically nuanced case. Michelle Cowan is a minor character with major impact, a portrait of the successful modern woman—career, loving husband, daughter at Brown—as a secret, Bovary-esque malcontent and sexual outlaw. She is the reason that her husband struggles to preserve the peace. ("There is something in her that is always threatening to undo it all," Sabbath realizes, "the warmth, the comfort, the whole wonderful eiderdown that is their privileged position.") Michelle is the only person who shares Sabbath's painfully conflated sense of sex and loss. Accustomed to being vibrant and attractive, having lived without reserve through her thirties and forties, she has suddenly awakened to being "fifty-five and seared with hot flashes," and to the feeling that "*everything* is racing off at a tremendous speed." Sabbath sees her menopausal flashes in an intensely sympathetic, even exalted, light: "Dipped, she is, in the very fire of fleeting time." (Or, less poetically, "It's no fun burning on a pyre at dinner.") And, unsurprisingly, he sees nobility in her refusal to go gently into unsexed darkness. Entirely different from Drenka in terms of class, education, and temperament, Michelle is another morally dedicated adulteress, a Molly Bloom refusing to let anything go: "Must everything be behind her? No! No! The ruthless lyricism of Michelle's soliloquy: and no I said no I will No."

However repellent Mickey Sabbath may be, though—considered as a man of flesh rather than of words, a befouler of white couches—he is clothed in Roth's most gorgeous and expansive language. It gives him stature, humor, color, and charm far beyond his naked self and turns him into a Whitman of negativity, a figure of engulfing if improper vitality. People may reasonably object to the idea of an old satyr rifling through a teenage girl's underwear drawer, but the catalogue that Sabbath makes of his findings is a thing of hilarity and joy:

> Brilliant hues of silk and satin. Childish cotton underpants with red circus stripes. String bikinis with satin behinds. Stretch satin thong bikinis. Floss your teeth with those thongs. Garter belts in purple, black, and white. Renoir's palette! Rose. Pale pink . . . Lace body stockings, *three*, and all black. A strapless black satin bodysuit with padded push-up cups, edged with lace and hooks and straps. Straps. Bra straps, garter straps, Victorian corset straps. Who in his right mind doesn't adore straps, all the abracadabra of holding and lifting? And what about strap*less*? A strapless bra. Christ, everything works. That thing they call a teddy (Roosevelt?

Kennedy? Herzl?), all in one a chemise up top and, down below, loose-fitting panties with leg holes that you slip right into without removing a thing. Silk floral bikini underpants. Half-slips. Loved the outmoded half-slip. A woman in a half-slip and a bra standing and ironing a shirt while seriously smoking a cigarette. Sentimental old Sabbath.

No surprise that Roth got these elements from a lingerie catalogue. But who in his right mind doesn't adore the abracadabra of such writing?

Sabbath isn't sentimental about much else, however, at least among the living. He thrives on antagonism: the real reason he can't leave this earth, he finally admits—it's the book's punch line—is that "everything he hated was here." There's a lot to hate, and Sabbath goes out of his way to make his hatreds hard to swallow. ("You'll do anything," Michelle tells him, "not to be winning.") Among his principal targets are the university feminists whose very purpose, he believes, is to deceive and deform their impressionable female students. Or, as Sabbath—at his most Miller-like—describes these puritanical enemies, addressing one such impressionable student, whose head happens to be buried in his lap: "these filthy, lowlife, rectitudinous cunts who tell you children these terrible lies about men, about the sinister villainy of what is simply the ordinary grubbing about in reality of ordinary people like your dad and me." Also despicable, of course, is the "stunted argot" that these students—among others—speak. (One group that doesn't come under attack, notably, is the Jews. Roth seems finally to have exhausted the subject in *Operation Shylock*.)

But Sabbath's list of bugaboos gets worse. Half a century after his idolized older brother was shot down over the Philippines—he died a few days later, with burns over eighty percent of his body—Sabbath reserves his fiercest loathing for the people he calls "the Japan*eez*." He flies into a rage at newspaper articles that report the most ordinary political events concerning the "little flat-faced imperialist bastards" and is only slightly less angry at New Yorkers eating sushi. This is not an entirely incredible position for a man of his generation and experience. ("You lost the right to fish, you bastards, on December 7, 1941.") But Sabbath holds to the offending theme with unremitting focus and tenacity. And Roth, peeking out from behind the mask, supplies a little antagonism of his own.

Michiko Kakutani, in a murderous review in *The New York Times*, noted the book's anti-Japanese vituperation and quoted Roth on "little flat-faced imperialist bastards." She chose not to mention the character of a female college dean named Kimiko Kakizaki, whom Sabbath refers to as "the Japanese viperina" after she fires him from his teaching job for sexual misconduct with a student. (From Sabbath's outraged point of view, he is guilty of nothing more than "teaching a twenty-year-old to talk dirty twenty-five years after Pauline Réage, fifty-five years after Henry Miller, sixty years after D. H. Lawrence, eighty years after James Joyce," and so on, back to Aristophanes.) Roth had deliberately shot off a few provocative rounds at Kakutani, in exchange for her review of *Operation Shylock*. The Japanese subtheme fit easily into Sabbath's thuggish Pearl Harbor pathology. "The Immaculate Kamizoko," Sabbath spews about his viperina: "Kakizomi. Kazikomi. Who could remember their fucking names. Who wanted to. Tojo and Hirohito sufficed for him." Kakutani, with a few more rounds in her own belt, concluded her review by suggesting that few readers would be able to finish this "distasteful and disingenuous book."

Other reviewers disagreed. In *The New York Times Book Review*, William Pritchard called it Roth's "richest, most rewarding novel" and found the scene of Drenka's final hours to be "as powerful as writing can be." Frank Kermode, writing with exceptional if not atypical erudition in *The New York Review of Books*, admired Roth's "Rabelaisian range and fluency" and evoked comparisons ranging from Thomas Mann and Robert Musil to Milton as he analyzed "this spendidly wicked book." *Sabbath's Theater* won the National Book Award, and even *People* magazine got into the act, describing Mickey Sabbath as "Roth's finest, fiercest creation." It's true, though, that many of these reviews came with a warning: Sabbath was not good company for everyone. Pritchard wrote that some readers—though he thought that they were wrong—would find the book "repellent, not funny at all." (Of course, as Kermode saw, taking this kind of risk is exactly what the book's genius—Roth's genius—is about.)

Despite the numerous curses that Sabbath gives and receives in the course of the book, not all of his feeling is for desecration. Far from it. He can be yearning and ardent, especially when he remembers the people of his past. Roth had written many strong secondary figures of old men in his novels. But *Sabbath's Theater* was his first work of fiction centered on an old man since "Epstein," the short story he wrote in his twenties, when the combination of decrepitude and appetite seemed good for a laugh (if a sympathetic laugh, even then). In the intervening years, of course, he had grown and changed; he had written *Patrimony*. Roth himself was turning sixty when Mickey Sabbath came into his head. His parents, like Sabbath's, were dead. He had written about visiting his mother's grave, in *Patrimony*, and even about trying to talk to her while he stood there. This is not to say that biography is the only key to the insistent themes of time and grief and death. The mad, snow-driven cemetery scene in *The Anatomy Lesson* was written more than a decade earlier. But the feelings in the cemetery have changed. The target of the raging energy has been displaced, from an incarnation of the father to the forces that have taken that father away.

To live long is, inevitably, to escape the world of family that one wished so much, in youth, to escape. But everyone else in the family escapes, too, eventually: all gone. Roth's love for his parents and his childhood was always present in his books, even when, as in the case of Alexander Portnoy, it was nearly overmatched by anger. Twelve years after *Portnoy*, Nathan Zuckerman assures his mother (in *Zuckerman Unbound*) that his childhood was a paradise. By the time of *The Facts*, in 1988, Zuckerman is berating Roth for having become "so tenderized" by his father's approaching death that he can't even remember the hard parts of having grown up his father's son. This is the transformation wrought by age: there is nothing more to fight or resist back in the past. Mickey Sabbath is sixty-four. The most beautiful passages in *Sabbath's Theater* are his memories of childhood. The paradise that Zuckerman merely suggested Sabbath raises up before us, his memories of life on the Jersey Shore rendered in hard, clean nouns—another magnificent catalogue—as essential as the things themselves:

> There was sand and ocean, horizon and sky, daytime and nighttime—the light, the dark, the tide, the stars, the boats, the sun, the mists, the gulls. There were the jetties, the piers, the boardwalk, the booming, silent, limitless sea. Where he grew up they had the Atlantic. You could touch with your toes where America began . . . In summer, the salty sea breeze and the dazzling light; in September, the hurricanes; in January, the storms.

They had January, February, March, April, May, June, July, August, September, October, November, December. And then January. And then again January, no end to the stockpile of Januaries, of Mays, of Marches. August, December, April—name a month, and they had it in spades. They'd had endlessness. He'd grown up on endlessness and his mother—in the beginning they were the same thing.

The chant of single syllables: the light, the dark, the tide. The sudden opening to the sea, booming and silent. The months, named and colored like a child's calendar. The starting over, the casual plenitude. It's possible that not since Proust has a writer so nearly captured Time.

"You could touch with your toes where America began." A small boy stands in the water off a rinky-dink New Jersey beach, the continent rising behind him. *Sabbath's Theater* is the book in which Roth rediscovered America: the mythic, grand-scale country of promises and principles, the America of his childhood indissolubly bound to the moral victory of the Second World War. This book is the first real result of his return home. "I was back embedded in American life and it was wonderful," he said on French TV, as a little Gershwin was obligingly brought up in the background. "All my memories were useful," he went on. "The American language was useful, strong, powerful in me." Although *Sabbath's Theater* is not a historical novel, it is the first of Roth's books in which history lifts the characters in its grasp, tosses them around, and tears them apart.

And it is the first book in which Roth claims America for himself. Young Alexander Portnoy envies the little boys named John and Billy, Smith and Jones, all the blond Christians who seem to him "the legitimate residents and owners of this place." ("Don't tell me," he insists, "we're Americans just like they are.") Roughly a quarter of a century later, Morris Sabbath has no doubts that he is American. It isn't only that he has paid the price: toward the end of the book, he literally wraps himself in the flag that was sent home with his brother's body—a big flag, with forty-eight stars—and sits on the beach and cries. Since Portnoy's childhood—since Roth's childhood—more recent immigrants have replaced the Jews' sense of foreignness and longing with their own. Sabbath, with his encyclopedic knowledge of the collected recordings of Benny Goodman and his command of the vernacular, is to his Croatian girlfriend what the *shiksas* were to Portnoy. She calls him her American boyfriend. And before she dies, she remembers their good times, when he would sing along to the music: "I was dancing with America," she tells him. "Sweetheart," he replies, "you were dancing with an unemployed adulterer." But she knows better. We know better. "You *are* America," she tells him. "Yes, you are, my wicked boy."

America Amok

"The epithet 'American Jewish writer' has no meaning for me," Roth told an interviewer soon after the publication of *American Pastoral* in 1997: "If I'm not an American, I'm nothing." This position was hardly new or unique. Few artists welcome the limitations implied by category, whether as Jews or blacks or women or any other subset of the species. And the American absolutism can be traced back to the opening words of Bellow's *Augie March* ("I am an American, Chicago born"), which had been so revelatory to Roth some forty years earlier. He also insisted, in the same interview, on French TV, that "being a Jew is just another way of being an American." He had never doubted this precept while growing up, whatever the doubts and insecurities voiced by his characters (or, for that matter, the doubts and insecurities voiced by the people who had once been so worried about his characters). He had been away from the country for long enough—and, in his early sixties, had lived long enough—to command a larger view. For Roth, the return to America was as fundamentally a literary move as it was a practical or emotional one. If he was not a writer, he was nothing.

American Pastoral grew out of some pages that he wrote in the early seventies and had kept in a drawer ever since. He pulled them out every time he started writing a new book, to see if he could figure out how to use them, but nothing had come to him until now, more than twenty years later. The pages were about a politically radicalized young woman who blows up a building as a protest against the Vietnam War. Why a woman? Because, unlike the angry young men of the anti-war movement, Roth explains today, the women acted without the threat of being drafted and becoming cannon fodder. There was a "purity to their rage," he says, which made them less immediately explicable and more compelling as a subject. In *The Facts*, he recalls that Maggie's daughter, Holly—whom he renames Helen—was so outspoken against the war during her high school years in New York that she became known as Hanoi Holly. (She did not, however, blow up any buildings.) Also vital to a book about the sixties, these women were a phenomenon unique to the times: "Women were active in the anti-war movement in a way that they had never been in the suffrage movement," he says. "They were openly violent. Young, college-educated women not afraid of violence—this was extraordinary in the history of American politics and American women."

He was particularly inspired by the case of Kathy Boudin, a young woman who became a prominent member of the violent anti-war group the Weather Underground. At the time the book was finally coming into focus, Boudin had been in jail for more than a decade, for her part in a robbery that had resulted in the murder of three people. Roth was acquainted with Boudin's parents—he says that Kathy "couldn't have had a more terrific childhood"—and he had been friendly with a family who lived across the street from the Greenwich Village town house that the so-called Weathermen accidentally blew up, in March 1970, when three members of the group were assembling a bomb in the basement. All three were killed; Boudin, who had been in another part of the house, escaped and went into hiding for years. The heroine of Roth's original story was a New Jersey high school student who blows up the Princeton Library. She was not an entirely unsympathetic figure. Back in 1970, Roth tells me, he was so frustrated with the war that—however figuratively—"I was pretty ready to set off a bomb myself." He had written fifty or sixty pages and got as far as the explosion, but he didn't know where to go from there.

The answer came to him, not surprisingly, in the figure of the father. Although Roth was exhilarated by the writing of *Sabbath's Theater*, he had grown heartily sick of Mickey Sabbath: the cynicism, the anger, the relentless darkness. He found himself longing to write about "a good man," he says, and he started with a name, or, rather, a nickname: "the Swede," recalled from an actual high school hero back in Weequahic, an all-star athlete whose triumphs in the mid-thirties were still legend in Roth's era, a decade later. ("We didn't have too many football heroes at Weequahic," he says. "It was still a new school, and it was a Jewish school. We had a great band.") He began to work out everything the name evoked: blond hair, blue eyes, strong jaw, a Viking look, stature, strength, general adulation. For whom is it easier to be good, after all, than one who has been given much and who mistakes his luck for the way of the world?

The Swede's physical attributes are all the more significant given that his full name is Swede Levov—he was born Seymour Irving Levov—an oxymoronic pairing of Aryan blondness and Jewish surname. His very existence is seen as an assimilative feat. For in the Jewish community of *American Pastoral*, being Jewish is not always viewed as just another way of being American. The handsome ballplayer—"as close to a goy as we were going to get"—is openly revered by his schoolmates as "the boy we were all going to follow into America, our point man into the next immersion." Because of his looks, he is understood by everyone to be at home in America the way that most Jews were not: "an American not by sheer striving, not by being a Jew who invents a famous vaccine or a Jew on the Supreme Court, not by being the most brilliant or the most eminent"—but merely by living and breathing. An American by rights, taking his place in "the ordinary way, the natural way, the regular American-guy way." For that alone he is a hero.

But it's also the times that make the Swede a hero. The Viking looks and the ethnic unlikeliness were part of the history of the real man, one Seymour (Swede) Masin—whose son wrote a book about him (*Swede: Weequahic's Gentle Giant*) roughly a decade after *American Pastoral* received a euphoric critical reception and won the Pulitzer Prize, granting the obscure high school athlete a kind of secondary fame. Of the real Swede's history, Roth used only the name and the athletic stardom; he knew nothing more. And this was all he needed to spur his invention. He began by moving his hero forward in time a few years, so that the Swede leads Weequahic High to victory after victory not in the mid-thirties but in the early forties, during the war. It's a slight adjustment that gives his athletic feats a new significance:

> The elevation of Swede Levov into the household Apollo of the Weequahic Jews can best be explained, I think, by the war against the Germans and the Japanese and the fears that it fostered. With the Swede indomitable

on the playing field, the meaningless surface of life provided a bizarre, delusionary kind of sustenance, the happy release into a Swedian innocence, for those who lived in dread of never seeing their sons or their brothers or their husbands again.

In compensating for unbearable losses—or, at least, in distracting from them—on the very days that newspapers were reporting Luftwaffe triumphs, the unwitting boy becomes "fettered to history, an *instrument* of history." This bond with history is perhaps, ultimately, the only thing he has in common with his daughter, the builder of bombs.

The story of the Swede does not come to us directly. The first quarter of *American Pastoral* is narrated by Nathan Zuckerman, who has been restored to Roth's oeuvre in a sadly reduced state: impotent and incontinent after prostate surgery, Zuckerman, now in his sixties, lives alone in a house in the Berkshires. (For the biographical record, Roth has not had prostate cancer. In the nineties, the disease hit his brother, though, and, he says, "just about every other one of my friends.") Zuckerman is wholly devoted to his work, inspired by the example of the now forgotten author E. I. Lonoff, whom, he reminds us, he visited in this vicinity many years earlier. At times it seems that Roth has written one immensely long and surging *roman-fleuve*.

Zuckerman's physical losses are not stressed. They are presented not as problems that he longs to overcome but merely as subtractions that have left him with no functional aspects of character—no life of his own—beyond his intellect, his memory, and his ability to tell a story. He retains his curiosity about the Swede, however, whom he worshipped as a boy, back in Weequahic, when—six years the Swede's junior—he was best friends with the Swede's obstreperous younger brother. On the basis of a recent dinner with the Swede, however, their first meeting in some fifty years, Zuckerman has scornfully dismissed his former hero as merely a "big jeroboam of self-contentment": a man who (unlike Zuckerman) has never known what it is like to be "enmeshed in obsession, tortured by incapacity, poisoned by resentment, driven by anger," and for whom life rolled out "like a fluffy ball of yarn." Zuckerman's decision to write the book we now hold in our hands is based on the fact that everything he thought he understood about the man was wrong.

Why does Roth bring in Zuckerman to tell the story? The pleasure of his company is almost enough to distract us from the question, particularly during the delicious set piece of a Weequahic High School reunion, a swirling ensemble of comedy and regret—"No," one former schoolmate admits, "a forty-fifth reunion is not the best place to come looking for ass"—where Zuckerman learns that Swede Levov is dead and that the youthful Apollo lived to become a latter-day Job. In fact, this first quarter of the book provides us with all the plain biographical facts about the Swede that we will ever have: after high school and a stint in the marines, he overcame his father's objections and married a beautiful Irish Catholic girl—Mary Dawn Dwyer, Miss New Jersey of 1949 and a contestant for Miss America—but was so fundamentally dutiful that he took over his father's glove factory in Newark rather than accept a contract to play professional baseball. When their daughter was born, he moved his family to an old stone house surrounded by a hundred open acres, forty miles west of Newark, far beyond both the old Jewish slum where his father grew up and the new Jewish suburban enclaves where his father urged him to live. His dream was too big for such confinements, a true American pastoral dream.

And then, one day in 1968, his daughter, Merry, aged sixteen, planted a bomb in the local post office—or, rather, at the single post office window in the local village's small, family-run general store. A man was killed. ("The kid who stopped the war in Vietnam by blowing up somebody out mailing a letter at five A.M.," the Swede's still obstreperous brother, Jerry, tells Zuckerman at the school reunion. "Little shit was no good from the time she was born.") Merry Levov spent twenty-five years in hiding, and although her father managed to see her from time to time, he never got over what happened. As a result of it all, the Levovs divorced. The Swede went on to have a second family—three healthy sons, about whom he spoke with insufferably platitudinous sunniness the evening that he and Zuckerman met for dinner. That was just a couple of months before he died of cancer, as Zuckerman now also learns. These are the facts. There are no mysteries to be solved. Except for the biggest mystery of all: who the Swede was, how he thought ("if," Zuckerman wonders, "he even had 'thoughts'"), and how he survived.

The Swede is just the kind of hero that Roth's critics—most notably,

Updike—had been demanding for years. ("Who *cares* what it's like to be a writer?") In many ways, Swede Levov is kin to Updike's own memorably nicknamed hero, Rabbit Angstrom: not a writer (like Zuckerman) or a professor of literature (like Kepesh) or a frustrated artist (like Sabbath, the arthritic puppeteer) but an athlete, a factory owner, a nonintellectual, part of mainstream American life. According to Jerry, his brother was exactly what he seemed to be: "a very nice, simple, stoical guy." "Bred to be dumb, built for convention, and so on." "Benign, and that's it." Hardly self-searching, at least until the bomb. And after the bomb? Does a person like that change? Or, to view it another way, is a person ever really simple and unthinking? For a writer, presenting this sort of character is a unique challenge. How do you plumb the depths of a person who either has no depths or lacks the wherewithal to plumb them? How do you express, in words, the feelings of someone who does not channel feelings into words?

It's a question of consciousness. And "the problem for most seriously ambitious writers," Roth believes, is, precisely, "how do you drive the wedge of consciousness into experience?" Speaking in a video interview with David Remnick, made for (but not fully aired by) the BBC, he continued, "If you neglect consciousness, you write popular fiction; if you have only consciousness without the gravity of experience, you have the failed experiment of Virginia Woolf, where consciousness so dominates the novel that it ceases to move through time the way a novel needs to." (This said, Roth is a great admirer of *Mrs. Dalloway*.) He expands on the subject, so essential to *American Pastoral*: "Fiction invents consciousness"—not that we don't all have a consciousness but that "in books it exists in developed language." And "the Mt. Rushmore" of this language, of course, is Joyce's *Ulysses*, from which Bellow, master of fictional consciousness, learned so much. The other American master Roth admires for this kind of interior endowment of his characters is Updike. "Rabbit Angstrom's consciousness is totally an invention," Roth concludes. "John's genius is to make it seem authentic."

But this isn't the method that Roth chose in *American Pastoral*. Rather than simply (or not so simply) endowing the Swede with his own authorial consciousness—à la Joyce, or Bellow, or Updike—Roth interposed the fiction-making mind of his longtime fictional novelist. You could call the method postmodern, or you could point out, as Roth does, that Joseph Conrad, who was post-nothing, employed a similar method with Charles Marlow, his tale-spinning sailor. "Telling the story this way was second nature for me," Roth says today; "it thickens the stew." In the more formal terms he uses to address a group of students, at Bard, he speaks of the "adventure of narration."

Zuckerman is neither an omniscient eye nor a participant in the story; rather, he is a fully conscious (if wholly invented) inventor of consciousness. "Anything more I wanted to know," Zuckerman says to himself near the end of the class reunion, "I'd have to make up." And we see him begin to make it up, bit by bit. (Or, as Roth puts it, "You see how the book is made, bit by bit.") A conjecture here, an alternative conjecture there, and then, after he has eased us into the notion that he is thinking *for* his hero as well as about him, and after warning us that all these conjectures may be wrong—if no more wrong than people usually are about other people—Zuckerman vanishes into the Swede without a trace.

"I dreamed a realistic chronicle," Zuckerman says, and transports us, like the Chorus in *Henry V*, straight into its midst: a long-ago summer morning when young Merry is always in her father's lap, and when paradise seems a reasonable reward for working hard, following the rules, and being brave enough to reject the suburbs. There is no Zuckermanian irony to ruffle the Swede as he exults in owning "a piece of America" or, striding across the fields, imagines himself as Johnny Appleseed. "Wasn't a Jew, wasn't an Irish Catholic, wasn't a Protestant Christian—nope, Johnny Appleseed was just a happy American." And so is Swede Levov, a big and happy American man in an American landscape, "going everywhere, walking everywhere." Roth's nod to the famous closing section of *Augie March*—"Look at me, going everywhere!"—is all the more touching for not having been deliberate. (One afternoon when he was enthusiastically quoting Bellow's finale, I mentioned that he had used one of these phrases for the Swede. He was momentarily surprised and then said, simply, "I guess I stole that from Saul.") But pleasure in the land comes from Roth himself, not from literature—from his own piece of America in Connecticut, seen here in bucolic splendor rather than under winter snow.

Every Saturday morning, the Swede walks the five hilly miles to the general store in the village of Old Rimrock—the intact, as yet unbombed

general store, with the American flag flying out front—to get a newspaper and sometimes milk and fresh-laid eggs. And then he turns and
walks back:

> past the white pasture fences he loved, the rolling hay fields he loved, the
> corn fields, the turnip fields, the barns, the horses, the cows, the ponds,
> the streams, the springs, the falls, the watercress, the scouring rushes, the
> meadows, the acres and acres of woods he loved with all of a new country
> dweller's puppy love for nature, until he reached the century-old maple
> trees he loved and the substantial old stone house he loved—pretending,
> as he went along, to throw the apple seed everywhere.

Roth is a master of the rapturous list. Like Mickey Sabbath's conjuring of the Atlantic shore of his childhood, or his catalogue of the bounty
of female lingerie, the Swede's account of his American paradise is a
godlike naming of things that requires no embellishment: there is sufficient beauty in the names themselves, and a sense of sublime abundance in the way the sentence tumbles on and on. Swede Levov lives in
America "the way he lived inside his own skin." He is intensely grateful
for the progress that began with his grandfather, an immigrant who
spoke no English, and continued through his father, who slowly built up
the factory, and culminates in his daughter, brought up in the old stone
house in the midst of all this beauty and abundance, on Arcady Hill
Road. How could he live anywhere except America? "Everything he
loved was here."

This love marks the Swede as the perfect opposite of Mickey Sabbath,
who is unable to carry out his long-planned suicide because "everything
he hated was here." (One wonders if Roth was also half remembering
Moses Herzog's tender comment on his own childhood: "All he ever
wanted was there.") Roth builds seriatim, book to book, offering up reversals and alternatives—counterbooks, counterprotagonists—and forg-
ing links in a continuing chain of thought. For the Swede, fate and
history and his daughter will work to expel him from paradise. Although he remains steady and controlled, the antithesis of Mickey Sabbath, he is no less an example of the "assailable man." Roth says that
this vulnerability, even of the apparently strong, is the essential subject
of these two very different books, although he didn't realize it for some

time. "Here is someone not set up for life's working out poorly, let alone for the impossible," Zuckerman observes of the Swede. But who is? "Nobody. The tragedy of the man not set up for tragedy—that is every man's tragedy."

The Swede's tragedy derives from the fact that his daughter hates America. She has made that clear, with her furious rhetoric, even before she plants the bomb. Her parents were against the war, too—the Swede even traveled to Washington with New Jersey Businessmen Against the War, if mostly to appease his daughter and deflect her anger. For the loving little girl has grown up to hate her parents, too—for being bourgeois capitalists, for continuing to live their superficial lives while the Vietnamese suffer. At sixteen, she can hardly tell her parents and her country apart. Among the most affecting scenes in the book are the face-offs between father and daughter: she, arguing with all the outraged moralism of youth; he, trying desperately to protect her from the potential consequences of her idealism. Neither seems completely right, or wrong; the author's understanding enfolds them both.

To keep Merry from getting into trouble, the Swede forbids her to go to New York to meet with other, older protesters. Instead, he encourages her to campaign against the war right there in stalwartly Republican Old Rimrock, where she might really have an impact. ("Bring the war home," he says. "Isn't that the slogan?") And she does. The result: the death of a beloved country doctor out mailing a letter before heading to work at the local hospital. And Merry vanished. Not that her father cannot imagine her wending her way home, "walking northwest into a horizon still thinly alive with light, walking up through the twilight call of the thrushes":

> up past the white pasture fences she hated, up past the hay fields, the corn fields, the turnip fields she hated, up past the barns, the horses, the cows, the ponds, the streams, the springs, the falls, the watercress, the scouring rushes . . . the meadows, the acres and acres of woods she hated, up from the village, tracing her father's high-spirited, happy Johnny Appleseed walk until, just as the first few stars appeared, she reached the century-old maple trees that she hated and the substantial old stone house, imprinted with her being, that she hated, the house in which there lived the substantial family, also imprinted with her being, that she also hated.

Roth has never been afraid of risk. He hadn't been afraid of anything, really, since *The Counterlife*, after which his freedom as a writer just seemed to keep growing. In this book, there are garlands of sentences that go on for nearly a page; there are paragraphs that go on for three pages. Unlike *Sabbath's Theater* or *Operation Shylock*, *American Pastoral* is filled with different kinds of writing, from this rhapsodic Johnny Appleseed poetry, whether illustrative of love or of hate, to a rigorous realism that tells us more about the manufacture of gloves than we might ever wish to know—but that gives us the *stuff* of these people's lives. The Swede's deliberately ordinary tenor of mind excludes the buoyancy and antic humor that characterized those earlier works and, particularly in the book's more expository middle section, inclines toward a flatness of tone that is nearer to that of *The Facts*. Not all of Roth's risks paid off equally. But this was a story different from any that he'd ever told before, and he had to tell it in its own way. This book, he says, no less than *Sabbath's Theater*, came as a kind of "outpouring"— "not that it wasn't hard work," he adds, "but I loved getting to my desk every day"—and it made him feel, well into his sixties, that he was beginning anew.

For one thing, he was taking on the subject of Newark with a fullness that he had never dared before. Not the thriving immigrant city of his idyllic youth—growing more idyllic in his memory year by year— but the city apocalyptically destroyed by its own long-cheated and suffering black citizens, during several days of riots, in the summer of 1967, when Roth has the Swede barricaded in his factory behind windows plastered with cardboard signs reading "Most of this factory's employees are NEGROES." Roth had touched on the squalor of post-1967 Newark in *Zuckerman Unbound*, in the rants of Alvin Pepler and in Zuckerman's own final ride through his old neighborhood, in a hired limo with an armed driver, saying to himself, "Over. Over. Over. Over. Over."

Some eight years before the riots, however, in *Goodbye, Columbus*, Roth gave us a very different and, in retrospect, extremely poignant view of the city in transition. Neil Klugman, on an errand, goes to visit Patimkin Kitchen and Bathroom Sinks in central Newark, in the old Third Ward, a neighborhood formerly Jewish but even then "the heart of the Negro section." And he is struck not only by the changes but by the continuity. The kosher delicatessens and the Turkish baths are hanging on; the lingering smells of corned beef and sour tomatoes now mix with the odors of auto-wrecking shops, a leather factory, and a brewery. Instead of hearing Yiddish on the streets, he hears the shouts of Negro children playing at being Willie Mays. The older Jews have died off and their prospering offspring have left for the mountains west of the city; and "the Negroes," Neil observes, "were making the same migration." Those left behind live in hopeless poverty. But Neil's only uncertainty is whether any new people will come to fill these streets when both the Jews and the Negroes have moved on.

Progress, of course, was not as reliable as he'd thought. In *American Pastoral*, the rampaging crowds don't torch the Swede's factory, because of those cardboard signs—put in place by the factory's black forewoman— but crowds of white vigilantes (or, the forewoman suspects, Newark cops) shoot out all the sign-bearing ground-floor windows. The factory stands, but in the middle of a burned, looted, and soon-to-be-emptied wasteland, as businesses deserted Newark en masse and virtually every- one who could get out got out. (Roth's parents had moved away years earlier, after both their sons had left home. In 1967, they were retired and living in Elizabeth.) By the time that Roth was writing this book, in the mid-nineties, Newark had lost a third of its population and no new people had come to fill its streets; the FBI ranked it the most violent city in the country. The city no longer holds that terrible title—it ranked at number twenty in the country in 2012—and it has its share of fans and boosters. But, in conversation, Roth compares his beloved Newark to Atlanta under Sherman or, worse, he says, to Carthage, be- cause of the finality of the destruction.

In *American Pastoral*, the bricked-up factories are as monumental and as culturally meaningful as the Pyramids: "as huge and dark and hideously impermeable as a great dynasty's burial edifice has every his- torical right to be." The spree that sealed the city's fate—"sirens going off, weapons firing, snipers from rooftops blasting the street lights, loot- ing crowds crazed in the street"—is evoked with the awful exuberance of freedom grabbed like goods through broken glass:

> Here it is! Let it come! In Newark's burning Mardi Gras streets, a force is
> released that feels redemptive, something purifying is happening, some-
> thing spiritual and revolutionary perceptible to all. The surreal vision of

household appliances out under the stars and agleam in the glow of the flames incinerating the Central Ward promises the liberation of all mankind. Yes, here it is, let it come, yes, the magnificent opportunity, one of human history's rare transmogrifying moments: the old ways of suffering are burning blessedly away in the flames, never again to be resurrected, instead to be superseded, within only hours, by suffering that will be so gruesome, so monstrous, so unrelenting and abundant, that its abatement will take the next five hundred years. The fire this time—and next? After the fire? Nothing. Nothing in Newark ever again.

James Baldwin warned of "the fire next time" back in 1963. Roth describes its arrival, four years later. The Swede refuses to close his factory and join the exodus, not because he is a hero but because he is afraid of giving his daughter one more reason to condemn him. ("*Victimizing black people and the working class and the poor solely for self-gain, out of filthy greed!*") But staying in Newark makes no difference; nothing makes any difference. Merry replaces the old Weequahic football pennant that she'd hung above her desk with a handmade poster labeled "WEATHERMEN MOTTO": "We are against everything that is good and decent in honky America. We will loot and burn and destroy. We are the incubation of your mother's nightmares." And then, in February 1968, seven months after the riot, she plants her bomb. (Roth was somewhat premature in suggesting Merry's engagement with the Weathermen. The group was not formed until 1969.) First the country, then the city, then the family. No escape. All apocalypse, all the time, and no end to the torturing questions.

The single overriding question for the Swede and, therefore, for the reader, is: how did Merry become so filled with hate? What did her parents do wrong? He thinks of many possible answers, and is informed or accused of even more, each painful in a different way. Growing up, Merry developed a serious stutter—humiliating, impossible to master— and the bomb was the way that she let out her rage. She is the ungainly daughter of two beautiful parents: more rage to be visited on an indifferent world. Or, perhaps, there was no personal rage: the bomb was the result of understandable trauma after she saw, on television, when she was very young, a Buddhist monk immolate himself in protest of the war. ("Do you have to m-m-melt yourself down in fire," she asked, "to bring p-p-people to their s-senses?") Perhaps they were too liberal as parents (this is his brother Jerry's nasty charge), or fatally insistent on a WASPy decorum that she could not resist blowing to oblivion (Jerry, again). Or, more tormenting still: the Swede impulsively kissed her on the lips once, when she was eleven. Could that be it? He had pulled away from her a little, physically, after that, just to make it clear that there would never be another transgression. Had he pulled away too far? Had she even noticed? He had loved her, her mother had loved her. But responsibility had to fall somewhere. Didn't it?

The answers that readers gave to these questions—their opinions of the arguments and the characters who make them—prompted a new look at Roth's position in regard to the upheavals of the sixties. He had long been considered a spokesman for the counterculture, however much he rejected the position, thanks to the unforgettable *Portnoy* and to the not-quite-forgotten *Our Gang*, in which Trick E. Dixon ends up campaigning for Devil, in Hell, on his claim of having turned Southeast Asia into Hell on earth. It wasn't difficult for some readers to view *American Pastoral*, with its anti-war heroine so out of control, as a social and political recantation. In *Commentary*, by then a home of liberal recantation, Norman Podhoretz wrote that he "detected in this book a born-again Philip Roth" who appeared to have "changed sides," and he claimed there was a question in the air: "Had Philip Roth turned into a neoconservative?" Outside of Podhoretz's assumptions, supporting the various movements of the sixties hardly meant supporting the Weathermen. Even the less ideologically entrenched, however, wondered if the book contained a condemnation of "the culture of liberal permissiveness," and assumed that the Swede's ideals of parenthood had created a monster.

Nixon aside, Roth aims to keep his books from representing any single position. "I don't write about my convictions," he insists. "I write about the comic and tragic consequences of holding convictions." There is hardly anything that he considers more crucial to his work. Indeed, one of the great strengths (and sources of confusion) in Roth's novels—as opposed to his political satire—is that he rarely takes an open stand. Countervoices clutter up every discernible argument, even shout it down. The long-simmering Jerry, for instance, finally unleashes the competitive little-brother fury of a lifetime, letting the Swede know, in no uncertain terms, that he has brought his fate upon himself, through both the hubris of his aspirations and his sentimental misunderstanding of the country:

> You wanted Miss America? Well, you've got her, with a vengeance—she's your daughter! You wanted to be a real American jock, a real American marine, a real American hotshot with a beautiful Gentile babe on your arm? You longed to belong like everybody else to the United States of America? Well, you do now, big boy, thanks to your daughter. The reality of this place is right up in your kisser now. With the help of your daughter you're as deep in the shit as a man can get, the real American crazy shit. America amok! America amuck!

Jerry has no doubts about anything. He possesses the strongest voice in the book, and he wields it like a weapon. Continuing his rant against the Swede, he provides readers with all the evidence that they might want to blame the catastrophe of Merry on liberal ineffectiveness:

> You're the one who always comes off looking good. And look where it's got you. Refusing to give offense. Blaming yourself. Tolerant respect for every position. Sure, it's 'liberal'—I know, a liberal father. But what does that mean? What is at the *center* of it? Always holding things together. And look where the fuck it's got you! . . . You made the angriest kid in America.

The trouble with Jerry's accusation is that we, the readers, have already seen the Swede maintain a firm line with his daughter. In forbidding her to go to New York, in insisting that she carry on her anti-war activities in their own small town, he is not being particularly permissive. True, he isn't the old-time grandfather pummeling his son into obedience in the basement. He persuades Merry through endlessly patient discussion—but, still, he gets her to do what he wants: restrict her activities to a safe and harmless place. And his actions literally blow up in his face.

Or, as Roth says to me about Jerry: "Of course, he's wrong." The character was tremendous fun to write—"to beat somebody down is wonderful!" Roth shouts, imitating Jerry, whom he freely describes as "a kind of brute"—but that doesn't mean he has any insights into his brother's life. "That's what you want to do if somebody is wrong," Roth adds. "You want to make him persuasive." (In *Operation Shylock*, a liberal Israeli journalist fears that the loudmouth settler leader will have just this kind of persuasive power if "Roth" puts him in a book.) But what has the Swede done wrong? The detailed realism of the book obscures a problem that goes back to Job, not to mention Kafka's Joseph K., who is arrested one fine morning without having done anything wrong. The Swede's search for an answer only adds to his anguish. Because there is no answer, or only an answer that doesn't solve anything. "He had learned the worst lesson that life can teach," Zuckerman concludes about his hero: "that it makes no sense."

Roth had no trouble suggesting the origins of pain and anger in troubled characters in earlier books: Lucy Nelson in *When She Was Good*, with her weak and drunken father, or even Alvin Pepler in *Zuckerman Unbound*, with his lifetime of corrosive disappointments. But Merry Levov is a child of the sixties, and the facts of history may be all that is required to explain her tragedy. *American Pastoral* is a book *about* a time in national history. The wartime sixties are not merely glimpsed in the background but constitute a force that "comes up and smacks you right in the face," Roth said in an interview on Dutch TV: "The history is vivid, gross, overwhelming." Talking about Kathy Boudin to me one day, he says that he believes "she wouldn't have killed anybody" had she grown up in another era. The same thing, he adds, is true of Merry: she would have stuttered, she would have rebelled, but it's highly unlikely that her rebellion would have resulted in anybody's death. "Somehow the moment joined with their temperamental rebelliousness," he says about the well-brought-up American kids who blew up buildings.

Merry's mystery is preserved, dramatically speaking, by a narrative that never presents her alone. We watch her develop through the Swede's eyes, we hear her voice as she argues with him, but we are never privy to her thoughts, and, once the trouble begins, we never follow her to wherever she goes when she leaves home. This is deliberately done: we have no more information than her bewildered father does; we are assaulted by the same uncertainties. This identification with the father, rather than with the child, may be seen as a shift in Roth's perspective, hardly surprising for a writer in his sixties. Yet even in the early seventies, just a couple of years after *Portnoy's Complaint*, Roth was unable to move forward with a book built principally around the bomber. He says that he was "too close to the war" at the time. But there is also a question of authorial temperament. Portnoy's rage is based on unseverable love; *Our Gang* is fiercely protective of a country under assault by its leaders. Roth is fully able to characterize the kind of destructive rage that Merry and her gang represent, or to satirize it, but it does not seem that he could comfortably inhabit it. In a serious book, he could apprehend the bomber only from the distance of another's eyes.

The tension of being confined within the limits of the Swede's mind becomes almost unbearable, however, with the appearance of another young female terrorist, who presents herself as an emissary from Merry, in hiding, and who calls herself Rita Cohen. Roth has described Rita, to his Bard students, as his hero's "real nemesis," and one can see why: she torments him sexually (Roth tells me that in writing Rita he had "the sex symbol of the Weathermen," Bernardine Dohrn, in mind), she cons him out of a lot of money, and she makes no sense in terms of anything that he ever thought he knew about young women, systems of values, or the human heart. As Roth sees it, she is the worst sort of ideologue: a figure incapable of change—fixed, immovable, a monomaniac. The Swede's lack of knowledge about her, or, especially, about her connection to Merry, is true to his point of view but also frustrating and sometimes confusing to the reader. (Is Rita protecting Merry? Is she exploiting Merry? Does she even *know* Merry?) She is ultimately too mysterious—a force, rather than a character.

Merry herself makes even less sense to her father when he finally locates her, on a tip from Rita, living in a horrific dump in downtown Newark, just an hour's drive from Arcady Hill Road. Emaciated, reeking of her own filth, she tells him tonelessly that she has killed three more people, out in Oregon, with another bomb. But she is now a Jain, part of an Indian religious sect that harms absolutely nothing: she doesn't wash because she reveres even vermin, she veils the lower half of her face with the foot of an old stocking to keep from inhaling microbes in the air. She speaks sensibly, without a stutter, and she is completely mad. The Swede, driven nearly mad himself, wants to bring her home. But he can't tell his long-suffering wife what he has found.

Dawn Levov is an unusual figure in Roth's work: a wholly loved and (for most of the book) loving wife. Dawn is proud, hardworking, self-invented—she rejects her given first name, Mary—and she dismisses her beauty pageant past as embarrassing and superficial. (Roth himself treats this past with considerable interest: the buzz of Atlantic City, the frighteningly long runway, the ever-present chaperones, and, of course, the gloves. A friend of his, the actor Ron Silver, had been having an affair with an ex–Miss America, and through her Roth met the more vintage Miss America of 1950, who schooled him in the elements of postwar pageantry.) Dawn isn't particularly funny or winning or unusual—she's no Drenka—but she's strong enough to have married outside her narrow Catholic milieu, and she is illuminated by her husband's love.

The book includes a few pages of the couple having passionate and loving sex, which Roth admits were not in his original drafts. One of the trusted readers to whom he gave the manuscript, Judith Thurman, told him that it was important to know about the couple's sex life. He had thought that it did not much matter—and, he tells me, "I wanted people to get off my ass about sex"—but he realized that she was right. And since "the cliché would be that he's such a square kind of guy and she's such a good Catholic girl that the sex would be inhibited," he says, he decided to go in the opposite direction and to make the Levovs "an exceptionally passionate married couple." Happily monogamous, too, until the bomb.

The Swede has one brief and unimportant affair in its aftermath, when Dawn has turned away from him, and from life. He has been leading her back to both ever since. He takes her to an expensive European clinic for a face lift—to erase the signs of grief—and he spends the night after the surgery on a bed beside hers, getting her through the pain. (Roth tells me that he based this scene on an experience that he had with his famous actress wife, and for a moment he's as enthusiastic as the Swede about the surgical restoration of a beauty's beauty.) He is building a new, modern house for him and Dawn to live in, because she can't bear the memories of Merry in the old one. The architect delivers a cardboard model, very like the model that Roth had made when he was intent on leaving his own memory-filled house. It turns out to be a terrible portent. On the same day that the Swede finds Merry, he realizes that Dawn is having a not brief, not unimportant affair.

They are giving a party. A barbecue, really, at the old stone house, since the Swede's parents have arrived from Florida for their usual end-of-summer visit—it is Labor Day 1973, five and a half years since the bombing—and the Swede has invited a few other couples whom the elder Levovs will be glad to see. He spies Dawn with the architect, in the kitchen, doing more than just shucking corn. The new house, he realizes, is being built not for him and Dawn but for them. He will be cast aside with the rest of her old life. Yet, in the very midst of these betrayals, with every reason for resentment and rage, he sits down and takes his wife's hand:

> There are a hundred different ways to hold someone's hand. There are the ways you hold a child's hand, the ways you hold a friend's hand, the ways you hold an elderly parent's hand, the ways you hold the hands of the departing and of the dying and of the dead. He held Dawn's hand the way a man holds the hand of a woman he adores, with all that excitement passing into his grip, as though pressure on the palm of the hand effects a transference of souls, as though the interlinking of fingers symbolizes every intimacy. He held Dawn's hand as though he possessed no information about the condition of his life.

Come what may, he continues to hold her hand right up until the end.

The party scene is a narrative tour de force. Beginning just after the book's personal universe has been reduced to its most claustrophobic—the father and daughter facing off in her tiny, airless room—it opens the view in all directions. Set on a terrace behind the old stone house, looking onto the surrounding fields, and with a dozen candles burning as night comes on, the scene is a much grander version of the Chekhovian late-summer dinner that concludes *The Professor of Desire*, and offers a deeper mixture of emotions. There are now ten at table—including a number of people we have never met before, each distinctively limned—plus the strongly felt specters of the child who is gone forever and, for the Swede, of the terrifying woman that she has become. People come and go, connive and betray, have arguments and assignations, in a Mozartean ensemble that extends over ninety-seven pages, with duets ceding to trios and septets, with tragedy punctuated by comedy (or is it the other way around?), while the Swede drifts in and out of his memories and seems entirely alone.

It has often been asked why Zuckerman does not return at the end of the book, to round off the story and perhaps to let us know what he has learned in writing it. Roth admits that he initially had such a conclusion in mind, "like the end of a television program," he tells the students at Bard. "It didn't dawn on me as quickly as it should have that this is a stupid cliché—a 'frame,'" he adds dismissively. "So I just decided he would get out of the way." (In support of this decision, he points out that the narrator at the beginning of *Madame Bovary*, a boy who went to school with young Charles Bovary, disappears after a few pages and is not heard from again.) Roth is clearly not interested in narrative formulas. Yet the closing party is in almost stately formal balance with the high school reunion near the book's beginning: two ensemble set pieces that surround the central story with warmth, humor, and a populous richness that does not so much cushion the blows—of Zuckerman's isolation, of the Swede's—as set them off.

This closing scene is bound to history from its opening words: "It was the summer of the Watergate hearings." The elder Levovs have been glued to the television, watching the hearings all day and the replays at night. Lou Levov, the Swede's father, is a ringer for the elder Mr. Zuckerman, or Mr. Kepesh, or Mr. Roth: opinionated, dominating, exasperating, profoundly humane. (Herman Roth, during the Watergate hearings, sent daily letters to the participants and once included a bar of soap in a letter to Kissinger, informing him that, after Cambodia, he couldn't wash his hands enough.) Whether Lou is carrying on about "Mr. Von Nixon and his storm troopers," or forcing a glass of milk and a piece of pie on the architect's alcoholic wife (pushing aside her glass of Scotch and feeding her, forkful by forkful), he is a powerhouse and (no surprise) nearly runs away with the scene. Yet Lou Levov is also a man besieged. These old campaigners against the world's disorder have always been besieged, the odds have always been against them, ever since Herman Roth had to leave school to earn a living. But they come through: they support their families, they do the job of what Roth, in *Patrimony*, called "making themselves American. The *best* citizens." This man has never felt uncertain that he is right about the way to live, or that, if he works hard enough, the right will prevail. Until now.

The strong but assailable man. Roth's feeling for him certainly goes back to Herman Roth, but it also goes back to Philip Roth, starting out in his twenties, target of the rabbis and husband of the undivorceable Maggie. The discussion that takes place at the Levovs' dinner table that evening is about politics, pornography, and decency—carried on with all the urgency of argument and opinion that characterized those years, when the world seemed to be spinning away. "This is the morality of a country that we're talking about," Lou says. And it does seem that nothing less is at stake when, late in the evening, Lou emits a very different cry—"Oh my God! *No!*"—that is a response not to Merry suddenly appearing in her rags, as the Swede imagines, but to the architect's drunken wife having taken the fork from Lou's aggressively well-meaning hand and stabbed the old man in the eye. Or nearly in the eye. Her aim is off by a luckily drunken inch. The scene has the crazy gut punch of slapstick, and the last sound we hear is laughter. Yet the once unassailable Lou Levov is suddenly face-to-face with the truth that his son is still trying to master: "He could not prevent anything." The undoing of these good men, no less than the fires of Newark, marks the end of a civilization.

Nevertheless, *American Pastoral* was considered so sympathetic to Merry that, a few years after its publication, Roth was asked to write a letter in support of the parole of Kathy Boudin. Although there are more differences than similarities between the figures—Boudin was in her thirties when she took part in an ostensibly political crime that involved killings, Merry in her teens—the parallels are clear. Yet he declined to write the letter. In part, he tells me, he felt ill equipped to judge the reality: "I'm a novelist, but I'm not Émile Zola." Stronger feelings emerge when we talk about the fact that Boudin was ultimately released, on her third request for parole, in 2003, and Roth says he believes that "she should have stayed in jail for the rest of her life." Merry Levov, however, as a careful reader of the book's first section will note, was never captured. After her father discovers her whereabouts, he continues to see her, in hiding, and to love her without cease until she dies. Books, as Roth is the first to point out, are larger than the people who write them. They contain possibilities—thoughts, emotions, kinds of wisdom, kinds of folly—that emerge, unplanned and unforeseen, from the writing itself.

Betrayal

S*abbath's Theater* won the National Book Award in 1995. *American Pastoral* won the Pulitzer Prize in 1998. In between the two, in 1996, Claire Bloom published *Leaving a Doll's House*, containing several chapters about her marriage to Roth that gained him more public attention than his own achievements. Although the memoir officially covered the span of Bloom's life, with accounts of her first two marriages and several glamorous affairs—Richard Burton, Laurence Olivier, Yul Brynner—no one (including Bloom) appeared to be much interested in anything but her "harrowing account" (in the words of the opening sentence of the Sunday *New York Times* review) of her life with Roth. The verdict was in even before the book was out. A month before publication, the *Times* ran an article titled "Claire Bloom Looks Back in Anger at Philip Roth," announcing that advance copies were already circulating and that gossip was "considerable." The *Los Angeles Times* reported a rumor that "Noo Yorkers" weren't even circulating the whole manuscript, just the "good part." *Vanity Fair* ran a chapter; *New York* magazine ran a cover story headlined "A Hell of a Marriage." The gist of the book, according to the *Times* article, was that Roth was filled with what Bloom described as "a deep and irrepressible rage" toward women and was—in the article's own summation of the charges—"a self-centered misogynist." This was clearly something that people couldn't wait to read.

Overall, Bloom had four chief and chiefly reported-on subjects of complaint. (1) Less than two years into their relationship, Roth had pressured her into asking her eighteen-year-old daughter, Anna, to move out of her London house. Although Bloom was an extremely successful woman in her forties, she writes, "the truth is that I was unable to oppose him," and was therefore "willing to jettison my own daughter." It was a grave mistake, although Anna "eventually" returned home. (2) Roth gave the name "Claire" to the character of the betrayed wife in the manuscript of *Deception*. This time, Bloom was able to oppose him, and to prevail. She reported that she still wore his "guilt offering" of "an exquisite gold snake ring with an emerald head from Bulgari on Fifth Avenue." (3) Roth's breakdown, in 1993—three years into their marriage—was, for her, an agonizing emotional roller-coaster ride, during which his behavior was unpredictable and often cruel. He accused her of being no help at all when he was ill. On one occasion, visiting him in the psychiatric hospital, she became so upset that she was kept overnight herself. (4) After deciding to end their marriage, Roth was unwilling to extend himself financially beyond the "unconscionable" terms (her lawyer's word) of their prenuptial agreement. The hundred-thousand-dollar settlement he finally offered did not even pay for a one-bedroom apartment in New York. In need of money, she was forced to take a job on a daytime soap opera.

There is much more, some of it fond, much of it ugly, all of it written by a woman who seems to be contending against herself—struggling to be less passive, more independent, a better mother—as much as against the frustrating men in her life. ("I knew that this should be simply an affair, but my needs overwhelmed my knowledge," she writes, not about Roth but about her second husband, who receives the nickname "the Unmentionable.") None of the men come off well, with the possible exception of Yul Brynner, who retains a handsome bravado, perhaps because he keeps his distance. Still, in a poor field, Roth—"spectacularly manipulative"; "a game-playing, Machiavellian strategist"—is easily the worst, and so it is rather dismaying when, toward the end of the book, after a meeting with Roth over coffee some eighteen months after the marriage ended, she reports herself distressed because he doesn't "want our old life back."

Bloom's indictment had a tremendous effect on Roth's personal reputation—perhaps more than anything since *Portnoy's Complaint*. Of course, not all reviewers were sold on her point of view. In the *London Review of Books*, Zoë Heller picked up hints that the pain in the marriage was perhaps more evenly inflicted than Bloom acknowledged—on the evidence of lines such as "I felt unfairly misunderstood and just started screaming"—and called the book a cautionary tale to female readers about "the dangers of economic dependence." But few reviewers questioned Bloom's facts or even conceded that they might be questioned. In the *Times* review, Patricia Bosworth noted that Bloom "has collected the facts—she draws on her journal, conversations with lawyers, psychiatrists and friends." (On the highly charged issue of Bloom's daughter leaving home, Roth offers the additional facts that Anna had gone to live in her school's residence hall, twenty minutes away, for a single semester. And that after her return he lived with both Anna and her mother for half of each year for another decade. So much for Machiavelli.) But for many readers, women especially, Bloom's account was confirmation of all the bad old accusations. There was undeniable pleasure in the idea that—in the teasing words of Marion Winik, in the *Los Angeles Times*—"Portnoy is getting his."

Still, there was only one assessment that really disturbed Roth. In 1999, John Updike published a single sentence about Bloom's book in an essay on literary biography in *The New York Review of Books*. Discussing the rise of a genre he termed the "Judas biography," written by a former spouse or friend to repay a grudge, Updike wrote, "Claire Bloom, as the wronged ex-wife of Philip Roth, shows him to have been, as their marriage rapidly unraveled, neurasthenic to the point of hospitalization, adulterous, callously selfish, and financially vindictive." Roth wrote a letter to the *Review*, suggesting a slight emendation of the sentence's all-important verb: "Claire Bloom, as the wronged ex-wife of Philip Roth, alleges him to have been . . ." Updike responded in print with an affable shrug, stating that the change was fine with him but that he thought his words conveyed "the same sense of one-sided allegations." Roth did not agree. The wounds had not entirely healed, and he felt betrayed by a friend who ought to have known better—who had actually *seen* them together and had told *New York* magazine, as Roth still easily recalls, "how proud and protective Philip seemed of her." He never spoke to Updike again.

Roth was stunned by Bloom's book. The last time he'd seen her, after all, was at that apparently friendly postdivorce date over coffee, in

March 1995. She'd written to him afterward to say what a good time she'd had—there was an exchange of several warm and mutually complimentary notes—and they had vaguely planned to meet again. In some ways, he still doesn't hold her fully responsible for the book: he had worked with her on an earlier memoir, an account of her acting career titled *Limelight and After*, and he says that she's too good a writer to have written anything as dreadful as this second memoir by herself. He thought of bringing a lawsuit. But then, he tells me, he knew that the issue would hang over him for years, and this wasn't where he wanted to put his energies.

He got out of New York, much as he had got out after *Portnoy*, leaving for the peace and quiet of Connecticut—"my private Yaddo." He was accompanied on weekends and vacations by a new steady girlfriend, a doctor just completing her residency, whom he had met in a movie line. (*Schindler's List*; mixed reaction.) She cheered him up by writing out a timeline of the events of his life, which showed Bloom's book as a tiny dot. This, he says, helped to put things in perspective. But, as with all novelists, if more openly so, Roth's books have a personal germ as well as an intellectual one. In *My Life as a Man*, he wrote—and demonstrated—that he was "as incapable of not writing about what was killing me as I was of altering or understanding it." Walking in the Connecticut woods, he tried to imagine an analogy for the way he felt now.

"To me it seems likely that more acts of personal betrayal were tellingly perpetrated in America in the decade after the war—say, between '46 and '56—than in any other period in our history": Nathan Zuckerman's former high school English teacher, Murray Ringold, is expounding on the period loosely called the McCarthy era, sitting on Nathan's back porch in the Berkshires in the summer of 1997. Murray is ninety years old. Nathan is sixty-four, and they are reminiscing about a man each loved in a different way—Murray's brother, Nathan's youthful idol—who had been denounced as a Communist in 1952 and died in ruin and disgrace. The analogy was workable. All that was required back then, after all, was an unsupported accusation from a supposedly reputable source to wreck a person's life. The historian Arthur Schlesinger had told Roth that there were probably as many acts of betrayal perpetrated during the Revolutionary War, but that was not an ideal period for a book set in Newark. And the late forties and fifties were Roth's era: he had started college in 1950, when Senator McCarthy produced his first public list of "Communists" in government; it was the first major public issue of Roth's adult life. During the Army–McCarthy hearings, in the spring of 1954, he rushed between his classes and the home of a teacher who owned a television, Bob Maurer, to watch McCarthy finally brought down. The issues had mattered to him then, and they mattered again now. His new subject was betrayal, public and private.

But few novels—and certainly not Roth's novels—follow a single line of thought: the process of composition is too long, the byways of memory and imagination too complex. *I Married a Communist*, published in 1998, is also about a boy's longing to become a man. In Roth's view, the subjects are not unconnected. He gives the young Zuckerman his own adolescent passions: the same books that Roth piled into his bicycle basket—baseball titles by John Tunis, *Citizen Tom Paine* by Howard Fast—are piled into Zuckerman's. The stirringly patriotic radio broadcasts that shaped Roth's sense of the purpose and beauty of language shape Zuckerman's desire to be a writer. There are several pages devoted solely to Norman Corwin's V-E Day broadcast, *On a Note of Triumph*, with its poetic vernacular and its mythicizing spirit. All that was required was to be twelve years old and sitting by the radio in 1945, Nathan recalls, to feel that "you flood into America and America floods into you."

It is the radio era in which the growing up and the betrayals take place, a fact as important as the different kinds of betrayal that the novel explores. Norman Corwin is Zuckerman's faraway boyhood hero, but the close-up heroes who come after him replace not only Corwin but Zuckerman's devoted yet disappointingly unheroic father. ("We lost Nathan when he was sixteen," Mr. Zuckerman tells people, sadly. "By which he meant," Nathan explains, "that I had left *him*.") Long before the events of *The Ghost Writer*, Zuckerman is seeking (and outgrowing) a whole series of spiritual fathers—men with big lives or big ideas, men with things to teach him—and betraying the father he loves. It's what he has to do on the way to achieving "the orphanhood that is total, which is manhood," he says. "When you're out there in this thing alone."

The romance of manhood in Roth's work has never been on fuller display, with the brave and the brawny viewed through young Nathan's worshipful eyes. In the opening pages alone, "masculine" and "male" and "manly" pile up thickly, as Nathan describes what it was like to have gruff, forceful Murray Ringold—Hero No. 1—as his high school

English teacher. An aberration in a profession filled with women, Murray, recently back from the army and the Battle of the Bulge, reveals both teaching and literature to be permissibly masculine pursuits. This was a signal realization for Roth, too. His grade school teachers had all been women (except for gym, which hardly mattered), and the impact of his first male high school teacher, Bob Lowenstein, was considerable. Lowenstein, too, was back from the war, but he didn't teach English; he monitored Roth's homeroom in freshman year, making announcements and taking care of school business. Still, even without the literary mentorship that Roth adds to Murray's powers, the example came through—when Lowenstein got back in touch in the early nineties, after more than forty years, Roth remembered him well and wrote back eagerly. His presence had been a kind of legitimization: the first real sign, Roth says, that "I could attach brains to manliness."

It isn't just Murray's emphasis on critical thinking—crucial as that is—or his innate "masculine authority" but his willingness to heave a blackboard eraser at a laggard student that releases the "masculine intensities" in boys like Nathan. Murray's biggest gift is to teach the tame and well-brought-up Weequahic boys to transgress, to subvert, to say, "I don't give a good goddamn"—in short, to be free. Whether he has taught anything to the girls is not a question Nathan thinks to ask. The ideal of manhood as freedom from the "cramped up and sivilized" world of women goes back at least to Huckleberry Finn, never mind to Alexander Portnoy. It's a rite of American literary adolescence, boys' division. For Nathan, who actually rather likes the civilized aspects of his mother's house, becoming a man is a matter of careful study and conscious effort, with rules of behavior that extend right down to the "manly" way to eat a piece of pie in a bar and grill.

Nathan's greatest mentor is Murray's brother, Ira Ringold: Hero No. 2, and the central figure of the book, a counterpart of Mickey Sabbath and Swede Levov. Ira is tied to the world not by love (like the Swede) or by hate (like Sabbath) but by a burning desire for justice and by the pleasure of exerting his will to get it: "Everything he wanted to change was here." Twenty years older than Nathan, Ira is a Communist by conviction and a radio star by circumstance. A giant of a man at six feet six, and the product of a brutalizing family—the only Jewish family in Newark's all-Italian First Ward—Ira left high school to dig ditches and to work in the zinc mines of northern New Jersey, then joined the army right after Pearl Harbor. Roth modeled Ira on one of the heroes of his own youth, a left-wing ex-GI named Irving Cohen ("*the* ex-GI in my life," Roth says), who had married Roth's older cousin Florence, a huge, rough guy who told stories about being beaten up in the army because of his outspoken views—as Ira is beaten up and called "a nigger-loving Jew bastard" for protesting army segregation. Roth admired the "manliness" of all the GIs coming home, but speaking about Irving Cohen in the Web of Stories interview, he says explicitly, "I brought to him my appetite to be a man." He sounds exactly like Nathan speaking about Ira, who "brought me into the world of men." There's a sense of nearly military induction into an idealized, wartime world of soldier-heroes that Nathan—like Roth—was too young to experience himself.

But Ira turns out to be disastrously flawed, and Nathan's ardor expires before he's out of high school. From the excitement of listening to Ira's colorful workman's lingo—expressions like "yellow-dog contract" are as compelling to the budding writer as Drenka's language is to Sabbath—and of admiring his camaraderie with actual working-class men, Nathan comes to see Ira less as a hero than as a psycho: uncontrollably angry, potentially violent, and wearyingly predictable in his political harangues. And that's long before he learns that Ira murdered someone, at sixteen, and was a diehard member of the Communist Party—an apologist "for Stalin's every villainy." The analogy with Roth's personal predicament doesn't hold, of course, since Ira is guilty of the charge of being a Communist, if not of further trumped-up charges of being a Soviet spy. (No one ever catches up with him for the murder.) It would have been too pat a story, Roth informs me—and too familiar— if Ira were completely innocent. It's the feeling of the era that Roth was after: the end of the golden age of heroism and the retreat into an ever-looming American darkness of irrationality, demagoguery, and lies.

Yet Nathan has learned that, even in a golden age, not all soldiers were heroes. That's part of his growing up, too. And Ira himself is finally shown to be no more a villain than he was a hero. He is, above all, a Roth protagonist of the late nineties: a man caught up in the grinding machinery of history. As Murray sees it, his brother was "an action machine," entirely gullible both politically and morally, and barely capable of self-reflection: "another innocent guy co-opted into a system he didn't understand."

Roth has once again set himself a narrative problem that clearly fascinated: how to render the consciousness of a man who is not entirely aware that he has one. The solution, this time, is even more complex than it was in *American Pastoral*, involving not one narrator but two. The discussion between Murray and Nathan turns out to be the book's controlling structure, straight to the end. The former student and teacher have run into each other after some forty years, when Murray, still avid for learning, enrolls in a summer course at a college in the Berkshires: Athena College, where E. I. Lonoff once taught, although either Roth or its administrators have modified its name, which used to be Athene. It's just a short distance from Nathan's isolated hillside home.

Nathan remains much as we last saw him: living alone in a modest two-room cabin, largely cut off from human contact, devoted to writing and nothing else. (The spartan cabin is based on Roth's writing studio, which stands a couple of hundred feet from his beautiful, spacious house; that's just one of the many differences between character and author.) Nathan is afraid even to invite his ancient friend to spend the night, out of fear of undoing his determined indifference to the intimate presence of another person. But he invites Murray back to talk—mostly about Ira—for six long summer evenings. Nathan himself takes over the tale from time to time, filling in his own experiences and at times inventing what he cannot possibly have known. Roth tells me that he sees Murray and Nathan "like two basketball players bringing a ball down the court, each dribbling for about fifteen seconds before passing the ball to the other," each adding pieces of the story to form a whole.

Two voices sounding in the dark. It's an ingenious scheme for a story that rests on memories of radio, and the book contains affecting tributes to the conjuring powers of speech—tributes that, to judge from Roth's oeuvre, are personal and heartfelt. ("The book of my life is a book of voices," Zuckerman tells us. "When I ask myself how I arrived at where I am, the answer surprises me: 'Listening.'") In practice, however, the scheme does not really work. I don't believe there is a book by Roth in which the voices are dimmer or less engaging, and in which, at the same time, they obscure the characters and actions they describe. Including Ira: the murder and the rages and the intractable beliefs are all painstakingly detailed but never dramatized. Saul Bellow complained to Roth, in a lecturing letter about the book, that Ira was "the least attractive of all your characters"—but the greater problem is that he never comes alive.

The book contains one wonderfully vibrant scene at a New York party; a couple of strong appearances by Nathan's always invigorating father; and a few occasions when Nathan and Ira make visits to local workmen—a taxidermist, a guy selling rocks outside a mine, an ex-GI with a mattress factory—whose distinctive voices make an impact and help bring the book to life. But there are too few such scenes of human commingling, or direct action, and returning to the narration feels like returning to a cage.

This is because, for the most part, Murray's side of the story consists of expositional chunks enclosed in quotation marks. He does not pass the ball back after fifteen seconds; his virtual monologues go on for ten or more pages at a time. And while Nathan initially tempts us with the promise that Murray, as a teacher, had a special talent "for dramatizing inquiry, for casting a strong narrative spell"—this is on page one—he later acknowledges that the voice has become "totally dispassionate," "more or less unvaried, mild," and marked by "a certain blandness." It is also stiff and oddly literary, even for a former English teacher. (It was so difficult to imagine a ninety-year-old saying, "His recourse to violence was the masculine correlate of her predisposition to hysteria—distinctive gender manifestations of the same waterfall," that I bought the audiobook to hear Ron Silver speak the part. Silver is marvelously adept, giving Murray a faintly Yiddish urban wise-guy edge that relieves his blandness. Much of the book, in fact, is aided by Silver's reading, which provides vocal tics and colors not seen on the page, although this particular line remains impossible.) Nathan's stories of his adolescence bring a steady pulse to the book, assured and energized. But when he joins in about Ira, he sounds hardly different from Murray: measured, calm, flat. There is a lot of wisdom in these pages, on subjects from families to utopianism, and some passages of profound beauty, but they are muffled by the steady narrative drone.

Roth claims that *I Married a Communist* is a favorite among his books, giving as his reason the fact that Ira Ringold is such an uninhibited, explosive character: "a hothead," as Roth likes to put it. He explains that there's a lot of freedom in writing about such a figure, a lot

of open emotional space. But he may also have something of a protective attitude toward a work that was not received with the seriousness
that he had poured into it—because of its incitement to exactly the sort
of gossip that he had sought to avoid by leaving the city, and which the
book roundly mocks in an aside about "the unifying credo of the world's
oldest democratic republic. In Gossip We Trust." Roth's outrage over
Bloom's book did not end with the evocation of an accusatory age. He
went much further than that, and he must have known that no reviewer
could resist the bait.

Ira Ringold is undone by his marriage to a beautiful actress with
perfect diction and an insufferable daughter—"a big adult baby who is
still living at home," and who cannot stop demanding that her mother
pay for maternal crimes long past. They are a closed family of two, with
emotional room for no one else. The daughter is a bully, verbally and
physically; the mother merely cowers in response. Ira is warned that
this monstrous child's unappeasable rage "will doom your household
from the start." And it does. But it is the wife, named Eve Frame, who
dooms everything else: culturally pretentious and a secretly Jewish anti-
Semite, she is giddily submissive to any show of strength. When the
marriage fails, she is persuaded by crusading right-wing snobs to write
a lurid exposé titled *I Married a Communist*—in which the term "Machiavellian" appears large.

The book is published in 1952, and Ira is blacklisted. A few years
later, Murray is hauled before a panel of the House Un-American Activities Committee, convening in Newark, and loses his teaching job.
(This was the actual experience of Bob Lowenstein, several years after
he was Roth's homeroom teacher; like Murray, he refused to "talk," and
was reinstated only several years later, as the result of a lawsuit.) In one
of the book's more animated scenes, Murray is defended in a courtroom
outburst by his fourteen-year-old daughter, Lorraine, a boldly virtuous
counterpart to Eve's wretchedly spoiled daughter, Sylphid—just as Murray's Bronx-born wife, Doris, is a salt-of-the-earth counterpart to Eve. It
was in the interests of a realistic world picture that Roth created this
second mother-daughter pair, he says: "It's not all betrayal."

There is a long if not quite noble tradition of literary revenge, from
D. H. Lawrence's malevolent portrait of Ottoline Morrell in *Women in
Love* and Doris Lessing's acid portrayal of her former lover Nelson

Algren in *The Golden Notebook* (Lessing even keeps his distinctive first name) to a fair number of pages of the collected works of Mary Mc-Carthy. Certainly, Roth meant to get his own back. But he neglects the vengeful program for a while when it comes to Sylphid—Roth, one recalls, likes to give his opponents the best lines—and she becomes, briefly, the most engaging presence in the book. ("We learn from Shakespeare that in telling a story you cannot relax your imaginative sympathy for any character," Murray tells Nathan, then adds, "But I am not Shakespeare.") Sylphid is the main reason that the New York party scene is so lively and engrossing. Seen in action, at last, and in a large ensemble, she is sly, honest, and very funny as she guides Nathan through a roomful of phonies who happen to be her mother's treasured guests. She's also extremely kind to poor "Nathan of Newark," bewildered by the cutlery and the doubtful edibility of his first artichoke. One anticipates further escapades, but it's not to be; the narrative corrals her back into her one-note relationship with her mother. Surely an author has the right to choose his subjects, but here the desire for revenge seems to contract Roth's novelistic freedom.

Reviews carried titles like "The Wrath of Roth" and "Roth Bites Back." Few failed to mention Bloom; *Publishers Weekly* dismissed the whole three-hundred-plus-page effort as "a thinly disguised vendetta." More than one reviewer pointed out that Roth had done himself more damage than Bloom had, and that he had gone a good way toward proving her charges. The word "misogynist" was back in common use, as even the most steadfast of Roth's admirers among female critics registered complaints. (No surprise, perhaps, that Roth got off easier with the men—Robert Kelly, in *The New York Times Book Review*; Todd Gitlin, in the *Chicago Tribune*—who saw the book largely as a "gripping novel" about politics.) In *The Boston Globe*, Gail Caldwell found a good deal to praise—including, I should say, the novel's joint narration—but found that the "caricatured demons" of Bloom and her daughter entirely overwhelmed the rest. In *The Guardian*, in Great Britain, Linda Grant went so far as to say that she would "rather read a dozen books of Rothian misogyny" than "a single page of Alison Lurie or Carol Shields or Margaret Atwood or Annie Proulx"—but make no mistake: "If there ever was a misogynist, Roth is one." (One cannot help recalling Harold Bloom grumbling over Doris Lessing's "crusade against male human beings.") And in a generally skeptical review in the daily *Times*, Michiko Kakutani—who had welcomed *American Pastoral* with ardent, ungrudging praise—found the new book "hogtied to a narrow, personal agenda" and a retreat to Roth's old "sexual wars and mirror games." Her review was titled "Manly Giant vs. Zealots and Scheming Women."

Despite his provocations, Roth was confounded by the renewed accusations of misogyny. He considers himself a man who loves women, and he counts many women among his close and lifelong friends. While Bob Lowenstein meant a lot to him as a teacher, his most important mentor in critical thinking was Mildred Martin, at Bucknell—who was one of those lifelong friends. He has certainly been angry at a few women in his life, but also at a few men. *I Married a Communist* is about many different things besides Eve and Sylphid. His books contain an immense variety of female characters, of every moral and emotional persuasion. And they are no more "good" or "bad" than his male characters; as a novelist, he couldn't afford to present things otherwise even if he thought that way, which he does not. His work was being misread by some contemporary feminists as it had once been misread by Jews—and for reasons not so very different, involving the depiction of flawed or comically conceived characters. With Henry Miller dead and Norman Mailer faded from view, he had become their major foil—a useful and perhaps necessary foil.

He had jabbed back at his feminist critics, it's true—but he championed the social and sexual freedom of women no less than he did that of men. Indeed, in his scheme of things, the freedom of men depended on women also being free. Surely that was clear if one read his books with an open mind, unimpeded by contemporary cant. And so he believed that he could explain himself—as he believed he could explain himself to a Yeshiva University audience in 1962—to a group of doubting and staunchly feminist college students in 1999. *I Married a Communist* is very much about the power of teaching, after all.

In the fall of that year, Roth agreed to join his friend Norman Manea in teaching a seminar on half a dozen of Roth's novels at Bard, the classes already referred to here. Each week, Manea led a session on a given volume, and the next day Roth came in to speak and answer questions. Manea habitually told Roth about the subjects discussed during the previous session, so Roth was aware, on the day that he was to talk about *I Married a Communist*, that the book had generated considerable anger among the young women in the class. There were about fifteen students in all, and women were in the slight majority, or perhaps it only appears this way on the videos that I've seen of the classes, because they do more of the talking. This was not the first time that dissatisfaction with various female characters had been expressed; in fact, such dissatisfaction had been a constant theme of the discussions.

Roth begins the class by lecturing on several subjects—the postwar period, narrative techniques, Joe McCarthy—and reads a passage about Murray's daughter, Lorraine, noting that her defense of her father is "the most touching single act of loyalty in the book." He appears apprehensive, and he is clearly responding to the objections that Manea has conveyed. None of the characters in the book are meant to be "likable," he tells the class; they are meant to be real. "I invented her," he says of Eve Frame, who betrays her husband, "but I didn't invent Linda Tripp." Nor did he invent daughters who hate their mothers: "But let's take a look at it. Don't be frightened of it." The class is relaxed, mostly quiet—there's a laugh just at the mention of Monica Lewinsky—and it is now open to questions.

At first, the students seem intimidated. But then a young woman speaks up, expressing the belief that Roth's male characters are "round" while his females are "flat"—or, at least, not as "grounded in complexity or sympathy." Roth asks her if she feels that way about Amy Belette/Anne Frank in *The Ghost Writer*, and she retreats, but the subject has been broached, and another young woman, her face angelic and her ear studded with tiny rings, offers a reformulation: "We are never inside the heads of the female characters—it's like a secondhand view." Manea reminds her that, at the *Sabbath's Theater* session, the students concluded that they could indeed get inside the mind of Drenka. ("I feel more about Drenka," she admits. Roth notes with relief, "I wasn't present at the *Sabbath's Theater* battle.") Roth asks to hear what was said during the previous session, and a male student ties himself in knots trying to explain something about "the nature and structure of gender relations . . . which I've taken very seriously." Pressing a point about dogma, Roth reads from a book about the trial of two Soviet writers accused of slandering the People by failing to present their characters as "good" citizens. "We're not putting you on trial!" the young women call out, comfortingly.

At times, though, the scene seems oddly like the satirical trial in *Deception*, particularly as Roth sums up and addresses complaints that have accumulated over several classes, yet seems never quite to be getting through. One student thought that Hope Lonoff was an "undeveloped character," he notes, apparently because she did not leave an unsatisfying marriage; another said she didn't find Maria Freshfield as "admirable" as she was meant to be. The underlying rub with these characters, Roth surmises, is that they "don't embody values that you respect"; like Eve Frame, they are "insufficiently forceful and assertive." But such women exist. Many types of women exist. And why has Lorraine been censored out of everyone's reading, he asks—because she doesn't fit the theory? Writers write about individuals, not about types. And if this is really a literary issue of "flat" and "round," why haven't these questions been raised about any of the male characters? Why hasn't anyone complained that Ira is a murderer? Finally, making no apparent headway, and exasperated: What if the women *are* flat? Or round? Why can't they go on to another subject? "What I really don't understand," he says, "is how this discussion hijacks every class."

An earnest young woman who has not yet said a word now volunteers: "Because of our ridiculous historical moment. Because all of our classes are about gender. I have to deal with lit classes where we talk about Joyce's portrayal of women, and Tolstoy's." She is clearly unhappy with this aspect of her education, and it seems momentarily that Roth's point about dogma has prevailed. And then one of the equally earnest young women who began the debate responds, suggesting that her generation is too liberated to identify with the female characters in *most* of the literature they read in school. Growing up, she says, she identified with the heroes in books, with the men, "and that creates some confusion." No one thinks of connecting her longing for a heroine with young Nathan's exhilaration at having a male teacher, after years of being taught by women; or with how much this sense of identification and legitimization meant to him.

Instead, Roth thinks of a connection with a different sort of lesson—a broader one, perhaps. Making a parable of his answer, he tells the students that, after growing up in "an extremely Jewish environment," he found that there were very few Jews in literature at all, aside from some figures "to make fun of" in T. S. Eliot or Hemingway. How could he be expected to "identify" with the characters of a Christian writer like Dostoyevsky? How? Through literature itself, he tells them—literature, in which we can identify with anyone and become larger than ourselves. But class time is nearly up, and the two sides seem to have fought to a draw. Not a truce. If nothing else, Roth pleads, finally, doesn't this discussion get to be *boring*?

Point of view is among the most crucial aspects of Roth's writing. "I found the right people" is a reason that he often gives for a book's particular power, but finding the right outlook on these people is even more important. With very few and rather compromised exceptions—some of the early stories, parts of *Letting Go*, *When She Was Good*—there are no omniscient narrators in his books. Always, *someone* is telling (or, as with Sabbath, channeling) the story, even when, as in *American Pastoral*, the storyteller obligingly disappears. This may be one reason that Roth sticks to the narrators who have been successful: his enormous bibliography clusters around a not enormous group of narrators' names. It's true that these storytellers are notably similar in their biographies to the author: Zuckerman, Kepesh, and, needless to say, "Philip Roth" are all male, all Jews who grew up in the thirties and forties. Even Amy Bellette's fantasy of being Anne Frank—a lengthy, dramatic, heartbreaking narration about a young woman, much of which takes place "inside her head"—turns out to be the fantasy of Nathan Zuckerman, although he is no more perceptible on the page than when he is telling the story of Swede Levov. The utterly free mind of Mickey Sabbath sets the tone for the freest of Roth's novels; the mind of the Swede brings forth a different kind of order, a different kind of thought, a different kind of sentence. Roth's way into a story is through a particular voice, a pair of eyes. But it's what these faculties convey that matters. Especially in these later books (and even in books with major failings, like *I Married a Communist*), there is an endless human carnival to be observed—a carnival of men and women, too. If the klieg lights are anchored in wartime New Jersey (they have to be anchored somewhere, don't they?), their beams sweep the sky.

Literature, which makes us larger than ourselves. In *I Married a Communist*, Nathan gets a lesson in the difference between politics and literature from his final mentor, a young college professor who dismisses Nathan's proud attempt at a Corwin-style radio play and argues, somewhat schematically, against making arguments in books. "Politics is the great generalizer," he begins, "and literature the great particularizer, and not only are they in an inverse relationship to each other—they are in an *antagonistic* relationship." The words that follow seem as close to a credo as Roth has ever written:

> As an artist the nuance is your *task*. Your task is *not* to simplify. Even should you choose to write in the simplest way, à la Hemingway, the task remains to impart the nuance, to elucidate the complication, to imply the contradiction. Not to erase the contradiction, not to deny the contradiction, but to see where, within the contradiction, lies the tormented human being. To allow for the chaos, to let it in. You *must* let it in. Otherwise you produce propaganda, if not for a political party, a political movement, then stupid propaganda for life itself—for life as it might itself prefer to be publicized.

Nathan's feet are now set on the path to holy art and Henry James and E. I. Lonoff's front door. And then onward to short stories and to books that will antagonize anyone who wishes to read an approvable message.

But if, for the writer, this is a book about starting out, it is also about ending up. Nathan has been cut down, sickened, sexually incapacitated—we learned of his prostate surgery in *American Pastoral*—and he insists that he no longer has a story to tell. "He's now of an age when people come to tell him their stories," Roth says to the Bard class, "not of an age when he's going to tell them *his*—an astonishing change." It seems possible that the eager, glowing students understand this part of his message even less (and, certainly, identify with it less) than with the other things he's said. Nathan explains his retreat from the world as part of a long tradition—the shack in the woods, the place where you go, in the end, to "absolve yourself of striving":

> The place where you disrobe, molt it all, the uniforms you've worn and the costumes you've gotten into, where you shed your batteredness and your resentment, your appeasement of the world and your defiance of the world, your manipulation of the world and its manhandling of you. The

aging man leaves and goes into the woods—Eastern philosophical thought abounds with that motif, Taoist thought, Hindu thought, Chinese thought. The "forest dweller," the last stage on life's way. Think of those Chinese paintings of the old man under the mountain, the old Chinese man all alone under the mountain, receding from the agitation of the autobiographical. He has entered vigorously into competition with life; now, becalmed, he enters into competition with death, drawn down into austerity, the final business.

This quietly wise and beautiful passage must be labeled, I suppose, "late Roth." Although Nathan is not finished yet.

The Fantasy of Purity
Is Appalling

Roth's condemnation of the American propensity for "gossip as gospel, the national faith" seemed uncomfortably prescient when *I Married a Communist* was released, in the fall of 1998, just eight months after Bill Clinton's affair with Monica Lewinsky had commandeered the nation's attention. But, as Murray Ringold points out, Senator McCarthy hardly originated the American show trial: rather, he took us "back to our origins, back to the seventeenth century and the stocks. That's how the country began: moral disgrace as public entertainment." Nothing had changed.

Although the public fiasco was sufficient reason for Roth to have Clinton on his mind, he had private reasons, too. Earlier that year, Clinton had secured an emergency visa for Roth's friend Emmanuel Dongala, a Congolese writer who had attended college in the United States in the sixties and had been unofficially adopted by Roth's close friends and Connecticut neighbors, C. H. Huvelle and his wife, Mary. Dongala—like Primo Levi, a chemist as well as a novelist—had returned to the Republic of the Congo, where he was the dean and a professor of chemistry at the university in Brazzaville and where he was trapped for months with his wife and children after civil war broke out. As a first step toward bringing him back to the United States, Roth alerted Leon Botstein, the president of Bard, who immediately offered Dongala a job. After attempts to get him a visa failed, Roth wrote a letter to Clinton—whom he had never met—but received no reply. And then William Styron took Roth to lunch at a Connecticut restaurant and mentioned that he was going to a ceremony at the White House the next day. Roth drove back to his house, got a copy of the letter, and asked Styron to put it directly into Clinton's hands: "Don't let him put it in his pocket. Make him read it right there." The visa came through the following day, and visas for Dongala's family soon afterward. That summer, Roth met Clinton at a party on Martha's Vineyard, and, Roth recalls today, the first thing the president said was, "Is your friend all right?" Clinton had just spent hours testifying about Lewinsky, and, Roth adds, "he looked battered, like he'd spent fifteen rounds with Muhammad Ali."

In November 1998, Roth was awarded the National Medal of Arts and attended a ceremony at the White House himself. It was just after the midterm elections, and the Democratic victory made it seem that the worst had passed, although the question of impeachment still hung in the air. The president and Mrs. Clinton, dispensing the honors together, appeared ebullient. The citation that Clinton read was thoughtful and apt: "What Dublin was to Joyce or Yoknapatawpha County was to Faulkner, Newark is to Philip Roth." But when he introduced Roth as a "grand old man of American letters," Roth, stepping forward to receive the medal, entered into a brief whispered exchange, which Clinton relayed into the microphone: "He just told me he really isn't that old. Hillary told him it was a literary expression."

Roth was already working on what amounted to a historical novel about that very year. After completing *I Married a Communist*, he told an interviewer for Dutch television, he'd begun to wonder: would it be possible to "treat 1998 the way you treat 1970 or 1948?" Culturally speaking, the moment seemed riveting, and it was a challenge to seize history as it was being made. He was not focusing on the Clinton scandal, nor was he writing about anyone directly affected by it—as Swede Levov had been affected by the events of his own time. Rather, he was exploring the country's "moral mood." Or, as he writes at the beginning of *The Human Stain*, published just two years later: "If you haven't lived through 1998, you don't know what sanctimony is." Much of the book takes place in the summer of that year, at the moment of "an enormous piety binge, a purity binge, when terrorism—which had replaced communism as the prevailing threat to the country's security—was succeeded by cocksucking," and when "life, in all its shameless impurity, once again confounded America." Nathan Zuckerman dreams of a mammoth Christo-like banner draped across the White House and emblazoned with the legend A HUMAN BEING LIVES HERE.

If *American Pastoral* and *I Married a Communist* are about people crushed by history, the third book of Roth's American trilogy is about people determined to escape it, by fleeing the past and strategically remaking themselves. The goal was hardly new to Roth's protagonists. As recently as *I Married a Communist*, Nathan Zuckerman recalls that, as a Jewish child, "I didn't care to partake of the Jewish character . . . I wanted to partake of the national character." But it is too easy to localize the national habit of escape: personal reinvention—what Roth calls "the high drama that is upping and leaving"—is one of the biggest American themes. It unites such unlikely representatives of our communal aspirations as Jay Gatsby, Alexander Portnoy, and the hero of *The Human Stain*, Coleman Silk, a light-skinned black man who passes for white throughout his adult life.

The issue for Silk is not self-hatred or hatred of his race: the issue is freedom. Freedom from all that his father endured. ("The impositions. The humiliations. The obstructions. The wound and the pain and the posturing and the shame.") Freedom from "society's most restrictive demarcations." Freedom from being part of a despised "they" and part of an equally tyrannous "we"—"the we that is dying to suck you in, the coercive, inclusive, historical, inescapable moral *we*." Silk has escaped from his race not because he longs to be white but because he longs to be unrestrictedly human. (It's difficult not to recall Alexander Portnoy, at fourteen, railing, "Jew Jew Jew Jew Jew Jew! . . . *I happen also to be a human being!*") To Zuckerman, who discovers the truth about Silk only after his death, there is something almost heroic in the way that he severed himself from his loved and loving but ineradicably Negro family, "in order to live within a sphere commensurate with his sense of scale." There is a faint echo here of the end of *Gatsby*, where Fitzgerald writes of man's glimpse of "something commensurate to his capacity for wonder" in newfound America itself. Coleman Silk's decision to cross the color line, made when he joined the navy in 1944, a month before he turned eighteen, makes him, in his own eyes—and in Zuckerman's— "the greatest of the great *pioneers* of the I."

It's clear why Silk becomes important to Zuckerman. The fact that

Silk pretends to be Jewish is an added irony, since Jewishness provides a convincing cover not only for his physical appearance—"the small-nosed Jewish type," Zuckerman initially sizes him up, "one of those crimped-haired Jews of a light yellowish skin pigmentation"—but also for the ostensible absence of living relatives and the uncertain origins of dead ones. What other group could have provided such a credible familial dead end? ("There was a whole generation of Jews like that. They never really knew.") Adding to the cover, his Jewish wife's abundantly frizzy hair promises a ready excuse for any racially telltale symptoms that their children might reveal. (Silk himself was circumcised, for hygienic reasons; his mother was a nurse.) But there are no symptoms. All four Silk children grow up with no doubts that they are fully white; the youngest, seeking his roots, becomes Orthodox. And when Silk is murdered, his killer has no doubt that he has eliminated a "two-bit kike professor" and a "Jew bastard."

Coleman Silk is a professor of classics, and *The Human Stain* is to some degree a campus satire, in the mode of Mary McCarthy's *The Groves of Academe* or Randall Jarrell's *Pictures from an Institution*. Like those earlier works, it has scores to settle. Betrayal is still on Roth's mind, although this time the subject is bound up not with politics but, rather, with the cultural politics that one might say have "hijacked" the discussion in American classrooms. (Roth had stopped teaching by this time; the Bard experience, he tells me, finished him off.) Professor Silk has twice run afoul of the Department of Languages and Literature of little Athena College, where he served as dean for many years and where, at nearly seventy, he stepped down from his position to return to teaching. In the first instance, a female student complained that the plays by Euripides assigned in his course were "degrading to women," and the head of the department—French, female, twenty-nine years old, with a degree from Yale and a vocabulary blighted by terms like "narratology" and "diegesis"—chastised him for "fossilized pedagogy," specifically for "the so-called humanist approach to Greek tragedy you've been taking since the 1950s." (Oh, for the good old 1970s, when all the Professor of Desire had to complain about were structure, form, and symbols.)

Second, and far more serious, when two students failed to show up for the first six weeks of class, Silk casually threw out the question "Do they exist or are they spooks?" Since the word "spook" has been used historically as a degrading reference to African Americans, and the students in question turned out to *be* African Americans, Silk found himself accused of racism. The charge was so ludicrous, yet so debilitating in its humiliations—meetings, hearings, investigations—that he treated it as a terrible joke until his healthy sixty-four-year-old wife died suddenly, of a stroke. It was then, after arranging for her burial and before quitting the college in a fury, that he came banging on Zuckerman's door, demanding the well-known writer's help. Because a book is the only way that such a thoughtful, law-abiding, cautious man—the opposite of Roth's last hero, Ira Ringold—can think of to obtain revenge.

Zuckerman turns him down. He barely knows this enraged man. And, of course, Zuckerman is a damaged man himself. Not owing entirely to the effects of cancer surgery but certainly aided by them, he remains confined to "a rigorous reclusion such as that practiced by religious devouts." He is sixty-five. It has been five years since he undertook this isolated non-life. In the first two books of the trilogy he remained true to his vows, keeping his distance from the action and serving essentially as a repository of memory or as an imagination-for-hire. Such a setup suited Roth at the time, and it suited Zuckerman. But five years is a long time to spend alone, and Coleman Silk stirs something in Zuckerman that opens him again to friendship, to participation in the story, and to the fears and dangers he had fled.

It's a dance, of all things, that seals the bond. What an unlikely scene for Roth: two men doing an impromptu fox-trot, on a porch in summertime, while on the radio Sinatra sings "Bewitched, Bothered and Bewildered." The impulse to dance comes from Silk, exhilarated by a new love affair that has finally wiped out the "spooks"-related bitterness—two years have gone by—and made him a new man. He is seventy-one and the woman is thirty-four: the summer of 1998 was notable not only for Clinton-Lewinsky but for the advent of Viagra, which the classics professor says should have been called "Zeus." Rapturously virile again, still possessing the strength and bounce of the high school boxer he once was—"a snub-nosed, goat-footed Pan"—Silk is as attractive to poor, unmanned Zuckerman as the manly heroes he worshipped as a boy. The pull of the Eros of life sweeps over him as Silk, shirtless in the summer heat, leads him dreamily across the floor. "I hope nobody from the volunteer fire department drives by," Zuckerman says. But, while the dance is not in any way a carnal act, he assures us, it is more than satire. As far as Zuckerman knows, it's his last romance.

The book that Zuckerman eventually produces, after Silk is dead—he tells us, before it's finished, that it's titled *The Human Stain*—is very different from the book Silk wanted him to write about how the college killed his wife. It is about race. It is about having secrets. It is about lust and rage—two old standby subjects that Silk himself elevates by tracing them, in his teaching, to the wrath of Achilles and the fall of Troy: Western literature born from a fight between two infuriated men over a girl. (It's enough to enlarge one's perspective on the ten-dollar pills that guarantee Silk's potency—and that's the idea.) Yet for all its differences from the book that Silk thought he wanted, *The Human Stain* embodies precisely the "humanist approach" that Zuckerman's hero—Roth's hero—lived for. Determinedly rational and informed by history, Roth's twenty-third book treats a wider range of human conduct and human failings than the author ever had before, and with a quiet sympathy unmatched in his earlier work.

Again and again, Roth introduces a figure who, in outline, suggests a comic pawn or a sociological stereotype—the chic young department head with her academic jargon; a long-abused woman who works as a janitor at the college; a disturbed Vietnam vet who is the janitor's ex-husband—and then adds layers of complexity that give them breath. Silk's young French nemesis, Professor Delphine Roux, turns out to be almost as brave a self-creation as Silk himself, and (equally surprising) more caring toward the students, more humane. If she is an ideologue, she is a disarmingly inept and uncertain one—no Rita Cohen, she is painfully if stumblingly open to change. Murray Ringold, in *I Married a Communist*, admits that he was unable to follow the Shakespearean counsel that "you cannot relax your imaginative sympathy for any character." In this book, Roth takes the lesson to heart.

While *The Human Stain* is an advance in social amplitude, it is also something of an old-fashioned novel. There are no narrative adventures, no doubling of characters, no battles with reality. The world is what it is, as firm and clear as the language Roth uses to describe it: straightforward language, with little patience for lyric lingering—the landscape poetry of *American Pastoral* is nowhere to be seen—yet both forcefully intelligent and shaped with ease. There's the fresh idiom of an old man finding himself "down to the last bucket of days"; of a young woman's "American flashbulb radiance." The typically unassuming use of terms like "string along" tempers even Nathan's mountaintop pronouncements: "The secret to living in the rush of the world with a minimum of pain is to get as many people as possible to string along with your delusions." Roth has accumulated a lot of wisdom over the years, and, if his tone has become more sober than ebullient, the results have their own satisfactions. Meticulously plotted, and with a climax of thriller-like tension, *The Human Stain* is characteristically Rothian only in that its hard-won wisdom is unapologetically shaped as a page-turner.

As a catchphrase, "the human stain" might initially be thought to refer to the evidence on Monica Lewinsky's notorious blue dress, so often is the affair discussed by various people in the book. ("She had the goods. Collected a sample. The smoking come.") And it does relate to Clinton, or, at least, to the banner that Nathan wants to drape across the White House. The person who comes up with the phrase is the book's heroine, Faunia Farley, who is the janitor at the college and the woman with whom Coleman Silk is having an affair. Tall, blond, from a rich and privileged background, Faunia isn't beautiful; she's drawn, thin-lipped, with an unsettling hardness to her gaze. But she was a beautiful child. She has become who she is—"exiled from the entitlement that should have been hers"—after being sexually abused by her stepfather from the age of five and, at fourteen, running away; at twenty, she married a dairy farmer, a Vietnam vet who started beating her when the farm went broke. (With painful irony, Silk uses the phrase "a gift of the molestation" to describe both Faunia's sexual skills and her emotional damage. It's a sign of the tendentiousness of present-day assumptions about Roth's attitude toward women that the often admirable professor Amy Hungerford, teaching a course at Yale on "The American Novel Since 1945," in 2008—it's available on YouTube— ignores both character and context to present Silk's words as flatly literal. Reminding her students—at Yale!—that "molestation is never a gift," she offers the phrase as proof that "Roth, in case you haven't noticed, is a very misogynist writer.")

If anything, Roth tries too hard to make Faunia an interesting woman; although she draws us in repeatedly—she's mocking, wounded, smart—the various aspects of her character never quite cohere. But this may be the result of the extreme nature of her life's experience, far outside both the everyday norm and the norm of Roth's fiction. Roth based her on a woman he knew in Connecticut, who, like Faunia, had been abused as a child and had run away to nothing. He tells me that he has come across many women with such stories in the countryside, women whose lives were stunted by family abuse or violent mates and who work at whatever jobs will pay the rent. The model for Faunia worked in an electrical supply store and lived, toward the end of her abbreviated life, in dingy industrial Torrington—in a "Torrington motel," two words that Roth says he cannot put together "without aching."

Roth made his heroine's situation even worse—"That's what novelists do," he says, shrugging—giving her two children who died in a fire when a space heater tipped over while she was parked out front in a pickup truck with a man. Two years and a couple of suicide attempts later, she keeps their ashes in a canister under her bed. Yet if Faunia is broken, she remains very much alive—Roth also gives her a stoic calm that is not exactly the same as strength but will do in its place. Faunia loves birds, especially crows, and she has a long and striking inner aria about what these widely unbeloved birds mean to her. "No crow goes hungry in all this world. Never without a meal. If it rots, you don't see the crow run away. If there's death, they're there. Something's dead, they come by and get it. I like that. I like that a lot. Eat that raccoon no matter what. Wait for the truck to come crack open the spine and then go back in there and suck up all the good stuff it takes to lift that beautiful black carcass off the ground." Faunia would very much prefer to be a crow.

When Faunia needs to secure her sense of calm she drives to the local Audubon preserve, where she communes with a caged, misfit crow, a bird that was hand-raised by humans and, when freed, is attacked by other crows because he doesn't know how a crow should sound; he learned to caw by imitating the schoolchildren who stood outside his cage imitating crows. "That's what comes of hanging around all his life with people like us. The human stain," Faunia says, without a hint of condemnation. *"That's how it is."* Like Roth, for whom this clear-eyed acceptance is one of life's great virtues, Zuckerman admires Faunia for acknowledging what other people pretend not to see, and he elaborates her thoughts into a near theology of impurity:

We leave a stain, we leave a trail, we leave our imprint. Impurity, cruelty, abuse, error, excrement, semen—there's no other way to be here. Nothing to do with disobedience. Nothing to do with grace or salvation or redemption. It's in everyone. Indwelling. Inherent. Defining. The stain that is there before its mark. Without the sign it is there. The stain so intrinsic it doesn't require a mark. The stain that *precedes* disobedience, that *encompasses* disobedience and perplexes all explanation and understanding. It's why all the cleansing is a joke. A barbaric joke at that. The fantasy of purity is appalling.

The fantasy of purity: it's an even more explicit version of the idea of "letting in the repellent" that Roth exemplified in Mickey Sabbath. Seen in a historical context, it's about the suffering that has been caused by this "insane" fantasy: sexual purity, racial purity, religious purity. (Primo Levi, in *The Periodic Table*, also praises impurity, for giving rise to "changes, in other words, to life," and to the dissension and diversity that fascism forbids.) It shouldn't come as a surprise by now that the most famous Jewish writer of our time is a devoted pagan. With no less an affinity for the Greeks than Coleman Silk—or Faunia Farley—Zuckerman continues to think about the human stain, and the image in which all of us were made:

> Not the Hebrew God, infinitely alone, infinitely obscure, monomaniacally the only god there is, was, and always will be, with nothing better to do than worry about Jews. And not the perfectly desexualized Christian man-god and his uncontaminated mother and all the guilt and shame that an exquisite unearthliness inspires. Instead the Greek Zeus, entangled in adventure, vividly expressive, capricious, sensual, exuberantly wedded to his own rich existence, anything but alone and anything but hidden. Instead the *divine* stain.

And what is the quest to purify, he asks, but *more* impurity?

Faunia loves the creature with the imitated voice and the fabricated life, as she loves Coleman Silk. Faunia, too, is a self-fabricated being, an impersonator: she pretends to be illiterate so that she can live untouched by expectations, at the bottom of the heap. And Silk loves Faunia. Not only her body, although that is plenty—there is a wry yet shimmering scene in which she dances naked for him, to Gershwin. He also loves her dignity and her gameness: "Because that is when you love somebody," he says, "when you see them being game in the face of the worst." Despite the difference in social status, she is his spiritual mate and his comrade-in-arms, so uninterested in judging that he's free to tell her his secret. And, at last, really to be free. Free from a lifetime of observing conventions and campaigning for legitimacy and preserving respectability: all the restrictions that he bought into when he took up full-time pretending. Faunia is the real "onslaught of freedom, at seventy-one"—barely in time.

And then Silk receives an anonymous letter: "Everyone knows you're sexually exploiting an abused, illiterate woman half your age." It has obviously been written by the tremendously addled Delphine Roux, in whose view the lowly janitor can signify no more to the professor than "a misogynist's heart's desire": "the perfect woman to crush." For everyone else in town, it's an easy leap from remembering that Silk was called a racist to believing him a misogynist now: "Simply to make the accusation is to prove it." We are back in the atmosphere of *I Married a Communist*. But we are also sited squarely in the summer of 1998, when "the righteous grandstanding creeps, crazy to blame, deplore, and punish, were everywhere out moralizing to beat the band."

"Everyone knows." These words, in Roth's work, are almost guaranteed to mean that what follows is outrageously wrong. Because most of what we know about anyone is wrong. If there is a great repeating theme in the American trilogy, this is it. But it's a theme that has long been embedded in Roth's work, in the matter of counterlives and counterarguments, in the multiplicities that we turn out to contain. "You must change your life." And if we hardly know ourselves, "what are we to do about this terribly significant business of *other people*?" Zuckerman poses the question in *American Pastoral*, after he realizes how wrong he has been in assessing Swede Levov—"That's how we know we're alive: we're wrong"—and decides to take up the Swede's story. To make up the Swede's story. It's a narrative technique and a philosophy: Zuckerman continually spinning a wholly convincing hypothesis about a character, then discovering his error and spinning it around another way. "*Nobody* knows," he insists, in *The Human Stain*. "You *can't* know anything. The things you *know* you don't know. Intention? Motive? Consequence? Meaning? All that we don't know is astonishing." So, again, he makes up a story, filling in the parts that are plainly blank.

(Did Faunia really know Silk's secret?) "For better or worse, I can only do what everyone does who thinks that they know. I imagine. I am forced to imagine. It happens to be what I do for a living." Zuckerman does what we all do, only better. And the rest of us don't get paid.

When *The Human Stain* appeared, in 2000, everyone seemed to know that Roth's hero was based on Anatole Broyard, a *New York Times* book reviewer who was known for his critical acumen before he became even better known as a black man who had passed for white, thanks to an essay by Henry Louis Gates, Jr., published in *The New Yorker* in 1996, a few years after Broyard's death. Like Silk, Broyard had made a painful break with his family and kept his secret even from his children, although, Roth points out, these were not uncommon elements in the history of "passing" in America, and Roth read many such histories before writing his book. (Roth never uses the word "passing" in *The Human Stain*, in order to stay as far as possible from these often told tales.) Roth had met Broyard a few times—oddly, he's pretty sure that Broyard was Maggie's writing teacher in a course at The New School, after she and Roth separated—and it's easy to see why his description of Silk as "an outgoing, sharp-witted, forcefully smooth big-city charmer" brought the critic to mind. But Coleman Silk's dilemma was inspired by somebody else.

The Princeton sociologist Melvin Tumin was not as glamorous a figure as Broyard, but he was a close friend of Roth's. A Newark-born Jew, Tumin worked in Detroit as the director of the Mayor's Commission on Race Relations before he went to Princeton, where, in the fifties and sixties, he wrote well-regarded books about racial segregation and social inequality. He was an old friend of Saul Bellow's—they were of the same generation, and both had studied anthropology at Northwestern. Tumin had endeared himself to Roth by fighting to end discrimination against Jews in the dining clubs at Princeton, where Roth taught in the early sixties. Over the years, Tumin was also a research consultant for the Anti-Defamation League of B'nai B'rith, and he directed a national task force on violence. And then one day in 1985, at Princeton, he used the word "spooks" in asking about two students who had failed to show up for class—two students he had never seen—and because, as it turned out, they were black, he was charged by the university with racism.

The irony could hardly have been greater if Tumin had been black himself—or so it seemed to Roth. The idea was also fostered, he explains to me, by Tumin's appearance, "with heavy lips and frizzy hair." (Just the kind of Jewish appearance that was useful to Coleman Silk as camouflage. In his physique, Tumin was big and heavy, nothing like agile, Pan-like Silk. But then, as Roth likes to say, making things up is what writers do.) After several disruptive and disheartening months of what Roth calls a "witch hunt," Tumin was vindicated of the charges. He retired from teaching in 1989. On his death, in 1994, the headline of the *Times* obituary was, "Melvin M. Tumin, 75, Specialist in Race Relations." Roth spoke at the funeral, paying tribute to his friend's life-long battles for tolerance. The following year, *Sabbath's Theater* was published, with a joint dedication: "For Two Friends: Janet Hobhouse (1948–1991) and Melvin Tumin (1919–1994)."

Roth is not reluctant to talk about the research he puts into his books, whether learning how to make a glove for *American Pastoral* ("It could have fit on my foot"), visiting zinc mines for *I Married a Communist*—"This is the best part of the work, it's like a vacation"—or going to a VA hospital to talk with Vietnam vets for *The Human Stain*. There was already a huge literature about Vietnam vets, of course, even larger than the literature of "passing," and that made it even harder to avoid overfamiliar scenes and stories. (Roth considers Michael Herr's *Dispatches* of 1977 to be "a masterpiece" and has taught it several times.) True as the memories of battle in Roth's book may be to memories he heard firsthand, they are uncomfortably close to accounts we've read elsewhere, and battle scenes are clearly not his forte. But other scenes go beyond the realm of common knowledge into the dramatically unexpected—for example, a scene of vets and families of the dead visiting the "Moving Wall," a half-scale replica of the Vietnam Veterans Memorial in Washington that travels around the country. Roth went to see the aluminum-paneled replica several times in Yonkers—he says that setting a scene at the big wall, in Washington, risked cliché—and he listened to local veterans who came to search out names in letters that are also half the original size. He asked questions, sometimes, of groups of two or three, and he wrote down the answers. He didn't have to embellish or even to "write it," he tells me: "Their speech was music."

Even more startling is a scene in which a group of crippled, shaking veterans makes a trip to a Chinese restaurant. Roth remembers how disturbed he was to learn about such restaurant visits from a friend who works in a psychiatric program for veterans with post-traumatic stress disorder. As therapy, how ridiculously prosaic it seemed; yet how difficult to undergo. The primary aim is not to eat but to stay calm. In the scene, the men are there to coach the newest, rawest, most incorrigibly violent member of the group—Faunia's ex-husband, Les Farley—in how to stay in his chair despite the Asian people all around him and the unbearable Asian food. ("The agony of the steam. The agony of the smells.") Victory means getting through the entire meal without running outside or vomiting in the bathroom or trying to kill the waiter as he softly approaches to refill the water glasses.

The specter of death is strong in *The Human Stain*. The reader learns early on that both Coleman Silk and Faunia Farley are dead; the book is conceived at Silk's graveside. And because Zuckerman himself has been so ravaged by disease, the defiant pleasures and the balm of sex are no longer open to him. In its place—as far as anything can replace sex—he has music. All kinds of music: the Sinatra song that he dances to with Silk, the Gershwin number that Faunia dances to—with trumpet by Roy Eldridge, it is a real black-and-white mélange—and the music that Zuckerman listens to, alone, every evening, which sounds to him like "the silence coming true."

Above all, there is the music on the last occasion that he sees Silk alive. Zuckerman has gone to Tanglewood on a Saturday morning, to an open rehearsal. The fact that he is there at all attests to the yearning for contact that his friend has roused. Silk has pulled away from him; a man in Silk's position can't risk too much closeness, especially with an inquisitive novelist who grew up perilously near to Silk's forsaken New Jersey home. But Silk is at the concert, too, with Faunia, sitting a few rows ahead. Zuckerman can sense that Silk has some great secret, although he does not yet know what it is. As he looks around at an audience filled with elderly tourists and retirees, Zuckerman's mind fills with thoughts of death. Not just his death, or Silk's: everybody's death. He visualizes "the blood vessels occluding under the baseball caps, the malignancies growing beneath the permed white hair, the organs misfiring, atrophying, shutting down." He can't stop himself. "The ceaseless perishing. What an idea! What maniac conceived it?"

And then the pianist, Yefim Bronfman, walks onto the stage and begins to play Prokofiev's Second Piano Concerto. And all morbidity is swept away:

> Bronfman the brontosaur! Mr. Fortissimo! . . . Yefim Bronfman looks less like the person who is going to play the piano than like the guy who should be moving it. I had never before seen anybody go at a piano like this sturdy little barrel of an unshaven Russian Jew. When he's finished, I thought, they'll have to throw the thing out. He crushes it. He doesn't let that piano conceal a thing. Whatever's in there is going to come out, and come out with its hands in the air. And when it does, everything there out in the open, the last of the last pulsation, he himself gets up and goes, leaving behind him our redemption . . . Our own lives now seem inextinguishable. Nobody is dying, *nobody*—not if Bronfman has anything to say about it!

But Bronfman, of course, has nothing to say about it. Silk's funeral, a few months later, concludes with the last movement of Mahler's Third Symphony, reducing everyone to tears. ("They pulled out all the stops. They played Mahler.") Although not even this great adagio, unfolding with "all of life's unwillingness to end," can prevent the cemetery from being the next stop.

The finale of *The Human Stain* is one of the most powerful scenes in Roth's work—terrifically tense, starkly beautiful, a clean and fully earned payoff to the story. Unlike the finale of *American Pastoral*, it's spare: the players are two men, Nathan Zuckerman and the man who murdered Coleman Silk and Faunia Farley, and who very likely knows that Zuckerman knows he did it. The place is a frozen lake on top of a mountain, a lonely outpost off the backcountry road where Zuckerman has parked his car in order to approach the killer—who is hunkered down in the middle of the lake, ice fishing. In part, Zuckerman approaches simply because he wants to be able to finish his book. But he is also compelled to look directly at the human extreme, the reality of evil. "Here he is," he thinks to himself, the way that "Philip Roth" in *Operation Shylock* thought about seeing John Demjanjuk in an Israeli courtroom. "Here is the killer," Zuckerman thinks. "He is the one. How can I go?"

But the face-off on this empty, ice-whitened stage is extremely dangerous. The men talk desultorily, about fish, about the lake, about the techniques of fishing. The killer sounds off about politics. ("That scumbag son of a bitch gettin' his dick sucked in the Oval Office on the taxpayer's money.") And then he lifts the steel-bladed auger that he uses to cut holes through eighteen inches of ice, to show Zuckerman—"You always gotta keep your blades sharp"—right up level with his eyes. And Zuckerman slowly, politely, begins to back away toward the shore, not entirely certain he will get there. When he feels safe, he looks back to see, in the last words of the book:

> The icy white of the lake encircling a tiny spot that was a man, the only human marker in all of nature, like the X of an illiterate's signature on a sheet of paper. There it was, if not the whole story, the whole picture. Only rarely, at the end of our century, does life offer up a vision as pure and peaceful as this one: a solitary man on a bucket, fishing through eighteen inches of ice in a lake that's constantly turning over its water atop an arcadian mountain in America.

The Human Stain was very well received—it won a host of awards, national and international—both in itself and as the final work in Roth's grand American trilogy. Whatever the individual criticisms, the trilogy is the fulfillment of an epic literary dream begun for Roth by Thomas Wolfe and fostered by writers from Dos Passos through Bellow. Perhaps because these books are more broadly "serious"—being about History—they are often taken to be the capstone of Roth's career, although it is equally possible to favor some of the more unruly and ecstatic earlier books, as I do. Yet to compare the snow scene at the climax of *The Anatomy Lesson*—the driving storm, the slapstick tragedy, the tumultuous energy and youthful power and the creative joy that spills out in the writing—with the still and frozen whiteness of this late winter scene, with its ominous control, its buried tragedy, its tensile energy and mature power and the creative joy that spills out in the writing, is to be stunned at a writer's development, and at a writer's persistence, and to be grateful to have both.

The Human Stain will give you a fair education in boxing, dairy farming, and ice fishing. In these late books, Roth has become a stickler for the material stuff of the old-fashioned novel, the real-world labor and activities that Zuckerman longed to be absorbed in, years ago—"everything the word's in place of." Talking with David Remnick for the BBC after the trilogy was completed, Roth expressed unusual enthusiasm for the long-disparaged Edwardian novels of John Galsworthy and Arnold Bennett, precisely because they include the kind of material heft that he now found useful in binding his creatures to the earth. Material heft but also unrelenting energy: he spoke, at the same time, about being inspired by the paintings of Jackson Pollock, in both their "pictorial substance" and the way they are "dramatized in every square inch." It's an odd pair of examples, combining the most traditional and the most abstract, matter and mind. Roth seems willing to grab hold of whatever works to bring the maximum life onto the page.

And what, finally, does the American trilogy say about America? That's a hard question to ask of a writer who builds his art from so many particulars and who likes to argue both sides of every question. The Swede's Johnny Appleseed dreams, Merry's anti-war fury, Ira's Stalinist delusions, Eve's betrayal and ethnic shame, Lorraine's young bravery, Coleman Silk's secret, Faunia's down-and-out dignity, Les Farley's derangement: and all bound together by Nathan Zuckerman—boy patriot, determined enlarger of the category of the human, and anguished recluse from real human beings. "The fantasy of purity," renewed over and over again—from the extreme anti-war Left, from the extreme anti-Communist Right, from the hypocritically puritanical everybody, to take the three books in order—is appalling. "But that's the great American blessing," Roth tells me when I ask how this phrase applies to the country. "It's a radically impure society." Coleman Silk's genealogical history, elaborated in two long pages of near Old Testament begats, includes runaway slaves, Lenape Indians who married Swedish settlers, and mulatto brothers from the West Indies who brought Dutch sisters from Holland to be their wives. And still, like most of the others, he made himself up. And still he was hounded and murdered for what he was and for what he wasn't. It's an unusually peaceful vision that concludes the trilogy: an arcadian landscape and the word *America*. And fear and danger and no sign of justice.

The Breasts

It is not surprising that Roth had death increasingly on his mind, although at sixty-seven he appeared to be the Yefim Bronfman of American literature. Ever since *The Ghost Writer* nearly two decades earlier, he had published one significant book after another, at a remarkable pace. Contrary to the examples of his great American predecessors—Fitzgerald, Hemingway, Faulkner—he expanded his range and his power as he aged, so that in his fifties and sixties he was producing some of his best work. Much of this productivity is attributable to absolute discipline; he had taken to calling himself, in the press, "a monk of writing." True, the American literary culture of alcoholism that compromised the careers of those earlier giants was largely gone (John Cheever aside). But it is difficult to imagine Herman Roth's son ever becoming a drunk, even though Roth claims to fully understand the need to ease the pain of work when it is going badly, which is much of the time. (When I ask him what he has instead of alcohol, he replies without missing a beat: "The misery.") Fueling the discipline is the feeling of how much he has to say and how urgently he needs to say it; and this was true no less after he completed the American trilogy than before.

But it seemed time to say things in a different way; to take a break from big, complicated books, and do something lean and direct, on the order of the short novels that Bellow had been writing in his later years. Roth says that he went to Bellow—the admired master, even then—to ask how he did it, but that Bellow only laughed. So here was a new challenge, just as writing a big book had been a challenge with *The Counterlife*. The economies of the shorter form, once so familiar, now felt to him like "fighting with one hand tied behind your back," he told Benjamin Taylor in an online video interview. And the question was, "How do you get a knockout punch?"

There's no doubt that with *The Dying Animal* he punched hard. For some readers, too hard: this book may have aroused more anger than any other work of Roth's career, particularly among female readers— beating out even *My Life as a Man*, although some adjustment should probably be made for the amount of attention given anything he published by this time. As the Yeatsian title suggests, the book is about death. And given Roth's view of life's most powerful opposing force, it is also about sex: he had been stressing the conjunction since *Sabbath's Theater*, in which goatish Mickey Sabbath arises from prose so sulfurously rich and a context so vastly tragic that he becomes a kind of Dionysian hero, exasperating yet noble in his refusals and his rage. Not so David Kepesh, a far more ordinary protagonist, whom Roth resurrected for the purpose from two earlier books. It is Kepesh—the Kafkaesque David K.—who, in *The Breast*, awakens one day to find that he's been turned into a one-hundred-and-fifty-five-pound mammillary object (or, rather, subject). *The Professor of Desire* filled in his life story before the transformation, concluding with his awful realization that long-term love and sexual desire are mutually exclusive and that he is on the verge of a torturous choice. In the years since we have seen him, he has gone on teaching—the trauma of breasthood apparently forgotten—and has even become a minor celebrity, appearing as a "cultural critic" on educational TV. But he has also undergone another metamorphosis, nearly as alarming as the first: Kepesh is seventy, transformed by white hair, a little potbelly, and a wattle. Still, he is a man who made his choice long ago, and he has stuck by it—until the crisis that prompts this book.

Sex and only sex and more sex, sex with new women every year, sex with his twenty-something female students of the present and his forty-something female students of the past, sex with no emotional attachments and with no threat, ever, of the torments of romantic longing or the imprisonment of marriage. Following a series of books in which Nathan Zuckerman was reduced to what he termed a "harmless eunuch,"

it's no wonder that Roth decided to return to Kepesh, the most relentlessly sexual of his serial heroes, for a book that he considers the third
in a series of "dreams, or nightmares, about sex": the Kepesh trio.

The overall subject, Roth says, is "the sexual side of the sixties"—
not Kathy Boudin's sixties but Janis Joplin's—and Kepesh is its living
product, despite the fact that he, like Roth, came of age well before the
liberating call. The anxiety of coming late to the party is, in fact, key to
the desperate importance the new freedoms have for a man—for a generation of men—who spent his formative years, as Kepesh says, as "a
thief in the sexual realm":

> You "copped" a feel. You stole sex. You cajoled, you begged, you flattered,
> you insisted—all sex had to be struggled for, against the values if not the
> will of the girl. The set of rules was that you had to impose your will on
> her. That's how she was taught to maintain the spectacle of her virtue.
> That an ordinary girl should volunteer, without endless importuning, to
> break the code and commit the sex act would have confused me. Because
> no one of either sex had any sense of an erotic birthright. Unknown.

So, in 1956, Kepesh got married, and had a son, and was living the
only life that seemed to be available—caged and miserable and sneak-
ingly adulterous—when the revolution hit. His son was eight at the
time of the divorce. "It was a difficult escape," he remembers, "and I
knew I could take only myself over the wall."

The Dying Animal is a coda to the American trilogy in the way that
The Prague Orgy was a coda to the earlier Zuckerman books, but it's a
more ambitious work, pungent and tough—an after-dinner digestif made
of bitter herbs. Like his predecessors, Kepesh has been sideswiped by
history; he was as unprepared for the sixties as Swede Levov. And, like
Coleman Silk, he refuses to accept the limitations he was born to: in
this case, sexual limitations rather than racial. His decision to change
his life is hardly as poignant as Silk's. He knows that he appears a bit of
a clown (especially at his age). But he sees his struggle as part of a
larger historical quest for personal freedom, and he's done his homework, tracing the origins of these kinds of freedoms back to an eighteenth-
century Massachusetts settlement called Merry Mount, where the
drinking and the dancing and the copulation with Indian women so

enraged the righteous Puritans of nearby Plymouth that the settlement's leader was jailed. Nathaniel Hawthorne wrote about this essential American conflict, declaring, "Jollity and gloom were contending for an empire." And they still are. The sixties were not an aberration but part of a tradition that was expunged from history. It came back, however, as it always must. The current problem, as Kepesh sees it, is that there is no spokesman representing "emancipated manhood." Poor potbellied Kepesh will have to do the best he can.

And he does, in a number of very explicit sex scenes. Roth has lost none of his desire to shock, or, rather, to keep the reader from becoming complacent: hence a scene of Kepesh roughly shoving his penis into a lover's not entirely welcoming mouth, and another of him drinking menstrual blood. (Zuckerman's old lesson from Kafka could serve as a legend: "If a book we are reading does not rouse us with a blow to the head, then why read it?") Still, *The Dying Animal* is not really about sex but about the ways we find to accommodate its disruptive power—and, indeed, about personal freedom. Nearly allegorical in its brevity and bareness, it verges on becoming a tract about the alternative sexual careers of modern heterosexual men.

The immediate alternative to Kepesh's example is provided by his son, Kenny, now forty-two, who hates his father and has determined to be everything that he was not: a loyal husband, a devoted father, a man who "must be admirable," as Kepesh sees it, "whatever the cost." And the cost is killing him. Sex, of the conjugal variety, has become "a heinous duty" long before it ceases entirely. Out of the bed, "arguments abound, irritable bowel syndrome abounds, placation abounds, threats abound," but the virtuous son cannot accept his father's advice and walk away. Nor can he indulge in the kind of casual adultery that his father practiced, so the mistress he has finally taken has become a virtual second wife—he recently flew down to Florida to meet her parents. Kenny is a prig, he is in agony, and all because of the father who failed him. "The consequences of my being what I am are long term," Kepesh observes, as though he had been born to an inalterable condition, like a hunchback or a psychopath or a king. "These domestic disasters are dynastic."

There is also the example of Kepesh's closest friend, the distinctly unsuffering George O'Hearn, a poet and a teacher at The New School, who has been married to the same woman all his life and is the father of four unalienated children. George keeps his lovely family tucked away in suburban Pelham, so that, at large in Manhattan, he can screw around with every woman he meets. "Marriage at its best," Kepesh observes, "is a sure-fire stimulant to the thrills of licentious subterfuge." No literary news here, of course, yet it is a message that no one ever seems to want to hear. It has been put forward, and assailed, at least since Tolstoy's attack on romantic love in *The Kreutzer Sonata* ("Every man experiences what you call love for every pretty woman") and Gide's *The Immoralist*, two tract-like stories about sex and marriage published a century and more ago. A book that Roth read and reread while he was writing *The Dying Animal* is Camus's *The Fall*, published in 1956, about a man whose several moral quandaries include a "congenital inability to see in love anything but the physical." Like so many of Roth's books, these are all in some measure tales of civilization and its discontents, of physical desire and social hypocrisy.

Yet if Roth seems to be arguing a case, he is not presenting a solution. He is presenting a problem, or a series of questions, and to critics who complain that he has sex (or anarchic male desire) too much on his mind, it might be pointed out that his questions are reasonably pertinent even now, when sex scandals are our only bipartisan political activity and such a large percentage of American marriages end in divorce. What is the way to balance sex and love, family and freedom? How should one live? Once again, readers will project an answer onto the page, if necessary—but Roth declines to come through. "The goal," he says, "is to position the book so that you *can't* answer these questions." Who, after all (apart from Tolstoy), has answers? The solution for the writer is the articulation of the book. But then, Roth is never content to leave a problem well enough alone: however thoroughly Kepesh justifies his philosophy, *The Dying Animal* is predicated on the fact that it has come crashing down.

For Kepesh has fallen in love. (He recalls Yeats's poem "Sailing to Byzantium" when he is at his lowest: "Consume my heart away; sick with desire / And fastened to a dying animal / It knows not what it is.") It began eight years earlier, when he was sixty-two and the girl, Consuela Castillo, was twenty-four, one of the students he regularly picks out from the seminar he teaches. And it began no differently with this

girl, who displayed any number of attractive qualities: a smoothly polished Brancusi forehead, a reverential attitude toward culture, perfect
posture—"She's not a slouching, unkempt, 'like'-ridden girl"—and the
oddly formal manners that are a result of her Cuban émigré upbringing. But Consuela's most remarkable feature is her breasts: "gorgeous
breasts," "a D cup," "round, full, perfect," "the type with the nipple like
a saucer . . . the big pale rosy-brown nipple that is so very stirring." It's
enough to make one think that Kepesh must dimly remember his earlier transformation. The affair lasted a year and a half; even while it was
going on, he found himself plagued by possessiveness and jealousy of
younger men. After she left, it took him three years to recover, and no
other woman has made up for her loss.

The story of their affair is told by Kepesh to an unidentified young
friend, in a monologue that easily breaks into other voices—it's structurally very like *The Fall*, or like Portnoy addressing his psychiatrist—
after Consuela reappears in his life. She is sick and seeking comfort.
The girl with the most beautiful breasts in the world has breast cancer.
She has already had chemo and is facing surgery. Since her father has
died in the intervening years, and her mother is too upset to help, she
has come to see her old lover, for just a few hours. She wants him to
admire her breasts again, and to photograph them. It is New Year's Eve
when she shows up, the turn of the millennium. (Kepesh imagines her
"too miserable and frightened to go to the party where she'd been invited and too miserable and frightened to be alone.") But after this visit,
three weeks pass. She doesn't come again. He doesn't know how to
reach her. Throughout this one-hundred-and-fifty-six-page monologue—
this tract about sexual freedom—he is waiting, anxiously, for the woman
to call.

Female critics, in particular—but not exclusively—were infuriated
with Kepesh, with his attitude toward women, and especially with his
emphasis on Consuela's breasts. Is this what men love women for?
(What kind of men?) Does Roth even know what love is? Why does he
insist on wasting his beautiful prose on such puerile stuff? Zoë Heller,
in *The New Republic*, wrote that "given his history, Kepesh would have
to down several tankards of menstrual blood before carping would be in
order" and complained that Roth's depictions of sex throughout his
work amounted to no more than "a serial case study in the *vagina dentata*

complex." Michiko Kakutani, in *The New York Times*, wrote that Consuela was "portrayed in highly patronizing terms," and Adam Mars-Jones, in *The Observer*, noted that she is "described alternately as if she was a zoo specimen and an art object." The book's strongest defender, Keith Gessen, in *The Nation*, declared straight out that "in his old age Roth has become Tolstoy"—because of the scope of his recent novels and because of his urgent need to communicate his particular truths, even to the point of forsaking his literary instincts in the process. For Gessen, *The Dying Animal* is more an essay than a work of fiction, yet valuable in the depths of meaning that it adds to Roth's previous work.

It's not difficult to understand the anger that Kepesh provokes. Roth seems at times to court it, as he courted the wrath of the rabbis, the *Times* critics, and the feminists. *The Dying Animal* is a blunt and unbeguiling work. If Kepesh has a virtue, it is his clinical, wholly unpoetic honesty, and he is principally honest about his sexual nature and all that he's done to stay clear of emotional attachments. He doesn't want to be good; he wants to be free. He doesn't dispute his ex-wife's assessment of his character. Except for George O'Hearn, he has no male friends—Kepesh's friends are his ex-girlfriends—since most men choose very different lives. "I am 'a limited man,' they tell me—they who are not limited." (On the subject of married men, Kepesh gives as good as he gets: "Their heroism is not only in stoically enduring the dailiness of their renunciations but in diligently presenting a counterfeit image of their lives.") He doesn't ask for sympathy. He knows very well that "I don't universally compel admiration." But it's one thing to say that Kepesh is limited or unlikable and another to say that he's unreal, or doesn't represent something real. Kepesh makes a specialty of saying things one should not say. And if only for this, it's worth listening to him.

Age has made Kepesh obsessive about everything that he will lose, including Consuela. Seeing her through his eyes is nothing like seeing Faunia Farley through Coleman Silk's: Consuela is an engaging presence—her voice has the old-fashioned lilt of her upbringing—but Kepesh is essentially blinded by her beauty, and he knows it. Racking his tortured brain to figure out how she has so affected him, he concludes, "Like a great athlete or a work of idealized sculptural art or an animal glimpsed in the woods, like Michael Jordan, like a Maillol, like an owl, like a bobcat, she'd done it through the simplicity of physical splendor." Is this demeaning? To her? It's an odd time we live in, surrounded by commercial images of youth and beauty—magazines, billboards, television—but in which literary accounts of beauty's power are found objectionable. True, Kepesh is not Baruch Spinoza. He is a man deeply bound up in the flesh. But he is not inhuman: when he learns that Consuela is sick, he is stricken by the thought that she has been alone and panicking. He worries that he might not be able to get an erection if she comes back to him, maimed. And he can't stop picturing a double-nude portrait, by Stanley Spencer, of the artist and his wife, in their mid-forties, just beginning to sag and slacken, and posed with "uncharitable candor" beside two pieces of raw meat, as if they were all in the same butcher shop window. Even the description is enough to make one want to turn away. And if only for this, it's worth looking.

There's an interesting contrast to Kepesh's experience in Alice Munro's celebrated story "The Bear Came Over the Mountain." Munro offers a portrait of one of the most indisputably loving husbands in modern fiction, a man who is devoted to his wife through old age and her descent into Alzheimer's, yet who also happens to have been, in his younger years, a compulsive philanderer. Indeed, he's a professor who was lured off the conventional path by the sexual free-for-all of the sixties, and saved from destroying his perfect marriage only by the growing vigilance of campus watchdogs and bewilderingly irate feminists. (As Gide's immoralist puts it, "Who's to say how many passions and how many warring thoughts can cohabit in a man?") Kepesh takes the path of the sixties in the opposite direction—a path that few have followed to its destination or have even asked exactly what that place might look like. Dedicated to following "the logic of this revolution to its conclusion," and to turning "freedom into a system," he has made his life into a radical experiment. And, like other radically "pure" systems that Roth has considered in his work, it is bound to fail:

> The great propagandist for fucking and I can't do any better than Kenny. Of course there is no purity of the kind Kenny dreams of, but there is also no purity of the kind I dream of . . . This need. This derangement. Will it never stop? I don't even know after a while what I'm desperate for. Her

tits? Her soul? Her youth? Her simple mind? Maybe it's worse than that—maybe now that I'm nearing death, I also long secretly not to be free.

Personal freedom also has its price, even for a man who slips "her soul" between "her tits" and "her youth" as though *that* were the embarrassing part of his confession.

These are the major concerns in what remains a minor book—and a flawed one. It hardly matters that Kepesh's personal history, related in *The Breast* and *The Professor of Desire*, doesn't match the history he is given here; he is given what he needs to tell this story. Or that, as the critic Mark Shechner has pointed out, no self-respecting, conservative Cuban parents would have named their daughter Consuela; the proper Spanish name for a woman is Consuelo. But even on its own terms, the book has shaky patches. There's a hurriedness that leads to awkwardness in the crucial scene of Consuela's return, when Kepesh is alarmingly quick (even for Kepesh) to ask to touch her breasts; it doesn't seem that this moment is meant to get a laugh. And there's an occasional digression that feels out of place or tonally flat: Kepesh's comparative analysis of the allure of a woman who has taken off her bra but not her skirt versus one still wearing only pants seems not so much frank as jarringly unbalanced when the woman undressing has just confessed to having cancer. Are these failings of the character or of the execution? Roth was, indeed, in a hurry to say what he had to say; *The Dying Animal* was published in the spring of 2001, just a year after *The Human Stain*. The voice is propulsive and close, and if there's an occasional translated European feel to the locutions, that's because lines like "She asked me to tell her about the beauty of her body" hardly seem possible anymore in an American book.

The country's sexual history is woven through the lives of the lesser characters, too. There's Janie Wyatt, a gypsy-costumed campus heroine of the sixties—a leader of "the first wave of American girls fully implicated in their own desire," part of the generation responsible for the sexual rights that women like Consuela take for granted. Janie is less a character than a symbol, though, like Delacroix's Liberty rushing forward with her breasts exposed; Roth, for all his championing of the revolution, deals best with people damaged by its failures. (In general, success is no more compelling for Roth, as a subject, than virtue.) A former girlfriend, Elena Hrabovsky, is a respected ophthalmologist, a kindhearted woman who is approaching middle age and wants to have a family but can't bear the boredom and humiliation of dating. "I sit there thinking, Please, Lord, just let me go home," she tells Kepesh; "It's rough out there, David." He is surprised to learn that several of his women friends have resorted to professional matchmakers, because the men they generally meet are "narcissistic, humorless, crazy, obsessional, overbearing, crude, or they are great-looking, virile, and ruthlessly unfaithful, or they are emasculated, or they are impotent, or they are just too dumb." No contradictory argument is made or evidence introduced. The upshot seems to be that marriage is one form of hell, but the post-revolutionary sexual situation can be another. Pick your poison.

The wife of one such "ruthlessly unfaithful" man makes a particularly vivid impression, even though she has only one scene and barely more than a single, if revelatory, line. George O'Hearn's wife, Kate, is in attendance at his deathbed, along with their grown children. Roth describes her as an imposing, white-haired woman, "attractively roundish, wry, resilient, radiating a kind of stubborn heartiness," yet profoundly worn down—whether by George's life or George's death he doesn't say. George himself, lying semi-paralyzed after a stroke, summons his wife to his bedside and begins to kiss her passionately—she returns the kisses—and then to fumble with his one good hand at the buttons of her blouse. Despite the presence of the family, their daughter calls out to Kate to assist him, and she does: first the buttons on the sleeves, then down the blouse's front. George is grasping at the cloth of her brassiere when he suddenly falls back on his pillows, breathing fast, his final act on earth cut short. It is a grand, touching, almost Victorian scene of the dying profligate redeemed. Immediately afterward, Kate, walking Kepesh down the driveway to his car, coolly deflates the drama, saying, with a weary smile, "I wonder who it is he thought I was."

Of course, Kepesh is no longer the man he thought he was. The ultimate lesson for the breast-obsessed connoisseur of female flesh is that he desperately wants to be at Consuela's side, even if the surgery means that she is about to lose her breasts entirely. Does this mixture of Eros and tenderness amount to love? The better question, surely (the Tolstoyan question), is: how long can it last? The Kepesh universe contains no model for sexually charged long-term love, a condition otherwise known as a happy marriage. Does Roth himself believe that the possibility exists? "Yes," he replies to my question, "and some people play the violin like Isaac Stern. But it's rare."

Yet Roth proposed marriage to the woman who was the model for Consuela. She wasn't Cuban, and she did not have cancer. But she was in her mid-twenties and nearly six feet tall, and she took his breath away. He was in his late sixties ("or maybe I was ninety," he throws in). He has never really been a "monk of writing," or of anything else. But for the first time in his life, he says, he felt jealousy. He knew that he was bound to lose her. And he did. That is his suffering on the page; it's fair to say, too, that those are her breasts. He was willing to take a chance on marriage, just to try to keep her away from younger men of the kind he used to be. Just to try to keep her. He portrayed a truly good marriage once, he recalls, with the Levovs in *American Pastoral*—because he enjoyed giving two such evidently proper people an exciting sex life, and because he wanted to deepen the tragedy when they are torn apart. Outside of literature, he knows a few men, his contemporaries, who are still passionate about their wives of several decades—his friend Al Alvarez, he says, is one. "I say to them," Roth says with surprising, quiet solemnity, "you are blessed."

Look Homeward, Angel

How clever Kafka was to have his metamorphosis take place
within a family. The family <u>stands for</u> the recognizable, we know
just what to expect from a family. Then comes the unexpected!
Must remember this and try it for myself sometime.

—Philip Roth to Jack Miles, December 2, 1977

The most startling sentence in *The Dying Animal* has nothing to do
with sex. It's part of a description of the international New Year's
Eve celebrations, seen on television, when Consuela visits her old professor on the eve of the year 2000: "Brilliance flaring across the time
zones, and none ignited by bin Laden." Since the book was published in
the spring of 2001, it seemed natural to ask Roth if he hadn't exposed
himself as the Mossad agent he had merely pretended to be in *Operation Shylock*: how else had he come to write about bin Laden months
before 9/11? His answer, far more logical, if less sensational, is that he
was struck by footage on TV, after the 1998 bombings of U.S. embas-
sies in Africa, that showed bin Laden walking through a military camp
while missiles and tracer bullets flared like fireworks against the sky.
The reference in *The Dying Animal* is not a warning, though—or, at
least, not a warning against what our enemies might inflict. Roth saw
the Western world's millennial celebrations as a release from our fears
that the twentieth century would bring even greater, nuclear destruction.

It had not happened. We had come through. Yet for Roth, this triumph had led to nothing nobler than an age of continuously televised trivialization. "No bombs go off, no blood is shed—the next bang you hear will be the boom of prosperity and the explosion of markets," Kepesh thinks. The country was entering a new and prosperous dark age.

And then came the attack on the World Trade Center. On the morning of September 11, 2001, Roth was in a swimming pool in the City Athletic Club in midtown Manhattan, where he regularly went to exercise and relieve his back pain. (Not to be confused with the famed New York Athletic Club, this club was established in 1909 to accommodate Jewish men excluded from the city's other athletic organizations.) He came out of the pool to hear the news. Leaving the building, he walked with the crowds up Sixth Avenue. He was glad to be in the city rather than off in Connecticut, and he had no thought of leaving: "I wouldn't have wanted to be alone." Cultural trivialization no longer seemed like such a pressing issue. For all his criticism of American cultural habits, Roth is obviously a product of the Second World War and a patriot. Over the next few days, he tells me, he became "furious with people like Susan Sontag who were blaming America and blaming the victims—people who said the deed was a result of American policy in the Middle East rather than a result of the way these people were brought up and abused by their own countries." He put a big American flag in his window, a full-wall window leading to a balcony that faces south over the city, with a clear view of the skyline.

It would be utterly mistaken to say that his politics had become in any way conservative. Roth is a man who closely values friendships and does not depend on or even particularly prize unanimity of opinion to keep them going. (One of the main activites he engaged in with Melvin Tumin, a political hawk, was arguing about Vietnam.) But he wasn't happy when his friend Ron Silver, the actor who had performed several of the audio versions of his books, cited the 9/11 attacks as a reason for converting from Democratic liberalism to fervent support of President Bush. Silver spoke at the Republican National Convention in 2004. A few weeks later, Roth and Silver had a heated discussion on the phone— Roth says that Silver complained of being blacklisted by liberals, which Roth considered a cheap shot at sympathy—and Roth broke off the friendship. He says that he shouted at Silver as he had never shouted at either of his ex-wives.

Roth began *The Plot Against America* in December 2000—a month before George W. Bush took office, after a contested election that, from many Democrats' point of view, was not contested enough. Roth's immediate inspiration was a sentence in a book by Arthur Schlesinger. After quoting from a speech made by Charles Lindbergh, in September 1941, in which he castigated American Jews for pushing the country toward war, Schlesinger observed that isolationist Republicans might have done better if they had joined together under Lindbergh, the nationally beloved record-breaking pilot and Nazi sympathizer. And Roth wrote in the margin, "What if they had?" And what if, instead of winning a third term in 1940, Roosevelt had been beaten by the young and charismatic, isolationist and anti-Semitic Lindbergh? A crucial election gone seriously wrong. After so many counterlives, why not a counterhistory?

He understood at once that such a history, wholly invented—a Lindbergh presidency, sympathetic to Nazi aims—had to be grounded in reality, specifically in the travails of a real family trying to get through its daily life. And he knew immediately that the family would be his own. This was a welcome aspect of the book, if not, in some ways, its heart. In an essay that he wrote on the book's release, in *The New York Times*, in 2004, he stated that it had given him "an opportunity to bring my parents back from the grave." This touching phrase recalls the "eruption of parental longing" that was his reason for writing *The Facts* some fifteen years earlier. Writing as an act of resurrection. The goal was to "restore them to what they were at the height of their powers in their late 30's," he went on, and to portray them faithfully, "as though I were, in fact, writing nonfiction." But there was one important difference: these modest, working-class American Jews now had to contend with a European-style fascist threat that legitimated all their Old World fears—that made sense of the paranoia that drove Alexander Portnoy to the couch, that made a *virtue* of the paranoia. Threatened, persecuted, put to the test, they had a chance to expand their simple decency into outright heroism, both physical and moral.

The savagery of history erupting into people's lives is a familiar subject in Roth's work by now. And even if the history did not happen, it is treated in the same way: not as a grand epic but as the chaos and disaster that ordinary people go through. The book is also clearly responsive to Roth's sore awareness of having grown up safe in America, at a time when Jewish children in Europe were suffering and dying, an awareness that runs from his earliest stories right through *The Ghost Writer*. On September 12, 2001, Roth published *Shop Talk*, a collection of previously published conversations with and essays about writers he admires. Given the publication date, and the fact that the slender book was not a novel, it received scant attention. But it is remarkable how many of its long, thoughtful discussions about history and literature are with people, or about people, whose counterlives he might have led: Primo Levi (Auschwitz, February 1944–January 1945); Aharon Appelfeld (deported with his father to a camp in Transnistria after the murder of his mother, in 1941, when he was eight; escaped and spent the next three years hiding in Ukrainian forests); Ivan Klíma (Terezín, December 1941–May 1945, aged ten through thirteen and a half); Isaac Bashevis Singer (fled Poland for America, 1935); Bruno Schulz (executed by a Nazi officer while walking through his village in Poland, 1942).

"I still remember my terror as a nine-year-old when, running in from playing on the street after school, I saw the banner headline CORREGI-DOR FALLS on the evening paper in our doorway and understood that the United States actually could lose the war," Roth writes in *The Facts*. *The Plot Against America* presents a different counterhistory, with potentially similar results for a Jewish family. In 1941, President Lindbergh signs nonaggression pacts with Germany and Japan; the Nazi foreign minister Joachim von Ribbentrop is an honored guest at the White House; and American Jews are subjected to a resettlement program reassuringly titled Just Folks, administered by the Office of American Absorption, which dispatches city Jews to the heartland to learn how real Americans live. Many Jews view the program as a design to break their ties as a community. Some Jewish families pack up and move to Canada; before long, others are killed in spontaneously occurring pogroms across the country. And much of this is seen through the eyes of young Philip Roth—looked back on by his older self, narrating unobtrusively—only seven years old when Lindbergh is elected, and nine when, in 1942, in a sudden deliverance, the president's plane mysteriously disappears. As a result, Vice President Burton K. Wheeler introduces martial law, the citizenry rebels, Roosevelt returns to office in a special election, and the country is set back upon the real and glorious way that made it possible for Philip Roth to grow up to be the man he is and the American he is, and to write this book. If the deliverance is disconcertingly abrupt and seems almost careless, one has the sense that Roth had already accomplished all he wanted, in the onset of historical mayhem and its effect upon people who would remain just as quietly ennobled when the world reverted to its proper course.

He never wanted to write this kind of a book, he says, "with Jews sitting around the kitchen table complaining about anti-Semitism." He shakes his head. "What am I, Neil Simon?" Even worse, "it's exactly the kind of book the rabbis once wanted me to write." He kept putting away the unfinished manuscript, thinking that he could not go through with anything so obvious. But then he'd take it out again and do some work, and little by little he began to feel that it was getting good. Part of what saved it for him was the restraint: Lindbergh is not turned into Hitler or into any sort of caricature—in fact, he departs in no significant way from his real political positions and recorded words. There are no American concentration camps, no murderous Nazi policies put into place. (Just Folks, which takes Philip's brother, Sandy, off to a Kentucky tobacco farm for a summer—a summer that he loves—has much the same intent as the real Philip did in going off to Bucknell.) The outright discrimination that occurs—the Roth family is turned out of a Washington, D.C., hotel when they are recognized as Jews—is, like the random anti-Jewish riots, the result of the ordinary worst coming out in ordinary people when their lowest instincts have been sanctioned.

But the real salvation of the book was Roth's invention of his family's downstairs neighbors, the tragically afflicted Wishnows, in every way a contrast with the hilariously afflicted Portnoys, who were also invented as neighbors to the strong and stable Roths. Mr. Wishnow dies horribly of cancer; Mrs. Wishnow goes to work and is ultimately transferred via the Just Folks scheme to Kentucky, where she is murdered by an anti-Semitic mob. Their son, Seldon—the smartest boy in Philip's class, lonely, hapless, too eager to please, and terribly frightened—has his childhood ruined, not unlike a European victim of the war. From a literary point of view, the Wishnows allowed for the diversion of pathos from the Roths, and especially from little Philip. Poor Seldon's desperate desire to be Philip's friend drives Philip crazy and gives him the opportunity to be bad—just the kind of opportunity Roth required. Philip is embarrassed by Seldon, he tries to avoid him, he plays mean tricks on him: he steals Seldon's clothing from his room, piece by piece ("How could I lose a pair of shoes?" Seldon wails; "How could I lose a pair of pants?"), and packs it into a cardboard suitcase, awaiting his escape to a non-disastrous, non-Jewish life in the Catholic orphanage a few streets away. But the most unbearable thing about Seldon is the tragedy that envelops him. Philip keeps Seldon from talking about his "terrifyingly dead father" by bombarding him with toilet jokes he learned at school. Nothing like a good toilet joke to fend off both the piety of victimhood and the sentimentalization of childhood.

Philip is a marvelously honest and practical child. (Roth's notes about the book contain the admonition "Read Huck Finn.") No matter what goes on in the larger world, he remains focused on his stamp collection; his fear of the Nazis is on a par with his fear of the ghosts lurking in the cellar. Forced to share a room with his cousin Alvin, whose leg was shot off in the war—Alvin volunteered for the Canadian army— Philip is horrified at having to see the artificial leg and, worse, the stump. (Roth had no cousin Alvin in reality; he based this particular childhood horror on the experience of sharing a room with his mother's dying, cancer-riddled older sister.) The transfer of Mrs. Wishnow to Kentucky, and her death, is the result of one of Philip's harebrained schemes to get rid of Seldon. Philip certainly didn't mean this to happen—he is overcome by remorse: "Let my family raise her son as their son from here on out. He could have my bed. He could have my brother. He could have my future." (Philip himself plans to run away, again, and get a job with the deaf-mutes who he's heard bend the pretzels at the New Jersey Pretzel Factory, and never speak another word.) This guilt is something that the grown-up Roth, narrating the book, carries for the rest of his life: "I did it. That was all I could think then and all I can think now." Even here he cannot escape his sense of astonishing luck at having lived the childhood that he lived and his feeling for those who were not so lucky.

Roth had doubts that he was writing this book for his usual

audience. The "what if" historical genre was not his métier, and he'd read hardly any of the books that critics cited in comparison. (There was one exception: Sinclair Lewis's fascist takeover tale of 1935, *It Can't Happen Here*, had been a favorite of his ever politically vigilant father. Swede Levov's father invokes it in *American Pastoral* in relation to Nixon—"The idea," Lou Levov says, "couldn't be more up-to-the-moment.") Much of the book has the quality of an old-fashioned adventure story, with cliff-hanging breaks that suggest a popular serial: "Don't you see, Uncle Herman . . . ," cries cousin Alvin. "He just guaranteed Roosevelt's defeat!" Although there are a number of the long and coiling half-page sentences that had become a kind of trademark—"It's like taking a ride on the subway," Roth says with a laugh, "you get on at one place and get off at another"—the writing, overall, is quick, supple, and unshowy. ("Shorten the sentences," his notes instruct; "relax the language.") It's the story that counts. Of course, there are striking turns of phrase: an insulting stranger in a Washington restaurant has a "holiday-goose of a belly," which Herman Roth is inclined to stab with his fork and knife. (The dangers of silverware in these books!) Roth has never failed to adjust his language to his subject: compare a sentence from *When She Was Good* with one from *Portnoy's Complaint* or *Sabbath's Theater*. So it isn't surprising that the central subject here—Roth's earnest, sincere parents—has touched the writing, too.

It's a far cry from the cheerful vulgarity of the Patimkins or the hysterical worry of the Portnoys or even the serene remove of the Levovs to this sober, essay-like explication of just who the Jews of the Roths' acquaintance were, as a community:

> These were Jews who needed no large terms of reference, no profession of faith or doctrinal creed, in order to be Jews, and they certainly needed no other language—they had one, their native tongue, whose vernacular expressiveness they wielded effortlessly and, whether at the card table or while making a sales pitch, with the easygoing command of the indigenous population. Neither was their being Jews a mishap or a misfortune or an achievement to be "proud" of. What they were was what they couldn't get rid of—what they couldn't even begin to want to get rid of. Their being Jews issued from their being themselves, as did their being American.

The final point, about Jews as Americans, is one that Roth had been getting at all along, in endlessly varied voices and guises, beginning as a tormented question in his early work and ending here, with an emphatic answer. There's a telephone conversation in the book, between Mrs. Roth and little Seldon, that restores an undreamed-of dignity to the figure of the Jewish mother offering food; Philip, listening, compares her saving strength with that of a "combat officer." And Herman Roth—in his last appearance in print—responds to the suggestion that the family move to Canada with the full-hearted declaration: "This is our country!"

What is Jewish writing? Does such a phenomenon exist? Roth took a crack at answering these questions in his *Paris Review* interview, in the mid-eighties, by denying that "the Jewish quality of books" had anything to do with subject matter. Rather, there was a certain recognizable sensibility: "the nervousness, the excitability, the arguing, the dramatizing, the indignation, the obsessiveness, the touchiness, the play-acting—above all the *talking*," he said, clearly enjoying himself as he described the stylistic qualities of his most recently published book at the time, *The Anatomy Lesson*. "It isn't what it's talking *about* that makes a book Jewish—it's that the book won't shut up. The book won't leave you alone." (Every Jewish writer who doesn't find the categorization ridiculous—or offensive—probably has his or her own definition. For Bellow, Jewish stories were those in which "laughter and trembling are so curiously mingled that it is not easy to determine the relations of the two"—in other words, a Bellow story.)

For all the outsized torment the characters undergo just for being Jews—there is more torment, in real terms, than in any other of Roth's books—*The Plot Against America* keeps its voice down. What need to shout when the enemy is real and near? By Roth's own definition, he hadn't written a "Jewish book" in years, and this very Jewish story is no exception. Indeed, it turned out to be one of his most broadly accessible books—direct, deeply engrossing, invoking both laughter and tears, without sex and with minimal masturbation, a book written by a genius although not a work of his genius, lacking the fire and the edge that Roth displays when he soars.

Roth took care in fitting his inventions to historical facts, and appended to the book both a twenty-page "True Chronology of the Major

Figures" and the text of the entire Lindbergh speech mentioned by Schlesinger, from September 1941, in which he denounced the British, the Jews, and the Roosevelt administration as "war agitators." But *The Plot Against America* hit the bestseller list in 2004 because of its implications for the present. Even the title, which Roth had lifted from a 1946 political pamphlet, seemed to have a post-9/11 ring. In *The New York Times*, Michiko Kakutani—who found the book "provocative but lumpy"—noted that the novel could be read as "either a warning about the dangers of isolationism or a warning about the dangers of the Patriot Act and the threat to civil liberties." But it was a column by Frank Rich, also in the *Times*, that really got things going. Announcing that the book was "riveting from the very first sentence: 'Fear presides over these memories, a perpetual fear,'" Rich compared this atmosphere to the "'perpetual fear'" that defined "our post-9/11 world" and to "the ruthless election-year politics of autumn 2004." Others saw Lindbergh's flight suit as a reference to Bush's getup for his "Mission: Accomplished" speech. And in *The New York Review of Books*, J. M. Coetzee asked whether Roth's novel of "America under fascist rule" wasn't really "about" America under Bush.

Roth, in his own essay in the *Times*, insisted that he had not written the book as "a roman à clef to the present moment"—even if he did consider George W. Bush "a man unfit to run a hardware store let alone a nation like this one." Still, he noted that Kafka's books had served as political inspiration to Czech writers who opposed Soviet rule in the sixties and seventies; this wasn't the way Kafka had meant his work to be read, but "literature is put to all kinds of uses." In conversation, Roth is careful to distinguish between fascism and Bush's merely "right-wing government." But he understands why his book was taken up as it was, politically. "There was this feeling of powerlessness we had about Bush," he recalls, "and no one of any consequence in the Democratic Party was speaking out. They grasped at this book as an articulation of their anger and frustration."

The Plot Against America, Roth concluded in the *Times*, had twin messages. First, that in spite of the general anti-Semitic discrimination by the Protestant hierarchy in the thirties, and despite the virulent Jew-hatred of the German American Bund, the Christian Front, Henry Ford, Father Coughlin, and, yes, Charles Lindbergh, it had *not* happened here—"How lucky we Americans are." And second, that our lives as Americans are "as precarious as anyone else's." It *might* have happened like this. "All the assurances are provisional," he wrote, "even here in a 200-year-old democracy." The election of George W. Bush had affirmed, for him, the lesson not just of this book but of all the books that he had been writing for years: "We are ambushed, even as free Americans in a powerful republic armed to the teeth, by the unpredictability that is history."

Ghosts

After winning two National Book Awards (*Goodbye, Columbus*; *Sabbath's Theater*), two National Book Critics Circle Awards (*The Counterlife*; *Patrimony*), two PEN/Faulkner Awards (*Operation Shylock*; *The Human Stain*), *Time* magazine's Best American Novel of the Year (*Operation Shylock*), the Pulitzer Prize (*American Pastoral*), the National Medal of Arts, the WH Smith Literary Award for the best book of the year in the United Kingdom (*The Human Stain*), the Prix Médicis étranger for the best foreign book of the year in France (*The Human Stain*), honorary degrees from Harvard and the University of Pennsylvania, and any number of other awards and prizes, Roth was back at the top of the bestseller list—right behind Stephen King and Dan Brown—for the first time since *Portnoy's Complaint* (which had won nothing). But a more durable honor was now coming his way: publication of his complete works by the Library of America, in its beautifully matched set of the canon of American literature, ushering Roth into a company that includes Herman Melville, Henry James, Edith Wharton, William Faulkner, James Baldwin, Eudora Welty, and Saul Bellow. The first two volumes of the works of Philip Roth were published in the fall of 2005, and six more were scheduled, to conclude when Roth turned eighty, in 2013. Only Welty and Bellow had previously received the honor in their lifetimes. And Roth hardly seemed to be slowing down. Indeed, his continuing rate of production meant that another volume eventually had to be added to the series.

Although the Library of America volumes contain no prefaces or critical commentary, there was new information to be gleaned from the appended chronology of the author's life and works. Assembled by the volumes' editor, Ross Miller, with the substantial aid of Roth himself, the usual list of publications and prizes was expanded and given emotional color by the frequent mention of friends he had made over the years. "1965: Begins to teach comparative literature at University of Pennsylvania . . . Meets professor Joel Conarroe, who becomes a close friend." "1976: In London resumes an old friendship with British critic A. Alvarez and, a few years later, begins a friendship with American writer Michael Herr (author of *Dispatches*, which Roth admires) and with the American painter R. B. Kitaj." "1980: Milan and Vera Kundera visit Connecticut on first trip to U.S.; Roth introduces Kundera to friend and *New Yorker* editor Veronica Geng, who also becomes Kundera's editor at the magazine." "1982: Corresponds with Judith Thurman after reading her biography of Isak Dinesen, and they begin a friendship."

This last entry offers a glimpse of a rather surprising habit of Roth's, considering his fame: often, when he reads something he admires, he sends a letter to the writer, who is just as often a total stranger. Thurman recalls her shock at receiving an enthusiastic note typed on a plain sheet of paper and signed "Philip Roth," and her reply, which began, "If you are Philip Roth the candlestick maker . . ." He is also a tireless champion of young writers and of struggling, not so young ones: Joel Conarroe, who went on to become Dean of the School of Arts and Sciences at Penn and later the president of the John Simon Guggenheim Foundation, has a thick file of Roth's recommendations for various jobs and awards. In sum, these entries hint at concerns very different from those of the notoriously solitary writer. One can't laugh as much as Roth has laughed in his life without accumulating friends.

By the time the chronology was published, a number of these friends were dying or dead: Janet Hobhouse, Melvin Tumin, Mildred Martin from Bucknell, Bob Maurer from Bucknell. "You think that's the end of it when your parents die," he says to me. "After that, you're done. Nobody's supposed to die anymore, right?" Veronica Geng was not only Roth's editor and friend but "the best humorist since S. J. Perelman," he declares, "only more quirky and *moderne*"; when Geng underwent surgery for brain cancer, in Sloan-Kettering, Roth would sit with her outside the hospital, where he had brought her in her wheelchair, so that, to the horror of the nurses, she could smoke. He joined a couple of other friends in covering her medical expenses and set up a fund, on the model of his Prague fund, to provide her with financial backup. She was staying in his Manhattan studio, recovering, when a seizure put her back in the hospital; she died on Christmas Eve 1997, aged fifty-six. Another hard death to absorb was George Plimpton's, in 2003; Plimpton was one of Roth's oldest friends and a man of apparently indefatigable energy. And then, hardest of all, Saul Bellow, in 2005.

Bellow was "the 'other' I have read from the beginning with the deepest pleasure and admiration," Roth wrote in the dedication to *Reading Myself and Others*, in 1975. On a personal level, the men were friendly enough in these earlier years and saw each other from time to time. Roth recalls that he and Bloom gave a dinner party for Bellow in London in 1986, when Bellow was in low spirits, recovering from the death of both of his brothers and the end of his fourth marriage; they also took him to a concert of late Shostakovich quartets, to cheer him up. (Not the most conventional idea of a pick-me-up, perhaps, but, Roth says, "I wanted him to hear something beautiful.") Bellow thanked him in a letter, since published, in which suffering and its musical relief are weighed in a typically unflinching formulation: "There's almost enough art to cover the deadly griefs with. Not quite, though. There are always gaps."

Yet, despite such occasions and communications, Roth felt that Bellow was generally guarded and kept himself at a remove. (One recalls Felix Abravanel's charm, in *The Ghost Writer*, "like a moat so oceanic that you could not even see the great turreted and buttressed thing it had been dug to protect.") The men did not become close until several years later. An entry in the Library of America chronology reads "1991: Renews strong friendship with Saul Bellow."

Roth credits a turnaround in Bellow's attitude—that is, the real beginning of their friendship—to Janis Freedman Bellow, whom Bellow married in 1989. Roth still recalls her supportive review of *Operation Shylock* and is convinced that it was she who got Bellow "to read me seriously." And he imagines her telling her illustrious husband, sometime after their marriage, "What's the matter, this guy really likes you, he really admires you, he wants to be your friend." Whatever she said, it seemed to work. No wonder that, in October 1995, Roth sent Bellow a letter, reading in its entirety, "Dear Saul, At last you've married a woman who understands me. Love, Philip."

Janis Freedman Bellow, a warm and easygoing woman who now teaches literature at Tufts University, insists that there was no need for her to coax her husband into reading Roth's work seriously. Together, she says, they discussed Roth's books endlessly—*American Pastoral* was a particular Bellow favorite—and, in fact, "the deepening of my appreciation of Philip's work would have come from Saul." Concerning the friendship, she believes that her husband was "hungering for a connection to Philip" and that she merely helped him let it happen. There was some tension between the men, she concedes, based on Bellow's sense of competition. He had a history of saying things he later wished he hadn't—this is a man who titled a story collection *Him with His Foot in His Mouth*—and he had said a few of these things to Roth. But he didn't want to be abrasive anymore. "I had that conciliatory gene," she admits, "but it's not like I was kicking him under the table."

During the early nineties, when Roth went to Chicago to visit his brother, Sandy, he also visited the Bellows; later on, in summer, he and a few other friends routinely got together at the Bellows' house in Vermont. Roth's feeling for Bellow's work approaches reverence. He speaks freely of having felt "swamped" by Bellow as a writer—"inspired but swamped" by "the uncanny powers of observation, the naturalness, the seeing into human faces." All in all, "he made me feel like an amateur." Roth thought that Bellow's last novel, *Ravelstein*, published in 2000, was deeply flawed, but Bellow was eighty-four when he finished it. "It's hard to write a book at eighty-four," Roth notes, "it's hard to remember from day to day what you've done." Slightly bending an agreement they had made about mutual candor, Roth told Bellow only that he couldn't properly evaluate the book because he was "out of sympathy" with the character of Ravelstein, as some people had been out of sympathy with Mickey Sabbath.

Roth stayed close to Bellow throughout the final, fading years. Even when things were at their worst, Roth was "a constant presence," Freedman Bellow recalls. He telephoned frequently. "That could be difficult," she says; "Saul could be repetitive, and a lot of people thought it wasn't worth it anymore." And the two would end up laughing. ("That

was the main bond," she adds, "the way they made each other laugh.")
Bellow had read *The Plot Against America* more than once, and he carried it around with him everywhere. "It was 'the Book,'" Freedman
Bellow says. "The cry around our house was, 'Where's the Book? Where's
the Book?'" About a week before he died, Roth tells me, Bellow called
to say that he'd had a dream about Lindbergh, in which Bellow said to
him, "Pardon me, sir, I don't mean to pollute you with my Jewish presence." By then, Bellow's condition had deteriorated so badly that, in
many ways, Roth says, he was "saved by death." But that didn't make it
any easier when it happened.

Bellow's death sent Roth into despair—"about him, about illness,
about dying," he says. Around the same time, in 2005, he underwent
back surgery, and continual pain compounded his dark mood. He'd already begun a new book, about an aging actor who has lost his powers;
it was based on Claire Bloom's experience of working with Ralph Rich-
ardson, who had told her after a performance one night that "the magic
is gone." Roth put this manuscript aside and, in the days after Bellow's
funeral, began something else. Too uncomfortable to work at his com-
puter, he wrote in longhand, very slowly, groping after what he wanted.
He remembered that his father, whose younger brother had died the
same year as his wife and several friends, had said to him, "Philip, I
can't look into another hole in the ground." In his Web of Stories interview, Roth says that he hadn't quite known what he meant and had offered to attend the latest funeral in his father's stead. But now he knew.
"I guess you reach a point," he says, "where you can't look into another
hole in the ground."

Everyman is a book about death and funerals and holes in the
ground, and about the illnesses that take us there. Extremely brief—a
novella, really—it was published with an ominous black cover that had
no pictorial image, and Roth was highly pleased that the book itself resembled "a tombstone." Indeed, the story begins at the funeral of the
central character and moves backward in time, brushing in the events
of his life. Familiar themes are starkly rendered as the aging hero
views the domestic chaos he has left in his wake: two angry, embittered
sons from a first marriage; a loving (if ultimately sexless) second marriage that he sabotaged for a sexual fling. He retains a good-hearted
daughter and a nearly heroic brother, but he is essentially alone as he

enters old age. Beyond his largely botched relationships, we know little of this man. Though he wanted to be a painter, he settled for a life in advertising—Roth alerted his brother that he was making use of some of his life's story—but his biography is composed mainly of medical disasters: a hernia operation when he is nine, a burst appendix at thirty-four, cardiac surgery at fifty-six, and an increasingly frequent series of hospitalizations for angioplasties, the installation of heart stents, and a defibrillator. Decades of health are duly noted and passed over as beside the point.

Like the fifteenth-century morality play from which it takes its title, *Everyman* is about the fate that claims us all: "the adversary that is illness and the calamity that waits in the wings." In the play, Everyman meets Death himself and speaks what Roth calls the best line in English literature between Chaucer and Shakespeare: "Oh Death, thou comest when I had thee least in mind." Unlike the medieval protagonist, however, Roth's Everyman does not believe in God or in an afterlife. He is a Jew, but that is a matter of no real significance. (His father owned a jewelry shop that he called Everyman's, to keep his Jewish name from alienating Christian customers; but by now the fact that Everyman is a Jew seems entirely unremarkable—in itself, perhaps, a remarkable fact.) The only paradise that he knows is his childhood, and the only hell he can imagine is giving up his life right here on earth. There is something invigorating in the book's relentlessness; Roth seems to be after the brutal directness of those holes in the ground.

Yet the construct loses power as the book goes on, because it isn't sufficiently enlivened. Everyman is, by the demands of his identity, entirely ordinary—"content to live by the customary norms, to behave more or less the same as others"—and the account of his trials is plain-spoken, medically precise, and somewhat stiff. In *American Pastoral*, Roth mediated the ordinariness of Swede Levov through Zuckerman's introspective sensibility. There is no mediation here. The third-person narration seems to issue from Everyman's point of view—"True, he had chosen to live alone, but not unbearably alone"—despite the fact that it outlasts his life and describes his funeral; the voice seems constricted by the man's own limitations. Praise, in this book, consists of words like "reliable," "amicable," "moderate," "agreeable," and "conscientious." There may be writers who find such qualities inspiring, but Roth's best gifts lie elsewhere. As he had feared when he took on shorter books, he seems indeed to be writing with one hand tied behind his back.

It is sometimes difficult to distinguish the book's plainspokenness from exhaustion, given the number of opportunities missed. What would Roth once have made of the surgeon, Dr. Smith, born Solly Smulowitz? (We learn here only that he "had grown up in the slums, the son of poor immigrants.") The redheaded nurse Maureen, from an Irish-Slavic family in the Bronx, has "a blunt way of talking that was fueled by the self-possession of a working-class toughie"—but we never hear her. There's a lot that we are asked to take on trust. Everyman, "in his joy at having survived" another round of surgery, thinks about his brother: "Was there ever a man whose appetite for life was as contagious as Howie's?" But we feel neither Howie's appetite nor our hero's joy, because Roth doesn't show them to us; and because the emotion isn't present in the language—as it was, so richly, in his masterpiece about living and dying, *Sabbath's Theater*. True, Roth was trying for something else: a short, intense dose of illness and the calamity of death, as experienced in a society that gives us plenty of time to see it coming.

Roth's *Everyman* is not an allegory, despite the title. It contains no blatant symbols and, certainly, no moral message. The very idea of calling the book *Everyman*, Roth says, came to him only after he'd finished a first draft without giving the hero a name. Yet there are aspects of the book that seem uncomfortably close to a fairy tale. Who would have thought that one could complain of a book by Roth that its characters are too good? He has portrayed good people many times, with vividness and truth—the warmhearted Norman Cowan in *Sabbath's Theater*, Swede Levov in *American Pastoral*, Roth's own parents in *The Plot Against America*—but brother Howie is a cardboard prince, not merely because he is a millionaire, happily married, irreproachably kind, and able to "play water polo as well as polo from atop a pony," but because of the breathless vantage from which this description seems to emerge. And he's not the only figure seen this way. Ever since *Portnoy*, Roth has balanced immense tenderness with rage, one emotion keeping the other in check. But this is a book in which, as Everyman notes, "the tenderness was out of control." Roth's narrator—and Roth himself—seems to be operating under the spell of mortality: an amalgam of gratitude, memory, troubled conscience, and longing. Roth has written about this phenomenon in *American Pastoral*, about the high-pitched admiration that takes hold of people in the limousine traveling behind the hearse.

There's a sense of great relief—and a welcome surge of energy—when the characters temporarily lose their constraints and let rip. Everyman sounds off about his unendingly bitter sons ("You wicked bastards! You sulky fuckers!"). The sweet and ingenuous second Mrs. Everyman—a character Roth based on Ann Mudge, his sweet and ingenuous girlfriend of the sixties, who restored his sanity after Maggie—catches her husband in an affair and throws him out. Her fury provides an interesting counterpoint to the views of marriage and sex so central to *The Dying Animal*:

> Oh, why go on—all these episodes are so well known . . . The man loses the passion for the marriage and he cannot live without. The wife is pragmatic. The wife is realistic. Yes, passion is gone, she's older and not what she was, but to her it's enough to have the physical affection, just being there with him in the bed, she holding him, he holding her. The physical affection, the tenderness, the comradery, the closeness . . . But he cannot accept that. Because he is a man who *cannot live without.* Well, you're going to live without now, mister. You're going to live without plenty. You're going to find out what living without is all about!

And he does. As he nears the end, it turns out that the cost of sex was pretty much everything. This may sound like an old man's philosophy—"late Roth"—but the knowledge was fully present in "early" Roth; it prompts the crisis that concludes *The Professor of Desire*, published back in 1977. Knowing the cost, however, does not alter the necessity of the choice or the pain of the results. For Everyman, sex remains the only part of life that kindles his curiosity, even if age restricts him to watching young women jogging past him on a boardwalk, while he yearns for "the last great outburst of everything."

Despite its disappointments, *Everyman* contains set pieces and minor characters that continue to haunt well after the book is closed: a woman with perpetual back pain who commits suicide; a woman who has been sobbing uncontrollably at funerals—upset by the fact that "she isn't eighteen anymore"—for fifty years. (Does one laugh or cry?)

One strong scene depicts a Jewish Orthodox funeral—the funeral of Everyman's father—during which the mourners themselves take up shovels and, one by one, fill the gaping hole in the ground, looking "like old-fashioned workmen feeding a furnace with fuel." This ritual process takes close to an hour, and it's a horrible sight; those who can't lift a shovel throw in fistfuls of dirt. Everyman wants to make them stop, but the process is unstoppable. Roth was describing Bellow's funeral, blow by blow, inch by inch of covering dirt, and the thoughts that he had at the time, he says, are the ones that he put into the book: "Now I know what it means to be buried. I didn't till today."

The climactic scene takes place in the same run-down cemetery, off the Jersey Turnpike, where Everyman has gone to visit his parents' graves. There is a gravedigger there, an amicable man willing to explain the mechanics of his job—a seven-foot spike to probe the spot, a wood frame to shape it—which is the nearest he can come to explaining its mysteries. (Gravedigging is to *Everyman* what glove manufacturing was to *American Pastoral*: an everyday job, requiring skill and patience, that helps make our lives appear intelligible.) Despite his lack of religious belief, Everyman speaks a few words to his parents aloud: "I'm seventy-one. Your boy is seventy-one"—words hardly eloquent, not remotely a prayer, the plain expression of a common (if astounding) fact. And he seems not at all surprised when his parents reply. "Look back and atone for what you can atone for," his father advises—for a moment coming close to the language of the medieval play—"and make the best of what you have left." The hero feels released from fear, although, as it turns out, he is almost out of time. The end of the book refuses any comfort. There is just the mother's reply, offering the only satisfaction to be had. "Good," she says to her boy, an old man himself now and about to die. "You lived."

A single line from *Everyman* has been taken up in newspaper articles as a catchphrase about old age, a species of folk wisdom. The line came to Roth while he was watching television reports of the evacuation of an old-age home during Hurricane Katrina, when people in wheelchairs and on stretchers were being loaded onto a boat, in swirling waters: "Old age isn't a battle; old age is a massacre." The feeling is carried forward into his next book, *Exit Ghost*—unsurprisingly, since it's not a feeling likely to recede with age. Yet despite the title and the subject, *Exit Ghost* abounds with charm, humor, and human complexity. Unlike *Everyman*, it is neither schematic nor sentimental but a startlingly buoyant if ruthless work about the bitter end.

The strength of *Exit Ghost* appears to derive from the presence of Nathan Zuckerman, whom Roth has revived one last time, if only to put the poor man through flaming hoops of shame and humiliation. For Zuckerman truly wishes to be revived: to be back in life again. After eleven years in his mountaintop retreat, basically alone, he has been inspired by the death of a friend named Larry Hollis to change his life, again. Hollis tried to push Zuckerman toward a less lonely and more active life: dinner invitations, Ping-Pong games, a gift of two kittens, who proved so distractingly adorable that Zuckerman had to give them back. (He has turned his back on life not because he is hardened to its charms but because he is too susceptible.) Hollis develops cancer on page twelve and commits suicide on page thirteen, but Zuckerman's account of the friendship is so genially matter-of-fact that the story is anything but grim. Zuckerman is older and sadder, as much inclined now to ponder as to explode, but no less witty or confidingly sympathetic— an instant intimate who picks up with us as though our own relationship with him had never been disrupted.

Newly roused, Zuckerman travels to New York to undergo a medical procedure that offers a chance of alleviating the incontinence that, along with impotence, he has endured since his prostate surgery nine years earlier, and that has become his major reason for keeping to himself. (There is nothing to be done about the impotence, and his memory seems to be failing, but getting out of diapers is a good opening shot at renewal.) Once he is in New York, walking the streets like Rip Van Winkle and grumbling about the ubiquity of cell phones, he discovers that "New York did what it does to people—awakened the possibilities. Hope breaks out."

Exit Ghost, published in 2007, is a sequel to Roth's novel of 1979, *The Ghost Writer*. Zuckerman shows no signs of remembering his interludes with Swede Levov or Ira Ringold or Coleman Silk, but he has never forgotten E. I. Lonoff, dead now for more than forty years, or the mysterious girl, Amy Bellette, whom he imagined as Anne Frank during a snowy night he spent at Lonoff's house in 1956. He was twenty-three. Instantly infatuated. The face. The voice, with its slight, untraceable accent. It's a voice he hears again almost as soon as he steps onto the elevator after leaving his urologist's office, at Mount Sinai Hospital, although the woman herself is unrecognizable. Amy Bellette is seventy-five, and, as Zuckerman discovers when he follows her to a nearby luncheonette, she has had brain surgery: taking off her hat, she reveals that one side of her head has been shaved and bears a raw serpentine scar running from behind her ear to her brow. What appeared to be a thin blue summer dress is a hospital gown that she has outfitted with buttons and a rope-like belt. Zuckerman decides to leave her in peace, although a complex series of events will soon bring them together, as Roth revisits and revises the earlier novel's large if airily borne concerns: youth and age, art and life, the flamboyance of the imagination and the claims of literature. All during the course of a single week, in the fall of 2004, while the city is reeling over the reelection of George W. Bush.

In the flush of the promise of physical renewal, Zuckerman impulsively answers an ad and agrees to swap his mountain retreat for an Upper West Side apartment, then goes to meet the young married pair of writers, Billy and Jamie Logan, who live there. Billy is boyish, modest, and deferential. Jamie is thirty years old, tall and slender, with a curtain of dark hair and a languid air. Zuckerman is seventy-one. Instantly infatuated. The face. The voice, with its slight, untraceable accent. (Texas, old money.) Jamie Logan isn't just a beauty: she speaks rapidly and quietly, "as highly complicated people will do." She might have stirred Zuckerman unbearably even had he touched a woman in the past eleven years, even had he not strenuously deprived himself of the sight of pleasures beyond his reach, before she presented him with all those pleasures in a single package, wrapped in a thousand-dollar cashmere sweater open to reveal a lacy camisole that looks surprisingly—he's been away from women's fashion also for eleven years—like lingerie. "Her breasts," he notes, "weren't those of an undernourished woman." Jamie is imperfect enough to seem utterly real—she has problems with her parents, worries about her writing, and doesn't know how to use "hopefully"—yet perfect enough to be slightly annoying. (When, on first reading the book, I sniffily complained to Roth about "overprivileged" Jamie, he gleefully replied, "You should hear what she says about you!")

Ridiculous for him even to think about her, of course. But this is Nathan Zuckerman, for whom the threat of being ridiculous is catnip:

There is no situation that infatuation is unable to feed on. Looking at her provided a visual jolt—I allowed her into my eyes the way a sword swallower swallows a sword.

All too fittingly, Strauss's *Four Last Songs* is on the couple's CD player when he arrives, elegiac music for a soaring female voice written by a very old man. (Were they already listening to it, he wonders, or did she put it on just for him?) It is playing, too, in the dramatic scenario that Zuckerman writes after encounters with Jamie during the next few days: a duet for male and female voices, titled *He and She*, described as "a play of desire and temptation and flirtation and agony." As the "agony" suggests, the play is not overtly sexual; the pair never touch. Instead, He and She discuss Conrad a good deal, and sometimes Hardy and a little Keats, as he begins to tell her what he feels and what he wants, and she replies as evasively as a flattered thirty-year-old woman can. Until their final exchange, which takes place on the telephone, when the tantalizingly young and desirable She suddenly announces (this is Zuckerman's play, after all) that she is coming right over to his hotel room.

Love and sex and flirtation and conversation and human warmth are not all that Zuckerman has renounced. Since 9/11, he has also sworn off newspapers, magazines, television news, and the consciousness of national events in any form. This is his way of preventing himself from becoming a "letter-to-the-editor madman," always roaring about the ways in which "a wounded nation's authentic patriotism" is being exploited by "an imbecilic king." It's his way of sparing himself "the despising without remission that constitutes being a conscientious citizen in the reign of George W. Bush." He has paid his dues in political outrage. Not so Jamie and her husband, with whom he watches the election results while they field phone calls from friends as confidence turns to predictions of doom. These are choice historical hours that Roth has captured, when, in New York, violated idealism gave way to theatrical despair. ("This is now the night before it all got worse!" Jamie cries; reports the next day are of people crying on the steps of the Forty-second Street library.) The young couple can't know what Zuckerman has learned, after living through the sixties assassinations, through Nixon, through Reagan. "It's a flexible instrument that we've inherited," he tells Jamie by way of reassurance. He follows with the most consoling words that he can summon about the country that has "enthralled" him for nearly three-quarters of a century: "It's amazing how much punishment we can take."

Exit Ghost is not just about old age but about the mystification between young and old—between the "no-longers" and the "not-yets." Mystification turns to antagonism when Roth confronts a subject that had attached to his later years as inevitably and about as pleasantly as death: biography. "It's just the way it's done now," Amy Bellette tells Zuckerman. "To expose the writer to censure. To compose the definitive reckoning of every last misdoing. Destroying reputations is how these little nobodies make their little mark." Amy has gotten in touch with Nathan in order to help her fend off a little nobody who is writing a biography of E. I. Lonoff, in which he intends to reveal a sexual transgression from Lonoff's early years as the key to the great man's work. Roth makes this newest of enemies as attractive as he can. Richard Kliman is twenty-eight years old, six feet three, handsome, virile (everything poor Zuckerman is not), and also reckless, smug, and blind with self-confidence: he is, in other words, Zuckerman concludes, "a passing rendition of me at about that stage," while Zuckerman himself—the elder and famously isolated writer—has turned into Lonoff. Zuckerman curtly refuses to support Kliman's project and tells him why: "Because the dirt-seeking snooping calling itself research is just about the lowest of literary rackets." To which Kliman has the perfect Zuckermanian retort: "And the savage snooping calling itself fiction?"

But there is no doubt about where the author's sympathies lie. Or about who he thinks will win. Although Zuckerman manages to frustrate the biographer's immediate scheme, he knows that, ultimately, there is little he will be able to do against the onslaught of "unknowing youth, savage with health and armed to the teeth with time." It's a stunning phrase, capturing the frightened, hunted feel of becoming old. The savageness of youth is built into the sound: the wicked kick at the end forces one to virtually spit out the alliterative joint of teeth and time. (The same alliteration works to much gentler but equally sensory effect in Mickey Sabbath's memory of being a child on the Jersey Shore: "You could touch with your toes where America began.")

Elsewhere in the book, the ease of the voice turns linguistic surprise into idioms so natural that you're not sure they haven't always existed: Jamie's adoring husband describes her in terms that make Zuckerman think, "It was as though he were telling me about somebody he had dreamed up in jail." Even the failure of words is eloquent. When Zuckerman is asked what it is like to be seventy, at a little birthday dinner given by his caretaker and his cook, at home in the country, he rises from his chair to tell them:

> "Think of the year 4000." They smiled, as though I were about to crack a joke, and so I added, "No, no. Think seriously about 4000. Imagine it. In all its dimensions, in all its aspects. The year 4000. Take your time." After a minute of sober silence, I quietly said to them, "That's what it's like to be seventy," and sat back down.

Time is the real subject of this book. The central love scene is not between Zuckerman and sexy Jamie but between Zuckerman and ravaged Amy Bellette—who suffers from the same disease and sports the same scar as Veronica Geng. The refashioned hospital gown, too, was Geng's, a gesture of her ironic, *in extremis* whimsy. And Amy has Geng's uncompromising passion for literature—it is her deepest bond with Zuckerman. This book is filled with ghosts. Near the end, Roth suspends the story for an eight-page disquisition on the extraordinary career and virtues of George Plimpton, whose death remains inconceivable to his old friend Zuckerman. It's the kind of interruption that a younger writer probably wouldn't dare, a formal disruption that pulls the story out of shape. But the pages on Plimpton are crucial: the original jacket cover was to have shown Plimpton himself, seated at the center of a party, in a restaurant. (It was changed because the photographer wanted too much money.) Plimpton is a force of life, like Zuckerman's friend Larry Hollis at the book's beginning. Both serve to amplify the questions that have driven Zuckerman since *The Ghost Writer* and that have now come to a crisis.

Art or life? To sit at a desk all day and "turn sentences around," as Lonoff did, as Zuckerman does, or to seek a livelier fate? The written world or the unwritten one? ("She: 'What have you given up your life for, then?' He: 'I didn't know I was giving it up.'") For Zuckerman, Plimpton—"a playful, debonair, deeply inquisitive man of the world, a

journalist, editor, and occasional film and television performer"—defined
the life well lived. "When people say to themselves 'I want to be happy,'
they could as well be saying 'I want to be George Plimpton.'" (In some
notes he made about the book, Roth compares Plimpton to the protagonist of Henry James's novel *The Ambassadors*, named Lambert Strether,
whose famous line is, "Live all you can; it's a mistake not to.") Zuckerman struggles to find the right word for the relation in which Plimpton
stood to him: "What is the word I'm looking for? The antonym of doppelgänger." The difference between them isn't one of counterlives, because Plimpton's life was never any kind of possibility for Zuckerman—or
for Roth—no matter what choices he might have made.

Intrinsic to Plimpton's success and bonhomie is the fact that he was
a member of "the monied Protestant hierarchy that had reigned over
Boston and New York society," Zuckerman states, "while my own poor
ancestors were being ruled by rabbis in the ghettos of Eastern Europe."
Plimpton provided Zuckerman with his "first glimpse of privilege and
its vast rewards":

> He seemingly had nothing to escape, no flaw to hide or injustice to defy or
> defect to compensate for or weakness to overcome or obstacle to circum-
> vent, appearing instead to have learned everything and to be open to
> everything altogether effortlessly.

Entirely unlike Zuckerman, brought up to a life of unstinting dili-
gence. Reverse the Plimpton formula—everything to escape, flaws to
hide, injustice to defy—and one has a fair idea of the driving forces
behind Plimpton's own "antonym of a doppelgänger," Zuckerman: the
Jewish writer who signed his life away to work. But Plimpton's death is
a great reproach to Zuckerman. He's suddenly ashamed of his long retreat, and, filled with regret for "all that I had squandered," he swears a
new responsibility to life. He will stay in New York, in the turmoil, in
the moment, in the drama.

And then, some twenty-five pages later, he packs his bag and flees.
Because the urological procedure did not succeed, because his memory
seems to be getting worse, and because even in his fantasy of Jamie
coming to his hotel room, what can he do with her when she arrives?
(How much humiliation can one man bear?) Zuckerman ends *He and*

She with He tearing out just as She is on her way—and by the time he writes it, he's back at home. It's a sorrowful ending for him, restored to his isolated cabin on a gray November morning and looking out from his desk over the silent, snow-dusted road. Roth reports himself rather pleased at having dispatched his best creature so cruelly. But there are some rare souls who believe that Zuckerman has made the better choice, and, in his heart, Roth seems to be one of them. In an interview in *Le Nouvel Observateur,* published in 1981, two years after *The Ghost Writer,* he said, "Art is life too, you know. Solitude is life, meditation is life, pretending is life, supposition is life, contemplation is life, language is life. Is there less life in turning sentences around than in manufacturing automobiles?" Or as Zuckerman puts it in *Exit Ghost*: "The unlived, the surmise, fully drawn in print on paper, is the life whose meaning comes to matter most."

Forging Ahead

And so "to forge ahead, into the twilight of my talent": Zuckerman, toward the end of *Exit Ghost*, is worried about having written a new book that is not quite satisfactory but that he finds himself unable to improve. Roth was seventy-four when *Exit Ghost* was published, to generally enthusiastic reviews (James Wood, in *The New Yorker*, called it "intricate, artful, and pressing") in the fall of 2007. He, too, was worried about how to forge ahead. He was writing the same number of hours every day, but he no longer had the mental stamina for a bigger book. After about six months, he says—rather than the usual two years or so that he worked on a book—he couldn't "complicate things any further." He had already completed another book, a short work that took just about five months, titled *Indignation*, but he wasn't sure how he felt about it, and, the summer before the release of *Exit Ghost*, he was going over it again and again. The criticism of some of the people he regularly relied on for initial feedback—by this time, I was one of them—underlined his worries. He had been hoping to add another big scene, but it wasn't working. Zuckerman, facing the same kind of problem, appeals to the contrasting examples of two of his heroes: Hemingway—who put aside any manuscript he couldn't finish to his satisfaction, either to work on later or to leave unpublished—and Faulkner, who gave every book his best and then, whatever the level of personal satisfaction, sent it out into the world to yield to readers whatever rewards it could. Zuckerman chooses Faulkner's way, and so did Roth. "This is the scale it is," he said about *Indignation*, and let it go.

Indignation is a modest but intense book and betrays none of its author's uncertainties. The writing is sure, simple, quickly moving. The fictional stakes are very high. The first sentence brings us simultaneously into the beginnings of the Korean War, in June 1950, and into the college career of the young protagonist, Marcus Messner. The war is not merely a backdrop. The following year, Marcus transfers from a local Newark college to rural Winesburg, in Ohio—Roth had read a new edition of Sherwood Anderson's stories just as he was starting to write—hundreds of miles from the insistent supervision of his father, whose fears for his only son's well-being have become intolerable. At Winesburg, Marcus enrolls in ROTC and abides strictly by the rules; his greatest concern is to avoid any trouble that could get him expelled and make him eligible for the draft. The components of the story are, of course, familiar: Newark, a school very much like Bucknell—with the same mandatory chapel attendance—and the interfering father. But the book's energy springs from the first youthful protagonist that Roth had attempted in some time. Innocent, brash, and, in fact, overwhelmed with indignation at any perceived injustice, Marcus, at nineteen, is younger and more raw even than Nathan Zuckerman when he came on the scene.

But Marcus is not Nathan Zuckerman, and *Indignation* is not a comedy, although it has many comic moments, most of them the result of Marcus's unknowing earnestness. Marcus's father is a kosher butcher, and Marcus grew up helping out in the shop; his story is steeped in blood from beginning to end. He will not become a writer, because he will not live long enough for the possibility to dawn on him. He is a wholly believable figure and, in his desperately proud and confused youth, rather heartbreaking (without ever being sentimentalized). The characters around him, though, are less credible: their motivations are obscure, and none seem designed to do much more than advance the story. Yet the book moves forward like a missile on a carefully plotted trajectory. Unable to provide the kind of accumulative detail that he had long considered basic to "the moral texture of fiction," Roth developed other methods. *Indignation* has the quality of a Voltairean moral fable, a latter-day *Candide*. It might be classified, with *The Dying*

Animal and *Everyman*, as a *conte philosophique*—and, the most harrowing of the three, it could be subtitled *A Soldier's Tale*.

Roth tells the story from Marcus's point of view, in the first person, even though—as Marcus himself tells us some fifty pages into the book—he has been killed in battle. Death, it seems, does not eliminate memory; death seems to be nothing *but* memory. And so Marcus, for eternity, is remembering all the trivial missteps and happentances that got him where he is: his first sexual experience (Roth makes the advent of the blowjob on the American campus seem a vital aspect of the country's social history); an argument with a roommate; a couple of tense meetings with the college dean of men; a campus snowstorm that unleashes the pent-up energies of several hundred sexually frustrated frat boys and turns into a riotous panty raid in bloodstained snow; Marcus's refusal to attend chapel services and his being caught paying another student to forge his name on the chapel attendance sheet. It's a brief history of meaningless infractions. Yet somehow, cumulatively, these events have led him to a numbered hill on a spiny ridge in central Korea, covered with corpses and more blood than he has seen since boyhood visits with his father to the local slaughterhouse.

The premise of the book is another "what if" situation, another counterlife. What if Roth's hectoring, continually worried, overprotective father had been right? What if Roth's magazine satire at Bucknell had got him expelled from school? The pages are filled with conscious portents:

> I envisioned my father's knives and cleavers whenever I read about the bayonet combat against the Chinese in Korea. I knew how murderously sharp sharp could be. And I knew what blood looked like, encrusted around the necks of the chickens where they had been ritually slaughtered, dripping out of the beef onto my hands when I was cutting a rib steak along the bone, seeping through the brown paper bags despite the wax paper wrappings within, settling into the grooves crosshatched into the chopping block by the force of the cleaver crashing down.

The language itself inflicts violence—the double "sharp," the almost Germanic snap of consonants ("encrusted around the neck," "the cleaver crashing down"), the buildup of "dripping" and "cutting" and "seeping," so that, in the end, even an innocent word like "crosshatched" seems ominous.

Marcus has good reason to worry about his fate, despite being a prudent, responsible, hardworking boy and an A student. In Ohio, he's traveled so far from his familial element that he's barely aware of his own maladaptation to the larger American world. Roth had never before depicted quite this sort of gropingly innocent outsiderness, or as pained a view of the poor Jewish boy's commitment to unstinting work. Marcus has to scrape and strain for everything: he has a single good set of clothes that he bought to match the clothes of a student in a photograph in the college catalogue; he works all weekend waiting on tables, and he isn't sure if the beer-sodden kids demanding his attention are calling out "Hey, you!" or "Hey, Jew!" He is so fearful of breaking the rules and being cast out—which means, in this case, Korea—that he won't masturbate in the school bathroom. But it isn't sex that finally does him in. Marcus is enraged when he has to sit through a sermon in chapel about "Christ's example"—enraged not because he's a Jew, he insists, but because he's a wholly rational atheist. It's typical of Roth that the college dean who is ultimately responsible for Marcus's dreadful death is not a villain: an ex-football star and a devout Christian, he is simply a man at home in a world where Marcus, fighting with his roommates and changing from room to room, literally cannot find a place. Their confrontation reveals not only the older man's sanctimony but his attempted fairness; not only the youth's independent-minded bravery but his inability to master his indignation and save himself.

So there's another "what if" situation: what if Roth, in college, had been unable to bear attending chapel, as Marcus, on a gut level, is unable to? Indeed, Roth tells me that he *couldn't* bear "the pieties and banalities of those clergymen who spoke to us." (He adds, however, with what seems an old and protective reflex, "the rabbi was the worst—he pronounced God with three syllables." It seems that to limit criticism to the Christians still implies resentment and a wholly repugnant sense of victimhood.) So did Roth refuse to attend? Did he pay someone to forge his name on the attendance sheet—apparently as common a practice at Bucknell as it is at Winesburg? "No," he replies to the question. "I went." He read in the pew—Schopenhauer's *The World as Will and Idea* and Carlyle's *On Heroes, Hero-Worship, and the Heroic in History,* he recalls. ("If a smart person mentioned a book, I read it.") But he didn't flash the covers: "I was defiant enough to read them but not defiant enough to advertise it." And while he says of chapel that at times "I thought it would kill me!"—it didn't. And he didn't always have such a bad time, either, given that "the girls were there en masse: long skirts and Peter Pan blouses and cashmere cardigans; they wore full slips." Now he is following the memory down a happier path: "Betty"—his girlfriend at Bucknell—"wore a full slip . . ." There were other things to think about. It's another lesson in the difference between autobiography and the raising of the stakes that is fiction. Marcus dies because he refuses to sit through Christian sermons—dies, in the simplest sense, of being a much less compromising and more defiant Jew than Roth ever was.

Despite the book's brevity, Roth doesn't hesitate to take on an entire era, casting a cold eye on its sexual repressiveness, its habits of surveillance, its provincial rectitude. Yet *Indignation* appeared to have a grim timeliness when it came out, in the fall of 2008, amid the public outcry over military casualties in Iraq and the government's refusal to allow the publication of photographs of homecoming coffins—both facts mentioned in the review by Charles Simic in *The New York Review of Books*. Roth had been inspired by a very different war, but this time he did not disclaim the parallels, as he had with the contemporary reading of *The Plot Against America*. "If you look in the newspaper at the names and ages of the soldiers getting killed in Iraq now," he said in an interview in the *Barnes & Noble Review*, "you find these terrifying ages like 19 and 22; it's just awful. And it was that particular awfulness of young death that engaged me." The college president's denunciation of students, following the panty raid—"A world is on fire and you are kindled by underwear"—seemed to some critics a fair rebuke to a citizenry as oblivious and as anesthetized by trivia as the Winesburg students, who are warned that "history will catch you in the end."

Marcus's address from the dead seems a strange venture into the uncanny. The dark, interior world in which he continues to exist, disembodied and alone, is to him an uncertain location between heaven and hell:

> It's not memory that's obliviated here—it's time. There is no letup—for the afterlife is without sleep as well . . . here there is nothing to think

about but the bygone life. Does that make "here" hell? Or heaven? . . . You can't go forward here, that's for sure. There are no doors. There are no days. The direction (for now?) is only back. And the judgment is endless, though not because some deity judges you, but because your actions are naggingly being judged for all time by yourself.

Is this a refutation of Marcus's atheism? A proof of it? Was Roth going soft and metaphysical in his later years, allowing for suggestions from beyond the grave? (And what of the voices that Everyman hears at his parents' graves? Maybe they were not, after all, only in his head?)

As we learn near the book's end, Marcus was wrong about being dead, although not about the battle. Suffering horribly from bayonet wounds that have nearly severed a leg and shredded his intestines, he has done all this remembering in a morphine haze: the drug hit his brain like a "mnemonic fuel." (The book's first chapter—almost as long as the book itself, extending straight through until this point—is titled "Under Morphine": we were told and still we didn't know.) And then, in chapter 2—barely seven pages long and titled "Out from Under"— Marcus really does die. Memory ceases, the medics pull his poncho over his face, and there is nothing more to be heard, except for his father's sobbing at the news, back in Newark. Absolutely nothing.

For Roth, who tells me that the book began with being "fed up with the politicians spouting about God," this nothing was an essential point, maybe *the* essential point. He remains as much a rational atheist as his nineteen-year-old hero. And while he has a warm appreciation for what he gained on an American college campus in the fifties—a solid education, lifelong friends—the social and sexual mores of the era is a subject that has yet to exhaust his indignation. (He sent a copy of *Indignation* to the woman he credits with "the only blowjob performed at Bucknell between 1950 and 1954." Roth says that he himself was flabbergasted, at the time—"This wasn't even on my list of fantasies"—and the girl, appalled at what she'd done, refused to go out with him again. More than half a century later, she replied with a gracious letter about her knee operation and her granddaughter, and reminded him that on their first date he had told her to read Thomas Wolfe.) A concluding "Histori-cal Note," a single paragraph long, relates that, twenty years after Mar-cus's death, as a result of the student movement of the sixties, "virtually all the strictures and parietal rules regulating student conduct," including mandatory chapel, were eliminated at Winesburg. If it's possible to intensify a sense of nothing—of futility, of the sheer randomness of fate—Roth does it here.

⚮

Even after he finished *Indignation*, Roth was feeling discontented, because he was having trouble getting something new under way. ("How long can you go without working on a book?" I asked him at the time. "Psychologically," he replied, "about two hours.") With shorter books, the gaps between were getting more frequent ("I hate the void"), and it was ever harder to summon the energy needed to start anew. He returned to the pages he'd written about a failing actor that he had put aside to write *Everyman*, and by late 2008 he had finished a very brief book, *The Humbling*, in which, for the first time in Roth's work, the protagonist commits suicide. (Mickey Sabbath spends an entire book trying to do himself in, but he is too bound to life to carry out the deed.)

It was a difficult time for Roth, with deaths and illnesses continuing to accumulate. William Styron, a close friend for decades, died in November 2006. Roth's brother, suffering a miserable array of illnesses, was in constant pain and not expected to live long. And in January 2009, John Updike died, at the age of seventy-six; he was precisely one year and one day older than Roth. They had started out nearly simultaneously: *Goodbye, Columbus* appeared the same year, 1959, as Updike's first novel, *The Poorhouse Fair*. A decade later, they had profitably scandalized the country with *Couples* (1968) and *Portnoy's Complaint* (1969). The two men had not talked in some ten years, however, since the falling-out over Claire Bloom's book. Maybe, Roth says now, he was a little "too raw" in his feelings then. In any case, he feels Updike's death as a serious loss—not so much personally but for the culture; he would like to have been able to read Updike on Obama, for example. In the weeks afterward, he speaks with great admiration about the way Updike spent his final months: "He was writing poetry!" Most impressive, he wrote a poem called "Spirit of '76" for what turned out to be his final birthday. ("Be with me, words, a little longer . . .") "Not complaining or whining in the end," Roth says, "but writing." One day that

winter, I asked Roth if he regretted having let so many years go by without resuming contact, and he replied, without elaboration, "Yes."

Not that they were ever close. Rather, they were what Roth calls
"friends at a distance," a description that seems to fit Updike's sense of
the relationship, too. (Asked if he and Roth were friends, in an interview in London's *Telegraph* just months before he died, Updike report-
edly gave a cryptic smile and answered, "Guardedly.") They were mutual
admirers, wary competitors who were thrilled to have each other in the
world to up their game: Picasso and Matisse. That's a very loose analogy, in which Roth would have to be Picasso—the energy, the slashing
power—and Updike would be Matisse: the color, the sensuality. (Roth
calls Updike the only American writer who ever approached the guilt-
less sensuality of Colette—a tremendous tribute.) The essential difference in their perspectives isn't so much Christian versus Jewish, or
believer versus nonbeliever, or small town versus city, although it involves all of these. As writers, their greatest virtues seem to arise from
different principal organs of perception, which might be crudely cate-
gorized as the eye and the ear. Updike was a painter in words—he
studied art for a year at Oxford—although the bleak loneliness of his
vision is often closer to Hopper than to Matisse. Roth is the master of
voices: the arguments, the joking, the hysterical exchanges, the inner
wrangling even when a character is alone, the sound of a mind at work.
There's not a page by one that could be mistaken for a page by the
other. But they are united in having spent a lifetime possessed by America. To go from Rabbit Angstrom to Nathan Zuckerman is, literally, to
go from A to Z in the history of the country in the years after the Second World War—the years in which, as Roth has said, "America discovered itself as America."

The day that I asked Roth about regrets, he was reminiscing about
times he had spent with Updike and other friends on Martha's Vineyard in the sixties, arguing about the war. Updike wrote in some detail
about those arguments—first, transformed into fiction in *Rabbit Redux*
(1971), and then in his memoir, *Self-Consciousness*, published in 1989.
In the memoir, Roth is portrayed as "on the dizzying verge of publishing
'Portnoy's Complaint'" and as looking "puzzled" by Updike's defense of
"Johnson and his pitiful ineffective war machine." At pains to understand his now embarrassing hawkishness, Updike recalls his revulsion

at the anti-war extremists of the era, particularly "the totalitarian intolerance and savagery epitomized by the Weathermen." For years, he carried in his wallet a slip of paper printed with a Weathermen slogan, the same lines (with small grammatical changes) that Merry Levov puts up on her wall: "We are against everything that's good and decent in honky America. We will loot, burn, and destroy. We are the incubation of your mother's nightmare." Broadening the subject to the morality of war, Updike notes that some religious systems recognize that merely to be alive is to kill: "The Jains try to hide this by wearing gauze masks to avoid inhaling insects." It's a startling conjunction of subjects: Roth, the Weathermen, and the Jains, all within six pages, published about five years before Roth began *American Pastoral*. It's hard not to see the tiny seed of Merry's terrible development here, and certainly it doesn't detract from Roth's monumental fictional construct to say so, or from the details that give it life: wretched Merry, in order to "do no harm to the microscopic organisms that dwell in the air," makes a mask from the foot of an old stocking. Yet it seems that Roth and Updike had a nourishing exchange, even from a distance.

Updike, who didn't review any of Roth's books after *Operation Shylock*, confessed his competitiveness in the *Telegraph* interview, implying that he felt it especially keenly at the time—October 26, 2008—"since Philip really has the upper hand in the rivalry as far as I can tell." It had not always been so. "I think in a list of admirable novelists there was a time when I might have been near the top, just tucked under Bellow," he went on. But it seemed to him that Roth's reputation had advanced, and that Roth "seems more dedicated in a way to the act of writing as a means of really reshaping the world to your liking." Whether this is meant as a virtue or a fault is not entirely clear. He admits that he has not read everything but considers himself "more of a partisan of the earlier books than the later." Still, Roth has been "very good to have around." One senses the earth-moving, bone-grinding effort behind this kind of lifelong production when Updike explains that, after fifty years of writing, he has recently begun to work on Sundays (it had been his only day off, "as a churchgoer") and then describes Roth as "scarily devoted to the novelist's craft."

For Roth, Updike's finest works are the third and fourth Rabbit books—*Rabbit Is Rich, Rabbit at Rest*—and the early stories. (Like

Updike, he doesn't claim to have read everything.) The books he likes least—"If he were here," Roth remarks, "he would say, 'Of course you do'"—are the ones about the Jewish writer Henry Bech. ("He puts all of his writing experiences into the life of this Jewish writer," Roth says, in his Web of Stories interview. "I'm not convinced.") But Roth is a tremendous admirer of Updike's whole career: the fortitude, the industry, the sentences, the fluency—the "gush of prose" that he believes Updike (like Bellow) had at his command. "I don't have the gush of prose," Roth tells me. "I have the gush of invention, dialogue, event . . . but not of prose." It's a distinction he seems to have thought about carefully. "Many days I was delighted to accept one page after six hours of work. On days when I'd have four or five pages they would not be fluent, and I'd have to spend four or five days working on them."

A listener must be careful not to take the mood of a moment as a sign of settled judgment; on other occasions, Roth describes the writing of some of his books—*Sabbath's Theater, American Pastoral*—as an "outpouring." But ultimately he is serious about how hard he works for what he gets and how different his process has been from Updike's or Bellow's. On the wall of his Connecticut studio, he keeps a chart of the alphabet, "to remind myself that it's only the alphabet, stupid—it's just the letters that you know and they make words." Still, he says, "I have to fight for my fluency, every paragraph, every sentence." And then he sits back and imagines a series of books he might have written in the Updike manner—*Rabbi, Run; Rabbi Redux; Rabbi Is Rich*—and he roars with laughter.

∞

There would have been little question about the winner of the PEN/ Saul Bellow Award for Achievement in American Fiction in 2009 if Updike had not died two months before the committee met. The award, given to "a distinguished living American author whose body of work in English possesses qualities of excellence, ambition, and scale of achievement over a sustained career which places him or her in the highest rank of American literature," was established by PEN and funded, in Bellow's honor, by private donors. It had been given for the first time in 2007, two years after Bellow's death, to Philip Roth. And because of the way the award is administered, Roth was part of the very small committee (along with Benjamin Taylor, then editing the Bellow letters, and me) assigned to determine the second winner. Roth takes this award very seriously. The fact that it's in Bellow's name is important to him. There was also the matter of some recent, stinging comments from the permanent secretary of the Swedish Academy, the organization that awards the Nobel Prize in Literature, criticizing the entire field of American writers as "too sensitive to trends in their own mass culture," and denouncing the culture itself as "too isolated, too insular" to allow for a role in "the big dialogue of literature." Roth was understandably incensed by the remarks. During committee meetings, he talks about how many great American writers there are and have been, saying, "It's amazing, in the company, that one can write at all." But he has never been much troubled by competition. The only real competitor of his generation, he says, was Mailer, who took his attitude from Hemingway. And, by the way—we are off and running now—he says he is immensely pleased to have discovered the word "papaphobia" in the thesaurus, when he was looking up "evil." It means "fear of the pope," although he likes the idea that it might also be used to mean "fear of Hemingway."

But living writers are the subject of discussion. There is a list. There is a lot of reading to do. (In a brief moment of giddiness, when we are down to two writers and no agreement, Roth suggests that we put the names in a hat—"I have Saul's hat in the closet!") Most interesting is not what Roth says about these writers but what he says about them in comparison with himself. In a discussion of a historical novel, he suddenly gets an idea: "Here's my book set in the nineteenth century: It was 1845 in the Weequahic section of Newark . . . World War Two was still almost a hundred years away . . ."

And finally there are two stacks of books on the table, one by Cormac McCarthy, the other by Don DeLillo. We have talked for a while, and Roth is quietly leafing through a couple of the books. "These guys are interested in extremes," he says, "nothing but extremes. They're the opposite of Cheever and Updike: Cheever, who tried to see real life in a brighter light, and Updike, who wanted to know every detail and nuance of it." And then, sounding rather sad, he says, "They make me look ordinary." (McCarthy won in 2009; DeLillo won the award the following year.)

On an extraliterary note, I have expressed some squeamishness during our sessions at the gruesome deaths of animals in McCarthy's *Blood Meridian*: the mules viciously kicked and shot or driven off the side of a cliff, the horse's skull crushed with a rock, the dogs drowned *and* shot. At the next meeting, when I ring the doorbell at Roth's apartment, he cries out cheerily from within: "Be right there, I'm just skinning a kangaroo!"

You Never Got Me Down

"**H**e'd lost his magic." It's the opening line of *The Humbling*, and Roth spins the idea outward from there. The aging actor at its center led an extraordinary life while the magic held, but the book is about what happens after it's gone. A renowned interpreter of Shakespeare and Chekhov, he began to freeze up onstage, to give terrible performances, and has finally accepted that he will never perform again. Very little of the pleasure that Roth takes in the theater is apparent here. This book is about a man coming to the end of his life, alone and unconsoled—like *Everyman*, like *Exit Ghost*, even like *Indignation*, although the man in that case is only nineteen. Unfortunately, the actor, Simon Axler, has neither Nathan Zuckerman's ironic humor nor Marcus Messner's fresh energy. Despite his stage credentials, Axler has something of the blank anonymity of Everyman. He has been reduced to little more than his disabilities—professional, psychological, and physical, including chronic back pain and a nervous breakdown that sends him to a psychiatric hospital for twenty-six days. *The Humbling*, published in 2009, is a book as strenuously reduced as its hero, and as depressive.

Axler suffers a double downfall. It should not be a surprise, with book number thirty, that the aging man fixes his hopes on a younger woman. Not, in this case, however, an impossibly, allegorically younger woman: Pegeen is forty to Axler's sixty-five. But Roth has added a twist that negates any chance of sexual salvation or even peace of mind. Pegeen is a lesbian, or has lived as a lesbian since her early twenties, and

Axler is tormented by the fear that she will return to her former life. Yet he has been alone for so long that he has no emotional resistance, and he is soon wildly in love. And because "in her company he had begun to be rejuvenated," he begins to dream about reconstructing his entire life: returning to the stage, having back surgery, even becoming a father—there is a scene in which he consults a doctor about the genetic hazards of fathering a child at sixty-five. The higher the hopes, the harder the fall. And this is a man who keeps a gun in his attic, and knows his Chekhov.

How agonizingly vulnerable Roth's men have become! Pegeen isn't much of a character, but that hardly matters: all that's required is for her to bring him a glass of water, and Axler starts to fall. ("Nobody had brought him a glass of water for a long time.") And she is soon doing much more, particularly since Axler's spinal condition "made it impossible for him to fuck her from above or even from the side." This is a woman who, in every way, stays on top. The book builds toward a series of in-your-face sex scenes, which begin the final chapter with a bang, so to speak, but feel forced and artificial, even dull, despite an energetic threesome and a strap-on green dildo. There's nothing wrong with providing a green dildo at this point in a very gray story, but this is the most perfunctory sex in Roth's work since the early sections of *The Professor of Desire*, which seem equally strained in an attempt to be outrageous. Sex, in the best of Roth, is part of life's relentless comedy, even when, as his heroes age, it becomes the great, tingling counterforce to death. But neither Axler's situation nor his temperament allows for comedy; even during the threesome, he's tempted to sit in a corner and cry. A note of wryness, at least, creeps in, when Pegeen, strapped for action, informs him that she has cheated on him with two female ballplayers and then eases his anxiety by performing fellatio on him as he thinks, "The oddity of this combination would have put off many people."

And it did. Roth himself wasn't entirely happy with the book, and he kept at it even after galleys went out for review. "Fixing the surface," he explained to me at the time: "making sentences better, more precise." These efforts were strictly for himself: it doesn't matter, he says, which version gets reviewed. He shrugs and laughs. The reviews, however, were exceptionally harsh. Leon Wieseltier, on *The New Republic* website: "There is no erotic abandon in Roth, not anymore; there is only conquest, and programmatic sex, and a sad prurience, and the bathos of a man who is most afraid of not getting laid." Not universally harsh, it's true: there's always someone to call a new Roth book his "best work in years" (Jesse Kornbluth, *The Huffington Post*). More notably, the feminist historian Elaine Showalter, in *The Washington Post*, praised the novel's "restrained eloquence" and used the occasion to make a larger statement on Roth's career, calling him "a literary colossus, whose ability to inspire, astonish and enrage his readers is undiminished."

Still, "enrage" turned out to be a key word. On the front page of *The New York Times Book Review*, Katie Roiphe opened an essay about male writers with an account of a friend who had thrown her copy of *The Humbling* into a trash can on a subway platform after reading one of the sex scenes—not because of feminist objections but because it was "disgusting, dated, redundant." Provoking rage was not, of course, a new experience for Roth. ("What is being done to silence this man?") But he hadn't done so in some time, and this development, in early 2010, was in some ways encouraging.

"You know, I'm an old man," he says. "And hating writers has gone out, as a style. It was around when writers were more combative. I guess I was supposed to be combative." It wouldn't be a bad thing, really—Salman Rushdie–style death threats aside—to have "a more vehement response to work, mine and others', back in the culture." To have books matter that much again. And so, I ask, is it still stirring in some way to get this kind of furious response? Does it start his own combative juices flowing? "Well," he replies, "it's true that it once gave me a subject." He pauses. "But if I had my druthers, I'd rather not be hated."

The truly disturbing aspect of *The Humbling* is Axler's continual brooding over how it feels to lose his talent. "You can get very good at getting by on what you get by on when you don't have anything else," he says, in a statement that applies almost too readily to these late novels, which, while a shadow of Roth's earlier works, maintain the narrative line of a master and the troubled insistence of a man who has not yet gleaned his teeming brain. In instance after instance, Axler's acting seems to be a stand-in for Roth's writing: "The initial source in his acting was in what he heard, his response to what he heard was at the core of it, and if he couldn't listen, couldn't hear, he had nothing to go on."

Axler describes the condition necessary for his art in the same terms that Roth uses to describe his own: "You're either free and it's genuine, it's real, it's alive, or it's nothing." And Axler concludes, "I'm not free anymore."

There is no older or more familiar trap in reading Roth's work, of course, than to mistake a book's voice for the author's autobiographical confession. The facts, as Roth has explained time after time, exist to be eviscerated by the imagination—as with Marcus Messner's path from chapel to grave. So, while it's true that Roth did have a torrid affair in these years with a forty-year-old former lesbian, he survived it perfectly well, and they are friends today. It's also true that he began to think about having a child and consulted a doctor about genetic feasibility— but this was a little later, and with a different lover. If this book were a conventional biography, there would be names and dates; that will come along, in time. What is important is that the affairs were becoming shorter and more difficult to maintain—just like the books. (In neither case, however, did the excitement show any sign of diminution.) And that Roth is a far braver and (needless to say) more resilient character than his hero. Axler, in the light of his artistic losses, quits the stage and, finally, uses the gun. At the time of the publication of *The Humbling*, Roth announced that he had completed another book.

Titled *Nemesis*, the book has none of the old exuberant freedoms, yet it is bracingly taut, engaging, and alive. These qualities did not come easily; Roth claims to have written thirteen drafts. ("This only happens when you're not getting it.") He hadn't had so much trouble working on anything since *My Life as a Man*. Published in 2010, the book is written with the blunt straightforwardness that characterizes all these late works—as though there were time for nothing but the basics—and takes up the same dark themes. In fact, Roth now decided to group, under the plural heading *Nemeses: Short Novels*, the quartet of *Everyman, Indignation, The Humbling*, and, finally, *Nemesis* itself, which is superficially the warmest yet ultimately the most savage of these small books. Roth does better with his younger heroes, in that he seems to feel obliged to fill out the worlds that they inhabit before everything is snatched away. Or maybe it's simply that these young men, unlike their isolated elders, still *have* worlds to inhabit. Better yet, neighborhoods: Bucky Cantor, the twenty-three-year-old protagonist of

Nemesis, is a gym teacher and the playground director at the Chancellor Avenue School, in the Weequahic section of Newark, in the summer of 1944. The prosaic charms of the place—the kids, the families, the hot dog joint—are a poignant setting for the hell that is unleashed.

Nemesis is a goddess of retribution in Greek mythology; she metes out punishment to those who have had an excess of good fortune, or who commit some other crime that provokes the envy of the gods. But Roth's heroes have not committed any crimes. They are punished because punishment is the human lot. Roth says today that a reasonable overarching title for his previous series of books would be *Blindsided: An American Trilogy.* We are helpless before history, aging, other people, our endless getting of everything wrong: the unknowable future. Roth has banged this drum again and again. He is intent on refuting not only standard religious claims about virtue and justice but the common and often misused notion, rooted in Freud's ideas about the Greeks and our own lives, that we are psychologically complicit in our fate.

He has been contesting these kinds of charges ever since Dr. Spielvogel, in *My Life as a Man,* accused Peter Tarnopol of getting into his awful marriage because his wife resembled his "phallic threatening mother"—a bit of "psychoanalytic reductivism" that sets off several furious pages of rebuttal. But Roth's insistence on our inability to see ahead and to choose—our essential innocence—has evolved, over the years, from a personal defense into a hard-earned theory of life. (Roth likes to quote Bellow: "Truth comes in blows.") Still, even today, he can get worked up about "the five-and-dime-store pseudo-Freudians"—I am quoting from some unpublished notes about his personal history—who "tell us that *we* make the future with our deliberate blindness and self-deceptions." The *Nemeses* quartet, and its last book, above all, demonstrates that our blindness is real, even if we are blind to that, too.

The nemesis this time is polio. Although the narrative's epidemic of the summer of 1944 is as fictional as Lindbergh's presidency, it is an easy premise to accept, eleven years before the vaccine became available. The threat of the disease had haunted Roth's childhood—or, rather, since it was particularly a killer of children, it haunted his parents during his childhood, as it did most parents of the era. Roth recalls that he and Sandy, healthy and well protected, didn't believe that anything could seriously hurt them. Bucky Cantor is not so lucky: his mother died in childbirth, his father disappeared, and although he was brought up by loving grandparents, his grandfather has died and he is more the caretaker of his grandmother than the other way around. There hasn't been so unparented a young protagonist in Roth's work since Neil Klugman in *Goodbye, Columbus* more than fifty years earlier.

Neil lived in Newark with an aunt and uncle, his parents having decamped to Arizona for the climate—a tactic that kept the author's mocking eye trained on less intimate familial targets (until he was good and ready for them). Both Neil and Bucky are just out of college, come from scrappy Jewish immigrant backgrounds, and fall in love with girls from well-to-do Jewish families above their station. But the distance from 1959 to 2010 is immense: the writer starting off with a flourish and a wisecrack, the writer nearing the end with a solemn warning and a shudder. There is very little mockery in *Nemesis*. The moment of its setting is historically fraught, filled with news of soldiers dying overseas—Bucky is exempt from the draft owing to poor eyesight—and children dying at home. This is as late as "late Roth" gets, and there is too much at stake to laugh.

Bucky, a jock and a gentle soul, is described, in fact, as "a humorless person, articulate enough but with barely a trace of wit, who never in his life had spoken satirically or with irony"—precisely the kind of challenge that Roth had been taking up since *American Pastoral*. Bucky isn't trusted to tell his own story, any more than was Swede Levov. Roth's use of third-person narration gives the book a cooler and more impersonal feel than any of the books in which a voice comes directly at us. The question of just who is telling this story—indeed, the sense that anyone in particular is telling the story—arises only with an occasional odd reference to the hero as "Mr. Cantor." This riddle is partially solved a hundred pages in, with the passing mention of "me, Arnie Mesnikoff," among the boys who got polio that summer. The history of this boy will come to have greater meaning. As with *Indignation*, Roth has tricks up his sleeve—old-fashioned tricks, but carried off so well that they make up for at least some of the interest and surprise that used to be part of the writing itself. ("You can get very good at getting by on what you get by on.")

Roth had reread Camus's novel *The Plague* before writing *Nemesis*, and several reviewers noted its influence. Camus, too, plays a trick with narration—it's a doctor, familiar from the start, who turns out to be telling the story—but Roth says that the idea of a narrating victim of his plague came to him only as he went along. Compared with Camus's magisterial allegory, Roth's novel seems crowded with noisily grieving aunts, awkwardly weeping fathers, and schoolboys stiff in their shirts and ties at an untimely funeral—all sweating mightily in "the annihilating heat of equatorial Newark," as relentless as the heat of Camus's Algerian port. Roth is ever striving for the particularity that is the novelist's greatest strength. (Bellow, writing to Roth in the late fifties, criticized one of Roth's stories because it relied too much on an idea. "Camus' *The Plague* was an IDEA. Good or bad? Not so hot, in my opinion.") Yet the "moral texture" of *Nemesis*, like that of the other books in this group, comes through in the handling of more overt moral questions, of the sort that Bucky is asked by one of those sweating, weeping fathers: "Where is the sense in life?" Or, as Bucky puts it to himself: "Why a disease that cripples children?" And, at his most urgent: "Where does God figure in this?"

Nemesis is about conscience and duty as much as it is about the randomness of fate. The question of moral responsibility has possessed Roth's heroes from the overthoughtful duo of *Letting Go* and the raging Portnoy—what else was he raging against?—to the battling father and son of *The Dying Animal*. Bucky Cantor is tortured by not being in the war, when all his friends are off and fighting; the same headline, COR-REGIDOR FALLS, that filled the young Roth with fear fills Bucky with terrible shame. It's a matter of manhood, in an era when manhood is a moral achievement; Bucky's grandfather had taught him "that a man's every endeavor was imbued with responsibility." Bucky proves himself by supervising some ninety children at a playground during the summer, as shrieking ambulances become more frightening than air-raid sirens, and as the epidemic gathers the force of a "real war too, a war of slaughter, ruin, waste, and damnation, war with the ravages of war—war upon the children of Newark." Bucky is an ordinary young man, but he is also heroic on a limited scale—a loving protector of the children who worship him.

Until he quits and runs away. His reasons aren't entirely clear; he startles even himself with his decision. The turning point comes when

he is visiting the house of his girlfriend, Marcia Steinberg. Marcia is no
Brenda Patimkin; a first-grade teacher, she is just as genial as Bucky,
and her family has not a trace of Patimkin-style vulgarity. Her father, a
doctor, is a man of "natural, unadorned authority," unfailingly kind and
wise. Marcia is away when Bucky makes his visit; she, too, is working
as a camp counselor, but in the Poconos, where the kids are healthy
and far better off than Bucky's Newark charges. Bucky, without a father
of his own, has come seeking advice, and is suitably awed by the family's house, with its "surfeit of bathrooms" (more than one) and its back-
yard garden. (Bucky is such a naïf that he thought only public parks had
gardens.) He isn't wildly ambivalent, like Neil at the Patimkins', or
wildly excited, like Portnoy at his college girlfriend's big American
house, which "might have been the Taj Mahal for the emotions it released in me"—there's no wildness in Bucky of any kind. He is just
quietly impressed, most of all by the sweetness of a rather symbolic
peach he is given to eat, which falls somewhere between the biblical
apple and Patimkin bounty. Add a phone call from Marcia that suggests
the pleasures of parentally unsupervised sex, and the next thing Bucky
knows, he has taken a job at Marcia's camp and left behind both the
sweltering city and its dying children. Bucky merely wants to have a
break, to feel a breeze, to get away from death. As Marcia tells him,
"This is simply prudence in the face of danger—it's common sense!"

The Poconos are a break for us, too. Blue skies, fresh air, a little
sweet-natured, very discreet sex on a nearby island—this book could
not be more different from *The Humbling*—and even a touch of humor
at the expense of an Indian-themed camp for Jewish children. ("It's our
medicine man," another counselor informs Bucky when, on Indian
Night, a figure in a commanding bird-mask appears: "It's Barry Fein-
berg.") But much of this material seems merely filler, a series of distractions meant to take our minds off the city streets and the attendant
worries about polio, so that we will be as shocked as Bucky is when a
teenage counselor in his cabin is stricken, just a week after Bucky arrives. The only conclusion, for Bucky, is that he is a carrier of the disease and has infected innocents both on the city playground and in the
bucolic mountains—several more campers quickly become sick—before,
finally, he succumbs himself.

Bucky is hospitalized and then in rehabilitation for more than a year, but he survives, physically crippled yet no worse off than many other polio victims of the time, including President Roosevelt and Arnie Mesnikoff. Arnie recognizes his old teacher on the street one day, in 1971, twenty-seven years after that awful summer—and more than a decade after the vaccine had virtually eradicated the disease, making the afflictions these men still bear seem even more gallingly gratuitous. It turns out that they have adapted to their fates in entirely different ways. And this difference, it seems, is the point and meaning of the entire story. Arnie has gone on to get married, to have children, and to start an engineering business that specializes in adapting buildings for access by the handicapped. Bucky, on the other hand, refused to marry Marcia all those years ago, certain that he had to free her of her obligation— that his last chance to be a man of integrity was to spare "the virtuous young woman he dearly loved from unthinkingly taking a cripple as her mate for life." He has lived alone ever since, cut off from everything that once mattered to him. And he has never stopped hating the God who made everything happen the way it did.

Nemesis is notable among Roth's books for containing a Hebrew prayer. True, Portnoy prays for his mother's deliverance from cancer— "Baruch atoh Adonai, *let it be benign!*"—and Neil Klugman has his own approach to the Divine: "I am carnal, and I know You approve, I just know it. But how carnal can I get?" But this is something more serious. "May His great Name be blessed forever and ever," the prayer reads, in part, in the English translation printed beneath the Hebrew text. It is recited at the funeral of a twelve-year-old, on an incineratingly hot day in Newark in 1944, when Bucky is already ablaze with his refusal "to swallow the official lie that God is good and truckle before a cold-blooded murderer of children." Ultimately, Bucky's search for explanations exceeds even Swede Levov's; his bitter retreat from life exceeds even Nathan Zuckerman's. The most harshly assailed of Roth's assailable men—assailed from within as well as without—he bases the rest of his life on a vision of God as

an omnipotent being whose nature and purpose was to be adduced not from doubtful biblical evidence but from irrefutable historical proof, gleaned during a lifetime passed on this planet in the middle of the twentieth century. His conception of God was of an omnipotent being who was a union not of three persons in one Godhead, as in Christianity, but of two—a sick fuck and an evil genius.

To Arnie, this is not blasphemy—Arnie thinks in terms of chance, not of God—but merely "stupid hubris": "the hubris of fantastical, childish religious interpretation." To Arnie's atheistic mind, Bucky's need to find a reason for everything is absurd. "He has to ask why. Why? Why? That it is pointless, contingent, preposterous, and tragic will not satisfy him." One tends not to think of Roth's work in theological terms, yet this endlessly troubling "Why? Why?" goes back to the very beginning, to the thirteen-year-old Hebrew school student of the story "The Conversion of the Jews," who pursues the story's rabbi with the same kind of irksome and unanswerable questions about God. Familiar, too, is the question of why one child is consigned to unspeakable suffering and death, through an accident of geography, while another child gets, so to speak, the Poconos—which, until the plot twist at the end of the book, is a green and perfect place where children grow up undisturbed: a "splendid sanctuary," an America. ("Why does He set one person down in Nazi-occupied Europe with a rifle in his hands," Bucky thinks, making the analogy wholly clear, "and the other in the Indian Hill dining lodge in front of a plate of macaroni and cheese?") And Bucky is hardly the first of Roth's protagonists to qualify for Arnie's furious condemnation as a "maniac of the why."

It seemed evident to me, on finishing the book, that Arnie is the saner man—by virtue of having salvaged a life out of meaningless catastrophe—and that Bucky suffers from what Dr. Steinberg, early on, calls "a misplaced sense of responsibility." But J. M. Coetzee took another view, in an especially thoughtful critique in *The New York Review of Books*. Bucky, he writes, in trying "to grasp God's mysterious designs," is the one who "takes humanity, and the reach of human understanding, seriously." He may be pigheaded and self-defeating, but he "keeps an ideal of human dignity alive in the face of fate, Nemesis, the gods, God." Camus also presents an argument about God, between the doctor and a priest, after they have observed the horrible death of a child and joined battle in, of all places, a school playground. The doctor, rather like Coetzee, divides the post-plague population into people who regain happiness because their desires are limited to human love, and those "who aspired beyond and above the human individual to-wards something they could not even imagine." The path for such people is, of course, much harder.

"I wasn't interested in the philosophical reverberations," Roth responds to these readings and their implications, "only in the psychological soundness." He finds that Coetzee takes a "grander stand" than he himself is able to do. ("It's a stand I would have taken as a younger man.") Yet his own assessment differs more in language than in kind, as he, too, defends Bucky's lonely resolve. He could have written a book about a man who was savvy and selfish enough to hang on to Marcia's love, Roth says, and to let her spend the rest of her life taking care of him—but *Nemesis* is not that book. Because, Roth tells me, Bucky is "bigger than that." And what if the woman wanted to take care of him? "There are some men who don't like being taken care of," he replies—"my brother, my father, being taken care of was a misery to them." And what if Bucky is wrong about his responsibility for spreading the disease? And even if he is responsible, he's really just another victim (as Arnie points out), isn't he? "Well," Roth says—pushed into a grander stand—"Oedipus wasn't responsible, either, in that he didn't know what he was doing. And Bucky, like Oedipus, chooses to live the way he lives, in recognition of the greatest fact of his life."

Nemesis concludes with a brief vision of Bucky at his youthful best, a latter-day Greek hero, showing his awestruck boys how to throw a javelin and counseling them to practice the three D's: "determination, dedication, and discipline." The contrast between the apparent invulnerability of youth and Bucky's later crippled state is somewhat heavy-handed—one recalls Roth's scorn for a "framing" structure for *American Pastoral*—but it underscores the book's fable-like quality, and it makes a fitting ending for the fable-like quartet. Certainly, there is much in these books that is genuine, real, and alive: the graveside scenes in *Everyman*, the confrontations between Marcus and the dean in *Indignation*, the radiating heat of a pestilent Newark summer in *Nemesis*. Yet one cannot help being aware of the formidable determination, dedication, and discipline that brought these books into being, and of the limitations that have been forged into new interests, methods, consequences. There is an invaluable lesson in seeing a powerful writer grapple with the constrictions of age—particularly a writer who takes these constrictions as a major subject—and continue to write books that rouse us with a blow to the head.

"The twilight of my talent": Zuckerman's self-abnegating phrase does not seem right for an artist who remained so relentlessly productive. What's certain, however, is that these final novels would have been filled out very differently at an earlier time in Roth's career. Is there a danger that a young reader coming upon these books will think that this is all there is to the work? At their best, these stripped-down tales appear to be attractive to an entirely new set of readers. Reviewing *Indignation* in *The New York Times Book Review*, David Gates remarked that he had a preference for Roth's "short, devastating sex-and-mortality novels," and in a review of *Nemesis* on the front page of the same publication, Leah Hager Cohen began by saying, "I wrote Roth off," and then went on to explain why she had become a convert and considered his latest books to be his best, possessing "all his brilliance, minus the bluster." Tina Brown, in an interview with Roth for *The Daily Beast*, also said that she prefers the later, shorter books, for their simplicity, directness, and urgency: "It feels like you are taken over in one mood." It seems to me that these books, although they are far more developed, bear comparison with Hemingway's late novella (and huge success) *The Old Man and the Sea*: easy to read, deeply engaging as storytelling, yet so simplified that they are equally engaging on the level of parable, ideal for the kind of elucidation that takes place in schools—or, today, in reading groups. If these are not Roth's best works, they may nevertheless last a long time.

"What the stories all have in common," Roth sums up, "is the cataclysm. Here are four men of different ages, brought down." Roth had weathered his own share. His beloved dead now included his brother: Sandy Roth died in May 2009, at eighty-one, while Roth was working on *Nemesis*. So many of his Connecticut friends were dead that winters in his house had become almost unendurably lonely. And then there were all those drafts of *Nemesis*: written, he said, because he was having so much trouble getting it right but also, it seems, because he couldn't bear to let it go. He didn't have another book in sight, a situation that he described, in the fall of 2009, as "painful," and he seemed to mean it viscerally. He was seventy-six, and it was just beginning to become clear that this would be the last novel he wrote. And then what?

The assailable man. The vulnerable man. The man who gets old, gets sick, can't perform anymore: the man brought down. We have been discussing this subject in his work, in a suitably encroaching twilight, with suitable seriousness, when the esteemed author suddenly rises and begins to act out the stunned and bloodied Jake LaMotta in *Raging Bull*. LaMotta has just been beaten to a pulp in the ring by Sugar Ray Robinson. He's lost the championship. He's dripping blood. But he's still on his feet and he's now staggering toward me, proudly wheezing out the words—Roth does an excellent De Niro—"You never got me down, Ray. You hear me? You see? You never got me down, Ray, you never got me down."

Afterthoughts, Memories, and Discoveries: At It Again

Roth also does a dead-on Marlon Brando as Mark Antony, reciting "Friends, Romans, countrymen," and getting remarkably far into the speech on the spur of the moment, as we walk through midtown on a sunny afternoon. He's orating to the Roman populace, and it's amazing how few people turn their heads. Later, he tells me that he watches *The Godfather* once a year and that he does it mostly for "the Daumier faces."

∞

It's easy to see all the mistakes in his past work, he says—much harder with the newer things. And the really early books make him squirm: the last, Israeli chapter of *Portnoy's Complaint*, for example. And don't even get him started on *Goodbye, Columbus*. "To begin with," he says, "Aunt Gladys would have been of my parents' generation, not an immigrant, so she wouldn't have talked that way—that's just wrong." Aunt Gladys was right about the absence of Jews in Short Hills, though. ("So when do Jewish people live in Short Hills? They couldn't be real Jews believe me.") Jews had moved from Newark to Maplewood and South Orange after the war, he tells me—"those were the suburban paradises"—but Short Hills was still off-limits. This was not a mistake but a way of covering for the real family he knew. The only character he's willing to stand up for is the girl, Brenda Patimkin. "She's young, she's decisive, she's playful, she's audacious," he says, just like the girl who inspired her. It's the voice of the hero, Neil Klugman, that he now finds "a bit smug." Where did that smugness come from? "Well, there was a lot of superiority going around about the suburbs. But I can't blame anybody else. That was just me."

∞

He sometimes quotes the last lines of *The Great Gatsby*, but admits that he has some reservations about the book: "It's a bit melodious for my taste." He believes that Hemingway was the stronger writer. I mention Fitzgerald's early draft of *Gatsby*, published about a dozen years ago, as *Trimalchio*, in which Gatsby's attitude toward Daisy is harsher than in the finished book, and Gatsby himself is less of a glowing Don Quixote. He replies, "It sounds like it was probably better that way."

∞

None of the other distinguished honorees can have felt more honored than Roth, the FDR baby and lifelong Democrat, to be awarded the National Humanities Medal, by President Obama, in March 2011. He is still excited when he shows me a video of the ceremony, beginning with the recipients of both the Arts and Humanities medals waiting in the White House Green Room—Joyce Carol Oates and Sonny Rollins among them—when suddenly the door opens and the president walks in. This was a break in protocol, Obama explains a little later, at the ceremony; he was meant to make a formal entrance into the East Room after the medal recipients were seated in the hall. But he says that he couldn't wait to see these people. And Roth is the first person the president sees: he lights up in recognition and breaks into a big smile as he calls out, "Philip Roth!" Roth replies exactly in kind, with the same tone of surprise and delight (what a surprise to see you here!): "President Obama!"

The ceremony is dignified, inspiring. The president, at the lectern, speaks feelingly of "thumb-worn editions of these works of art and these old records," works that "helped inspire me or get me through a tough day or take risks that I might not otherwise have taken." American art, he proclaims, is one of the country's major "tools of change and of progress, of revolution and ferment." He speaks jointly of the works of Harper Lee—an honoree who was not present—and Roth, an unlikely pair who have "chronicled the American experience from the streets of Newark to the courts of Alabama." After a tribute to Lee's teachings about racism, the president says, quietly sly, "How many young people have learned to *think* by reading the exploits of Portnoy and his complaints?" There is a double wave of laughter: at first, people are laughing to themselves, and then—after Obama has taken a long, deadpan pause—there is a second, bigger swell when they realize that everyone else is laughing, too.

Finally, it is time to present the awards. A military officer recites a very brief summary of each recipient's achievements. Two of Roth's books are cited: *Portnoy's Complaint*, of course, and *American Pastoral*—"which won the 1998 Pulitzer Prize." (The young officer mispronounces the word "pastoral," but then no one has told him how to pronounce the name W.E.B. Du Bois in the citation for the biographer Arnold Rampersad.) Up on the stage, Roth stares out at the crowd, as though trying to fix the moment in his mind. The president says a few confidential words as he lowers the medallion, on its red ribbon, over Roth's bowed head. Roth tells me that Obama said, "You're not slowing down at all." And that he had replied, "Oh yes, Mr. President, I am."

∞

He's had a lot of back pain in recent years and is facing major surgery. It's the spring of 2012, and I speculate that, when he has recovered and is pain-free and back in Connecticut, he may yet write another novel. He sighs and says, "I hope not."

∞

We are talking about his first wife, Maggie, and I ask if he really believes, as Nathan Zuckerman claims in *The Facts*, that she was responsible for releasing him from the role of a pleasing, analytic good boy who would never have been much of a writer—that, in a literary sense, he owes her big. At first he seems taken aback, and then he growls, "Nathan Zuckerman was making it up. I don't owe her shit."

He expands on the subject. "She interrupted my life and took a part of it away," he says, quietly now. "She also changed it forever." He is currently recovering from back surgery, and when the subject comes up again a few months later, and he is feeling healthier and stronger, he says that Zuckerman was right. But today he is thinking about more than the work.

He has just seen Ann Mudge, his girlfriend of the mid-sixties, and is under the spell of counterlives past. He hadn't seen her in more than forty years. "The only person who could write this, it isn't me, it's Proust," he says. She is six months older than him—that makes her eighty, as we speak—and has been long and happily married. "She was a little old white-haired lady I wouldn't recognize in the street," he says, "until she sat down and began to speak, and then I began to see her face. And you know what never changes? The facial expressions—they're exactly the same."

They broke up in 1968, before the publication of *Portnoy*—just months after Maggie's death. Because "I had just flown the coop," he says, and had to be free.

They had talked for hours, remembering. "Thank God I'm not writing anymore, because I'd be driving myself crazy, trying to get it down.

"Maggie took up the years from twenty-three to thirty-five. If I hadn't married Maggie, I would have married someone else—probably Ann. We would have had a kid, I would have fooled around, we would have got divorced, if I'd followed the normal pattern. Who knows? But life would have been different."

This day, at least, he concludes, "I wish it had never happened. Even if she gave me everything."

✺

At first, he didn't know what to do. With *Nemesis* completed, he found himself, for the first time in more than half a century, unchained (as Zuckerman says of Lonoff) from his talent. He made lists of possible subjects for books, but none of them seemed compelling. He was afraid he would become depressed, would suffer from the lack of occupation, would be unable to cope with life without the daily application of his energies to the written page. But none of these things happened. He was utterly surprised to find that he felt free.

✺

He is besotted with the eight-year-old twins of a former girlfriend, especially the girl. The boy is wonderful, he likes trucks and baseball, but

Roth and the girl are writing books together. This was her idea. She is extraordinarily smart and verbally advanced, he says, "although I don't want to sound like a grandfather." Each of the authors writes a sentence a day, taking turns. The first thing he does in the morning is check his e-mail to see what she has sent him. They have already completed a couple of books. He whoops with delight at her reply to his suggestion that they have gone far enough with a particular story: "No, it's not enough!" Such brashness, such eagerness, such playfulness! He can't stop marveling, and wonders if "growing up with feminism so fully established" might account for the confidence of this "dazzling child"?

❧

The joys of a non–writing life: phone calls and letters to friends, exercise, reading political histories and biographies. Tony Judt's *Postwar*, Simon Sebag Montefiore's book on Stalin, books on Stalin and Hitler by Alan Bullock and John Lukacs, the three volumes of Arthur Schlesinger's study of FDR, several books about Eleanor Roosevelt, Sean Wilentz's *The Age of Reagan*, Robert Caro's latest volume on Lyndon Johnson, David Nasaw's biography of Joseph Kennedy. There was a mild furor in the literary press when he was quoted as saying that he doesn't read fiction anymore, and it's true that a lot of his time is taken up with books like these.

But he is also reading fiction—or, rather, rereading the books that mattered so much to him when he was young: "Because I asked myself, 'Am I never going to read Conrad again?'"

There is also Turgenev, including the letters and biographies; there is Faulkner, confirming for him that *As I Lay Dying* is "the best book of the first half of the twentieth century in America" and that, reading the first fifty pages of *Absalom, Absalom!*, "you might as well be a kitten caught in the yarn." Hemingway, of course: *In Our Time* ("Talk about magic, that's magic"). And *A Farewell to Arms*: "a nearly perfect book—no, a perfect book. The blending of the war and the love affair is extraordinary, and it has all this aggressive male banter, like a faint echo of the war. But it's the love affair I'm a sucker for, the way they joust at each other in the beginning, until she says, 'Do we have to go on and talk this way?'" And the later Hemingway, so underrated. *Islands in the Stream*: "He'd never written about having children like this before." And even *The Garden of Eden*, which was cobbled together posthumously from his papers and shows him "coming clean about sex, which I don't think he ever did before."

Greatest lines in literature: In *Crime and Punishment*, Dunya, Raskolnikov's sister, goes to see Svidrigailov in his apartment. Svidrigailov is an appalling character, a villain—"with," Roth says, "a sinister, devil-like charm." He's cornering Dunya, "literally manipulating her into a corner of the room," threatening rape. (Roth has written about this line in *Operation Shylock*, but all he's thinking about now is how much he likes it.) "And he's just about to make a move when she pulls a pistol out of her purse—and it's then that he has the greatest line in literature," Roth declares: "'That changes everything.'" He repeats the line with gusto—"'That changes everything!'"

"The other really great line," he says, clearly enjoying himself, is in *Ulysses*, when Bloom sees Gerty MacDowell on the beach. "He doesn't yet realize that she's a cripple. He's standing there watching her from maybe thirty yards away. He's got his hand in his pocket, and I think he's cut the pocket out of his pocket—didn't he? If he didn't, I'm going to use that sometime. But the next line is"—dramatic pause—"'At it again.'"

"'At it again'! That combination of resignation, delight, and tolerance! That's what I want it to say on my tombstone," he concludes. "At it again."

⚭

He has received a few old family photographs from a cousin on his mother's side—among them one of his mother in her wedding dress. It's a beautiful photograph, showing Bess Finkel on the day that she became Bess Roth—February 22, 1927—wearing an elegant gown with a long gossamer veil that trails over a rather grand staircase edged with greenery. He remembers, vaguely, the photo displayed among many others on the sideboard, near the dining table, during his childhood, but he hasn't seen it in more than half a century. The real discovery, however, comes when he says to his cousin that he assumes the photo was taken in a rented hall—where, he also assumes, the marriage took place—and she replies that, no, this is the Finkel family home.

His mother was quite well-off as a child. It is a shock. She grew up in a big house on North Broad Street in Elizabeth. (The houses are mostly gone now.) And suddenly he begins to solve a family mystery that he never even realized was a mystery: why his father's side of the family so dominated his childhood and why he saw so little of the relatives on his mother's side. He saw plenty of his mother's three sisters and of her brother, Mickey. But his mother's father had three brothers, who lived with their wives and children not very far away; and these people he never saw at all.

The Finkels were prosperous. The four brothers ran a fuel business in Elizabeth—coal and, later, oil—and he can now remember seeing the big trucks with Finkel Fuels across the sides. As he pieces it together, his grandfather Finkel—Philip, for whom he was named—had a falling-out with his brothers in 1928, took his share of the business in cash, and lost it all in the Crash. The big house was sold in 1929. His grandfather's death a couple of years later left his widowed grandmother in tough circumstances; apparently, the brothers refused to come to her aid. Hard feelings; broken relations; family schism. But Bess Finkel had grown up, before any of this happened, in circumstances that he had never remotely imagined. He knew that she had finished high school, unlike his father, and that she had trained to be a legal secretary. But he had never realized quite how far down she stepped to marry Herman Roth.

The feuds, the coal business, the money, the house, the loss of the money—"It doesn't matter to me personally," he says. "I had plenty of family. But think of what I missed out in the writing!"

∞

He is recalling the little Irish girl he loved when he was twelve. One Sunday, he was visiting a cousin, also named Philip—his Aunt Ethel's son, born a year before him and named after the same grandfather—up in Pelham, with his family. It was summertime, and he was having such a good time playing baseball with all the new kids—he remembers impressing them with his long ball—that his parents let him stay on for a few days. He used to sing "Peg o' My Heart" to the little girl. ("It's your Irish heart I'm after," he croons, rather nicely, now.) "I had a terrific crush on her," he recalls. And then he adds, thoughtfully, "I could get them."

I laugh because this seems so obvious.

"Could you get them?" he asks. Well, yes, of course. (Doesn't everyone?)

"That's why we went into literature," he concludes.

◦✕◦

A few years back, a developer was threatening to build forty-four houses on land across the road from Roth's Connecticut house, and, as he says, he "dug into my pocket" and bought the land himself. He now owns almost two hundred and fifty acres, and he seems to know every tree on them. He has become a connoisseur of bark and lichen. On the day that I arrived for a visit, in the summer of 2012, Roth's close friend and neighbor Mia Farrow was there with him to greet me, and we took a walk along a wide path mown through open fields. As Roth (literally) showed me the lay of the land, it felt as though Daisy Buchanan were floating along beside us.

And that was not the only literary shiver. Over there—Roth's writing studio—is Zuckerman's lonely two-room cabin, and here are Lonoff's giant maple trees. Lonoff's apple orchard is down to just a few living trees, but the fruit is sweet. And the candlelit dinner, on this late summer night, in the presence of the actress and the writer and with crickets chirping in the background, is as Chekhovian as anything in *The Professor of Desire*.

Conversation over dinner turns to the Obama-Romney battle and, in particular, to concerns over campaign financing. I mention that one of Romney's backers, Sheldon Adelson, owns the Sands Hotel in Las Vegas, and Farrow replies, laughing, "I once got married at the Sands!" Roth is wholly delighted—"You mean to Frank Sinatra?!"

She has a wedding picture on her cell phone.

◦✕◦

Old habits die hard. He is no longer writing all the time but, somehow, pages are piling up. Not fiction, though. He says that he hasn't the strength anymore "to keep pulling something out of nothing." Instead, there are notes, thoughts, corrections: so many things have been written about him, so many of them wrong, and they are already hardening into history. These are writings for the record, for the future. A letter to Wikipedia, attempting to correct its claims about his inspiration for

The Human Stain, and subsequently published on *The New Yorker* website, has generated an astonishing amount of outrage. He's seen enough outrage. Better to keep his head down. He's written a wonderful account of the American writers who shaped his youth—it's about them, not about him—but he's done it just for the pleasure of doing it. He can't stop writing, can't stop turning life into words.

∞

Both Roth's agent and *The New York Times* tried to be discreet about the reason for a recent interview, but Roth was quick to sniff it out: the *Times* is updating his obituary. He is not in the least put out by the idea; it's hardly as though he hadn't thought about what's coming next. But there is one thing that disturbs him. The *Times* will, of course, use *Times* reviews in summing up his career. "Even in death," he says, "you get a bad review!"

∞

We are standing outside Carnegie Hall, during intermission, on a beautiful spring evening. The Emerson String Quartet has just performed, first excerpts from Bach's *The Art of Fugue* and then Shostakovich's String Quartet no. 15. Roth, who rarely misses an Emerson concert, has invited several friends to join him, and other friends who happen to be in the audience have been coming by to say hello. These include an elegant older woman with red hair, still extremely attractive, who goes far back in his life—her name is Maxine Groffsky and she was the inspiration for Brenda Patimkin. (Roth recalls that the hair was once incredibly beautiful, "the color of an Irish setter," and he thinks that she may have been flirting with him tonight: "Maybe we'll have an affair every fifty-one years.") Bowled over by the gorgeously death-haunted Shostakovich, he admits that he has never really liked *The Art of Fugue*. "Too obsessive-compulsive," he says. And then, directly to Bach: "You've figured it out already! You can stop!" To us, he elaborates on his agitation: "He's like a guy constantly checking his pockets, or worrying that he left the pilot light on!" Who had any idea that Bach could be so funny?

The second half of the program is Beethoven's String Quartet in B-flat Major, op. 130, played with its original ending, the Grosse Fuge, the most formidable fugue in Western music: wild, dense, dissonant, intensely dramatic, even argumentative, running the emotional gamut. The performance is electric, and coming out of the theater, Roth says that now he understands why we listened to the Bach: "the Beethoven is like Bach on drugs!" We are all more than a little punchy as we head off into the city streets, and soon we are laughing so hard that we can hardly walk, as Roth—master of literary countervoices, I can't help but think—continues to expand on the fugue: "How crazy all those voices are! Like four lunatics in an asylum! Four madmen screaming away all on their own and then . . . they turn out to be together!" He tells one of our company, a psychiatrist, that under non-musical circumstances she would have to give each of them a shot. "Four guys who all think they are God!"

People peel off in various directions, and then, standing on Eighth Avenue, he is hailing a taxi, arm raised high. It's a bit of a wait, and now strangers passing by are saying hello. A gray-haired man crossing the avenue launches in. "Hi, I've loved everything you've done for the last fifty years," he says, and quickly adds, "I'm older than I look." Roth, who has been quietly humming to himself, emerges from his thoughts in time to respond, "I'm older than I look, too." Another man crossing the street simply reaches up to Roth's outraised hand, grabs it, and says, "Bravo, Maestro!" (This is still the Carnegie crowd, musically minded.) This happens too quickly for Roth to respond, or to fully relinquish the music going through his head. He doesn't seem pleased or displeased; he hardly seems to have noticed. And now I can distinctly make out the melody issuing from him, the crazy, crossing voices, as he stands in the New York night, traffic flashing by, humming the Grosse Fuge.

Acknowledgments

My first and deepest thanks to Philip Roth, of course, for writing the books and living the life.

My tremendous gratitude, as well, to a number of people who have helped to make the book possible, and who have bestowed a tremendous range of gifts along the way.

Jonathan Galassi, for continuous support, steadying intelligence, and an unerring ear; and everyone at Farrar, Straus and Giroux—especially Miranda Popkey, Jonathan Lippincott, Mareike Grover, Devon Mazzone, Jeff Seroy, and Lottchen Shivers—for their meticulous and caring work.

Robert Cornfield, a wise man who led me through the thicket of worries from journalism to books.

Ann Goldstein, who knows more about the English language than anyone I know, and who lent her exceptional good sense and grace to every page—an ally and a wonderful friend.

The extremely generous friends of Philip Roth who shared their memories with me: Janis Freedman Bellow, Joel Conarroe, Barbara Sproul, Benjamin Taylor, and Judith Thurman.

My dear friends Robert Gottlieb and Mindy Aloff, who read the manuscript and made important suggestions. Also my dear friends Alastair Macaulay and Alex Bevilacqua, who listened with patience and responded with unfailing insight. And thanks to all for their sustaining company and conversation.

Bonnie Yochelson, for a great day driving around Newark in the rain.

Hermione Lee, for invitations, conversations, and encouragement.

Dr. Jeffrey Liebmann, who makes it possible for me to continue to see the pages.

Shiva Rouhani, who turned a photographic ordeal into a party.

Catherine von Klitzing, for gourmet nourishment.

Allegra Kent, for the beauty and the history and the peonies.

Jim Pappas, master bookseller, whose table on Columbus Avenue was a site for so many treasured meetings with so many people, including Philip Roth.

My extraordinary family, the people who really hold me together: Julia Pierpont (a brilliant writer, whose first novel will be published in 2014), Shirley Roth, Allan Roth, Bob and Mary Pierpont, Doris Garcia, and Diana Garcia. In family, as in friends, I have been hugely blessed.

And especially my husband, Robert Pierpont, who has read these pages almost as many times as I have, and who has provided no end of encouragement, love, and strength.

Works by Philip Roth

Goodbye, Columbus and Five Short Stories (Boston: Houghton Mifflin, 1959)

Letting Go (New York: Random House, 1962)

When She Was Good (New York: Random House, 1967)

Portnoy's Complaint (New York: Random House, 1969)

Our Gang (Starring Tricky and His Friends) (New York: Random House, 1971)

The Breast (New York: Holt, Rinehart and Winston, 1972)

The Great American Novel (New York: Holt, Rinehart and Winston, 1973)

My Life as a Man (New York: Holt, Rinehart and Winston, 1974)

Reading Myself and Others (New York: Farrar, Straus and Giroux, 1975)

The Professor of Desire (New York: Farrar, Straus and Giroux, 1977)

The Ghost Writer (New York: Farrar, Straus and Giroux, 1979)

Zuckerman Unbound (New York: Farrar, Straus and Giroux, 1981)

The Anatomy Lesson (New York: Farrar, Straus and Giroux, 1983)

The Prague Orgy (published as the epilogue to *Zuckerman Bound*, including *The Ghost Writer, Zuckerman Unbound,* and *The Anatomy Lesson*) (New York: Farrar, Straus and Giroux, 1985)

The Counterlife (New York: Farrar, Straus and Giroux, 1986)

The Facts: A Novelist's Autobiography (New York: Farrar, Straus and Giroux, 1988)

Deception: A Novel (New York: Simon and Schuster, 1990)

Patrimony: A True Story (New York: Simon and Schuster, 1991)

Operation Shylock: A Confession (New York: Simon and Schuster, 1993)

Sabbath's Theater (Boston: Houghton Mifflin, 1995)

American Pastoral (Boston: Houghton Mifflin, 1997)

I Married a Communist (Boston: Houghton Mifflin, 1998)

The Human Stain (Boston: Houghton Mifflin, 2000)

The Dying Animal (Boston: Houghton Mifflin, 2001)

Shop Talk: A Writer and His Colleagues and Their Work (Boston: Houghton Mifflin, 2001)

The Plot Against America (Boston: Houghton Mifflin, 2004)

Everyman (Boston: Houghton Mifflin, 2006)

Exit Ghost (Boston: Houghton Mifflin, 2007)

Indignation (Boston: Houghton Mifflin, 2008)

The Humbling (Boston: Houghton Mifflin, 2009)

Nemesis (Boston: Houghton Mifflin, 2010)

Index